HENRY V

HENRY V
THE CONSCIENCE OF A KING

MALCOLM VALE

YALE UNIVERSITY PRESS
NEW HAVEN AND LONDON

For information about this and other Yale University Press publications, please contact:
U.S. Office: sales.press@yale.edu   yalebooks.com
Europe Office: sales@yaleup.co.uk   yalebooks.co.uk

Typeset in Adobe Garamond Pro by IDSUK (DataConnection) Ltd
Printed in Great Britain by TJ International Ltd, Padstow, Cornwall

Library of Congress Cataloging-in-Publication Data

Names: Vale, M. G. A. (Malcolm Graham Allan), author.
Title: Henry V : the conscience of a king / Malcolm Vale.
Description: New Haven : Yale University Press, 2016.
LCCN 2016006349 | ISBN 9780300148732 (cloth : alk. paper)
LCSH: Henry V, King of England, 1387–1422. | Great Britain—Kings
   and rulers—Biography. | Great Britain—History—Henry V, 1413–1422.
Classification: LCC DA256 .V35 2016 | DDC 942.04/2092—dc23
LC record available at http://lccn.loc.gov/2016006349

A catalogue record for this book is available from the British Library.

10 9 8 7 6 5 4 3 2 1

To avoid the peril to conscience that might result from our giving, and he receiving, the said hospital . . . unless the title was clear in law and conscience.

> (Henry V, on the grant of the hospital of St Anthony, London,
> to William Kynwolmersh, at Mantes, 20 June 1419)

He is now at the final point and conclusion of his labours and, through God's grace and the help of his allies and friends, shall soon bring his war to an end . . . [and] what good and profit might arise if there were peace and rest among Christian princes . . .

> (Henry V, diplomatic instructions, at Saint-Faron-les-Meaux,
> 18 December 1421)

CONTENTS

ACKNOWLEDGEMENTS

When first approached by a publisher and asked whether writing a book on Henry V would be an attractive proposition, my initial reaction was distinctly negative. Given the nature and extent of the existing literature, it seemed that yet another 'Life of' would be surplus to requirements. Had everything not already been said about the king and his reign? And was a biography of a medieval ruler actually achievable in any case? But, on reflection, it occurred to me that a rather different approach to the subject might yield fruit. One problem of medieval biography lies in the difficulty of penetrating the layers of, on the one hand, eulogy and near-hagiography and, on the other, of criticism and denigration, produced by contemporary writers. While the accounts, views and opinions of chroniclers, annalists, moralists and others can never be completely ignored, their testimony can often tell us as much about them as about their subject.

I decided to look elsewhere in a search for reliable evidence that might give us access to Henry V's thoughts, attitudes, aims and motivations. In many ways he embodied, as well as exercised, what might be called the 'conscience of kingship' – hence my subtitle. It has recently been argued that 'the conscience of the prince was at the centre of fifteenth-century political decision-making'.[1] If so, then a prince actively engaged in the decision-making process, as Henry V clearly was, might provide us with a good test case. To discover how and why that conscience operated, or failed to operate, and what may have lain behind the decisions he took, there is no alternative but to return to the original sources. No historical source can ever be entirely objective, but the surviving archival and documentary material, partial and incomplete as it often is, does at least possess a certain neutrality, or absence of evident prejudice, bias or distortion. So my initial lack of enthusiasm has been overcome by the decision to attempt a study of Henry V drawing largely upon the archival evidence (which is reasonably extensive) for his own personal involvement and intervention in matters both public and private. How successful I have been must be left to the reader to judge.

My first acknowledgement must therefore be to Heather McCallum, of Yale University Press, for commissioning the book, and accepting that it would take a form that did not correspond to what was at first envisaged. I am also very grateful for the support of many colleagues, and for their expressions of interest, sometimes leading to invitations to talk about Henry V to groups of scholars, students and members of the general public. In this latter respect I am especially indebted to Rowena Archer, Brigitte Bedos-Rezak, Hugh Doherty, Nicholas Vincent, John Pitcher, Mark Whittow and Hannes Kleineke. For very useful references and generous giving of their time, I am indebted to Hannah Skoda, Michael Tait, Julian Gardner, Patrick Lantschner and Adrian Ailes. Institutional support has come from my College, St John's, Oxford, whose Governing Body elected me, in retirement, to an Emeritus Research Fellowship. The staffs of The National Archives, Kew; the British Library; the Bodleian

---

[1] J. Catto, 'The Burden and Conscience of Government in the Fifteenth Century', *TRHS*, 17 (2007), p. 84.

Library, Oxford; the Guildhall Library; Eton College Library and Archives; and the Westminster Abbey Muniments, have been unfailingly helpful. Moral support, as well as constructive comment, has been provided by Anne Wheeler and Timothy Vale. Kind friends and colleagues have saved me from making slips and mistakes, but for any errors that remain, I am entirely responsible.

ABBREVIATIONS

BIHR	*Bulletin of the Institute of Historical Research*
BJRL	*Bulletin of the John Rylands Library*
BL	British Library
BNF	Bibliothèque Nationale de France
Bod. Lib.	Bodleian Library
CCR	*Calendar of Close Rolls*
CPR	*Calendar of Patent Rolls*
ECR	Eton College Records
EETS	*Early English Text Society*
EHR	*English Historical Review*
Foedera	T. Rymer, *Foedera*, 20 vols (London, 1727–35)
JWCI	*Journal of the Warburg & Courtauld Institutes*
L&P	*Letters and Papers illustrative of the Wars of the English in France,* ed. J. Stevenson, 2 vols (RS, London, 1861 4)
l. s. d	Pounds, shillings, pence sterling
n.d.	No date
Oxford DNB	*Oxford Dictionary of National Biography*
P & P	*Past & Present*

PMLA	*Proceedings of the Modern Language Association*
PPC	*Proceedings and Ordinances of the Privy Council*
PRMA	*Proceedings of the Royal Musical Association*
RCAHMW	*Royal Commission on the Ancient and Historical Monuments of Wales*
RP	*Rotuli Parliamentorum*
RS	Rolls Series
TNA	The National Archives, Kew
TRHS	*Transactions of the Royal Historical Society*
VCH	*Victoria County History*
WAM	Westminster Abbey Muniments

PRELUDE
BAPTISM OF FIRE

On 21 July 1403, the usurper Henry IV, king of England, fought and defeated his baronial opponents – the Percy clan of Northumberland and their supporters – in a bloody battle at Shrewsbury. On the field, fighting with him, was his eldest son, the sixteen-year-old Henry, prince of Wales, the future Henry V. As a great future exponent of the devastating effectiveness of archery fire, which was to win him the victory at Agincourt in 1415, Henry had an early, direct, personal experience of its effects. He was on the receiving end of missile fire from enemy longbowmen. It was to be a distinctly unchivalrous baptism of fire. At some point in the battle, the prince seems to have raised the visor of his helmet and, as a result, sustained a serious arrow wound to his exposed face. The wooden shaft of the arrow was soon removed, but the metal arrowhead had entered just below the cheekbone, lodged itself in the back of the skull, and proved immovable. According to the surgeon John Bradmore,[1] who, some time later, operated on him, the prince had been

---

[1] See S.J. Lang, 'Bradmore, John (d.1412)', in *Oxford DNB* (Oxford, 2004; online edition Jan. 2008); and 'John Bradmore and his book *Philomena*', *Social History of Medicine*, 5 (1992), pp. 121–30.

struck in the face with an arrow beside the nose on the left side, which arrow entered from the side, and the head of the said arrow, after its shaft was extracted, remained in the back part of the bone of the head to a depth of six inches . . .[2]

Henry was taken, with the arrowhead still firmly embedded in his skull, to the castle of Kenilworth, where he was to spend the next few months. Despite the efforts of the king's physicians and surgeons to remove it by applying ointments, poultices and heat to the wound, the object could not be extracted. A London surgeon, John Bradmore, was then summoned. By applying an instrument that he had invented, in the form of a vice- or pincer-like extractor, Bradmore successfully removed the arrowhead.[3] He then averted the risk of a potentially fatal spasm by repeatedly massaging therapeutic ointments into the prince's neck. Miraculously, sepsis did not apparently set in and Henry slowly recovered. But he had come very close indeed to death.

The fact that he was not killed outright, and that the arrow had not penetrated any part of the brain or other vital organs in the head, may have been because it was a stray round, deflected in its flight, so that its impact was lessened. Whatever the case, it was considered that God's grace had spared the prince. This was his baptism of fire as a soldier. The experience could not have been without its after-effects. Some disfigurement must have resulted. Even fully healed a wound of this depth and severity must

[2] The prince 'in facie juxta nasum ex sinistra parte fuit percussus, que quidem sagitta intravit . . . ex transverso, et capud dicte sagitte, postquam sagitta fuit extracta, stetet in posteriori parte ossis capiti secundum mensuram vj uncharum . . .': BL, MS Sloane 2272, fo. 137r. The extract is from John Bradmore's treatise on surgery, the *Philomena*, printed in S.J. Lang, 'The Philomena of John Bradmore and its Middle English Derivative: a Perspective on Surgery in Late Medieval England' (University of St Andrews unpublished Ph.D. thesis, 1998), p. 66.
[3] For details of the procedure and of Bradmore's instrument (including a drawing) see H. Cole & T. Lang, 'The Treating of Prince Henry's Arrow Wound, 1403', *Journal of the Society of Archer Antiquaries*, 46 (2003), pp. 95–101; J. Cummins, 'Saving Prince Hal: Maxillo-facial Surgery, 1403', *Henry North History of Dentistry Research Group Publication* (2006) [http.// historyofdentistry.co.uk/index_htm_files/2006N].

have left a prominent scar. The surviving profile portrait of Henry[4] shows the left-hand side of his face, which has prompted speculation as to whether the wound was in fact on the right side. Unless the portrait is (as is entirely possible) an idealised version, the absence of any sign of a scar might suggest that Bradmore was not referring in his account to the *patient's* left side, but to his own, as he faced the prince. Whatever the reality was, the immediate healing process took twenty days, but Henry was effectively out of action for the best part of a year. We can only speculate upon the effects of the trauma he had undergone. He was not to participate in another pitched battle for twelve years – and that would be his last.

This book seeks to explore aspects of Henry V's character, personality and behaviour which lie outside the traditional and stereotypical depiction of him as a soldier, a warrior-king par excellence. It is largely based on the evidence for the king's direct, personal involvement and intervention in the wide range of matters with which he was obliged, or chose, to deal. It also attempts to uncover, as far as it is ever possible to do so, the workings of his mind and their translation into political behaviour, religious observance, and patronage of the peaceful arts. Issues of conscience, duty, justice, mercy and charity, as well as expediency, ruthlessness, ambition, self-awareness and single-mindedness, are all raised by the evidence considered. Although some of these are certainly present in Shakespeare's *King Henry V*, his great play is essentially a work of fiction, albeit fiction of genius. It has, however, set the tone for much subsequent interpretation of the 'real' Henry V and, despite its manifestly fictitious nature, continues to

---

[4] No fifteenth-century original survives, but copies exist in various collections. The copy in the Royal Collection, Windsor, has been dated by dendrochronological analysis to *c*.1518–23. See J. M. Fletcher, 'Tree Ring Dates for some Panel Paintings in England', *Burlington Magazine*, 116 (1974), pp. 250–8. For another copy, now in the National Portrait Gallery (NPG–545), dated to the late sixteenth or early seventeenth century, see *Complete Illustrated Catalogue. National Portrait Gallery, London*, ed. D. Saywell & J. Simon (London, 2004), p. 296.

inform the popular image of the king as warrior, if not warmonger. It would be an absurdity to contend that the king did not display an aptitude for warfare and its waging. Whether he liked it or not, or felt most at home in camp and castle, always in the company of fighting men, is a different matter. There is another Henry V . . .

INTRODUCTION

It pleases lesser mortals to detect the Achilles' heel of the great ones that
live in the world's eye.

(K.B. McFarlane)[1]

This book is not a biography. There have been many attempts at a
biographical treatment of the life of Henry V of England (1413–22).[2]
From them, he has – in the great majority of cases – emerged as one of
the 'great ones that live in the world's eye'. But the search for the Achilles
heel, and the urge to cut a 'great' historical figure down to size, certainly
continues to please mortals, lesser or not. Henry V has been seen as a 'deeply
flawed' mortal, but one who achieved extraordinary things in spite of manifold weaknesses and mistakes.[3] Those achievements have given him legendary status, perpetuated by Shakespeare's *Henry V*. Hence, as with his

---

[1] K.B. McFarlane, 'Henry V: a Personal Portrait' in his *Lancastrian Kings and Lollard Knights*
(Oxford, 1972), p. 132.
[2] See below, pp. 10–13 for a brief survey of the existing secondary literature.
[3] See I. Mortimer, *1415: Henry V's Year of Glory* (London, 2009; 2nd edn 2010), p. 551.

near-contemporary, Joan of Arc, the legendary character tends to carry far more significance and meaning in today's world than the 'real' historical figure. And it is to that 'real' historical figure that this book is directed. It is concerned less to measure success and failure, or to identify merits and defects, than with an attempt to discover, explain and understand how and why that figure thought and acted as he did. It also tries to set the king into a much broader context, necessitating what may seem to be digressions from the mainstream subject-matter of a royal 'Life'. But the significance of some of his thoughts, beliefs and actions can only be explained contextually and when set against a broader perspective.

The last twenty or so years have seen the appearance of a cluster of books on the life and reign of Henry V (born in 1386, died aged thirty-five in 1422; reigned for just nine years and five months). The rate of production has increased significantly over the past five years, especially as the celebration of the anniversary of the battle of Agincourt in October 2015 approached. Given Christopher Allmand's scholarly volume in the Yale English Monarchs series (first published in 1992, with a new edition in 1997), the recent contributions by Juliet Barker on *Agincourt* (2006) and *Conquest: the English Kingdom of France* (2009), as well as Ian Mortimer's *1415: Henry V's Year of Glory* (2009), the king and his times clearly continue to exercise a fascination for readers. The narrative history of his reign has been told and retold many times. The rights and wrongs of his war in France, the quality of his military leadership, the nature and extent of his religious convictions, bigoted or not – all these issues, and many more, have been described and discussed at great length. As an 'iconic' event in British national history, his victory at Agincourt has, moreover, acquired symbolic overtones. The brave defiance displayed by an island nation, in the face of overwhelming odds, was thought to be exemplified in that victory. Endlessly repeated, the same (or very similar) evidence is brought out to illustrate and justify arguments which often have less to do with the fifteenth century than with an author's own time, its assumptions and preconceptions.

What, then, can be said about Henry V that is in any way new or original? The most common image of the king, if such exists, in the mind of the general public, is probably that derived from Shakespeare's *Henry V*, especially as played on screen by Olivier or Branagh. In 1944, Laurence Olivier was commissioned to direct what was in effect a wartime propaganda film of *Henry V*, with a musical score by William Walton; acclaimed by critics at the time, it subsequently achieved the status of a classic of the cinema. It was dedicated 'to the Commandos and Airborne Troops of Great Britain, the spirit of whose ancestors it has humbly attempted to recapture'. The reference back, from present to past, was not unprecedented. Continuities had been perceived, during a previous world war, between the qualities of 'our bowmen' at Agincourt and the 'musketry' of British infantry in 1914, 'and so it has been from the wars of Marlborough and Wellington down to the present'.[4] In elevated prose, a writer on the battle of the Marne (1914) could emphasise that continuity:

> Just 500 years before, and almost upon this very ground, had Harry of
> England met and broken, in fair shock of battle, the chivalry of France
> . . . On Crispin's day 1914, was England once again embattled against
> an enemy . . .[5]

In 1989, when the next acclaimed film version of *Henry V* appeared, directed by Kenneth Branagh, a 'grittier', more realistic treatment of fifteenth-century warfare was presented to audiences. To some extent, this corresponded with changes in historians' perceptions of the historical Henry and the nature of his war in France. There was now a growing body

[4] A. Corbett-Smith (Major), *The Marne – and after* (London, 1917), p. 132.
[5] Corbett-Smith, *The Marne*, p. 236.

of critical voices.[6] Historical writing was no longer quite so concerned with Henry's 'Englishness', his charisma, and his supreme military qualities, which placed him beside Marlborough, Wellington, Churchill and Montgomery as one of the nation's greatest commanders and war leaders. But the urge to evaluate, judge and deliver a verdict on the king, against any number of largely contrived benchmarks, remained (and remains) strong. Do we need to adopt what are often arbitrary, absolute criteria in our attempt to arrive at a better understanding of our human subject?

One answer may lie in a rather different approach to the man and, above all, to our sources for his life and reign. A major aim of this book is to seek and find, with some certainty, evidence for the direct personal intervention and involvement of the king in all the manifold activities undertaken by a fifteenth-century ruler. In Henry V's case, we are fortunate to have at least some of that evidence. The screen of administrative process, and the layers of bureaucracy that often lie between the medieval (and modern) ruler and his subjects are, in some cases, lifted and pared away under Henry V. The king's wishes, his strength of will, the exercise of his conscience, and his direct involvement in matters of all kinds, can be seen in the surviving documentation. Some of this was now consistently expressed in the English language, rather than in Latin or Anglo-Norman French: for example, letters issued under his personal seal, the signet, some carrying his 'R.H.' (*Rex Henricus* or *Roy Henry*) sign manual or cipher; diplomatic and other memoranda composed by the king himself, sometimes with annotations in his own hand; his responses to the many

---

[6] See, for example, K. Dockray, *Warrior King. The Life of Henry V* (London, 2004; 2nd edn 2007), esp. pp. 225–35. Also W.M. Ormrod, *Political Life in Medieval England, 1300–1450* (Basingstoke, 1995), esp. pp. 136–7, partially retracted in his 'Henry V and the English Taxpayer' in *Henry V: New Interpretations*, ed. G. Dodd (Woodbridge/York, 2013), pp. 214–17. Censorious criticism of Henry V is not, however, an entirely recent phenomenon. In 1878, for example, Bishop Stubbs thought that 'the war of Henry V in France must be condemned by the judgement of modern opinion': William Stubbs, *The Constitutional History of England in its Origin and Development* (5th edn Oxford, 1896), p. 275. French historians, not unexpectedly, have been almost unanimously condemnatory.

petitions received from his subjects; and entries in his financial accounts, some of which he personally inspected. In many of these documents, some of which, evidently, were dictated, we can hear the king himself speaking. So what we see, and hear, is a king in action – action that is sometimes, but not always, borne out by the narrative and chronicle sources. The chronicles are, of course, often laden with bias and prejudices which the more 'neutral' governmental, administrative and financial sources do not share. It is one intention of this book to concentrate closely upon these latter kinds of evidence and to produce a picture of Henry V that may differ in important respects from at least some traditional and current views.

Among those views, his military, chivalric and patriotic qualities still, inevitably, loom large. But even among those who laud his military genius and contribution to the greatness of 'our island's story' Henry V does not escape criticism. Some historians have not been slow to judge the king for what they perceive to be his warmongering; for drawing the infant English nation into a continental war which, they contend with the benefit of hindsight, proved ultimately unsuccessful and deeply damaging to the monarchy and the English people. Rather than concentrating on the serious (and perhaps God-given?) task of establishing English supremacy over the whole of the British Isles – including Scotland and Ireland – thereby hammering a unitary nation state into existence, they claim that Henry's war aims in France were a distraction both for him and for his successors. So the continental lands which he and they acquired or regained, and attempted to hold, proved to be leeches and parasites, draining England of its precious lifeblood in men, money and supplies. Such is the critical view.[7]

---

[7] For a convenient summary of the critical view of Henry's life and legacy see Dockray, *Warrior King*, pp. 237–42. For (qualified) criticism of the long-term implications of Henry's fiscal policies and creation of a 'war state' see Ormrod, 'Henry V and the English Taxpayer' in *Henry V: New Interpretations*, ed. Dodd, pp. 187–216, where the relatively high yields and general lack of resistance to Henry's taxation should not be used to 'suggest that the system operated in the 1410s was economically sustainable in the long term or that, by extension, the evolving and ambitious war aims of Henry V were at all realizable' (p. 214).

Another approach seeks to set Henry V into a rather different context. Here was an English king who took the claims inherited from his Plantagenet predecessors to hold both titles and lands in France much further than any previous sovereign. For the first time, a potentially plausible, politically feasible, dual monarchy of England and France was in the process of formation when Henry died, prematurely, in 1422.[8] It would become England's greatest commitment and obligation in Europe until Britain's entry into the European Economic Community 550 or so years later. This book argues that Henry's war with France was certainly a calculated venture, concerned to assert, implement and realise his claims to sovereignty over that kingdom. Yet it was not solely a cynical, opportunistic adventure in defence and fulfilment of those claims, but also formed part of a higher purpose. The two kingdoms were to be united, once a civil war within France had, by both military and diplomatic means, been brought to an end, in a joint war (and perhaps diplomatic) effort against heretics and infidels. Had Henry lived longer, whether that war, and that diplomacy, would have targeted the heretics of Bohemia, the Mamluks of the Holy Land or the Ottoman Turks – or all of them – has to remain an open question.

Yet the inherent implausibility of such an Anglo-French union, when seen in the light of subsequent history, seems obvious. But there was nothing inherently implausible, in the fifteenth – and sixteenth – centuries about multinational and multi-state political formations, whether they

---

[8] It is, unusually, a French historian who has recently appeared to suggest that the possibility of a durable Anglo-French dual monarchy was not totally out of the question: 'the dream of a double monarchy vanished, although it is difficult to know what would have happened had Henry V, by far the best soldier of his time, lived longer than he did'. See J-P. Genet, 'The Government of Later Medieval France and England: a Plea for Comparative History' in *Government and Political Life in England and France, c.1300–c.1500*, ed. C. Fletcher, J-P. Genet & J. Watts (Cambridge, 2015), p. 2.

were styled 'empires' or not. This book, therefore, bases itself on such evidence as we have for Henry V's motives, intentions and assumptions, and tends to take issue, at certain points, with the thesis of the inevitable unsustainability, and predictable collapse, of the Lancastrian dual monarchy of England and France. Clearly Henry V's death, only two years after he had been recognised as 'heir and regent of France' (1420), played a critical part in shaping the future of the union – but the precise nature of that part needs reconsideration.

Another major aim of the book is to shift some emphases. It is to move them away from the military ethos that Henry V is said to have enshrined towards a less monolithic and stereotypical frame in which to set his life, his aims and his objectives. We certainly see the king at war. But at war in its widest aspects, including Henry's apparent talent for military organisation, as well as the measures he took to contain, and sometimes counter, the worst effects of warfare. The king is also seen as diplomat – here I underscore his close personal attention to his role on the European stage; and as a ceremonial figure, which is illustrated from the copious documentation of his concern for, and use of, ritual. We also investigate what appears to have been Henry's conscious and purposeful promotion of the use of English, for the first time in the history of English government since the Anglo-Saxon period, as well as his personal interest in the language of diplomacy. Two chapters on both the temporal and spiritual aspects of his relations with the Church stress the significance of this dimension of his activities, which claimed much of his time and energies. A section on the king and the peaceful arts redresses a balance which undue emphasis on his martial and coldly pragmatic qualities sometimes tends to upset and distort. Patronage of some art forms, and active participation in others, such as music, adds another dimension to a far more complex personality than often meets the eye.

Fundamental to the picture put forward here are two further themes: first, an emphasis upon the king's own part in the everyday business of government.[9] We can trace and chart this through the surviving archival sources, perhaps to a far greater extent than with any previous English ruler. Secondly, and most importantly of all, we can see Henry as a religious and moral reformer. It is argued here that his deeply held religious convictions, and his concern for the state of the Church, were exceptional in a ruler of his type and time. His application to the business of, in effect, overseeing the government of the Church within his dominions, and of reforming it, was central to the exercise of his kingship. Ecclesiastical and devotional matters ranked very highly indeed on his scale of priorities. He lived at a time when reform of the Church in Western Christendom was constantly in the air. He was a man of his time in that respect. But he went well beyond the normal bounds of a secular ruler's place and role. If he had ever been given a choice of career, much of the evidence seems to suggest that the vocation of priesthood, preferably accompanied by the tenure of a great prince-bishopric, might have satisfied him. What may seem to us his exaggerated piety and hyper-orthodoxy, however, had their causes. It was imperative for him to set his face against the Lollard heresy associated with the Oxford scholar John Wycliffe (c.1330–84), whose doctrines profoundly influenced the contemporary Czech heretic Jan Hus and his followers. England was viewed by many in fifteenth-century Europe (including the popes) as the seedbed of the most pernicious deviation from Catholic orthodoxy that they had witnessed outside the openly heretical kingdom of Hussite Bohemia. This book will therefore picture Henry as a devout, though thoroughly pragmatic, religious leader as well as a calculating military commander– a potent and, in less responsible hands, dangerous combination. And this was played out on the international as well as the national stage.

---

[9] For recent observations on the personal ability, or inability, of later medieval English and French kings to 'perform a handful of key tasks' see J. Watts, 'Conclusion' in *Government and Political Life in England and France, c.1300–c.1500*, ed. Fletcher, Genet & Watts, pp. 369–71.

It will be obvious that this book differs from many of its predecessors in a number of ways, not least in its structure. This is not a narrative biography. It is a thematic study of personal rule, direct action and the exercise of power by an individual who, by any measure, possessed some exceptional qualities. It raises questions about the part played by myth and legend in our 'national' histories, both English and French. It questions interpretations that play down the role and contribution of a powerful individual to the ebb and flow of events, however much he may have been at the mercy of impersonal forces. It considers issues such as the relationship of Church and State, and of the interplay, and sometimes the collision, of the sacred and the secular, and of conscience and political necessity. It discusses the use of languages at different times, for different purposes and in different contexts. Finally, it poses questions, if not always directly, then (it is hoped) in the mind of the reader, about the 'what might have been[s]' of history. To appreciate the extent – and limitations – of the evidence upon which this book is based, a brief survey of both the primary sources and secondary authorities for the king and his reign is necessary.

As with any other medieval ruler, our primary evidence stems largely from two kinds of source. The first is found in the narrative accounts of chroniclers, both ecclesiastical and secular. By Henry V's reign, however, the great medieval tradition of monastic historical writing and commentary on contemporary, as well as past, events was beginning to wane. Chronicles stemming from essentially urban sources, such as town chronicles, as well as guild records, heralds' narratives, newsletters and correspondence of all kinds, had begun to appear beside the time-honoured accounts of national and local events composed in monastic houses, such as the abbey of St Albans, throughout the Middle Ages. Use has certainly been made of them in this book, but they have not provided the major part of the material upon which it is based.

A second category of primary source, which this book prioritises, warrants very close and sustained attention: that is, the archival and documentary records. The historian of later medieval England is fortunate in having an unrivalled body of such material in The National Archives, much (though by no means all) of it published in the great series of Chancery enrolments (the Calendars of Patent Rolls, Close Rolls and so forth). A vast array of other documentation is also available, ranging from administrative and personal correspondence, wills and testaments, diplomatic reports and memoranda, to virtually complete (with some exceptions) sets of financial accounts for all the great departments of state, the king's household, the armies and navies which he led to Harfleur, Agincourt and subsequent engagements, and for England's overseas possessions (Aquitaine, Normandy, Calais, and Lancastrian France). Such a wealth of evidence provides a valuable control on the narrative sources, as well as giving us insights into aspects of the king's life and actions which the chroniclers, biographers, eulogists and memoir-writers do not touch upon. This book, as noted above, draws extensively on such information, much of it unpublished, and much of it under-used by previous writers. There is no reason why it should not be deployed to recreate a picture of the king's life as it was lived from day to day, and as a reliable source for what actually happened. It is used here as perhaps the most immediate of sources for the king's own, direct, personal intervention in all kinds of business. If his presence is recorded, if his cipher or sign manual is there, and (even more so) if the document, or part of it, is 'by mine own hand', it is proof enough of that attention to detail, application to business, and personal concern for justice by which Henry V can be shown to be exceptional among rulers. The archival deposit should never, ever, be dismissed merely as the desiccated residue of government and administration. The king can often be seen in action here – more vividly, in some instances, than in the contrived and rhetorical narratives of the chroniclers.

The reign has attracted a copious secondary literature, which tends to be rather disproportionate to its actual length. A selective overview of recent – and not so recent – books about the king and his reign must begin with the work of J.H. Wylie and W.T. Waugh, entitled *The Reign of Henry V*, in three volumes (Cambridge, 1914–29). This narrative account is packed with detail, and replete with full scholarly apparatus, and is a veritable mine of information. An early attempt at analysis of Henry's major French campaigns after the victory at Agincourt is found in R.A. Newhall's *The English Conquest of Normandy, 1416–1424. A Study in Fifteenth-century Warfare* (New Haven, 1924). This was a pioneering study of Henry V's war effort, firmly based on the original sources, especially those of military organisation and finance. E.F. Jacob's *Henry V and the Invasion of France* (London, 1947) is a useful 'Home University Library' book, written as part of a series intended for the general reader, and still valuable as a basic introduction. In another category is Christopher Allmand's sound and scholarly account – *Henry V* (New Haven/London, 1997; first published 1992) – with a very readable narrative and analysis of many aspects of the reign. This is the 'standard' account to date. The subsequent history of Henry's conquest of Normandy is traced in Allmand's *Lancastrian Normandy, 1417–1450. The History of a Medieval Occupation* (Oxford, 1983). This takes the story up to the end of the Lancastrian regime in the duchy. A very substantial, indeed seminal, contribution to the subject of Henry as king, organised on a thematic basis, is still to be found in G.L. Harriss (ed.), *Henry V: the Practice of Kingship* (Oxford, 1985; 2nd edn Stroud, 1993). This contains ten valuable essays by leading scholars on many aspects of the reign.

More recent work has tended to turn towards the military dimension of the reign and there has been a heavy and sustained concentration on the battle of Agincourt and its aftermath. This has produced a number of interesting studies, studies that differ substantially in their treatment and conclusions. Anne Curry's *The Battle of Agincourt: Sources and Interpretations* (Woodbridge, 2000) is a book of extracts from the sources, in English translation, for a student readership, but with a helpful interpretative essay and commentaries on the texts and documents. Her edited volume on *Agincourt 1415* (London, 2000) is a collection of essays by various authors on the techniques of warfare, tactics and strategy, with detailed accounts of the uses and functions of archers and archery. Among the more recent studies that tend to adopt an overtly critical attitude towards the king, Keith Dockray's *Warrior King. The Life of Henry V* (London, 2004; 2nd edn 2007) led the field until the work of Ian Mortimer appeared. Dockray's book is a popular biography, but contains substantial treatment of the posthumous and subsequent – especially Shakespearean – reputation of the king. The book is, by and large, critical of both the reign and its legacy which 'in the last analysis, was bleak'.[10] Pursuing the Agincourt theme, Juliet Barker's *Agincourt* (London, 2006) became a major popular success, and may become the 'standard' account of the battle. She takes issue with the work of other historians at some points, for example concerning the numbers actually engaged at Agincourt. The book is heavily military in emphasis – but this is both inevitable and justified, given its subject and the nature of the material used.

The recent work of Ian Mortimer, *1415: Henry V's Year of Glory* (London, 2009; 2nd edn, 2010) sets out substantially to revise our assessment of Henry V and does not shrink from controversy. But the book is also interesting on account of its structure. It is organised as a kind of journal, on a daily basis, covering just over one year of the reign. Events taking place outside England, not only in France but, in particular, at the great council of the Church at Constance, are chronicled. Mortimer tends to take issue with the Oxford historian K.B. McFarlane's assessment of Henry, including his conclusion that he was 'the greatest man that ever ruled England'. Less controversially, and following her *Agincourt* (2006), Juliet Barker gave us *Conquest. The English Kingdom of France* (London, 2009). This is a broadly narrative account, beginning with Henry's invasion of 1417, which then tells the story of Lancastrian France until its demise in the 1450s. The book mainly follows a traditional pattern, chronicling the regime's early successes culminating in what is deemed to be its inevitable decline and fall.

---

[10] Dockray, *Warrior King*, p. 242.

Renewed interest in Henry and his rule has recently resulted in a volume of scholarly essays, which may come to form a companion to the earlier *Henry V: the Practice of Kingship* (1985). *Henry V: New Interpretations*, ed. G. Dodd (Woodbridge, 2013) provides an overview of recent work, with a useful Introduction (by Christopher Allmand) outlining the main trends in thinking about the king and his reign in recent years. Its emphasis is – with a couple of exceptions – largely on the English aspects of the reign, especially on its financial basis and fiscal practices, but essays on Henry's household, his Chapel Royal, his suppression of Lollardy, and his chivalric reputation, broaden the canvas. His rule – as well as his campaigning – in France, as both Regent and as ruler in Normandy, which has not always received the attention it deserves, is usefully broached in a contribution (by Neil Murphy) on Henry's relations with the towns in Normandy and Lancastrian France. As chapter 5 in the present book on Henry and the Church in Normandy attempts to suggest, treatment of this aspect of the reign demands further research. His concern to confirm the privileges and liberties of both towns and churches implies an appreciation of the need to win the inhabitants of his French conquests to his side. Seeing Henry V as a French ruler, as well as an English sovereign and a European statesman, forms an essential dimension to any fully rounded picture of the king.

In creating that picture, this book attempts, as far as is ever possible, to draw conclusions about Henry V and his legacy. An effort is made to avoid resorting to what Bishop Stubbs, in 1878, called 'the judgement of modern opinion'.[11] The abstract judgements of subsequent generations can some- times distort rather than illuminate the past. Notions of 'good' or 'bad' kingship, it is suggested, do not necessarily help our analysis, because they often refer to abstract, anachronistic or inappropriate criteria, or bench- marks, for a ruler's conduct. Nor is an attempt here made, by a 'lesser mortal', to cut the king down to size. The prime source of evidence lies in

[11] See above, p. 4, n. 6.

the archival material that reveals the degree to which the king was personally involved, and directly intervened, in matters of all kinds. It is therefore
a study of rule at its most personal. Anachronistic concepts of nationalism
and 'modern' state formation are held back in favour of what (it is hoped)
is a more appropriate view of the fifteenth-century context. A degree of
realism about the circumstances in which this remarkable man found
himself is introduced: the extent to which he was able to shape and mould
them to his advantage, and the degree to which opportunism ruled his
behaviour, is assessed. Was this a Machiavellian ruler living a century
before Machiavelli (1469–1527)? But, as McFarlane observed, Henry 'was
not the one Machiavelli in an innocent world'.[12] Or was there a higher
cause which shaped his actions? Did Henry's professed wish to unite
England and France in a peaceful union, which would result in a joint
campaign to recover the Holy Land from the infidel, really determine his
motives and behaviour? We can conclude that the able war leader, and
pragmatic military organiser, may have been a far more complex and
interesting figure than some of the extant literature might lead us to
believe. It has recently been said that 'as hard as they might try, historians
will continue to struggle to overturn the basic view that Henry V was an
extraordinarily capable and successful king'.[13] Insofar as any verdict
emerges from this book, it will not dissent from that view. But there are,
perhaps, other issues with which historians may spend their time and
energy struggling. The creation of a plausible and convincing context and
explanation for a ruler's behaviour is one of them. And, to explain that
behaviour, it is not always necessary to invoke tests of capability, inca-
pacity, success or failure. Abstract judgement is not always the most helpful
tool of historical analysis.

---

[12] McFarlane, 'Henry V: a Personal Portrait', p. 126.
[13] G. Dodd, 'Henry V's Establishment: Service, Loyalty and Reward in 1413' in *Henry V: New
Interpretations*, ed. Dodd, p. 64.

Chapter 1

THE EVERYDAY BUSINESS OF KINGSHIP

Also . . . King Henry V used every day, when full royal estate was not kept after dinner, to have a cushion laid on the 'cupborde', and there he would lean for the space of an hour or more to receive petitions and complaints from whomsoever would come.

(*The Ryalle Book*, c.1460)[1]

What did a later medieval English king do all day? What was his daily round and routine? What did 'personal monarchy' really mean? Henry V, of whom it has been said that he 'kept personal control of every branch of government',[2] chose to exercise one important facet of that

---

[1] 'The Ryalle Book' (c.1460) in *The Antiquarian Repertory*, ed. F. Grose & T. Astle, 4 vols (London, 1807), i, p. 314: 'Also . . . Kinge Henry the Vth used every day that none estat was kept aftur dener, but to have a quyschyne laid on the cupborde, and ther he wold lene by the space of an houre or more to resave bills and compleynts off whomsoever wold come . . .' *The Ryalle Book,* which includes a manual of procedures for the king's chamberlain and the ushers of his Chamber, has been re-dated from the reign of Henry VII to c.1460. See D. Starkey, 'Henry VI's Old Blue Gown: the English Court under the Lancastrians and Yorkists', *Court Historian*, 4 (1999), pp. 1–28, esp. pp. 12–13. See also J. Stowe, *Annales of England* (London, 1952), pp. 549–50 for a similar account.

[2] K.B. McFarlane, 'Henry V: a Personal Portrait' in his *Lancastrian Kings and Lollard Knights* (Oxford, 1972), p. 117. McFarlane's essay was first delivered as a lecture to the Oxford branch of the Workers' Educational Association in November 1954.

control in the domestic setting of his household. Not only, as the popular imagination might picture him, on the battlefield, in the camp or at the siege, but going about the normal everyday business of fifteenth-century kingship. Even the greatest of military leaders could not afford to ignore or neglect the other obligations they had to those over whom they ruled. Some form of dialogue and exchange between a ruler and his subjects was an essential requirement and duty of kingship, whether conducted directly or through intermediaries. A breakdown of that dialogue could, in England, contribute to the downfall of a monarch, as it had done under Edward II in 1327 and Richard II in 1399.

Henry's practice, inherited from his father, Henry IV, of informally receiving petitions from his subjects on days when the formal 'keeping of estate' (or royal ceremony) by the king did not apply, played an important part in this process. As *The Ryalle Book* tells us, this reception by the king – in person – of supplications and complaints took place in the Great Chamber after dinner in the Hall, and represented the exercise of personal monarchy at its most direct. The everyday business of kingship certainly had its formalities, but it was also conducted more informally, in parallel with the institutionalised procedures associated with Council, Parliament and the great departments of state. An image of the king standing, leaning on a cushion placed on the 'cupboard' (in fact a sideboard or table) in the Great Chamber, upon which gold and silver plates of spices and cups of wine were set out, imparts a near-domestic character to one of the vital functions of a fifteenth-century ruler.[3] Much has been made of the increasing 'bureaucratisation' of government during this period, but this image of the king reminds us that his household still remained a power

---

[3] For a tapestry ('1 pece darras') 'pur le cuppebord, del estorie "Dune dame qe harpe"' in the inventory of Henry V's goods taken after his death, in 1423, see *RP*, iv, pp. 214–41, no. 693 [TNA, C 65/85, m. 15r]. Unless otherwise stated all references to original archive material in this book relate to documents in The National Archives, Kew (TNA).

centre, providing that space around a ruler which was the scene of his daily activity.[4]

To hear, assess, adjudicate and respond to petitions (the 'bills and comp-leynts' of *The Ryalle Book*) were among the most significant activities of a king or prince, often conducted on a near-daily basis.[5] It has recently been observed that 'the late medieval period was an age of the petition *par excellence*'.[6] This chapter will therefore concentrate on this aspect of Henry V's exercise of kingship, as well as on some of the more formal and ritualised daily expressions of his power and authority. But in order to understand the ways in which Henry exercised that authority, we need briefly to outline the largely bureaucratic processes through which the king's decisions, however spontaneous, were translated into actions. To some extent, the nature of those decisions could be shaped and determined by the very procedures, with their accompanying constraints, to which a ruler and his advisers, officers and civil servants had to conform. There remained, of course, considerable scope for the exercise of the king's prerogative, and of those qualities of justice, reason, conscience and charity which he was exhorted to cultivate and display. Conscience and duty certainly had their parts to play.[7]

---

[4] For the role played by members of Henry V's household in political life see D. Morgan, 'The Household Retinue of Henry V and the Ethos of English Public Life' in *Concepts and Patterns of Service in the Later Middle Ages*, ed. A. Curry & E. Matthew (Woodbridge, 2000), pp. 64–79, esp. pp. 69–72.

[5] For recent literature (which is extensive) on the petitioning process see M. Ormrod, 'Murmur, Clamour and Noise: Voicing Complaint and Remedy in Petitions to the English crown, *c*.1300–1460' in *Medieval Petitions: Grace and Grievance*, ed. W. M. Ormrod, G. Dodd & A. Musson (York, 2009), pp. 135–55; G. Dodd, *Justice and Grace: Private Petitioning and the English Parliament in the Late Middle Ages* (Oxford, 2007); 'The Rise of English, the Decline of French: Supplications to the English Crown, *c*.1420–1450', *Speculum*, 86 (2011), pp. 117–50; 'Kingship, Parliament and the Court: the Emergence of a "High Style" in Petitions to the English Crown, *c*. 1350–1405', *EHR*, 129 (2014), pp. 515–48; and his 'Thomas Paunfield, the Heye Court of Rightwisnesse and the Language of Petitioning in the 15th Century' in *Medieval Petitions*, pp. 222–41. The standard work on petitions received by Parliament at this period remains A.R. Myers, 'Parliamentary Petitions in the 15th Century', *EHR*, 52 (1937), pp. 385–404, 590–613.

[6] G. Dodd & S. Petit-Renaud, 'Grace and Favour: the Petition and its Mechanisms' in *Government and Political Life in England and France, c.1300–c.1500*, ed. C. Fletcher, J-P. Genet & J. Watts (Cambridge, 2015), p. 240.

[7] See below, pp. 60–1, 138, 169–72; also, for a stimulating survey, J. Catto, 'The Burden and Conscience of Government in the Fifteenth Century', *TRHS*, 17 (2007), pp. 83–99.

It has been said of Henry V that 'his inclinations were despotic . . . and like most successful despots he knew when to unbend'.[8] But the king's authority, however authoritarian or autocratic he might appear, was not unconstrained, nor was it absolute, in either theory or practice.[9] In England, the power of the crown was essentially subject to the limits imposed upon it by Magna Carta (1215), and its subsequent confirmations and revisions. It was – in this respect, but not others – essentially unlike the power of, for example, the Italian despots of the same period. The Visconti, Sforza and Malatesta were in effect absolved from the laws, were not bound to observe statutes, and could tax without consent. In 1334, for example, Malatesta 'Guastafamiglia', his brother Galeotto, and their heirs were granted *plenitudo potestatis* ('fullness of power') by the general council of the commune at Rimini.[10] They were thereby 'absolved from obedience to all statutes, and empowered to proceed against anyone, *ad sui comodum pro libito voluntatis* ('to their advantage on account of the freedom of [their] will').[11] Similarly, the Visconti at Milan had, by the mid- to late fourteenth century, acquired 'acknowledged title to absolute power'.[12] In fifteenth-century France, the king, it was likewise thought, 'has no other control over him than the fear of God and his own conscience'.[13] Arbitrary rule in the French manner had created what has been described as an 'unwieldy tyranny'.

[8] K.B. McFarlane, 'Henry V, Bishop Beaufort and the Red Hat, 1417–1421', in *England in the Fifteenth Century. Collected Essays*, ed. G.L. Harriss (London, 1981), p. 79. The article was originally published in 1945.

[9] For another view, rejected in the present book, which sees Henry V as an 'absolutist monarch', see I. Mortimer, *1415: Henry V's Year of Glory* (London, 2010), esp. pp. 318–19, 542–3. Also see below, pp. 59–61.

[10] See P.J. Jones, *The Malatesta of Rimini and the Papal State. A Political History* (Cambridge, 1974), pp. 63–6.

[11] P.J. Jones, 'The End of Malatesta Rule in Rimini' in *Italian Renaissance Studies*, ed. E.F. Jacob (London, 1960), p. 222.

[12] See D.M. Bueno de Mesquita, 'The Place of Despotism in Italian Politics' in *Europe in the Late Middle Ages*, ed. J.R. Hale. J.R.L. Highfield & B. Smalley (London, 1965), p. 302 and, for further discussion of the nature of Visconti/Sforza despotism, pp. 316–20.

[13] Quoted by P.S. Lewis, 'France in the Fifteenth Century: Society and Sovereignty' in *Europe in the Late Middle Ages*, ed. Hale, Highfield & Smalley, p. 279; and p. 300 for the 'unwieldy tyranny'.

In England, things were different. Henry V's power was moderated, and sometimes bridled, not only by Magna Carta and the laws, enshrining the need for consultation and consent, but also by the sheer bureaucratic processes of the king's own government. Much – though by no means all – of later medieval 'governance' (the act or process of governing) was reactive, prompted and spurred by request, petition and complaint. But the manner in which a king might react, and the reasoning behind that reaction, was in part determined by the boundaries imposed by what we might call procedural due process on a ruler's assumptions and behaviour. Established rules and principles, part and parcel of the daily functioning of government, had an important part to play. In the study of power and its exercise, the supposedly dry-as-dust details of administrative history have, whether we like it or not, a central and fundamental place.[14] Its recent comparative neglect, in company with diplomatic history, has left historical writing deprived of a vital dimension. To understand and explain the assumptions and behaviour of the powerful, we have to come to grips with the formal processes whereby their decisions were expressed, transmitted and implemented. There is simply no alternative, whatever the technicalities and apparently arcane issues involved, to the close study of those processes and their documentation. A bitter pill, occasionally sweetened and enlivened with anecdote and illustrative example, has sometimes to be swallowed.

The practice of addressing requests, petitions and supplications to rulers dated more or less from time immemorial. It was a part of that process whereby the mercy, clemency or simply judgement of a sovereign, a prince or lord might be appealed to, over and above any formal legal or

[14] Although it in effect concludes in 1399, the masterpiece in this respect remains T.F. Tout, *Chapters in the Administrative History of Medieval England*, 6 vols (Manchester, 1920–33). Tout's account of the privy seal, however, moves at some points into the fifteenth century. For a more recent plea for the centrality of administrative history, advocating the need to focus upon institutions and administrative systems, rather than individuals, their ideas and motivations, see G. Dodd, 'Patronage, Petitions and Grace: the "Chamberlain's Bill" of Henry IV's Reign' in *Henry IV: Rebellion and Survival, 1403–1413*, ed. G. Dodd & D. Biggs (Woodbridge, 2008), pp. 105–34, esp. pp. 105–6.

judicial procedure regulated by courts or other bodies. This was an aspect of rule at its most personal, which had been exercised by biblical kings, oriental potentates, Roman emperors and governors of many kinds, thereby expressing and endorsing their ultimate authority. There were many medieval rulers who were represented, and sought to present themselves, as latter-day King Solomons, the great biblical law-giver, whether receiving petitions and homage, and dispensing justice, under oak or elm trees, or through much more formal procedures. Henry II of England (1154–89), as duke of Normandy, had held court, negotiated settlements, and received homage and supplications in the shade of a great elm at Gisors, which became the victim of an act of arboricide by Philip Augustus of France in August 1188.[15] A more celebrated instance was that of Louis IX of France (1226–70) sitting, sometimes on the ground, under an oak in the Bois de Vincennes or in the garden of his palace on the Île-de-la-Cité, hearing and adjudicating petitions from his subjects. In the biography of the king by Joinville,[16] an image – soon to become iconic – of Louis was presented, eliciting the observation from a modern historian that the Vincennes oak represented a 'place of the king's personal justice, and of access for his subjects to the public exercise, in the open air, of the principal kingly function'.[17] This was an 'idealised model of a direct, personal monarchical government . . . which he [Joinville] opposed to a contemporary model of a bureaucratic monarchy'.[18] Under Henry V an attempt was

---

[15] See J.-F. Lemarignier, *Recherches sur l'hommage en marche et les frontières féodales* (Lille, 1945), pp. 73–113, 104; also the intriguingly entitled article by L. Diggelmann, 'Hewing the Ancient Elm: Anger, Arboricide and Medieval Kingship', *Journal of Medieval and Early Modern Studies*, 40:2 (2010), pp. 249–72 which discusses, among other matters, Philip Augustus of France's destruction of the elm at Gisors.

[16] See Jean de Joinville, *Histoire de Saint Louis*, ed. N. de Wailly (Paris, 1874), p. 35.

[17] J. Le Goff, *Saint Louis* (Paris, 1996), caption to Illustration 4: 'le lieu de la justice personelle du roi, de l'accès pour ses sujets à l'exercise public en plein air de la principale fonction royale . . .'

[18] Le Goff, *Saint Louis*, p. 484, n. 4: 'un modèle idealisé d'un gouvernement monarchique direct, personnel . . . qu'il [Joinville] oppose au modèle contemporaine d'une monarchie bureaucratique'. Further references to this image of St Louis are on pp. 484–5, 603, 702–4.

being made – apparently with some success – to perpetuate that model of personal government, idealised or not. But to deal effectively with the sheer volume of request and complaint demanded, in addition, more bureaucratic structures and procedures.

In later medieval England, the practice of petitioning for favour, compensation, dispensation or redress had been, to a large degree, formalised and institutionalised. The process of supplication could assume a variety of forms. Beside the quasi-domestic, informal ritual which we have already observed, conducted by Henry V in the king's Great Chamber, petitions were presented, written on parchment and, to a lesser – though increasing – extent, on paper, in different settings and contexts.[19] All, however, fell broadly into one of two fundamental categories: first, requests for, or complaints about, the redress of perceived grievances which could not be resolved by the normal processes of the common law; and, secondly, requests for the simple grant of favours, benefits or dispensations. Petitions presented directly in the king's Chamber, or elsewhere when the king was present in person (e.g. at the Tower of London, Westminster, Canterbury or Kenilworth), became known as 'chamberlains' bills'.[20] Once dealt with, they were signed and endorsed by the chamberlain, then sent to, and kept by, the privy seal office. To implement the decisions stemming from them, a privy seal writ, addressed by the king to the Chancellor, the Treasurer or other high-ranking officers, was normally required, commanding the appropriate action. Hence the eventual issue of formal, official letters patent or close (in Latin) in the king's name by the Chancellor, under the large and impressive great seal of the kingdom, could only be initiated and

---

[19] Although now divided, sometimes artificially, among various archival classes, a large number of surviving petitions, and material relating to them, can be found at The National Archives in TNA, SC 8 (Ancient Petitions), SC 1 (Ancient Correspondence), C 81 (Chancery Warrants), C 49 (Parliament Rolls, for common petitions) & E 28 (Privy Seal and Council Files). These have provided the main source of evidence for this chapter.

[20] See Dodd, 'Patronage, Petitions and Grace . . .', pp. 105–34.

certified by writs and letters of warranty under the smaller privy seal.[21] This process was of vital importance, because so many of a ruler's decisions, and their translation into practice, were subject to its terms and procedures. The sheer volume of privy seal business had by the fourteenth century generated its own bureaucratic department – the privy seal office. Like the Chancery, it had its permanent seat in London. Under Henry V, the office consisted of fourteen clerks, including the poet Thomas Hoccleve,[22] skilled in the rhetorical arts and techniques that had been introduced into the process whereby letters, writs and diplomatic documents were drawn up.[23] It also serviced the king's council, and was vital to the routine business of government when (as under Henry V) the king was absent abroad. The establishment of routine was a key part of later medieval government, as it relieved the not inconsiderable burdens on the ruler.[24] The cogs and wheels of the English administrative system thus revolved around the deployment of various wax seals – the great and privy seals, and (increasingly) the king's personal seal or signet – creating an

---

[21] The processes involved in warranty are set out in detail (drawing largely on evidence from Henry IV's reign, 1404–5) in A.L. Brown, 'Authorization of Letters under the Great Seal', *BIHR*, 37 (1964), pp. 125–56.

[22] For Hoccleve's literary output see *Hoccleve's Works, The Minor Poems*, i, ed. F.J. Furnivall, *EETS* Extra Series, lxi (1892); ii, ed. I. Gollancz, *EETS* Extra Series, lxxiii (1925); *Hoccleve's Works, The Regemen of Princes*, ed. F.J. Furnivall, *EETS* Extra Series, lxii (1897); & J.H. Fisher, *The Emergence of Standard English* (Lexington, Massachusetts, 1996), pp. 33–5. His work, both poetic and bureaucratic, has attracted an extensive secondary literature. See E. P. Knapp, *The Bureaucratic Muse: Thomas Hoccleve and the Literature of Late Medieval England* (Philadelphia, 2001) & H.K.S. Killick, 'Thomas Hoccleve as Poet and Clerk', unpublished University. of York Ph.D. thesis, 2010.

[23] For the workings and personnel of the privy seal office see J. Catto, 'The King's Servants' in *Henry V: the Practice of Kingship*, ed. G. L. Harriss (Oxford, 1985; 2nd edn Stroud, 1993), pp. 79–82. Also A.L. Brown, 'Privy Seal Clerks in the Early Fifteenth Century' in *The Study of Medieval Records: Essays presented to Kathleen Major*, ed. D. Bullough & R.L. Storey (Oxford, 1971), pp. 260–81. Hoccleve was rewarded with pensions from both Henry IV and Henry V, which continued into the reign of Henry VI: E 403/655, m. 4r (May 1422); E 403/658, m. 4r (Feb. 1423).

[24] This was as common in the Italian despotisms of the period as in monarchies. See, for example, Bueno de Mesquita, 'The Place of Despotism in Italian Politics' in *Europe in the Late Middle Ages*, ed. Hale, Highfield & Smalley, pp. 301–31, esp. pp. 320–1, for the place of routine in the government of the Visconti and Sforza of Milan.

interlocking machinery of grants, warrants, patents, writs and mandates whereby actions were ordered, implemented and authenticated. And the record-keeping activities of departments such as the privy seal office assisted the admittedly patchy and partial survival of these documents (in part a result of the Whitehall fire of 1619 which destroyed many dating from before c.1386) to this day.[25]

There were, therefore, under Henry V, a number of types of petition which were presented and dealt with in and by different offices and departments.[26] Of this large body of surviving documentation, the greater part can be divided into three main classes: first, the so-called 'Chancery bills', addressed to the Chancellor, some of which were sent on to the king for adjudication; second, the 'chamberlains' bills' presented, as we have seen, directly to the king in his Chamber; and, lastly, Parliamentary petitions, presented in Parliament, falling into the two groups of 'private' and 'common' supplications. Private petitions came largely from individuals; common petitions from corporate bodies and groups such as merchants, clergy, the burgesses of a town, the members of a guild, fraternity, university or even a garrison, and other collective entities. Some of these, as well as some petitions from individuals, were presented on their behalf by members of Parliament from the shires and boroughs. Under Henry V, in the 1421 Parliament, the Commons 'interceded' for a substantial number of petitioners, and they could represent the interests of certain groups, such as the merchants of the Staple at Calais, or specific members of both clergy and laity.[27] The king could also receive supplications from the

---

[25] S. Thurley, *Whitehall Palace: an Architectural History of the Royal Apartments, 1240–1690* (London/New Haven, 1999), pp. 65–80 for the Banqueting House fire of 1619; also Brown, 'Authorization of Letters under the Great Seal', p. 126.

[26] For what follows see Dodd, 'The Rise of English, the Decline of French', pp. 118–22; Myers, 'Parliamentary Petitions', pp. 385–96, 590–4, 612–13. Dating from between the later thirteenth and later fifteenth centuries, 17,629 petitions can be found in The National Archives. See, for an online source, http://www.nationalarchives.gov.uk/documentsonline/petitions.asp

[27] *RP,* iv, p. 53 (1414); 80 (1416). The Parliament Rolls are available online, as PROME: www.sd-editions.com/PROME or www.british-history.ac.uk>Sources>Primary.

Commons in Parliament, as a collective entity, describing themselves as 'his poor Commons' ('ses poveres communes'). Sometimes petitions would be received from other groups of the 'commons', such as 'les communes' or 'les communaltes' of specific shires.[28] The identities of Parliamentary petitioners were thus extremely diverse.

Of all types of supplication, those presented in Parliament, received by Chancery clerks, then 'tried' (or assessed) and filtered for the king's attention by specially appointed auditors, were perhaps the most formal in their manner of presentation and format. Some could be resolved by the 'triers' themselves, but others were passed on to the lords in Parliament, the council or the king for a response. Many were enrolled, with replies, for record on the Parliament Rolls. It had become customary for the Chancellor, at the end of the Parliamentary sermon he preached to members at the beginning of every session, to invite petitions. The Parliament Roll of 1414, for instance, stated that 'the Chancellor said that because . . . the king wishes that right and full justice be done to all his subjects, both rich and poor, if there is anyone who wishes to complain about any harm or wrong done to them, which could not be remedied by the common law, they should submit their petitions, between now and next Saturday, to the assigned receivers . . . the names of whom, and also of the triers of the same, follow below'.[29] By whatever means their petitions were presented and received, all petitioners were expected to adhere to certain epistolary and supplicatory forms, formulas and conventions. These were very largely in Anglo-Norman French but also, under Henry V, they began to be composed in English. Responses to such requests are often found written on the dorse (back) or face (front) of the petition itself (as had been the case from the later thirteenth century onwards). But, from the mid- to late

---

[28] *RP*, iv, p. 14 (1413); Myers, 'Parliamentary Petitions', pp. 390–7.
[29] *RP*, iv, p. 34 (1414).

fourteenth century, writs under one of the king's smaller seals, authorising grants to be made in reply to petitions, were, increasingly, issued. This meant that the response to the petition could now be contained within the writ, summarising the content of the request, which was then attached to the original petition and sent forward for action to the privy seal office. But the crucial practice of endorsement, whereby the king's wishes were recorded on the petition itself, sometimes in his own hand, continued. It is here that we can see the king himself in action, without any shadow of doubt as to his personal involvement in the particular decision that was reached. This is therefore among the most vital of our types of evidence for Henry V's conduct of the everyday business of kingship.

A striking feature of the petitioning process under Henry V was the increasingly widespread use of a practice which may appear as merely an administrative or archival detail, but which carried important implications. During his reign, the king's signet emerged as the preferred instrument by which warrants for action by the Chancellor, as custodian of the great seal, and by the Keeper of the privy seal, normally both high-ranking churchmen, as well as other officers, were normally initiated and authenticated.[30] The signet, which could be mounted on a finger-ring, had become the most personal of the king's smaller seals over the course of the previous century. It had originally emerged in 1311–12, described as the king's 'secret' seal, when his council had taken over control of the privy seal during one of the crises of Edward II's reign.[31] The king had therefore to have some instrument at hand in order to seal his private correspondence. Under Edward III, the secret seal became known, after 1367, as the

---

[30] For an examination of the signet and its uses at this period see J. Otway-Ruthven, *The King's Secretary and the Signet Office in the xvth Century* (Cambridge, 1939; repr. 2008). The surviving letters under the signet at this time are listed, calendared and summarised in *Calendar of Signet Letters of Henry IV and Henry V*, ed. J.L. Kirby (London, 1978).

[31] See P. Chaplais, *English Diplomatic Practice in the Middle Ages* (London, 2003), pp. 97–8, 100.

signet and was used for diplomatic and other correspondence, especially for matters in which the king had a special interest or which were 'close to his heart'.[32] In time, as the signet became more 'official' and institutionalised, it became customary for the king to adopt, in addition, a sign manual or signature which he himself wrote on signet letters to demonstrate that they represented his will, or that he was particularly concerned by their contents.[33]

The increasingly frequent appearance of the autograph sign manual 'RH' ('R[ex] H[enricus]') or 'HR' ('H[enricus] R[ex]') indicated the king's personal presence and involvement in the most immediate of ways.[34] The signet – or signets, as there were more than one of them – however,

---

[32] Chaplais, *English Diplomatic Practice*, pp. 100–1. The formula 'this oure writing procedeth of oure certain science and hert' is found in signet letters, signed with the sign manual, under Henry VI. See Otway-Ruthven, *The King's Secretary and the Signet Office*, p. 26. See below, chapter 2, pp. 72–3, 76–8.

[33] Edward II had used the privy seal to similar effect during the crisis that was to lead to his deposition. In a letter to his loyal nobles and towns in Gascony, dated 23 Sept. 1326, Edward told them to ignore letters purporting to represent his son's (Prince Edward's) wishes, but in effect stemming from those with malicious intent around him, as they 'contained certain things contrary to our will'. He had already informed the towns, in a letter dated 27 June that, as well as the Latin text under the great seal, he was sending a French version under the privy seal. They could then be assured that it was an authentic and genuine expression of his will. See M. Vale, *The Origins of the Hundred Years War. The Angevin Legacy, 1250–1340* (Oxford 1996), pp. 245–6; & C 61/38, mm. 6v, 4v. [www.gasconrolls.org/edition/calendars/C 61].

[34] The first recorded appearance of Henry's sign manual appears to be in Apr.–May 1415 (E 101/69/7, nos 509–10). Otway-Ruthven, however, thought that the use of the sign manual 'does not become usual until the reign of Henry VI' (*The King's Secretary and the Signet Office*, p. 25). The sign manual is first recorded under Richard II. See Chaplais, *English Diplomatic Practice*, pp. 100–1 & below, pp. 27, n.35, 64, 65–7. A similar chronology for the emergence of the sign manual or signature is found in France, where the period *c.*1360–1400 can be seen as a turning point in its favour. See B. Fraenkel, *Signature: genèse d'un signe* (Paris, 1992) & by C. Jeay, 'Pour une histoire de la signature: du sceau a la signature, histoire des signes de validation en France (xiiie–xve siècles)', *Labyrinthe. Actualité de la Recherche*, 7 (2000), pp. 155–6 [http://labyrinth.revues.org/739]; 'La Naissance de la signature dans les cours royales et princières de la France (xiiie–xve siècles)', in *Auctor et Auctoritas. Invention et conformisme dans l'écriture médiévale*, ed. M. Zimmermann (Paris, 2001), pp. 457–75; *Des Signatures et des rois: du signe de validation à l'emblème personnel (France, xiiie–xve siècle)* (Paris, 2003); 'La Signature comme marque d'individuation. La chancellerie royale française (fin xiiie–xve siècle)', in *L'Individu au Moyen Âge. Individuation et individualisation avant la modernité*, ed. B.M. Bedos-Rezak & D. Iogna-Prat (Paris, 2005), pp. 59–78. See below, pp. 63–4, 65–7, 277–8.

remained the king's own personal instrument whereby his will and wishes were made known.[35]

Like the privy seal, but unlike the double-sided great seal, the signet was single-sided, often applied to the surface of a document rather than appended on a tag, cord, or tongue of parchment. The relative scarcity of complete surviving impressions may in part be accounted for by this practice: a *plaqué* or *en placard* seal cracked, flaked and disintegrated far more easily than an appended seal. Such was the frequency with which the signet was now used, and the volume of business that came its way, that (as with the king's other seals) it called for bureaucratic support. By the early fifteenth century a small signet office, with a staff of at least five clerks under Henry V, had evolved.[36] The king's secretary acted as its head and as formal keeper of the seal. By Henry's reign, the signet was often referred to in the documents to which it was applied by the Latin formula 'a tergo' or 'a targo' (literally, 'by', or 'on, the back' or 'dorse' of the document) (Lat. *tergum, targum*). In his last will, made at Dover on 10 June 1421, before his departure for the last time to France, Henry referred to his 'signeto aquile a tergo' ('signet of the eagle on the dorse'), as well as his 'signeto armorum nostrorum' ('signet of our [heraldic] arms').[37] A surviving wax impression of a heraldic signet (described as a 'secret' seal), on a document dated in June 1414, shows a small circular seal, in red wax, on a tag, with a shield of arms within it, inset with a circular band, or fender, of

[35] Some contrast with the reign of Henry IV is suggested in Brown, 'Authorization of Letters under the Great Seal', p. 141: under Henry IV 'the signet seems to be going through a period of relative unimportance, perhaps in reaction to its extensive use by Richard II'. The position appears to have been significantly changed under Henry V.

[36] See Otway-Ruthven, *The King's Secretary and the Signet Office*, pp. 106–25. Also her 'The King's Secretary in the Fifteenth Century', *TRHS*, 4th ser., 19 (1936), pp. 81–100, esp. pp. 88–9.

[37] ECR, MS 59, fo. 6r, edited and printed in P. Strong & F. Strong, 'The Last Will and Codicils of Henry V', *EHR*, 96 (1981), pp. 79–102. For discussion of Henry's various wills, see below, pp. 84–6, 240–6, 255–8. I am indebted to Professor Brigitte Miriam Bedos-Rezak for her advice on sigillographic questions and the interpretation of diplomatic formulae.

twisted rush.[38] On 8 June 1421 he had sealed another document, also at Dover, 'under our signet of the eagle, in the absence of our other'.[39] In March of that year he had also referred to the use of 'our signet of theegle in absence of our oothir signet' in two letters, issued at Weobley and Shrewsbury.[40] There was clearly more than one signet used by the king, but each appears to have carried sufficient and equivalent authority to authenticate and validate letters and writs.

The use of smaller seals to add validity, weight and strength to documents issued under greater seals of majesty or dignity seems to have emerged in the later twelfth and early thirteenth centuries. Sometimes these took the form of counterseals, whereby the smaller 'secret' seal was impressed on the back (*a tergo*) of a wax impression of the larger seal. To understand the motives and influences behind Henry V's use of the signet, which sometimes appears to have been used as a counterseal, we need to take account of such developments in sealing practice and diplomatic. Despite assumptions to the contrary, they were by no means irrelevant to the manner in which power was exercised, projected and expressed by a ruler. The function of the counterseal was set out very clearly in, for example, charters and letters issued by European episcopal chanceries from the mid-thirteenth century onwards. In January 1259, a letter of Otto von Lonsdorf, bishop of Passau, carried the following explanatory postscript:

> And let it be noted that this is the first letter where we have had our secret [seal] impressed on the back of our seal [of dignity], which [secret seal] contains a wolf within a shield, engraved as a device, and the superscription reads: SECRETUM ECCLESIE ['secret (seal) of the Church']. On account of this, we henceforth judge all letters written on our

---

[38] E 30/1531: instructions to ambassadors to the duke of Burgundy, at the castle of Pontefract, 25 June 1414.
[39] C 81/1365, no. 31: 8 June 1421.
[40] C 81/1365, nos 28, 29: 7 & 11 Mar. 1421.

behalf, with our seal depending from them, to be false, unless that seal has the aforesaid shield [of the wolf] impressed upon the back [*a tergo*].[41]

A similar practice was followed by the bishops of Breslau (Bratislava) in the fourteenth century, when an *inspeximus* of twelve episcopal letters, dated 2 March 1347, referred to

> one letter, that is to say the largest, to which is appended, on a silken cord, the seal of lord Henry, lord bishop of Breslau, having green wax on its face and common [*communem*] wax on its back [*a tergo*] . . . and a second letter which has two seals appended on silk, having green wax on their face and common wax on their back [*a tergo*].[42]

English monastic and episcopal chanceries appear to have adopted similar practices. Thus the round counterseal of St Mary's (Augustinian) abbey at Leicester bore the legend around its circumference: 'We are placed on the back [*a tergo*] and we are thus a sign of witness'.[43] The archbishops of York acted in a similar fashion. The archbishop's counterseal was used 'against' his seal of dignity (the equivalent of the royal great seal) to strengthen the validity of an instrument or document. The seal used for this purpose was the *Secretum* (secret seal) in the thirteenth century, superseded by the archbishop's signet in the fourteenth, which was used for private letters and

---

41 See *Monumentorum boicorum collatio nova*, 29 (Augsburg, 1831), p. 131: 'Et notandum quod hec est prima littera ubi in sigillo a tergo secretum nostrum imprimi fecimus, quod Lupum in scuto, pro signo insculptum continet, et superscriptionem continet. SECRETUM ECCLESIE. Quapropter omnes litteras ex parte nostri scriptas cum pendent sigillo nostro, nisi ipsum sigillum a tergo predictum scutum impressum habeat, falsas exnunc inantea judicamus . . .'

42 See *Codex Diplomaticus Silesiae, hrsg. vom Vereine für Geschichte und Alterthum Schlesiens*, Bd 10, *Urkunden des Kloster Kamenz*, ed. P. Pfotenhauer (Breslau, 1881), no. CC: 'quarum uni, scilicet majori, est appensum in corda sericea sigillum domini Henrici domini episcopi Wratislaviensis, in facie habens ceram viridem et a tergo communem'; the second letter 'habebat 2 sigilla in serico pendencia, in facie viridem ceram et a tergo communem habencia'.

43 See 'Houses of Augustinian Canons: Leicester Abbey', *VCH, County of Leicester* (London, 1934), ii, pp. 13–19.

other business, sometimes on its own.[44] As in the case of the smaller royal seals, the signet was attached to documents 'the contents of which were of special interest to the archbishop'.[45] Unlike other episcopal seals, which were oval, the signet was a round seal, often bearing the heraldic device of its owner or a personal emblem such as Archbishop Kemp's eagle arising (1450). It could also act as a counterseal, and Kemp, when bishop of London, issued letters under 'his great seal, with an impression of the signet of the same bishop on the back [*in dorso*] of that seal'.[46]

It is noteworthy that Henry V's signet, or signets, could also act as a counterseal when used in conjunction with other seals. But they – especially the 'signet of the eagle' – could be used alone, applied to the back of letters, warrants and other documents, impressed upon a cross or star of red wax, sometimes protected with a fender of twisted rush.[47] The address and addressee of such letters were recorded on the back, or dorse, of the document, which was closed by the signet. Hence the warrants issued under the signet by Henry V still bear traces on their dorse of the application of the signet (in red wax) even though the *plaqué* seal itself has perished.[48] When the signet of the eagle was being employed on its own, the king would sometimes indicate its use 'in the absence of our other [signet]'.[49] But this did not appear to affect its validity, or authenticity, as an instrument for the expression of his wishes.

The signet of the eagle may have originated as the king's personal seal of warranty for duchy of Lancaster business after the Lancastrian usurpation

---

[44] See J.P. Dalton, *The Archiepiscopal and Deputed Seals of York, 1114–1500* (York, 1992), pp. 6–9.

[45] Dalton, *The Archiepiscopal and Deputed Seals*, p. 9.

[46] *Register of Henry Chichele, Archbishop of Canterbury, 1414–1443*, ed. E. F. Jacob, Canterbury & York Society (1938–47), iv, pp. 256, 261: 'sigillo suo magno cum impressione signeti eiusdem episcopi in dorso ipsius sigilli'; Dalton, *The Archiepiscopal and Deputed Seals*, p. 9.

[47] See Otway-Ruthven, *The King's Secretary and the Signet Office*, Plate II, facing p. 24, & pp. 25–6.

[48] Many of the warrants under the signet in e.g. C 81/1365 have such traces on their dorse.

[49] See also above, pp. 28–9.

of Richard II in 1399.[50] Warrants from the king, activating the other seals of the duchy, were normally issued under it. But it was to become the king's personal and secret seal of choice, for many types of business, under Henry V. Surviving wax impressions are of great interest, as the image of the eagle set into them appears not to be engraved on metal (usually on gold, silver or silver gilt) but cut from a stone, perhaps an ancient gemstone or antique intaglio, set within a later medieval surround.[51] This was not an unusual practice for personal seals, and a number of these gem or cameo seals survive.[52] The image on it is of a double-headed eagle – an imperial symbol used by the Byzantine emperors from an early date, and then by the medieval German, and later Austro-Hungarian and Russian emperors.[53] Symbolising temporal authority – and conferring it on both Church and State – the twin-headed 'signet of the eagle' may have been a natural seal of choice and preference for Henry V. It might even tell us something about his conception of kingship and of his dual role in both secular and ecclesiastical matters. Around the more deeply set image of the eagle runs

[50] See *PPC*, vi, p. cxlvii; *RP*, iii, p. 442. The signet of the eagle is last recorded in use in 1509, for the sealing of Henry VII's will.

[51] See W.S. Walford & A. Way, 'Examples of Medieval Seals', *Archaeological Journal*, 18 (1861), pp. 49–55 & illustration on p.49 of a surviving impression from the will of Henry VI (1447) in the Archives of King's College, Cambridge. The authors noted that signs of heavy use on the wax impression suggested that the seal matrix may have been made much earlier than the 1440s, probably 'soon after 1400' at the latest (p. 55). For gem-seals see M. Henig, 'The Re-use and Copying of Ancient Intaglios set in Medieval Personal Seals, mainly found in England: an Aspect of the Renaissance of the 12th Century' in *Good Impressions: Image and Authority in Medieval Seals*, ed. N. Adams, J. Cherry & S. Robinson (London, 2008), pp. 25–34.

[52] See M. Dalas, *Corpus des Sceaux français du Moyen Âge 2: Les sceaux des rois et de régence* (Paris, 1990), p. 152 (eagle counterseal of Philip Augustus); p. 209 (signet of John the Good); R. Kahsnitz, 'Staufische Kameen' in *Die Zeit der Staufer*, ed. R. Hausherr (Stuttgart, 1977), v, pp. 477–520. I owe these references to Professor Julian Gardner. The archbishops of York also possessed secret seals, used as counterseals, made from antique intaglios, such as the three bearded men's heads on the counterseal of Archbishop Roger de Pont-l'Eveque (1154–81), bearing the Christianised legend: 'Caput nostrum trinitas est' ('our head is the Trinity'): Dalton, *The Archiepiscopal and Deputed Seals*, p. 7.

[53] See also the eagle counterseal of William II of Holland, as King of the Romans, in 1248: *Corpus Sigillorum Neerlandicorum: De Nederlandse Zegels tot 1300* (The Hague, 1937–41), no. 523.

a raised, engraved legend in the Latin of the Vulgate, quoting the beginning of a passage from the Old Testament Book of Deuteronomy: 'Like an eagle that stirs up its nest and hovers over its young, that spreads its wings to catch them, and carries them aloft. The Lord alone led him [Moses]; no foreign god was with him' (Deuteronomy 32: 11–12).[54] Deuteronomy was closely associated with Henry V by the author of the *Gesta Henrici Quinti*. Speaking of the king's personal piety, he wrote:

> This prince . . . wrote out for himself the law of Deuteronomy in the volume of his breast; and may God, of his immeasurable mercy, grant that, as he [Henry] began, he may read it all the days of his life, in order that he may learn to fear the Lord his God . . .[55]

Not only was the king to 'learn to fear' God, but so were his people. It has been pointed out that 'learning to fear', in this context, may bear a further meaning. It may also imply fearing God through the agency of the king, the embodiment or 'avatar of Moses, who in Deuteronomy lays down in detail the canons of an orthodox way of life for a disobedient people'.[56] Now the legend inscribed on the signet of the eagle is taken from the 'Song of Moses' or 'canticle for the remembrance of the law', describing God's care for His people and His awakening of their consciences to His law. Linked to this particular text, the image of the eagle might also be applied to the nature and practice of kingship. God's fostering of, and care for, the people of Israel is compared in Deuteronomy chapter 32 to that of the

---

[54] 'Sicut aquila provocans ad volandum pullos suos, et super eos volitans, expandit alas suas, et adsumpsit eum atque portavit in umeris suis' (Deuteronomy 32: 11). The legible portion of the legend on the seal reads: 'V.' sicut Aquila provocans ad volandum p[ullos] . . .'

[55] *Gesta Henrici Quinti. The Deeds of Henry the Fifth*, ed. & tr. F. Taylor & J.S. Roskell (Oxford, 1975), p. 155.

[56] Catto, 'The Burden and Conscience of Government', p. 97; Deuteronomy 32: 5–7, 44–52, esp. v. 46: 'And [Moses] said unto them: set your hearts unto all the words which I testify among you this day, which ye shall command your children to observe to do, all the words of this law'.

eagle for its young. But the chapter goes on to chronicle the punishments which God metes out to those who stray from His commandments and who follow false gods and beliefs. The eagle may, of course, signify nothing more, in this context, than the majesty and authority of empire and kingship. But its association, on the signet of the eagle, with this particular biblical text may have possessed further meanings for Henry V and the Lancastrian monarchy.

The significance of the eagle in the ideology of Lancastrian kingship and its legitimation has also been stressed in studies of the English coronation ceremony.[57] In 1399, apparently for the first time, the new, usurping king was anointed with oil from an ampulla, or sacred vessel, contained within a golden eagle. The oil, or so the legend went, had been given in a phial to St Thomas Becket, during his exile in France, by an apparition of the Virgin Mary. This was a clear attempt to imitate the French myth whereby the coronation oil of the French monarchy had been sent from heaven to Clovis, to be kept at Rheims and used to sacralise the person and office of the king. The story of Becket's reception of the oil gained many accretions, including that of the 'oil-containing eagle', and prophecies gathered round it. An English king anointed with it would 'love Holy Church with a fuller love', and he and his successors would

> recover the lands lost by their forefathers, as long as they have the eagle and the phial. Now there will be a king of the English who will be the first to be anointed with this oil: he shall recover by force the land lost by his forefathers, that is to say, Normandy and Aquitaine. He will be the greatest among kings, and he it is that will build many churches in the Holy Land, and will put all the heathen to flight from Babylon . . .

[57] See L.G. Wickham Legg, *English Coronation Records* (Westminster, 1901), pp. xxxvii–xxxviii, 69–70; J.R. Planche, *Regal Records* (London, 1838), pp. 87–8; C. Wilson, 'The Tomb of Henry IV and the Holy Oil of St Thomas of Canterbury' in *Medieval Architecture and its Intellectual Context. Studies in Honour of Peter Kidson*, ed. E.C. Fernie & P. Crossley (London, 1990), pp. 181–90.

and as often as he carries this eagle on his breast [that is, through anointing] he will have victory over all his enemies and his kingdom will be ever increased.[58]

For the coronation ceremony of 1399, at which Henry V's father was anointed, an eagle of gold, enclosing the ampulla, was said to have been taken out of the Tower of London, where Richard II had placed it. Although its existence had apparently been known – it had been housed at Poitiers since the reign of Edward II – it was only used, for the first time, to consecrate and legitimise the usurping Henry IV.[59] The eagle thus became an important element in the official propaganda of the new Lancastrian monarchy. The signet's eagle image may have been adopted as part of that mythical ideology. No example of the seal's metal matrix survives, but wax impressions confirm its relatively small size, although none of the four gold rings listed as 'signets' in the inventory of Henry V's effects after his death can be identified with it.[60] Nevertheless, it was evidently the instrument of authority that the king kept close by him, if not on his person, and was in very frequent daily use.

The ease and immediacy of action implied by the use of the signet allow us to witness the king's will, thoughts and assumptions very much at first hand. A class of signet letters, as well as a body of memoranda and diplomatic instructions under the signet, quite independent of any association with petitions, also evolved. Many were composed by the king himself, and in them he expressed his own views and wishes. One of the clerks of the signet office would normally draft them, but many bear all the signs of dictation by the king and, in some cases, there are signs of direct

---

[58] Legg, *English Coronation Records*, pp. 170–1, from Bod. Lib., Ashmole MS 1393, fo. 52.
[59] For the legend and its communication to Edward II by a letter of Pope John XXII in June 1318 see Legg, *English Coronation Records*, pp. 69–76; Wilson, 'The Tomb of Henry IV and the Holy Oil', pp. 182–3, 186. The eagle and the oil had, it was claimed, then been discovered at Poitiers by Henry of Grosmont, later first duke of Lancaster, in the 1340s, and handed over by him to the Black Prince, whence it descended to Richard II.
[60] See *RP*, iv, p. 214 for the 1423 inventory.

intervention in his own hand.[61] In August 1417 these signet letters began to be composed in English, identified as 'Chancery Standard' or 'Chancery English' by some linguistic scholars, rather than in the Anglo-Norman French of the past.[62] The use of the signet became steadily more wide-spread and common, activating such procedures as, for example, the king's initial response to supplications; ordering warrants for the issue of letters of protection, safe conduct and safeguard; certifying acts of homage performed by the major landholders and magnates of the kingdom; restoring their temporalities to bishops and, above all, enabling the grant of pensions and annuities, benefices, offices, lands, pardons and ward-ships, for which the recipients and beneficiaries had petitioned the king. Central to this process was the creation and perpetuation of styles, conven-tions and formulas of supplication, in Anglo-Norman and then also in English, to which the suppliant had to conform.

The format and manner in which petitions to the king were drawn up, and by whom, have been much debated.[63] Some undoubtedly origi-nated, at least in draft or verbal form, in the suppliants' personal input. But it seems that clerks, attorneys and other legal representatives, acting on behalf of their petitioner-clients, would employ professional scribes and other clerks residing around Westminster to ensure that a client's request was duly and appropriately rendered and presented in the correct

---

[61] See below, pp. 62–6, 72–8. For the king's role in composing these letters and instructions see McFarlane, 'Henry V: a Personal Portrait', pp. 117–19. Also J.H. Fisher, *The Emergence of Standard English (Lexington, 1996)*, p. 9: 'Henry V must sometimes have given the clerks rough drafts and/or approved finished versions'.

[62] See Fisher, *The Emergence of Standard English*, pp. 8–20, and, for criticism, M. Benskin, 'Chancery Standard' in *New Perspectives in English Historical Linguistics II*, ed. C. Kay, S. Horobin & J. Smith (Amsterdam, 2004), pp. 1–40; M. Richardson, 'Henry V, the English Chancery and Chancery English', *Speculum*, 55 (1980), pp. 726–50; also G. Dodd, 'Trilingualism in the Medieval English Bureaucracy: the Use – and Disuse – of Languages in the Fifteenth-century Privy Seal Office', *Journal of British Studies*, 51 (2012), pp. 253–83. See below, chapter 3, pp. 89, 108, 112.

[63] See, for what follows, Dodd, 'The Rise of English, the Decline of French', pp. 120–1, 131–4; 'Kingship, Parliament and the Court; the Emergence of a "High Style" in Petitions to the English Crown, c. 1350–1405', *EHR*, 129 (2014), pp. 527–30, 542.

form. Exemplars and models of petitions were to be found in commonly used manuals and formulary books.[64] In some cases, especially of those suppliants of humble social origins and modest income, it seems that – given the striking uniformity of style and language found in many of their petitions – scribes and copyists were directly employed, probably at relatively little cost. Robert Gunthorpe in 1419, a London 'servant and carter' who worked for a certain Robert Hawkyn, provides us with a good instance of a suppliant of relatively low social origins seeking pardon from the king in a petition drawn up in the correct Anglo-Norman form and idiom.[65] It also reveals the king acting in favour of those of humble status who might find it difficult to gain redress through the courts because of their expense, and by reason of the obstacles in the way of getting their voices heard. His replies to petitions from the humble might instruct his officers to 'do unto them both right and equity, and especially so that the poorer party shall suffer no wrong' (April 1419).[66] A 'poor tenant' is not to be wronged in any way, and the king's officers are to ensure that 'he have all that he ought to have of right in this matter' (July 1420).[67] A poor woman is to receive justice 'ye more favourably considering the poverty of the said Margery' (May 1421).[68] Lowliness and poverty must not, in Henry's mind, deter or prevent suppliants from seeking his justice and mercy.

Hence Robert Gunthorpe, carter, told the king that he was carrying a consignment of ale, destined for the king's household, to the Tower of

---

[64] A good example of such a formulary is found in *Anglo-Norman Letters and Petitions from All Souls MS 182*, ed. M.D. Legge (Anglo-Norman Text Society, Oxford, 1941). There appears to be no surviving example of a formulary for Middle English letters and petitions from before the mid-fifteenth century. See below, chapter 3, pp. 108–9.

[65] E 28/32, no. 61: 14 February (?)1419 & see Appendix 1 (3), p. 282.

[66] C 81/1365, no. 4: 'that ye do unto hem bothe right and equite, and in especial that the porer partye suffer no wrong'.

[67] C 81/1365, no. 19: 'that no man doo hym wrong in no way . . . and that he have al that he aught to have of right in this matere . . .'

[68] C 81/1365, no. 30: 'ye more favourably considering the pourete of the saide Margerye'.

London. As he approached the Tower with his cart – in effect a brewer's dray – the horses suddenly took fright. They had heard, he said, the roaring of the king's lions, housed in the menagerie in the Lion Tower, a barbican in the outer ward of the Tower, built by Edward I.[69] At this, the cart overturned, the barrels of ale broke open and all of it was lost. Without the king's grace and mercy the hapless carter would have to pay for the loss and, because he was 'only a poor labourer who had to work for his living, and had nothing with which to pay . . . for the said ale',[70] he begged the king for pardon. The petition was endorsed, in the chamberlain's hand: 'the king has granted it'. By what means Robert Gunthorpe's supplication reached the king, and by whom it was drawn up, we shall never know. A professional hand was clearly at work. Not only in the city of London but even out in the 'provinces', however remote, there were lawyers and clerks, acting for suppliants, who had been trained in London at the Inns of Court and who were perfectly conversant with such practices.[71] The dialogue between ruler and subjects, however direct it might be, thus demanded – on both sides – its intermediaries.

Henry V's reputation for just judgment and the even-handed administration of justice was not confined to his English kingdom. In April 1419, his Gascon subject Charles de Beaumont, the Alferez of Navarre, told him, admittedly hopefully, that 'you never fail to render justice to anyone who asks it of you'.[72] This was not pure flattery on Beaumont's part. Seeking justice directly from the king was normally achieved by petitioning. The partial survival of records of the king's council, kept by the privy seal office, allows us to see how this particular function of the royal prerogative was exercised and implemented. The written endorsement of

---

[69] See G. Parnell, *The Tower of London* (London, 1993), pp. 40, 54 & see below, Appendix [3.].

[70] 'Il nest pas forsque un povre [la]borer de travailler pour sa sustenance, et rienz nad dont a paier ne satisfaire pour ladicte cervois': E 28/32, no. 61.

[71] See Dodd, 'The Rise of English, the Decline of French', pp. 120–1, 146; Benskin, 'Chancery Standard', pp. 2–3.

[72] *Foedera*, ix, p. 742: 28 Apr. 1419.

petitions, giving a very brief, if not exceedingly laconic, note of the king's responses, sometimes with an order to the appropriate officer to implement those decisions, was crucial. It is worth examining that process in some detail. In the surviving minutes of the council meeting of 29 March 1415, for example, a memorandum of the endorsements on petitions delivered to the king ran as follows:[73]

> [On a petition from the troublesome Thomas Paunfield of Chesterton, Cambridgeshire.] Let it be ordered that the pursuit [of the case] cease, because the party [Paunfield] has been outlawed.[74]
>
> [From Roger Moigne, draper.] Committed to the Chancellor so that he may, in his visitation [of the case] seek the truth of the matter and relate it to the king.
>
> [From Richard Welby of Multon and William Porter of Holbech, chaplain.] Let their petition be sent to the council of [the duchy of] Lancaster to inform them of the matter and so that they can report upon it to the king.

In these three cases, the council has submitted petitions to the king for his consideration and response. This could be a simple 'Le Roy le voet' ('The king wishes it'), 'Le Roy ne le voet' ('The king does not wish it'), 'Le Roy la grante' ('The king has granted it'), or an order to forward the petition to a third party, for subsequent report back to him. In the great majority of cases, petitions were endorsed with the phrase 'Le Roy la grante', 'Le Roy a grante toute la bille' ('The king has granted all the petition'), or other such terms, sometimes in English. Relatively few were refused or rejected,

---

[73] *PPC*, ii, p. 149.

[74] See also SC 8/23, no. 1143 for Paunfield's long petition to the Parliament of 1414; also *RP*, ix, pp. 57–61 & Dodd, 'Thomas Paunfield, the heye court of rightwiseness and the language of petitioning in the 15th century' in *Medieval Petitions: Grace and Grievance*, ed. W.M. Ormrod, G. Dodd & A. Musson (York, 2009), pp. 222–41.

as far as we can tell from surviving examples. But a significant minority carried the order to refer the case to another appropriate party or parties, before the king's final decision. It was a common and marked characteristic of Henry's generally prudent and cautious approach, and of his apparent determination that full information be received upon which his final response could be based. In some instances, the council played an important role in the process. In May 1416, its minutes recorded a decision to 'speak to the king' so that 'henceforth, petitions by which forfeitures are requested could, if it pleases him, be endorsed and sent to his council'.[75] The council's advice would then be given, to the benefit of all parties.

The interaction between king and council was an essential element in Henry's government.[76] We can trace it through the surviving council records, and the concrete detail they provide gives us some idea of the close relationship between royal initiative and reaction and conciliar input and action.[77] The council minutes reported that the king, present in person at the Tower of London on the morning of 12 April 1415, had, under the signet ('a tergo'), ordered the council to go away and discuss ('a estre comunees') certain matters. These included the sending of letters to 'his adversary of France'; as well as letters to Jean, duke of Berry and to Master Jean Andrieu, counsellor and secretary to Charles VI of France; and the issue of safe conducts to an impending French embassy. They were also to consider the terms of Master Philip Morgan's commission to negotiate with the French; to inspect the king's instructions to his ambassadors 'lately sent to the emperor [Sigismund]'; and to speak to the earl of Salisbury concerning the duchy of Guyenne, about which he had been summoned to appear before the council on the next Monday (15 April). Lastly, if that were not enough, the mayor of London was to be summoned

---

[75] *PPC*, ii, p. 200.

[76] For a similar degree of interaction under Henry IV, especially in relation to petitioning, see Dodd, 'Patronage, Petitions and Grace', pp. 121–2.

[77] For the council, its clerk and its records see Catto, 'The King's Servants', pp. 79–82.

to discuss the provision and sale of armour and weapons in the city. It was, after all, the prelude to the Agincourt expedition.[78] The council acted promptly. On the afternoon of the same day (12 April), they reassembled at the house of the London Dominicans, at Blackfriars, between the Thames and Ludgate Hill, having probably come up the river by barge from the Tower. The minutes recorded the presence of Chichele, archbishop of Canterbury, the dukes of Bedford and Gloucester, the bishops of Winchester (as Chancellor) and Durham, the earl of Dorset and the keeper of the privy seal (John Prophet, dean of York).[79] The business exactly conformed to the schedule set out by the king, and copies of letters relating to the negotiations with France had already been drawn up by the bishop of Durham (Thomas Langley). These were to be shown to the king. The Chancellor was to draw up a commission for Morgan, while letters of safe conduct for the French embassy, to last until 8 June 1415, were prepared. These were indeed issued, on 13 April. The councillors still had to see the instruction to the ambassadors to the emperor; and the earl of Salisbury was summoned to be before them on 15 April. Lastly, the mayor and some aldermen of London appeared before them on the afternoon of 12 April, and the mayor was charged to ordain that, in London, 'armours should be sold at a lower price than they currently are' and was to report back to the council, also on Monday 15 April.

Further instances of the process, not necessarily related to petitions, whereby the council sent proposals to the king for comment and response, can be seen in the council minutes of 25 February 1416.[80] Matters 'to discuss with . . . the king, by his council' were noted: these included a dispute between two Gascon lords – those of Lesparre and Labarde; the appointment of ambassadors to go to Calais to negotiate a treaty with

[78] *PPC*, ii, pp. 153–4.
[79] *PPC*, ii, pp. 154–6.
[80] *PPC*, ii, pp. 191–4.

Flanders; the arrival of ambassadors from the archbishop of Cologne; the situation in Ireland, and the terms of Lord Furnival's lieutenancy there; and the issue of letters to the emperor and other German princes. Who should be assigned to carry them? It was noted that the king specifically wished that 'Aquitaine King-of-Arms carries the letters addressed to the emperor, to the general council [of the Church at Constance], and to the kings, princes, dukes and other princes of the Empire'. It may not be coincidental that a herald associated with the overseas possessions of the English crown should be appointed as a messenger to those powers of Christendom whose support Henry was eager to enlist in his plans and schemes for a Lancastrian continental empire. At this time, the position of Aquitaine, or Guyenne, King-of-Arms was held by William Bruges, who was soon to become premier herald of the kingdom as Garter King-of-Arms.[81] Gloucester herald was meanwhile to take letters to the Iberian kingdoms: Castile, Portugal, Aragon and Navarre, while Master Peter, the king of Denmark's secretary, currently in London, would bear letters to his own sovereign. Lastly, the king's opinion was to be sought by the council on arrangements for the reception of the Emperor Sigismund in England, due to take place in April 1416.[82] The impression given by such evidence is that business was being expeditiously dispatched, and that most of that business related to diplomacy and foreign affairs. There was nothing insular about Henry V's government. Given the apparent efficiency with which its procedures worked, it is hardly surprising that his reign was viewed by at least some contemporaries as a gold standard for government and administration.[83]

The evidence thus presents us with a picture of constant interaction between king and council, with both sides referring to each other on

---

[81] See C 81/1137, no. 28: protection for 'William Brugges, alias dictus Guyen', Rex armorum' to go abroad in the king's company, for one year: 22 May 1417.

[82] *PPC*, ii, pp. 193–4.

[83] See Catto, 'The Burden and Conscience of Government', p. 98 for Henry's reign as a 'gold standard for good government'. Also, Morgan, 'The Household Retinue of Henry V', pp. 67–9.

matters both major and minor. The king's wishes and commands are noted, and the council minutes carry the evidence of his personal and direct oversight of its business. The phrases 'le Roy voet' ('the king wishes') and 'soit parle au Roy' ('the king should be spoken to') constantly recur.[84] Some issues were clearly productive of extended discussion or negotiation – between 6 and 9 March 1417, for example, rates and modes of payment for those serving in the king's impending French campaign were resolved between king and council. On Saturday 6 March, proposals from the council about payments and allowances (in the form of advances) for the first and second quarter-years' service were received in writing by the king.[85] The council was concerned about precedents. They asked whether those still accounting on behalf of the dead at Agincourt (in October 1415) were to be given retrospective allowances for the wages of that relatively small group for the entire second quarter-year of their service, or only up to their date of death. The king replied that they should be treated 'like the others who are living' ('come les autres qi sont en vie'). And what of those who, the council pointed out, although they would be prepared and ready to serve in the king's forthcoming expedition, were forced to remain in England through lack of shipping? Were they to claim any allowances and advances? The king's response was a firm negative. New proposals were then drawn up (on the same day), and submitted to the king, who read them 'in his secret chamber', before four members of the council, at the Tower.[86] These were agreed, with one exception, on which the king would take further advice. At a subsequent council meeting, held at the Tower on Tuesday 9 March, the king reiterated his decision that 'those who for lack of shipping . . . shall remain in England shall not have any allowance'.[87] A strict and uncompromising approach to military

[84] *PPC*, ii, pp. 198, 199, 200, 219, 221, 226, 229.
[85] *PPC*, ii, p. 226. The king's reply was 'Le Roy ne le voet'.
[86] *PPC*, ii, p. 227.
[87] *PPC*, ii, p. 229.

finance – as well as to military organisation and discipline – was, as we shall see, one of Henry V's strongest points.

Custody of a king's seals – the instruments of power – was a major issue, especially during reigns in which there were lengthy periods of royal absence from England.[88] Trust in the king's regents, lieutenants and deputies was at a premium – misuse or abuse of the seals could wreak havoc. Henry V was absent from the English kingdom for a total of five years, two months in a nine-year reign. His father, during his reign (1399–1413), had never left the country. Richard II (1377–99), spent eleven months, two weeks outside England, mainly in Ireland. Edward III (1327–77), despite his active prosecution of the war with France, had only spent approximately three years, six months, two weeks abroad during a reign of fifty years. All of these rulers had tended to spend relatively short, discrete periods abroad; Henry V differed markedly from them in being out of England for a single unbroken period of three years and seven months, in Normandy and France (23 July 1417–1 February 1421), followed by another continuous stretch of one year and three months at the end of his nine-year reign (10 June 1421–1 September 1422). This was something of a reversion to a style of government not seen on any scale in England since the time of the Angevins (1154–1216) or at least that of Edward I (1272–1307). Edward had spent one unbroken period of three years, three months in France and Aquitaine (13 May 1286–12 August 1289). Under Henry V, his absences meant that duplicates of the great and privy seals had to be made: the great seal and privy seal 'of absence' were kept, in England, by the Chancellor and the keeper of the privy seal respectively. A great seal and privy seal 'of presence' were kept at Rouen.[89] Personal use of the privy seal 'of presence' was made by the king at certain periods, beginning in mid-1417, during his time in

---

[88] For the following details of royal absences from Edward I to Henry V see *Handbook of British Chronology*, ed. Powicke et al. (3rd edn London, 1986), pp. 35–7.

[89] For examples, see *Foedera*, ix, p. 760; *PPC*, ii, pp. 241–3 (seals 'of absence'); *Foedera*, ix, pp. 628–31 (seals 'of presence'). Noted in Chaplais, *English Diplomatic Practice*, pp. 199–200.

France and Normandy.[90] Privy seal letters, in Anglo-Norman French, were certainly issued by him at Caen, Rouen, Vernon, Mantes, Meaux, Paris and other places during his French campaigns and residences.[91] Otherwise, only the king's signet, or signets, remained with him – another reason for the increasing importance of signet letters as instruments of the royal will.[92] And from August 1417 onwards, Henry's signet letters, quite unlike those issued under the privy seal, were in English, not French.

As a direct expression of the king's will, the signet was always – literally – close at hand. The king's secretary, its formal custodian, was in daily attendance upon him. It therefore was used with great flexibility, relatively unconstrained by bureaucratic rigidities. The scope of letters under the signet was very wide, ranging from important memoranda and secret diplomatic instructions to the most humdrum of matters. Thus Robert Rolleston, keeper of the great wardrobe, received personal orders under the signet from the king in 1421 to deliver items of armour from the wardrobe to 'John Hampton, sergeant of mine armoury'. These included vambraces and rerebraces, buckles, poleyns, sallets with visors, bacinets and red silk lining for them, some to be given to Henry's household knights and esquires, such as Edmund Beaufort, William Bourgchier and John Meredith of Glyn Dwr.[93] The signet could be employed when the king was in transit, on water as well as on land. In July 1417, signet letters were issued 'dedens nostre nef' ('on board our ship') as the king sailed from

[90] C 81/666, no. 880: privy seal letters at Caen, 24 May 1418; also no. 888: 'en nostre hoost devant Roan', 22 Oct. 1418.
[91] See, for examples C 81/667, nos 908, 951, 963; C 81/669, nos 1113–23, 1133, 1136, 1141–2, 1145–51, 1166, 1179, 1183–4, 1192–3.
[92] See Otway-Ruthven, 'The King's Secretary in the Fifteenth Century', p. 88: the signet office, accompanying the king, was 'the natural means of communication with the administration in England'.
[93] E 101/ 407/3, no. 7: with traces of the signet, n.d., prob. summer 1421. See also no. 3 for a certificate endorsed by Henry, Lord Fitzhugh, as chamberlain, to John Hampton, for the delivery of items of armour, dated 2 Mar. 1420. Also E 101/407/4, fos 3v–4r for Hampton's account, as king's armourer, which refers to the provision of pieces of armour, banners, trumpet banners, pennons, daggers and ostrich plumes. These, it was said, were listed in three 'signet bills' and a privy seal writ of 27 Nov. 1421, directed to Fitzhugh.

Portsmouth to Normandy.[94] Meanwhile, all matters (generally of a more routine kind) which could be dealt with by the council at Westminster, under Gloucester or Bedford as regents or 'protectors' of the kingdom, were expedited in England under the great and privy seals 'of absence' *in situ*. Everything else was subject to the king's personal use of the signet and a steady flow of letters, writs and warrants went back and forth across the English Channel. At certain periods, Rouen and other places in Normandy and northern France became the effective power centres of the English kingdom, as well as of the French possessions and conquests. Just as the Thames provided a regular highway for the king's movements in and around London, so the Seine became a major thoroughfare for him in Normandy. In June 1421, the master of his 'rowebarge', the *Esmond del Tour*, was paid for serving the king, with thirty-four other mariners, for six weeks 'on the river Seine or elsewhere where it shall be pleasing to his will'.[95] Where the king was, there lay the power.

On 4 September 1416, Henry was at Sandwich, about to set sail for Calais, where he was to spend just under six weeks. It was necessary to ensure that the great seal 'of absence' for the kingdom was safely entrusted to the relevant officer of the Chancery in London so that it could be properly deployed during the king's absence. A detailed report, in the form of a witnessed memorandum, of the procedure by which this was achieved, survives.[96] Henry was lodged at Sandwich in the house of the prior and convent of the Carmelite friars. In 'a certain outer chamber', and in the presence of Archbishop Chichele, Thomas Langley, bishop of Durham, and others, at 10 a.m. on 4 September, Henry ordered the Chancellor, Henry Beaufort, bishop of Winchester, to deliver the great seal to Simon Gaunstede, clerk, keeper (or master) of the Chancery Rolls. This was in accordance with the king's previously issued letters under the signet,

94 C 81/1364, nos 30, 31: 26 July 1417.
95 E 403/651, m. 11r :18 June 1421.
96 *Foedera*, ix, p. 385.

addressed to the keeper, in the Chancellor's absence. After sealing two letters – of urgent business – with the great seal, Beaufort put the matrix into a leather bag, sealing the bag with an impression of his own signet, in white wax, 'containing the image of the Holy Trinity'. He then gave the bag to his clerk John Mapleton, for immediate delivery to Gaunstede in London. The seal matrix, in its bag, arrived there post-haste later that day, at night 'around the time that the clock struck nine' together with further signet letters ordering Gaunstede to take possession of the great seal. The seal was then used until 12 October 1416, four days before the king returned from Calais, when Gaunstede delivered it back to Beaufort, as Chancellor, in his chamber at the priory of the Blessed Virgin Mary at 'Suthwarke' (Southwick, Hants), about two miles from Porchester, between 6 and 7 p.m. that day.[97]

An analogous procedure took place just before Henry's next departure for France, on 23 July 1417.[98] Another memorandum tells us that Beaufort, now outgoing as Chancellor, delivered the great seal (the 'magnum sigillum aureum'), in a leather bag, to the king, at Southwick priory, 'in a certain chapel of the Blessed Virgin Mary, over the lower gate' there. This took place between 2 and 3 p.m., in the presence of Chichele, Thomas Langley, as newly appointed Chancellor, Humphrey duke of Gloucester, Henry, Lord Fitzhugh (the king's chamberlain), John of Arundel, Lord Maltravers, Sir Walter Hungerford, Simon Gaunstede, and others. The king then gave the seal to Langley, as Chancellor, who took it 'as far as Wykeham' (Wickham, Hants), issuing letters patent and writs under it on the same day. There could be no interruption in the deployment and use of the seal, and the extremely precise recording of the witnessed dates, times and places at which it changed hands is an index of this overriding concern.

Personal control of the processes of government required constant vigilance and regular intervention on the part of the king. Letters and warrants

---

[97] For Southwick priory see *VCH, County of Hampshire* (London, 1903), ii, pp. 164–8.
[98] *Foedera*, ix, p. 472.

under the signet cascaded on to the desks, as it were, of Henry's regent in England, and of the Chancellor, the keeper of the privy seal, the Treasurer, the barons of the Exchequer and other officers. These could carry a definite sense of urgency, and a requirement for prompt action. In March 1416, the king wrote (in English) under the signet to John Radcliffe, knight, lieutenant of Calais, and Richard Woodeville, esquire, concerning a loan which they were immediately to 'entreat and induce' from the Company of the Staple there. The request was to aid 'the setting out of our great army into our realm of France' and, the king told them, '. . . in this matter we pray you that you fail in no manner whatsoever'.[99] The promptness of the king's response to events, expecting a similarly prompt reaction from his officers and servants, can be gauged from signet letters sent as military and naval conditions changed, especially just before his departures for France. On 29 June 1417, when Harfleur was under siege by the French, John, earl of Huntingdon, as admiral, had defeated and captured some Genoese carracks in a sea fight off the pays de Caux (Normandy).[100] These were relatively large, ocean-going vessels, useful as troop, horse and provisioning transports for expeditionary forces. On 12 July, at Southampton, the king issued one of his last signet letters in French. Addressed to the Chancellor, Henry Beaufort, the letter enclosed a schedule listing new names 'devised by us for the four carracks recently taken . . . by the earl of Huntingdon and others . . . together with the names of those who will be [their] masters', to serve in the forthcoming expedition.[101] So, Henry ordered, the *Vivande* was to be rechristened the *[Saint] Paul;* the *Pynele* was to become the *Christopher,* and the *Galeas Negre* the *Andrew.* Significantly, all were now to bear the names of saints, joining a fleet of

---

[99] E 28/31, no. 6: Mar. 1416: 'in this mater we pray you that ye faile as in no maner wyse'.
[100] C. Allmand, *Henry V* (New Haven/London, 1992; 2nd edn 1997), pp. 113, 224, 227.
[101] 'Les noms par nous devisez des 4 carrakes jatarde prinses . . . par le conte de Huntyngdon et autres . . . et les noms de ceulx qui seront maistres de mesmes les carrakes pour nostre service en iceste nostre prouchein voyage, a laide de dieux': C 81/1366, nos 17, 18: 12 July 1417. The name given to the fourth vessel is lost, as the document is damaged at that point.

twenty-seven ships in which the *Litill John* and the *Swan* were heavily outnumbered by the *Jhesus*, the *Trinite Roiale*, the *Holygost*, the *Marie* (four vessels so named), the *Agnes, Anne, George, Gabrielle* and *Nicholas*.[102] Similarly, Henry's 'great ship', the *Gracedieu*, constructed at Southampton, was 'consecrated' by Benedict Nichols, bishop of Bangor, in July 1418.[103] It was with God's grace and God's aid, and by the intercession of his saints, that victory at sea, as well as on land, was to be achieved.

An even greater sense of urgency was conveyed by a signet letter of 30 March 1422, from Rouen, to Humphrey, duke of Gloucester and the council in England, headed, as was the common form, 'By ye kyng':

> Right trusty and well-beloved brother, right worshipful and worshipful fathers in God, and trusty and well-beloved, we send unto you with these our letters a roll under our signet containing certain articles advised by our well-beloved knight John Tiptoft, seneschal of our duchy of Guyenne, for the governance of our said duchy, and the answers given by our council here upon the same art[icles]. For which reason we wish that you execute the said answers as far as it appertains to you. *And [we wish] that this be done in such a manner that our seneschal and mayor of Bordeaux be not delayed in our realm of England, but speeded hence as far as is possible, as our trust is in you, for it is very necessary that their departure be hastened in every possible way.*[104]

---

102 C 81/1364, nos 34–5: signet letter at the castle of Touque, 12 Aug. 1417, in English, listing the names of ships and their masters, and ordering the payment of annuities to them. Some of the Genoese ships bore the names of their merchant owners, e.g. for Golestan Pynele [*Pinelli*], merchant of Genoa, see *CPR, 1377–1381*, pp. 283, 307, 311, 356, 360. A ship called the 'Little John of Rye' (*parvus Johannes de Rya*) had brought supplies to the besieged English at Harfleur at this time, after the defeat of the Genoese. See F. Taylor, 'The Chronicle of John Strecche for the Reign of Henry V (1414–1422)', *BJRL*, 16 (1932), p. 158.

103 E 403/636, m. 11r: payment of expenses of 100s. to him, sent by the king's council from London to Southampton to consecrate the vessel (16 July 1418).

104 SC 1/43, no. 161: 30 Mar. 1422: '*and that this be doon in such wyse that oure seneschal and maire of Bourdeux be nat tarried yn oure Rewme of England, but hasted al that is possible, as oure truste is to yow, for hit is grete necessite that thaire goyng be hasted al that may be doon*'. My italics.

The requirement to act 'in all haste' is a recurrent theme of many of these missives. In February 1419, Langley, as Chancellor, was informed by the king of a possible Castilian naval raid on English ports. Writing, again, from Rouen, Henry told him that the Castilians, in alliance with the dauphinist French, intended to 'burn and destroy our ships and the navy of our land', especially at Southampton. Langley was therefore instructed: 'by the advice of our brother of Bedford, and of others at your discretion, [that] you ordain in all haste for the governance of our land, and for the safeguard of the security of our said vessels at Southampton . . . and that those of the ports and of the sea coast all around be warned about this in all haste'.[105]

The king's orders under the signet bear extensive quotation. Behind the formulas and epistolary conventions to which they conform, an authentic voice can be heard, expressing itself in an English singularly devoid of artifice and rhetoric. We may have here a record of Henry's actual spoken language; perhaps for the very first time, a ruler's spoken voice breaks, in English, through the bonds of bureaucratic and scribal convention. In June 1418, writing from Bernay in Normandy, the king urged Langley to act promptly, and

> we wish that, in all possible haste, you ordain that as many ships as will suffice for the shipping of the prior of Kilmainham, with 200 horse and 300 foot, be sent to Waterford in Ireland out of our port of Bristol, to come to us in all haste, with God's grace. And that this be not left undone in any way, as our trust is in you.

---

[105] SC 1/43, no. 162: 12 Feb. 1419: '. . . by thavys of oure brother of Bedford, and of other suche as semeth to youre discreccion, [that] ye ordenne *in alle haste* for ye gouvernance of oure lande, and for ye saufwarde of seurkepyng of oure saide vesselx at Hampton . . . and that thay of the portes and of ye see coost al about be warned hereof *in alle haste* . . .' My italics. For the original text see Appendix [1.].

A further signet order, dated the next day, added as a postscript to the same letter, and written from the abbey of Bec-Hellouin, continued in the same vein:

> Furthermore, we wish and pray you that in every way you hasten the said shipping for the same prior, and [that] they who shall come to us with him tarry for no other reason than lack of shipping.[106]

The letter was endorsed at its base with a note of agreement (in French) by the king's council at London, immediately ordering the issue of a commission under the great seal to Robert Russell, mayor of Bristol and John Hexham, clerk, to arrest ships at Bristol to transport the Irish contingent.[107] They were to ensure that the ships were to sail *a toute haste* to Waterford, and then to the king 'to serve him in the parts of France where he is at present'. The war effort in no way excluded the clergy from its demands, either in terms of manpower or of money. The Hospitaller prior of Kilmainham was merely one among many of its members required to aid and advance Henry's war in France.[108]

A frequent refrain found in the letters under the signet was Henry's injunction to his lieutenants and officers to ensure, to the best of their ability, that a case was settled without further recourse to an already very busy and hard-pressed ruler. In July 1419 he wrote to his brother Bedford, as 'keeper' ('wardein') in England, enclosing a petition from an allegedly dispossessed husband and wife in Kent, which he had received. Bedford was instructed to

---

[106] C 81/1364, no. 59: 3 & 4 June 1418. They were to 'come to us *yn al haste* with goddes grace. And that this be not left yn no wyse, as oure trust is to you' and 'ferthermore, we wol and pray yow that for anything *ye haste ye said shipping* for ye same priour, and [that] they that shal come to us with him taryen for noon other but for lacke of shipping'. My italics.

[107] For a payment of wages to the ship-masters and sailors concerned see E 403/636, m. 9r (June 1418).

[108] For a payment of a 'special regard' to him, on the king's order, see E 403/638, m. 1r (17 Oct. 1418).

call unto you our justices and, by their advice, ordain that both parties named in the aforesaid supplication be justly judged, so that neither of them have cause to complain hereafter for default of justice.[109]

Sometimes the action – or inaction – of his deputies in England during his absence was not altogether pleasing to the king. In November 1418, he wrote to Bedford, under the signet, from 'our host [army] before Rouen', about the violation of truces with the duke of Brittany by some of his subjects. The security of the narrow seas and the Western Approaches very much depended upon these agreements. Henry wrote, chiding his brother: '. . . As we suppose that you do not remember in what manner, and how often, we have charged you by our letters that good and hasty reparation were ordained and made at all times for such attempts . . . by our subjects', the king was nonetheless surprised that no action had been taken. Henry demanded that the Chancellor be summoned by Bedford to inspect the duke of Brittany's letters of complaint (which the king enclosed). They were then to 'send to us *in haste* all those persons that are our subjects' for an explanation of their behaviour to the king in person. Remedy was also to be provided by Bedford in all other cases relating to truces so

that no man have cause hereafter to complain . . . for default of right doing . . . nor that we have cause to write to you as we have done for such reasons, considering the great occupation that we otherwise have.[110]

---

109 E 28/33, no. 5: at Mantes, 12 July 1419: Bedford was to 'calle unto yowe oure justices and by thaire advis ordeineth that bothe parties nempned in ye forsaide supplicacion have right, soo that nouther of thaim have cause to compleine hereafter for defaute of justice'.
110 *PPC*, ii, p. 243; from BL, MS Cotton Julius B. VI, fo. 35: 29 Nov. 1418. Bedford was told 'as we suppose it is not of youre remembrance in what wise, and how ofte, we have charged yow by oure lettres that good and hasty reparacion and restitucion were ordained and made at al tymes of suche attemptats . . . by oure subgettis'. Remedy was to be provided so that 'no man have cause hereafter to compleine . . . for defaute of right doing . . . ner we cause to write to yow allweye as we doon for such causes, considering the grete occupacion that we otherwise have'.

An evidently displeased king, with other business – such as the reconquest of Normandy – very much on his mind, would not tolerate any sign of slackness or procrastination, let alone negligence, on the part even of his most loyal lieutenants. The Chancellor, most frequent recipient of orders and warrants under the signet, was similarly treated: in September 1417, Henry, at Caen, had told Langley, as Chancellor, to issue letters under the great seal granting the late Master Richard Dereham's prebend at Chichester to the king's signet clerk, Robert Shirington. Nothing had been done by early November, and the king wrote again, this time from Alençon, evidently displeased with Langley, reminding him of the matter, about which 'we have written to you before this time'.[111]

On occasion, there was cause for direct intervention by the king in order to rectify errors in previous letters. In April 1419, writing under the signet from Vernon, Henry ordered the reissue of letters patent by the Chancellor in favour of Piers Garney, esquire, granting him 'the keeping of the lands and tenements that were Hugh Fastolf's, knight, that is taken by God'. The initial letters were invalid because the value of the late knight's lands and tenements was not given, and also because some of such custodies had been assigned for the expenses of the king's household. But the letters were to be reissued under the same date as the first grant 'for it is our will that he have such letters patent as may be viable and reasonable to him'.[112] Again, an error, detected in letters granting possession of lands held by 'Isabelle', wife of the late Nicholas Kyriel, knight, to Sir Thomas Kyriel, was to be rectified. The grant was invalid, as 'the wife of the late Nicholas was called Elizabeth, not Isabelle as was contained and written in our letters'.[113] Vigilance, sometimes prompted by petition from an aggrieved party, had constantly to be exercised over grants and their terms – although the Chancery might issue the relevant letters, only the king

[111] C 81/1364, nos 39, 40: 30 Sept. & 2 Nov. 1417.
[112] C 81/1365, no. 3: 28 Apr. 1419.
[113] C 81/667, no. 908: at 'our castle of Vernon', 27 Nov. 1419.

could (unless he had delegated or deputed those functions elsewhere) cancel and reissue his own letters patent.

The royal will did not, however, operate in a completely autonomous fashion. Advice was often sought by the king when resolving a case presented in a supplication. In 1414, a petition from a group of his own tenants, who claimed to be menaced by Sir Richard Stanhope of Rampton, over rights of pasture at Darlton and Ragnall (Notts) was endorsed: 'Because the subject of this petition concerns free tenure [*francetenement*], the king wishes to be advised about this'.[114] A related petition from a married couple at Wympleton (Notts) referred to Stanhope's unacceptable behaviour, which had led to him being 'so much feared by the common people in the said county that they dare not do anything against his will or intentions, for fear of death or loss of goods'. Stanhope – evidently something of a menace to persons and property in his locality – had been brought before the king and the lords spiritual and temporal, and the petition had been read to him, but he denied the charges.[115] Advice was clearly needed from the common lawyers. Similarly, a petition to the Commons in Parliament, passed on to the Lords and then the king, about the practices of foreign 'brokers' who were forcing up the prices of foreign merchants' goods, was endorsed 'the king will seek advice'.[116]

In some cases, the king, rather than asking for further advice, decided that one or more of his officers in England might satisfactorily resolve an issue without further direct intervention by him. In May 1418, writing under the signet from the castle of Caen, Henry told Langley, as Chancellor, that he had received a petition (which he enclosed) from Roger Waltham, for a grant of the office of baron of the Exchequer, in place of the late Robert Sandford. The Chancellor was told that the king had considered

---

[114] SC 8/23, no. 1128; *RP*, iv, p. 293; also see *CPR, 1413–1419*, pp. 62–3.
[115] SC 8/23, no. 1129.
[116] SC 8/24, no. 1183.

that he [Waltham] might be in a position to do us better service in another occupation than that in which we have put him, for our profit, as you may be more clearly informed by the said supplication. So we wish that you see and understand clearly all the matter contained therein, and ordain such provision thereupon as seemeth best at your discretion, for our profit and advantage in this case.[117]

Similarly, in August 1418, the Chancellor's discretion was to be exercised in 'the full execution of right' over a 'reasonable' supplication from the prior and convent of Bath.[118] In April 1419, Janico Dartasse, esquire, who had petitioned the king, was to have 'such writs as may lawfully be had and such as you [the Chancellor] thinketh reasonable in this case'.[119] At higher levels of state affairs, some degree of delegation was also essential. Thus, again in April 1419, the king told Langley, as Chancellor, that he had appointed Sir John Radcliffe as constable of Bordeaux and captain of the strategically vital castle of Fronsac. The Chancellor was to take the advice of Bedford and the council in England, and 'treat and accord with . . . [Radcliffe] for his abiding there, so that he may do us good service as it seemeth best to their discretions for our advantage and the profit of the country, and that you speed him in all the haste that you can'.[120] Although, as we have seen, Henry kept a very tight personal control over matters of government, he was clearly prepared to allow his higher-ranking servants some necessary degree of discretion.

Other cases, however, demanded the king's personal presence and attention. Henry himself insisted upon this: unlike some of his predeces-

---

[117] C 81/1364, no. 51: 1 May 1418: 'that he might be of power to doo us better service yn other occupacion, as we have sette hym ynne for oure prouffit, as ye may be more clerely enfourmed by the saide supplicacion. So we wol that ye see and understand clerely al ye matere contened therynne, and thereupon ordeine such provision as hit semeth best to youre discrecion, for oure prouffit and avantage yn this cas'.

[118] C 81/1364, no. 66: signet, at the siege of Rouen, 30 Aug. 1418.

[119] C 81/1365, no. 1: signet, at Vernon, 6 Apr. 1419.

[120] C 81/1366, no. 13: signet, at Rouen, [–] Apr. 1419. See also E 404/35/119. Radcliffe's formal appointment, dated 16 May 1419, is in C 61/118, m. 9.

sors, it seems that he required no prompting or imploring from his officers, advisers and councillors. He was no Edward II, sometimes notoriously unwilling to attend to affairs of state. In September 1418, writing under the signet from the siege of Rouen, he sent the Chancellor a petition received from the abbot and convent of St Mary Graces beside the Tower of London, ordering him to show 'all the favour and ease that may be done, in law and conscience' to the house. But the final resolution of the matter was to be delayed 'until we may ordain at our coming home, with God's grace, to put it in rest and quiet'.[121] In the event, the abbot and convent had to wait until his return in February 1421. The formula about the king's intentions upon his return was often repeated. In June 1419, the Chancellor was exhorted to ensure that the revenues of the hospital of St Anthony in the city of London were not spent, but that he should 'keep them still wholly until our coming home, with God's grace'.[122] Again, in the following month, he told the Chancellor that the disputed election of a provost for Oriel College, Oxford, should be 'put in respite until our coming home, with God's grace' and that the college was to be 'put . . . in such governance as seemeth best according to your discretion . . . until our coming'.[123] One potential, and sometimes actual, disadvantage of the king's long, three-and-a-half-year absence abroad may have lain here: the conclusion of English business might be long delayed, while a very considerable burden of responsibility was necessarily laid upon his regents, officers of state, lieutenants and deputies. That responsibility could include the summoning of Parliament and the oversight of appointments and elections to offices throughout England. Hence, in October 1420, Henry

---

[121] C 81/1346, no. 68: 21 Sept. 1418. The Chancellor was to show 'al the favour and ese that may be doon, by lawe and conscience' and the matter should not be resolved 'unto that we mowe ordeyne at oure coming hoom, with goddes grace, to put hit yn reste and quiete'. See below, chapter 5 for discussion of the case.
[122] C 81/1365, no. 6: signet, at Mantes, 20 June 1419.
[123] C 81/1365, no. 8: signet, at Mantes, 7 July 1419.

wrote to Humphrey of Gloucester, as regent in England, from the siege of Melun, that

> it is our will and intention that you . . . summon Parliament, to be held on Monday 2nd December, for certain reasons of which we wish you to be informed in all haste. And we also wish and charge you that you see that the Justices of the Peace, sheriffs, escheators, coroners and such officers as shall be appointed be able and worthy persons . . . and be not troublers in their regions, and that they be chosen without brokerage[124] or favouritism, or any other unlawful means, according to the statute and ordinances made thereon.[125]

Recent experience of 'troublers', such as Sir Richard Stanhope, in the shires, may have had some part to play in shaping the king's 'will and intention' in these concerns.[126]

Direct intervention was often more urgently demanded, in cases of violence and dispossession which called for a speedy resolution. In July 1419, for instance, the king had received, at Mantes, a request from

> our poor liegeman John Bone, according to which supplication we wish that you [the Chancellor] let him have what right and law dictates . . . but [also] that the other side be well advised not to heed . . . the suggestions . . . of he who calleth himself parson of Wortham, until

---

[124] Brocage, brokage: brokerage; use of an agent. The king's concern was clearly with the procedures whereby the officers of local government were appointed and elected.

[125] C 81/1543, no. 21: headed 'By ye kyng', under the signet, 'in oure hoost afore Melun', 8 Oct. 1420: 'it is oure wil and entente that ye . . . [summ]on parlement, to be holde Monday ye second day of Decembre next, for certaine causes ye which we wol do you to have knowlech of in al haste. And also wol and charge you that ye se[e] that justices of the pees, shereves, eschetours, coroners and suche officers as shul be maad, be such persones as ben able and worthy . . . and that ben no treublers in thaire contrees, and that thay be chose[n] without brocage or favour of persones, or any other unleeful meanes, after ye statut and ordonnances maad thereupon'.

[126] For Stanhope see above, p. 53; below, pp. 58–9.

such time as the real truth of his accusations is clearly examined and known . . . for the aforesaid parson is held to meddle in such matters.[127]

Such instructions tend to reveal a (perhaps surprising) degree of acquaintance by the king with individual cases, and a willingness to seek and deploy information which might help to resolve the issues. Some of these cases had a previous history, well known to the king. Perhaps one of the more heartfelt of Henry's responses to a petition comes in a letter of 22 May [1421], on paper, to the Chancellor, under the signet of the eagle, at Lambeth. The text is worth citing in full, as – like some other of Henry's peremptory missives – it reveals his character and tone of voice, particularly, as McFarlane has pointed out, that 'abruptness with which he expressed his will'.[128] Headed 'By the king', the letter goes straight to the point:

Chancellor. There is a certain Thomas Walwayn's wife, who has made a grievous complaint to us about Sir John Scudamore, and although we had ordained both parties to be before us or our council, in order to have knowledge of the matter in debate between them, and to make an end of it, it is now the case that we cannot make an end thereto at this time . . . considering our hasty departure from here, we wish that [not] withstanding that we suppose she standeth not in the right, because s[he is?] a rather slanderous woman, and also that we do not wish to be burdened with her weighty pursuits, that you send for both of the said parties to come before you on such a day that seems reasonable to you, to hear the said controversial matter, and make an end of it, as we shall

---

[127] C 81/1365, no. 9: 11 July 1419: petition from 'oure poure ligeman Johan Bone, upon which supplicacion we wol that ye doo hym to have that that right and lawe wollen . . . but that thothersyde beeth wel avysed [not to heed] . . . ye suggestions . . . of him that calleth himself person of Wortham, unto ye tyme ye verray trowthe be clerely examined and knowen of his accusacions . . . for ye aforesaid person is holden to besy in suche materes'.

[128] McFarlane, 'Henry V: a Personal Portrait', p. 118.

tell you tomorrow more fully by word of mouth. But at all events give them their day when they shall be with you.[129]

There could hardly be a more direct and abrupt expression of the royal will. But, despite the king's suspicion that the exasperating and allegedly 'slanderous' petitioner 'standeth not in the right', the case was nonetheless to be heard before the Chancellor. Skidmore (or Scudamore), the Herefordshire knight who was the subject of the complaint, was serving Henry in France and was to become celebrated (and ultimately disgraced) by marrying the daughter of Owain Glyn Dwr.[130] In similar interventionist vein, in November 1420, during his siege of Melun, the king was exercised once again by the behaviour of the troublesome, 'unruly and truculent' Nottinghamshire knight Sir Richard Stanhope. Despite his position as a county MP and JP, Stanhope had already been the subject of complaints in 1414.[131] In November 1420 he was again intimidating, and attempting to dispossess, local people in the county, and was the subject of a petition from one of the king's servants, John Hertishire, who was serving with him in France. Stanhope, it was claimed,

---

[129] SC 1/43, no. 159: 22 May 1421 [misdated, according to a note in the file, to 1419]. Thomas Walwayn, a Herefordshire esquire, had died at some time between 9 May 1415 and the probate of his will on 20 May 1416. His long and interesting will (in English) survives, in which he bequeaths extensive landed property and movable goods to his wife and chief executor, Isabella. The subsequent case, involving Sir John Skidmore, concerned rights to the possession of the manor of Langeford (Herefordshire). See *The Fifty Earliest English Wills in the Court of Probate, London, A.D. 1387–1439*, ed. F.J. Furnivall (*EETS*, lxxviii, 1892), pp. 23–6. Also, for earlier petitions from Thomas Walwayn himself, see SC 8/249, no. 12428 & C 81/580, no. 1279 (1399). For the original text of the letter see below, Appendix [2.].

[130] Sir John Skidmore (Scudamore) (c.1365–1435) of Kentchurch, Herefordshire, served the crown in both Wales and France. His eldest son, another Sir John, was among the very few members of the English knightly class killed at Agincourt. Skidmore senior appears to have retained Henry V's favour, despite complaints made against him, throughout the king's lifetime. See *The Chronicle of Adam of Usk, 1377–1421*, ed. C. Given-Wilson (Oxford, 1997), pp. 256–7; *CPR, 1416–1422*, p. 218.

[131] See above, p. 53, 56. Also *The History of Parliament: the House of Commons, 1386–1421*, ed. J.S. Roskell, L. Clark & C. Rawcliffe; entry for Sir Richard Stanhope (c.1374–1436): www. historyofparliamentonline.org/volume 1.

prevents and disturbs him and his attorney, wrongfully and against law and conscience, from . . . occupying a place with certain rents in the town of Clayworth in the county of Nottingham . . . about which, if it is so, we are in no way well pleased . . . [and] as our said servant has continually remained in our service since we came into this land, you are to see and ordain that he has no wrong done to him by the said Stanhope, nor by none other . . . until our coming home, with God's grace, into the realm of England, so that we may if need be attend to the said matter ourself, knowing that we write in a similar way to our brother of Gloucester on the same affair . . .[132]

In just under three months' time, the king would be back 'home' in England, prepared, if need be, to settle this case – and others. Meanwhile, the able and ambitious men whom he had left in charge of such everyday business were to investigate the charges and attempt to resolve them. That they often did so is evidence that the king's trust in them was well placed; and perhaps their fear of, and respect for, his displeasure was justified.

In a much-quoted passage, the chronicler Jean de Wavrin, from the Burgundian Netherlands, summed up Henry V's reign and character, stressing the fear with which he was regarded. The king, wrote Wavrin,

was a wise man, and expert in everything that he undertook, and extremely strong-willed . . . and he was so much feared and dreaded by

---

[132] C 81/1365, no. 26: at Melun, 5 Nov. 1420: Stanhope 'letteth and destourbeth hym and his attourne wrongfully and ayenst lawe and conscience, to . . . occupie a p[lace] with certain rentes with ynne the town of Cliworth in the conte of Notyngham . . . of which thing, if hit soo bee, we ben no thing wel pleased . . . as oure saide servant hath continually abiden in oure service sith oure commyng in to this lande, yat ye see and ordeine yat he have no wrong by the said Stanhapp', ner by noon other . . . unto oure commyng hoom, with goddes grace, in to the reaume of England, so yat we may if nede be doo entende to the same matere oureself, wittyng yat we write semblable unto oure brother of Gloucestre upon the same matere'.

his princes, knights, captains and all manner of people, that there was no one, however close to him, nor favoured by him, who dared to disobey his ordinances, especially among the English; and so were those of the kingdom of France, of whatever rank, who were under his obedience and domination, reduced to a similar state; and the main reason for this was because he punished those who did the contrary, and infringed his commands and ordinances, harshly and without mercy; and he maintained the discipline of chivalry [*de chevallerie*] very well, just as the Romans once did.[133]

Wavrin may well have been thinking, in particular, about the notorious and punitive severity with which Henry enforced military discipline and applied the usages of war. But there was clearly a widespread fear, palpable in some cases, of incurring the royal displeasure – although the royal wrath and anger could be very tightly controlled and calculated. And, in fearing the king, his subjects were, in his own mind and in those of some of his contemporaries, also learning to fear God. Whatever he might have wished to be, Henry V was no despot; there were, no doubt, many things which he may have had more will than strength to do.

The promptings and prickings of conscience also played their part.[134] The exercise of what has been called a 'disciplined conscience' in the public sphere, which could not always be reconciled with private, sometimes self-indulgent, individual consciences, has been seen as an important contribution of the early fifteenth century to the business of statecraft. Although there was by this time an extensive theory-based, and especially theological, body of thought, from the works of St Bonaventure (1221–74) and

---

[133] Jean de Wavrin, *Recueil des croniques et anchiennes istories de la Grant Bretaigne*, ed. W. Hardy (RS, London, 1868), ii,p. 429.
[134] See below, chapter 5, pp. 169–72. Also, for what follows, Catto, 'The Burden and Conscience of Government', pp. 97–9.

St Thomas Aquinas (1225–74) onwards,[135] on the subject of conscience and its workings, its application to the rough and brutal world of politics was not based on abstract principle. The devotional tract and the confessor's manual may be better guides to the 'disciplined conscience' of laypeople than the more abstract works of moral philosophy and theology. The everyday experience of advisers, councillors and confessors also played its part. In Henry V's case, that conscience was tempered and tested in the refiner's fire of political realities. It was no stranger to the apparent cruelties and acts of ruthlessness which were sometimes thought to be necessary. But that did not make him a Visconti, Sforza, Este, Malatesta, Gonzaga or Montefeltro.[136] Like them, he knew what the fate not only of tyrants (or would-be tyrants), but also of those who usurped them, could be. As the French were pleased to point out, the English killed their kings.[137] The Burgundian Wavrin may thus have credited Henry, whose legitimate dynastic title was by no means entirely unblemished and secure, with far greater naked and unbridled power than could ever have been exercised by him. The burdensome business of English kingship did not encompass absolutism – and down the road to despotism, however enticing it might be, English rulers went at their peril.

---

[135] See J.V. Dolan, 'Conscience in the Catholic Theological Tradition' in *Conscience: its Freedom and Limitations*, ed. W.C. Bier (New York, 1971), pp. 9–19; D.C. Langston, 'The Spark of Conscience: Bonaventure's View of Conscience and Synderesis', *Franciscan Studies*, 66 (2008), pp. 317–36.

[136] For an exploration of the evolution of Ludovico (Il Moro) Sforza of Milan's conscience, and related matters, see D.M. Bueno de Mesquita, 'The Conscience of the Prince', *Proceedings of the British Academy*, 65 (1979), pp. 417–41 (repr. in *Art and Politics in Renaissance Italy*, ed. G. Holmes (Oxford, 1993), pp. 159–83). For a penetrating analysis of the nature of Malatesta despotism see Jones, *The Malatesta of Rimini and the Papal State*, esp. pp. 317–38.

[137] See P.S. Lewis, 'War Propaganda and Historiography in Fifteenth-century France and England', in his *Essays in Later Medieval French History* (London, 1985), p. 205: '. . . the Lancastrians were usurpers, . . . the Yorkists were usurpers and . . . the English were all murderers anyway'; also 'Two Pieces of Fifteenth-century Political Iconography: (b) The English Kill their Kings', in *Essays in Later Medieval French History*, pp. 191–2.

Chapter 2

'IN MINE OWN HAND'

THE PERSONALISATION OF KINGSHIP

With Henry V . . . we enter on a period in which it is not unusual to find the royal wishes set out in the king's own hand, especially matters too secret for another's knowledge. To read a man's own words is to know his mind more intimately than at second-hand.

(K.B. McFarlane)[1]

McFarlane's ability to produce what he called a 'Personal Portrait' of Henry V was made possible, in part, by the existence of evidence 'set out in the king's own hand'. The lens or filter introduced by second-hand reporting or purposeful obfuscation (by chroniclers or bureaucrats) was offset, and sometimes eliminated, by such evidence. English kings were known, on relatively rare occasions, to have used their own hand in correspondence since the youthful Edward III agreed, in 1330, to write the words 'Pater sancte' ('Holy father') on those of his letters of recommendation to Pope John XXII that he 'took particularly to

---

[1] K.B. McFarlane, 'Henry V: a Personal Portrait' in his Lancastrain Kings and Lollard Knights (Oxford, 1972), p. 117.

heart'.[2] A single surviving example of Edward III's use of a signature is also to be found in an enrolment of a letter appointing proctors and nuncios to treat with Castile in June 1362.[3] But the autograph endorsement of surviving letters and other documents, or their annotation – let alone their actual composition – in the ruler's own hand, was very rare before the reign of Henry V.[4] At earlier periods, actual physical contact between rulers and the documents written out and sealed in their names had been relatively slight, if not non-existent. Henry II, when confirming the liberties and immunities of St Albans abbey, was said 'physically to have touched the charter of settlement issued by the abbot . . . and to have placed on it a silk thread from his own cloak . . . presumably as a cord for the application of the seal: perhaps the closest that most medieval kings came to a physical gesture of assent to their own written instructions or commands'.[5] Otherwise, with the exception of the occasional application of a cross or other mark, sometimes in the king's autograph, to the most formal and solemn of charters issued between 1066 and the early years of Henry II's

---

[2] See, and for what follows, P. Chaplais, *English Diplomatic Practice in the Middle Ages* (London, 2003), pp. 100–2. The autograph 'Pater sancte' was a secret code to enable the pope to identify those recommendations for appointment to ecclesiastical office which carried the king's warm support. Edward was not yet master in his own house at the time, as his mother Isabella, and Roger Mortimer, were effectively in control. The more general subject of rulers' literacy is discussed in V.H. Galbraith, 'The Literacy of the Medieval English Kings', *Proceedings of the British Academy*, 21 (1935), pp. 201–38 (repr. in his *Kings and Chroniclers* (London, 1982), pp. 78–105). For literacy in England at an earlier period see M.T. Clanchy, *From Memory to Written Record: England, 1066–1307* (2nd edn Oxford, 1993).

[3] C 76/45, m. 6: 'scripturam "E. Rex" manu domini Regis propria factam ['the writing "E. Rex" (Edwardus Rex) done in the lord king's own hand']'; *Foedera*, iii, p. 657; P. Chaplais, *Essays in Medieval Diplomacy and Administration* (London, 1981), XXII, pp. 181–2 & Appendix. The original letter does not survive. I was reminded of this reference by M. Claude Jeay.

[4] For some examples of handwriting, in facsimile, for Richard II and Henry IV see W.J. Hardy, *The Handwriting of the Kings and Queens of England* (London, 1893), pp. 13–18. Specimens of Henry V's hand are on pp. 19–29.

[5] N. Vincent, 'The Great Lost Library of England's Medieval Kings? Royal Use and Ownership of Books, 1066–1272' in *1000 Years of Royal Books and Manuscripts*, ed. K. Doyle & S. McKendrick (London, 2014), p. 83, citing *Gesta abbatum monasterii S. Albani, a Thomas Walsingham . . . compilata*, ed. T. Riley (London, 1867–9), i, p. 156: 'cui etiam rex manum suum apposuit, nam laqueum pallii sui pro testimonio apposuit'.

reign (*c*.1154–65), all written documents issued in the king's name were authenticated only by wax seals.[6]

It is a contention of this book that the use of the autograph sign manual, or the signature, as well as the annotation and endorsement of documents by the king himself, advanced very markedly during Henry V's reign. This was, it is argued, in large part a direct result of royal choice and initiative. So was the introduction of English, to a far greater extent than had ever been the case before, as a language of government.[7] Richard II's reign (1377–99) had certainly seen the occasional use of the sign manual in the abbreviated form 'Le roy R[ichard] s[econd]' or his signature 'Richard'. Like the 'secret' seal under Edward II, Richard's sign manual, together with the signet, represented the personal will of the king – a will which, for at least some of his subjects, was exercised unjustly and (some claimed) tyrannically. From such practices, it was thought, despotism might be born. But the usage had taken root. Whether fully literate or not, rulers were now expressing their will through their own handwriting. There can, however, be little doubt of the very high levels of literacy within the usurping house of Lancaster.

Henry V and his brothers have been described as 'the most bookish group of royal princes in medieval England' and their education was thorough: Henry was learning Latin by the age of eight, when he was bought Latin grammars.[8] Of his father's literacy there can be no doubt. Henry IV (1399–1413) could write in his own hand in Anglo-Norman French and in English. In a signet letter of October 1403 he also quoted the Latin tag *necessitas non habet legem* ('necessity has no law') in his own hand, followed

---

[6] See Vincent, 'The Great Lost Library . . .', p. 84 and n. 85. The practice of applying this kind of sign manual had been discontinued by *c*.1170.

[7] See also below, chapter 3, pp. 88–9.

[8] McFarlane, 'Henry V: a Personal Portrait', pp. 115–16. For the schooling of the medieval English upper classes see, in general, N. Orme, *From Childhood to Chivalry: the Education of the English Kings and Aristocracy, 1066–1530* (London, 1984).

by an autograph postscript in Anglo-Norman.[9] Henry IV had also employed a sign manual, resembling a royal cypher, formed by the initial letters 'H. R.' (*Henricus Rex*) or 'R.H.' (*Rex Henricus*), and the signature 'Henry'. This practice was followed, on a larger scale, by his son. Why was this so, and what lay behind Henry V's apparent readiness to endorse and subscribe letters with his own hand? Some clues to an answer may lie both in recent past precedent and in his own desire that his will should be fully expressed and authenticated not only by the arguably impersonal application of a seal, but also by a personal validation. He appears to have expected other rulers to act likewise.

To try to understand the conditions from which a greater use of the sign manual or signature emerged requires a brief excursion into the reign of Richard II. Clearly, this development formed part of a common European movement.[10] In France, a turning-point in its favour occurred during the period *c.*1360–1400. Recent French scholarship has tended to conceptualise it as a sign of a growing movement of 'individuation' and 'individualisation'.[11] McFarlane's researches, followed up by those of Nicholas Orme, demonstrated that in England the tendency had begun, if anything, rather earlier.[12] The literate layman had certainly arrived at various levels of both government and society, with significant consequences for both Church and State. So the emergence of the sign manual and signature may represent one facet of a rising level of lay literacy, which was already well under way by 1350, if not much earlier, in the higher and middle reaches of society. Visual identification of individuals,

---

[9] The two examples are in TNA, C 81/1358, no. 4B & C 81/1362, no. 46. See H.C. Maxwell-Lyte, *Historical Notes on the Use of the Great Seal of England* (London, 1926), pp. 129–30. Henry rendered the Latin quotation as *nessescitas non habet legem*.

[10] See below, pp. 109–15.

[11] See, most recently, C. Jeay, *Signature et pouvoir au Moyen Âge*, Mémoires et documents de l'Ecole des Chartes, 99 (Paris, 2015).

[12] See K.B. McFarlane, *The Nobility of Later Medieval England* (Oxford, 1973), pp. 41–8, 228–47.

by means of their more naturalistic portraits or 'likenesses', had also begun to be made.[13]

But there were pragmatic, as well as more general cultural reasons for these innovations whereby identity could be individualised. It was thought that wax impressions even of personal seals affixed to documents were not always sufficient to guarantee their authenticity. Nor, it was claimed, did they fully express the personal wishes or intentions of the writer, normally mediated through a clerk or scribe. Writing to his officers in England, especially those at the ports and points of entry, Richard II could therefore issue letters of safe conduct and protection to the king of Navarre and his entourage, concluding with the note that 'in witness of this we have had our seal put to these present [letters]. And to the end that it should more clearly show that this proceeds from our conscious will [*de nostre conscience*], we have written our name here with our own hand . . .'[14] Although such letters were already – or also – sealed, they were given greater weight and authority, it seems, by the addition of the king's personal mark, whether by the sign manual or signature. Even more telling, perhaps, was another instance from Richard's reign, which gave precise grounds for the use of the king's own hand. Early in 1395, a disputed and contested election to the see of Exeter was in full cry. The king had already made his wishes well known to the electoral body, naming his candidate for the office. But, writing to an anonymous recipient (as the letter is found in a formulary of letters and petitions) the king stated that some of the canons of the cathedral 'have said that our said letters did not conform to our will, and

---

[13] See, for the origins and functions of the portrait at this time, A. Martindale, *Heroes, Ancestors, Relatives and the Birth of the Portrait* (Maarssen/The Hague, 1988); also, more recently, M. Grzeda, 'The Pre-History of Portraiture in Central Europe', seminar paper, University of Hamburg, 2012 (www. academia.edu/2051095/The Portrait of Rudolf IV of Austria); & Jeay, 'Pour une histoire de la signature', p. 156. Also above, p. 64.

[14] *Anglo-Norman Letters and Petitions*, ed. Legge p. 157, no. 107: 'En tesmoign de ce nous avons fait mettre nostre seel a ces presentes. Et affin que mielx appere que ce vient de nostre conscience, y avons nostre noum escript de nostre main'.

were not sealed under our signet, because . . . our signet had recently been newly made and changed . . . [and that] it was unknown to them'.[15] But the dean and chapter were to be reassured that 'our signet, letters and will are all in agreement'. In a subsequent letter to the canons of Exeter, the king told them that he had been informed that 'some of you have openly said that the said letters were not ours, and this was because you did not recognize our signet', as it had been changed. But he assured them that the letters had indeed been issued 'under our signet, entirely of our own will and true knowledge'. They were to agree to elect his nominee, and so that they knew 'that this is our will, we have written our name on these letters, and in our own hand'.[16] Again, it was not thought sufficient simply to seal the missives with the signet, especially since there had been an alteration in its form. They had to be validated further by inserting the king's own name.

The extent to which personal promises, commitments and undertakings could (it was hoped) be strengthened by the addition of signs manual and signatures to proposals and agreements was exemplified in Henry V's dealings with John the Fearless, duke of Burgundy, in September–October 1416. The two princes, plus the emperor Sigismund, met at Calais.[17] A series of drafts and memoranda, stemming from those meetings and listing the 'articles which the duke of Burgundy shall promise to the king', survives

[15] *Anglo-Norman Letters and Petitions,* p. 171, no. 115: 'ont dit que noz dites lettres ne passerent de nostre voluntee, ne ne estoient ensealez desoubz nostre signet pur ce . . . que mesme nostre signet, que de nostre mandement estoit ore tard de novel fait et chaungez . . . [et] a eux estoit desconeuz'. But 'noz signet, lettres et volunte de tout saccordent'. Cited by Chaplais, *English Diplomatic Practice,* p. 101, n. 137.

[16] *Anglo-Norman Letters and Petitions,* p. 172, no. 116: 'les uns de vous avez overtement dit que les dites lettres nestoient pas nostres, et ce a cause que vous naviez pas conissance de nostre signet'. But the letters were confirmed to 'estre passez soubz nostre signet de nostre pleine voluntee et verraie conissance' and so that they were to know that 'ce est nostre voluntee, noz avons escriptz en cestes noz lettres de nostre mein'. In the event, Richard's nominee – his secretary Roger Walden – was not appointed, and Edmund Stafford was provided to the bishopric on 15 Jan. 1395. Cited Chaplais, English Diplomatic Practice, p. 101, n. 137.

[17] See Allmand, *Henry V,* pp. 109–12.

in various forms.[18] One of these sets out the steps whereby Burgundy's undertakings could be made more binding and more difficult to deny, avoid or evade, with the words:

> To the end that everyone knows that these articles proceed from his own pure and free will, and that he wishes to keep and observe them, at every point, without ever acting to the contrary, the duke shall swear [to them] and promise, on the faith and loyalty of his body, without fraud or malice, and shall write them out in his own hand, sign them with his sign manual, and apply the privy seal of his arms, the day and place etc [of issue], just as it is in fact.[19]

The draft is accompanied by a blank sheet of paper, with the note at its base: 'Things written in the king's hand concerning the duke of Burgundy', with some remaining traces of a seal (probably the signet) in red wax.[20] Apparently unnoticed by historians, the draft's indication of the king's direct involvement in the negotiations could not be clearer. He was also, it seems, largely responsible for devising the ways employed to attempt to compel the slippery and elusive duke to keep his word.[21] That some, admittedly limited, degree of success was achieved appears evident from John the Fearless's draft letter, dated October 1416, promising to observe

---

[18] See *Foedera*, ix, pp. 394–5; E 30/1068, 1273, 1609; E 28/32, nos 65, 66.

[19] 'Et au fin que chascun sache que cestes articles precedent de sa pure et franche voluntee, et qil le voet garder et observer en chascun point sanz jamais de venir a lencontre, jurera et promectera le dit duc, par la foy et loyaute de son corps, et ce sanz fraude ou mal engin, et les escrira de sa propre main, et ou son signe manuel le signera, et metera son prive seal de ses armes, le jour et lieu etc, ensi qil est de fet': E 28/32, no. 65: draft memorandum, 1 folio, on paper, damaged, n.d., but clearly Sept.–Oct. 1416.

[20] E 28/32, no. 66: 1 folio, paper, endorsed: 'Choses escrites de la main du Roy touchant le duc de Burgoigne'. Traces of a seal *en placard* appear between the words 'du' and 'Roy'. The (otherwise blank) folio may have acted as the cover or wrapper of the main document, sealed with the signet, in effect *a tergo* (on the dorse).

[21] The author of the *Gesta* was similarly suspicious of the duke and his behaviour. See *Gesta Henrici Quinti*, ed. Taylor & Roskell, pp. xlix, 175.

the terms of the Calais agreement.[22] This was 'written in our own hand and sealed with our privy seal', as set out in the articles above.[23] The letter stated:

> So that everyone shall know that these our letters stem from our full and free will, and that we wish to keep and observe them completely in every point, without ever doing or acting to the contrary in any way, we swear to, and promise, them by the faith and loyalty of our body and by the word of a prince.[24]

In the event, an overt Anglo-Burgundian alliance did not result at that time. This had to wait for the duke's murder in 1419, and his son's subsequent fulfilment of what were to a large extent the terms of the Calais negotiations of 1416. But the fact that Henry chose to put such an emphasis on securing promises signed by the duke, in his own hand, suggests that he expected other rulers and princes to act as he himself often, and increasingly, did.

The most striking – and in many ways the most remarkable – of the king's known correspondence written in his own hand was a letter, now

---

[22] It has been argued that this paper document, and others associated with it, 'are merely projects emanating from the English Chancery' (P. Bonenfant et al., *Philippe le Bon: sa politique, son action* (Brussels, 1996), pp. 143–5). But comparison of watermarks suggests that some at least may have emanated from the Burgundian secretariat. See E 30/1068 & 1069, with watermarks representing a pair of scales with triangular pans & C.-M. Briquet, *Les filigranes, dictionnaire historique des marques de papiers de leur apparition vers 1282 jusqu'en 1600* (Leipzig, 1923), nos 2398, 2399–2406, 2412, 2413 for instances of paper with a similar watermark found at Dijon (1417), Alost (1419), Damme (1421) and elsewhere in the Burgundian dominions. Also, for paper manufacture in the region, F. Gamier, 'Production et diffusion du papier bourguignon aux xve et xvie siecles', *Annales de Bourgogne*, 79 (2007), pp. 211–28, esp. p. 217.

[23] E 30/1068: 1 folio, paper, a copy or draft: 'escrit et signe de nostre propre main et sealee du prive seal de nos armes'; & *Foedera*, ix, p. 395: 'escriptes de notre main et sealeez de notre prive seal', at Calais, Oct. 1416.

[24] E 30/1068: 'Et affin que chascun sache que cestes noz lettres precedent de nostre pure et franche volunte, et que nous les volons garder et observer en toutes en chascun point, sanz jamais de faire ou venir alencontre en aucune manere, nous le jurons et promettons par la foy et loiaute de nostre corps et en parole de prince'.

apparently lost, with which a bemused Pope Martin V was presented at Rome in June 1422. The Vatican Registers (in the Archivio Secreto) contain a later transcript of a letter from Martin to Henry V, alluding to 'certain letters, which are said to be in your own hand, and in the English tongue [*idiomate anglicano*], explained to us through an interpreter'.[25] In continental Europe, English was still largely unknown as a written and spoken language until the eighteenth century. The pope could have had no knowledge or understanding of it. The letter from Henry concerned an alleged slight and insult suffered by Thomas Polton, bishop of Chichester, currently the king's representative at the papal court. He had, it was claimed, been treated 'less honourably than befits a royal envoy [*oratori regio*]' as a result of the seating order recently drawn up for a public consistory, or assembly, which he had attended. It has been observed that precedence was the 'tenderest spot of medieval diplomacy'.[26] It appeared that the envoy of Juan, king of Castile and León, had been preferred to Polton, Henry's representative.[27] The ensuing dispute over precedence between Polton and the Castilian envoy had allegedly 'brought the two men to blows'.[28] A slight to Polton, it was implied, was a slight to the royal majesty itself, and the pope's reply was conciliatory. By way of explanation, but not

---

[25] See J. Haller, 'England und Rom unter Martin V', *Quellen und Forschungen aus italienischen Archiven und Bibliotheken* (1905), viii, pp. 294–6; cited Chaplais, *English Diplomatic Practice*, pp. 100, 133. The text, an eighteenth-century copy, referred to 'certis litteris, que tua propria manu scripte dicuntur in idiomate anglicano, per interpretem nobis expositis', and is dated 13 June 1422. No record of it has been found in the *Calendar of Entries in the Papal Registers relating to Great Britain and Ireland, 7: 1417–1431*, ed. J.A. Tremlow (London, 1906) under that date.

[26] J. G. Dickinson, *The Congress of Arras, 1435: A Study in Medieval Diplomacy* (Oxford, 1955), p. 38.

[27] The pope stressed that it was not his decision that the Castilian envoy should be given precedence over Polton, thereby harming Henry's royal dignity: 'Et propterea existimare non debes nostrum judicium fuisse, ut orator carissimi in Christo filii nostri Johannis Castellie et Legionis regis illustris oratori tuo anteponeretur, et aliquanter tua dignitas lederetur' (Haller, 'England und Rom', p. 295).

[28] Harvey, 'Polton, Thomas (d.1433)', in *New Oxford DNB*. Polton had, as a young man, previously been involved in an affray at Oxford in 1394, leading to the death of another student, for which he was charged but pardoned.

of excuse, he told Henry that common opinion at the curia was that Polton was not Henry's fully empowered envoy and plenipotentiary (*orator*) but merely his proctor (*procurator*), in which capacity he had first come to the papal court. The curial officials were clearly ill-informed about Polton's current status. The pope assured the king that in future he would ensure that any representative of Henry who came to the curia would be assigned the appropriate place, according to the long-standing ceremonial rules of precedence, 'on account of your honour [*pro honore tuo*]').[29]

Whether Henry's letter in English was directly addressed to the pope or came in the form of a missive to Polton from the king, which he then expected his representative to translate for the pope's benefit, is not entirely clear. Time was short, and the king may have had little stomach for an elaborate exchange over a matter about which the sensitive and self-important Polton might have felt more strongly than he did himself.[30] Henry was, moreover, to die two months later, and may already have been suffering from the terminal illness which he had contracted at the siege of Meaux. But it would have been most unusual and undignified, if not offensive, to have communicated directly with the Holy Father in this way. And Henry, as far as we know, was a scrupulous observer of protocol in these matters. It would not, after all, have been difficult for Polton to have translated the letter *viva voce* into Latin for the pope – indeed he may well have been the interpreter to whom reference was made. Whatever the case, the incident was exceptional: there is no other recorded example of the king writing in English, in his own hand, to anyone other than his own

---

[29] Haller, 'England und Rom', p. 296: 'quod cuicunque, ad nos venienti tuo nomine, locum pro honore tuo debitum assignari mandabimus, secundum cerimonialia et instituta prefate curie diu servata'.

[30] For Polton's role at the council of Constance and at the papal curia at this time see below, chapter 5, pp. 173–4. For a recent biography of Polton see Harvey, 'Polton, Thomas (d.1433)' in *Oxford DNB* (Oxford, 2004) [http//www.oxforddnb.com/view/article/22482]. For Henry V's relations with Martin V at this time see M. Harvey, 'Martin V and Henry V' in *Archivum Historiae Pontificiae*, 24 (1986), pp. 49–70.

kinsmen, kinswomen or subjects.[31] We cannot, at this stage, infer that it represented an outburst of royal anger in the language in which he perhaps felt most comfortable; or that he was, in effect, defiantly answering one alleged slight with another. The whole matter remains mysterious, and the search for the controversial letter, and for some trace in English archives of the pope's reply, continues. But it does confirm the view, expressed by the king himself, that the use of one's own hand and of one's own language or mother tongue was a guarantee of authenticity and sincerity. And the pope, it seems, took the point.

In another of the matters that he held very 'close to his heart' – the safekeeping and guarding of his French and Scots prisoners, of whom there were no fewer than seventy-six in July 1422 – he was equally insistent.[32] One of the most notable, and noted, surviving records of what is assumed to be Henry's autograph is part of a letter, attributed to the king's own hand,[33] written probably in February 1418 to Thomas Beaufort, duke of Exeter. It is, again, worth quoting in full, as it conveys very well the king's direct style of address and manner of speech.

> Furthermore, I wish that you consult with my brother [Bedford], with the Chancellor, with my cousin of Northumberland, and my cousin of Westmoreland, and that you keep good order in my northern marches; and especially as regards the duke of Orleans, and all the remainder of my French prisoners; and also for the king of Scotland, because I am

[31] For further discussion of the language issue, see below, chapter 3, pp. 89–90, 96–9.

[32] The custody of his prisoners was a matter of constant concern, as is reflected in the many payments made to that end. See, for instance, E 403/636, m. 7r: payment to a physician for medicines supplied to treat the illness of the lord of Estouteville, the king's prisoner in the castle of Moresend (Northants) (25 May 1418). For their number see E 403/655, m. 10r (July 1422).

[33] The hand here attributed to the king appears less well formed and practised than in some other examples. The possibility that this fragment of the letter may be a copy or draft by another hand cannot entirely be ruled out. But the content and style of the text clearly indicate Henry's authorship.

secretly informed by a man of right notable estate in this land, that there has been a man of the duke of Orleans in Scotland, who agreed with the duke of Albany that, this coming summer, he will bring in the puppet of Scotland[34] to stir up what he can, and also that ways may be found of abducting especially the duke of Orleans, and also of the earl, as well as the remainder of my aforesaid prisoners, that God forbid. Wherefore I wish that the duke of Orleans shall still be kept within the castle of Pontefract, without going to Robert's place[35] or to any other disport. For it is better that he lack his disport than that we lose all the remainder [of the prisoners]. Do as you think fit.[36]

If the rest of the letter had survived, we could probably add it to the corpus of surviving instruments of the king's will under the signet and sign manual. As it is, its style and spelling correspond well enough with the examples of his written interventions which have been more securely identified. Although the hand in which it is written may not be that of the king, its content could hardly have been of anyone else's devising. Henry's continuing concern for his French prisoners was also exemplified by his

[34] The 'Pseudo-Richard II' whose appearance in various guises was supported by Scottish plots. See Allmand, *Henry V*, pp. 309–10 and, for Henry's dealings with Scots prisoners and hostages, P.J. Bradley, 'Henry V's Scottish Policy: a Study in Realpolitik' in *Documenting the Past. Essays in Medieval History presented to George Peddy Cuttino*, ed. J.S. Hamilton & P.J. Bradley (Wolfeboro/Woodbridge, 1989), pp. 177–95, esp. pp. 187–90.

[35] Orléans had been held at Pontefract since the summer of 1417 (*CCR, 1413–1419*, p. 395). 'Robert's place' was Methley Hall, held by the Lancastrian retainer Robert Waterton, where Orléans had been permitted to 'disport' himself by hunting. See McFarlane, 'Henry V: a Personal Portrait', pp. 118–19; also *Calendar of Signet Letters of Henry IV and Henry V*, ed. J.L. Kirby (London, 1978), no. 881.

[36] BL, Cotton MS Vesp. F iii, fo. 8: paper, imperfect, n.d., probably *c*. Feb. 1418. For the original text see below, Appendix 1. Printed in *Original Letters illustrative of English History*, ed. H. Ellis, 1st ser., 2nd edn [i], pp. 1–2; *Titi Livii Foro-Juliensis, Vita Henrici Quinti Regis Angliae*, ed. T. Hearne (Oxford, 1726), pp. 99–100; transcript (late seventeenth century) in Bod. Lib. MS Smith 82 (S.C. 15688), p. 3. The identification of Thomas Beaufort as recipient rests on a letter of his to Thomas Langley, the Chancellor, dated 2 Mar. 1418, in which Beaufort acts according to the king's instructions and passes them on to Langley. See *Lettres des Rois, Reines et autres personnages des cours de France et d'Angleterre*, ed. J.J. Champollion-Figeac, 2 vols (1839–47), ii, pp. 396–7. For an illustration of the document see Allmand, *Henry V*, Plate 15.

dealings with one of the most high-born and politically significant of them. In September 1420, Jean, duke of Bourbon, his prisoner since October 1415, swore not to leave his place of captivity, and to 'remain . . . the said king's loyal prisoner as long as he [the king] pleases'.[37] At Henry's insistence, he signed a recognisance of his oath with his own hand, as well as sealing it with his seal of arms, in the presence of his keepers. The personal seal alone was evidently now regarded as, perhaps, conveying a less binding guarantee of adherence to an agreement. The sign manual or signature did not entirely replace it, but was becoming an essential adjunct in certain kinds of transaction.

One of the earliest surviving instances of the king's use of his autograph sign manual, in conjunction with a document, in English, written in his own hand, dates from the prelude to the Agincourt campaign, in April–May 1415. Endorsed 'R.H.'('Rex Henricus'), this fragmentary note relates to the drawing up of indentures with his captains, and is attached to the indenture subsequently made on 19 June 1415 with Richard Beauchamp, earl of Warwick, as captain of Calais.[38] Henry's note appeared to concern the terms of the indentures, especially the provision of one-third of the gains of war which was to go to the king. This, he ordered, was to be specified in the indenture. His concern for the mechanisms of military organisation and recruitment was also borne out by a signet order to the keeper of the privy seal, John Wakering, which must date from between 24 November 1415 and 7 July 1416. The king stated:

We wish, for certain notable reasons that move us, that you send unto us, clearly written in a roll, the names of all the captains, with their

[37] C 47/28/7, no. 10: 16 Sept. 1420, with the signature 'Jehan'. The duke declared that 'En tesmoin' de ce jay signe ceste lettre de ma main et mis le sain[g] de mes armes'.

[38] E 101/69/7, no. 509: paper, autograph, n.d., damaged. The partially legible text reads: '. . . endenture passe as hit is here maad . . . hit hath been used in ye . . . when hit was wel gouverne[d] . . . ye [. . .]e thryde to ye kyng then be hit speci[fied in ye] endenture, and ellis yif hit hath not pass[e]d hit under this fourme aforesaid. R.H.' The indenture with Warwick is dated at Westminster, 19 June 1415 (E 101/69/7, no. 510).

numbers [of men], who have indented with us for this present voyage . . .[39]

Inspection of documents, as we shall see when considering Henry's dealings with the Church in Normandy, was very much part of the everyday business which he undertook.[40] In December 1418, for example, he had sent for 'various letters . . . and evidences' which were in the keeping of Thomas Elmham, the chronicler, prior of Lenton (Notts) at that time.[41] They were dispatched to him at the siege of Rouen. We do not know what these were, but may assume that they related to his claims to the duchy of Normandy and crown of France. Scrutiny of documents and records was not to be left entirely to his officers and agents. In July 1421, for instance, it was agreed by the king's council, in England, that Robert Rolleston, keeper of the great wardrobe, and others, were to inquire into certain items on the accounts of the late keeper, John Spencer. These were to be found

[i]n certain rolls of John Spencer's accounts, seen by the king at Calais, and signed and marked in his [the king's] own hand . . . [and they] should conduct a diligent inquisition, certifying to the council of the lord king all that will be found by inquisition, and especially concerning those things where the king has himself written in the margin these

---

[39] PSO 1/4, no. 220: 'We wol, for certain causes notable that meveth us, that ye sende unto us clerely written yn a Rolle, ye names of alle ye cappitaines, with thaire nombres, that han endented with us for this present voyage . . .'; signet, paper, headed 'By ye kyng', addressed to the bishop of Norwich, keeper of the privy seal, or his deputy. This can be no one other than Wakering, who held the bishopric from 24 Nov. 1415 onwards, and was keeper of the privy seal from 3 June 1415 until 7 July 1416. The letter is dated 'at oure towne of Caleis', 4 May [?1416]. If this is so, then, intriguingly, the document suggests that Henry may have been at Calais to meet the emperor Sigismund. There is no other recorded reference to his presence there. See Allmand, *Henry V*, pp. 104–5.

[40] See below, chapter 5, pp. 175–86.

[41] E 403/638, m. 9r: payment to a messenger for obtaining 'diversis litteris Regis et evidenciis' from the prior of Lenton and bearing them to the king in Normandy (7 Dec. 1418). For Elmham see 'Elmham, Thomas' in *Oxford DNB* (Oxford, 2004). Elmham had produced a history of the kings of England (1416) and a metrical chronicle of the life of Henry V.

words: 'to be inquired into'[*ad inquirendum*] in his own hand, as well as other things in the said rolls marked at the head with a black sign [*punctu nigro*] in the king's hand.[42]

The first occurrence of the personal examination and checking of their household and other accounts by English kings has often been attributed, following Francis Bacon's *History*, to Henry VII (1485–1509).[43] The above evidence to the contrary, which makes Henry V the first 'businessman-king' or 'bureaucrat-king' is incontrovertible. Similarly, the formula *inspeximus* ['*we* have inspected'] in at least some of the formal documents and letters patent issued in his name, seems to have meant exactly what it said.

The value placed by the king on the use of the signet, and of his own hand, is also exemplified by two other sources: diplomatic instructions and memoranda, as well as his own wills and the codicils to them. In January 1417, Sir John Tiptoft was at Constance, as Henry's envoy to the council there. A set of instructions, in English, which the king sent him from England on 25 January, was specific and complex. They concerned secret negotiations which Henry had had with his Agincourt prisoner, the duke of Bourbon, over his potential release and its terms. This had important implications for the future of Henry's war effort in France, in which he also

---

[42] *PPC*, ii, p. 289: minutes of the council, 4 July 1421; original in BL, Cotton MS Cleopatra F. III, fo. 173. The king had been at Calais between 4 Sept. and 16/17 Oct. 1416 and also, very briefly, early in June 1420 (Allmand, *Henry V*, p. 162). Spencer's accounts as keeper of the great wardrobe survive for 1 Oct. 1415 – 1 Oct. 1416 (E 101/406/26) where a reference to 'certain items' (*certarum parcellarum*) in the roll which were the subject of allowances conceded and promised by Henry V to Spencer's widow, as his executor, might have some bearing on the issue of the annotated and 'marked' entries in his accounts. The reference is dated 16 Feb. 1423 (m. 1v). Copies of the relevant items (*parcellas*) were seen by the king's council on that day. Rolleston had become keeper of the wardrobe by 10 June 1419 (E 101/407/1: great wardrobe account, 10 June 1419–10 June 1420).

[43] See *Francis Bacon*, ed. B. Vickers (Oxford, 1996), p. 178. Bacon (1561–1626) said that he had 'seen long since a book of accounts of Empson's, that had the king's hand almost to every leaf by way of signing, and was in some places postilled [annotated] in the margent with the king's hand likewise'. For Henry VII's chamber finances see D. Grummitt, 'Henry VII, Chamber Finance, and the "New Monarchy" ', *Historical Research*, 72 (1999), pp. 229–43, esp. pp. 240–2 for Henry's personal oversight and signing of Chamber accounts.

saw a role for Sigismund.[44] The instructions were also highly secret and confidential, and would be viewed as classified material today. Henry told Tiptoft that he was to divulge the content of his instructions only to 'my brother' the emperor Sigismund, and that no one was to

> have knowledge thereof, without my special order, from my own mouth, or else written with my own hand and sealed with my signet . . . [as this was] one of the most secret things that concerns me . . .[45]

To reinforce the point, the king concluded that 'because of the secretness of this matter, I have written this Instruction with my own hand, and sealed it with my signet of the Eagle'.[46] The use of a 'secret' seal for confidential matters was, similarly, adopted by others in positions of authority – Archbishop Chichele, for example, employed a secret seal for his private correspondence with the pope. But such were the risks of interception of letters, and of the theft of an envoy's belongings, that the most vital parts of diplomatic and other messages were often omitted from their written instructions, to be committed to memory for oral delivery.[47]

Although, unlike the previous case, not entirely written in his own hand, another striking example of the king's direct and interventionist manner in affairs of state was a memorandum and aide-mémoire (in effect

---

[44] For Henry's diplomacy with the Emperor and the German princes at this time see below, pp. 120, 133–4, 188–9, 268–71, 273–4.

[45] *Foedera*, ix, pp. 427–8; P. Chaplais, *English Medieval Diplomatic Practice, Part 1:1: Documents and Interpretation* (London, 1982), pp. 98–101, no. 65. No one was to have 'wittyng thereof, without myn especial commandement, of myn owne mouthe, or els written with myn owne hand and seelyd with my signet . . . [as this was] one of the secreest things that touchis me . . .' There is a contemporary MS copy, paper, partially damaged by the Cotton fire, in BL, Cotton MS Calig. D. V, fos 16–17r.

[46] *Foedera*, ix, p. 428: 'for the secreness of this matere, I have written this Instruction with myn owne hande, and seled hit with my signet of thEgle'.

[47] See, for examples from correspondence with the papal curia, M. Harvey, *England, Rome and the Papacy, 1417–1464: the Study of a Relationship* (Manchester, 1993), pp. 86–7.

a 'to-do' list) which he drew up late in 1420.[48] Described as 'Memoires', this remarkable document outlines the tasks which the king set for himself before his impending return to England in the aftermath of the treaty of Troyes (May 1420). The use of the first person singular is telling – the aide-mémoire, on paper, was evidently written out by a French secretary, or at least one with considerable fluency in 'court' French. It bears all the signs of dictation. The king refers to 'mon partement vers Engleterre' (my departure for England), 'ma venue en Engleterre' (my coming to England), and to 'les deniers de ceulx de France que je paieray a beaux frère et uncle de Clarence and Excestre' (the money of those of France that I will pay to [my] fair brother and uncle of Clarence and Exeter). Apparently unnoticed by historians, the memorandum bears the endorsement 'a tergo', meaning that it was drawn up and validated under the signet of the eagle. At its foot are two further lines, in English, in another hand, which bear such a strong resemblance to surviving examples of the king's own autograph that they might be included in the known corpus of such material. They read: 'Also to sende to court for thabbot of West[minster]' and 'Also thider for the Rendu [?] of the Chaterhous etc'. We may have here yet another instance of the king at work, in what today might be called the most 'hands-on' manner.

Such examples could hardly give a clearer indication of the importance which he accorded both to his favoured seal – the signet of the eagle – and to his own hand in matters of the very highest political and diplomatic significance. But this did not only apply to the higher reaches of statecraft. In the everyday, humdrum business of government, Henry V used the signet and sign manual probably as no other ruler had done before him.

---

[48] E 30/1619: paper, watermarked with a crossbow, 1 folio. The document warrants very close scrutiny. Although undated, it must be before 28 November 1420, as it refers to the fact that neither the town of Abbeville nor that of Montreuil had taken the oath to the treaty of Troyes (fo. 1r). Abbeville did so on 28 November, Montreuil on 30 November. See Allmand, *Henry V*, p. 147.

The occasional addition of a brief note of the king's wishes beside the autograph sign manual or cypher indicates a quite exceptional grasp of detail on the king's part.[49] In June 1421, a response to a petition from Elizabeth, wife of William Ryman, for the grant of a Sussex manor, bears the autograph endorsement 'RH, yelding 4d by yeere' (yielding 4d yearly).[50] Another petition of the same month from John Kingsley, esquire, restoring Cheshire revenues granted him by Henry's brother Thomas, duke of Clarence before his death earlier that year, was endorsed: 'R.H. In the form and manner that our brother's letters state, while we so wish'.[51] A very similar endorsement is found on a petition from William Troutbeck, esquire, also datable to 1421.[52] The responses to two further petitions were endorsed by the king: 'R.H. we wish that he have the 20 marks according to the content of this bill, and the office during our will' and 'R.H. we have granted this bill yielding to our Exchequer 4d per year at the accustomed terms'.[53] In January 1422, a petition from John Hereford, the king's 'povre servitor' (poor servant), for an annuity from the 'wood or enclosure called Lythewode', held from the abbot and convent of Shrewsbury, was endorsed: 'R.H. We have graunted this bille'.[54] Micro-government was clearly at work here.

The very ordinary and uncontroversial nature of these signet letters, and the regular, everyday use of the sign manual, have been commented

---

[49] Such additions also survive, in very small numbers, from the reign of Henry IV, e.g. the endorsement 'H.R. Nous prions penser de la mer' on a signet letter dated 15 Feb. 1405, concerning the flight of Constance, Lady Despenser and the children of Roger Mortimer, earl of March: BL, Cotton MS Vesp. F III, fo. 5; *Calendar of Signet Letters*, ed. Kirby, no. 936.

[50] E 28/34, no. 19 : 6 June 1421. Presumably a yield to the Exchequer of 4d p.a., probably at certain terms of the year.

[51] E 28/33, no. 10: 9 June 1421: 'In the forme and manere that oure brethers lettres purporteth whil us lust'. Copy in BL, Cotton MS Vesp. F. XIII, fo. 27; & see *PPC*, ii, pp. 315–16.

[52] *PPC*, ii, pp. 315–16; original in BL, Cotton MS Vesp. F. XIII, fo. 27.

[53] *PPC*, ii, p. 302 (petition of William Pomeroy, esquire, 16 Sept. 1421): 'R.H. We wol he have ye 20 mar[k]s after ye contenu of this bille and thoffice during oure wille'; pp. 304–5 (petition of John Feriby, 16 Oct. 1421): 'R.H. we have granted al this bille yeldyng to oure eschequer 4d. by yeer at termes accustumed'.

[54] E 28/36, no. 19: 5 Jan. 1422. The dorse bears traces of a seal in red wax.

upon.[55] But this did not mean that the daily business with which they dealt was thought to be insignificant or trivial, especially in the eyes of the king's subjects. A king had to be seen to rule as well as reign – and ruling, in the fifteenth century, could mean the assumption of personal control, or at least close supervision, of every area of government. The knowledge that the king was addressing the issues that most affected the daily lives of his subjects, both greater and lesser, could only contribute to fostering the all-important loyalty and allegiance which a usurping dynasty so much needed.[56] If those issues were addressed in what was perceived to be an even-handed manner, and were broadly representative of his subjects' experiences, a ruler could be assured a degree of security.[57] From the humblest to the greatest, direct access to the king's grace, mercy and judgment was a vital element in ensuring stability in unstable times. Delegation was, of course, essential – but the ultimate authority rested with the king. Personal intervention and involvement in what may appear to us as minor and insignificant matters, while at the very same time dealing with major affairs of state, characterised Henry V's government. Especially after his full-scale conquest in France had got under way in the summer of 1417, it was imperative that his English subjects were assured of the king's continued concern for English issues. The stream of signet letters sent after August 1417 from France, in English, concerning English business, surely demonstrated that the king was not neglectful of his subjects' needs and demands.[58] In December 1418, for instance, a large number of his signet letters were sent from Normandy to England and then dispatched to 'bishops, lords and other magnates' in the

[55] See, for example, Allmand, *Henry V,* p. 363: 'Consideration of the content of Henry's signet letters underlines how uncontroversial they were, and that the signet letter was now an administrative device, not a political one as it had been under Richard II'.

[56] See G. Dodd, 'Patronage, Petitions and Grace the "Chamberlain's Bill" of Henry IV's Reign' in *Henry IV: Rebellion and Survival,* ed. G. Dodd & D. Biggs (Woodbridge, 2008)', pp. 132–4.

[57] For the nature and effects of usurpation on English kingship see J.L. Watts, 'Usurpation in England: a Paradox of State-growth' in *Coups d'état a la fin du Moyen Âge,* ed. F. Foronda, J-P. Genet & J-M. Nieto Soria (Madrid, 2005), pp. 115–30.

[58] For examples, see above, pp. 35, 44–5; also below, chapter 3, pp. 81, 106–7, 121–5.

Welsh and Northern marches.[59] In April 1421, two signet letters were sent 'in great haste' to Sir Thomas Carewe and John Hawley, esquire, relating to the king's urgent business.[60] Furthermore, it is estimated that only about one-tenth of these letters have survived and, of the 120 or so extant signet letters sent after 1417, 100 were written from France, dealing largely with English affairs.[61] This application to everyday business, as well as the espousal and pursuit of higher causes and wide-ranging ambitions, was a hallmark of Henry V's practice of governance. Despite the burdensome demands it made not only upon the king himself, but on his advisers, officers and agents, some of them considered it the 'gold standard' by which other regimes might be judged.[62] Archbishop Chichele's Statutes (6 April 1443) for his beloved foundation – All Souls College, Oxford, founded in 1438 as a 'Lancastrian war memorial'[63] and dedicated to the king's memory – waxed eloquent on the subject of the kingdom of England's former greatness 'even in our own times'. The reference must have been to Henry V's reign when, Chichele observed, both the secular and clerical *militiae* ('knighthoods' or 'soldieries') 'competing with each other in pious emulation, made the kingdom of England, by its merit, formidable to its enemies, and resplendent and glorious among nations abroad'.[64]

[59] E 403/638, m. 8r (3 Dec. 1418).
[60] E 403/651, m. 1r (15 Apr. 1421).
[61] See *Calendar of Signet Letters,* ed. Kirby, p. 5.
[62] See above, p. 41. The sign manual, sometimes with brief further endorsements in the king's own hand, is found on the following 'routine' documents, including petitions, signet orders and other letters: E 28/32, no. 20; E 28/33, nos 57 & 58; E 28/34, nos 10, 19, 39, 72; E 28/36, no. 19; C 81/1364, no. 38; *PPC*, ii, pp. 302, 304–5, 315–16. They date from September 1417 to January 1422.
[63] See *VCH, County of Oxfordshire, iii, University of Oxford,* ed. H.E. Salter & M.D. Lobel (London, 1954), p. 175.
[64] See 'All Souls College' in *The Statutes of the Colleges of the University of Oxford,* ed. F.A. Bond, 2 vols (Oxford/London, 1853), p. 11: 'rememorantes magnificentiam et honorem quibus predicta utraque militia, pia aemulatione se invicem excedere contendentes, dudum etiam nostris temporibus inclitum Angliae regnum adversariis merito formidandum effecerat, et apud nationes exteras splendidum praedicaverat ac plurimum gloriosum'. See also E.F. Jacob, 'The Warden's text of the Foundation Statutes of All Souls College, Oxford', *Antiquaries Journal,* 15 (1935), pp. 420–31. Also see the essays in *Unarmed Soldiery: Studies in the Early History of All Souls College. The Chichele Lectures, 1993–1994,* ed. J. Catto et al. (Oxford, 1996).

It has been argued that the reign provided a touchstone for later policy, and that the king embodied 'an ethos of public life defined as the realization of a king-led war-enterprise'.[65] In the conduct of the higher affairs of state, moreover, the king's insistence on taking personal responsibility for all decisions, and the actions that flowed from them, received expression through the personal stamp or mark which the sign manual and the signet represented. What might be considered part of the private sphere – personal and secret seals and other means of identification, which under both Edward II and Richard II had been used, controversially, to deal with contentious matters[66] – now acquired a public face.

Similarly, the private and public spheres met and overlapped when the king put his mind to the making of his will. How were his last wishes in life to be validated and given the authority which they demanded? In the concluding lines of his first will, made on 24 July 1415 at Southampton, before his departure on the Agincourt campaign, he stated:

> We have drawn up the present page, and the present testament, in writing, containing our last will, as written above, and sealed [*signari*] it with our privy seal and signet, and appended our great seal, and have confirmed it [*fecimus roborari*] by subscription in our own hand.[67]

The 'subscription', as its name implied, consisted of words written under the main text of the will, which concluded:

[65] D.A.L. Morgan, 'The Household Retinue of Henry V and the Ethos of English Public Life' in *Concepts and Patterns of Service in the Later Middle Ages,* ed. A. Curry & E. Mathew (Woodbridge, 2000)', p. 68.

[66] See Allmand, *Henry V,* pp. 362, 363, for comment. Also above, pp. 25–6, 64.

[67] *Foedera*, ix, p. 293: 'presentem Paginam, sive praesens Testamentum, voluntatem nostrum ultimam continens, suprascriptum, in scriptis redigi, ac sigillo nostro private et signet sign [a]to signari, nostrique Sigilli magni appensione, et propriae manus nostrae subscriptione fecimus roborari'. No original, or contemporary copy, of the will survives. Rymer's transcription is from a manuscript dated 1681 in Gonville & Caius College, Cambridge, MS 392 (2), pp. 1–10.

These [words] are written in the king's own hand, that is to say: 'This is my last will subscribed with my own Hand, R.H. Jesu Mercy and Gremercy, Ladie Marie help.'[68]

The use of the sign manual 'R[ex] H[enricus]', coupled with the signet, and reinforced with both the great and privy seals, gave no doubt of the authenticity and authority of the will. The pious invocation : 'Jesu, Mercy and Gremercy' (Graunt merci), is found in the devotional literature of the time.[69] 'Ladie Marie help' was a common phrase, often used as a talisman, deriving from the multiple prayers to the Virgin which proliferated at the time, many stemming from the *Obsecro te* (I beseech thee) page of Books of Hours. 'Help me, Mary' is, for example, found engraved on armour, with other protective inscriptions.[70] That these words were written in the king's own hand suggests a desire on his part to demonstrate beyond any doubt that the will was his and his alone, and – perhaps – that no clerical or other intermediary, ecclesiastical or secular, had intervened between Christ, the Virgin and Henry himself. The layman's voice was here asserting itself, invoking the aid of the Virgin at the hour of death.

In his second 'will' (in English), which is in fact a declaration of his wishes for the administration of certain duchy of Lancaster lands, and the payment of debts, dated 21 July 1417, Henry guaranteed its authenticity and authority, by stating:

[68] *Foedera*, ix, p. 293: 'Haec scripta sunt propria manu Regis, viz . . .' The king's words are in English.

[69] For one example see *The Book of Margery Kempe*, ed. B. Windeatt (Woodbridge, 2014), p. 118 where the Carmelite friar William Southfield of Norwich (d.1414), was treated to a long account of Margery's 'meditacyons' and 'felyngs' by her, to which he replied: ' "Jhesu, mercy and gremercy! Syster", he seyd, "dredeth ye not of yowr maner of levyng, for it is the Holy Gost werkyng plentyrowsly hys grace in your sowle".'

[70] See, for a breastplate made at Innsbruck *c*.1510, inscribed 'HILF MIR MARIA' (Help me Mary) (Tower of London Armouries, III. 1246), C. Blair, *European Armour* (London, 1958), fig. 254, p. 221. Biblical texts were also used for talismanic purposes, such as the passage from Luke 4:30: '*Jesus autem transiens per medium illorum ibat* (Jesus however passed right through the midst of them)' engraved on an armour at Churburg castle of *c*.1390. See Blair, *European Armour*, p. 171.

And in witness that this is my full will and intent, I have set hereto my great seal, and my seal that I use for the governance of my inheritance of Lancaster. And I have subscribed with mine own hand these present indented and divided letters, and close them under my privy seal . . .[71]

This time, his 'subscription' to the will took the form, in his own hand: 'This is my ful wille god knoweth. R.H.'[72] Again, the personal avowal, and use of the great and privy seals, the sign manual, and signet (if that is what is meant by the duchy of Lancaster seal) gave maximum force and strength to the king's expressed wishes. He also referred, in the text of the will, to a means whereby his feoffees of some Lancaster lands should know his true, last wishes, in the event of changes being made to the 1417 will. His last, final will might contain changes, 'of which they may be certified by my letter, subscribed with my own hand and sealed with my seal'.[73] This 'certificate', in the king's hand, appears not to have survived, and there is no surviving copy.[74] But, as we shall see, what was described as a codicil, dated 9 June 1421, was attached to the king's last will, which he signed and sealed at Dover the following day, before his next, and last, voyage to France.[75] The 'codicil' was described (in February 1426) as 'a certain paper schedule, written in the king's hand, and sealed [*signato*] with his signet of the eagle,

---

[71] E 23/2: 'And in witnesse that this is my full wille and entente, I have set herto my grete seel, and my seel that I use in the governance of myn heritage of Lancastre. And I have subscribed with myn owen hand thes presentes lettres endentet and inpartit, and do close hem under my prive seel . . .'; original; parchment, indenture; 2 tags for seals (lost), traces of a seal in red wax on dorse; English, with some minor deletions and interlined insertions. The king described it as his 'wille and entente'. Printed in *A Collection of all the Wills . . . of the Kings and Queens of England*, ed. J. Nichols (London, 1780), pp. 236–43.

[72] E 23/2 & Nichols, *A Collection of all the Wills*, p. 242. The dorse has the rubric: 'Voluntas metuendissimi domini nostri regis inti[manda] feoffatis suis in certis dominiis hereditatis Lancastr' (p. 243).

[73] E 23/2 & Nichols, *A Collection of all the Wills*, p. 238: 'the whiche thai may be certifiet of be my lettre, subscribed with myn owen hand and enseelet with my seel'.

[74] The issue is discussed at some length in P. Strong & F. Strong, 'The Last Will and Codicils of Henry V', *EHR*, 96 (1981), pp. 80–2.

[75] See below, pp. 85–6, 241–3.

enclosed within the said testament'.[76] This is now lost. But we know (from the record on the Parliament Roll) that it ended with the following words:

I have made this will myself, and written it in haste with my own hand, all interlined and blotted as it is, the ninth day of June [1421].[77]

This must have been the 'certificate' which Henry promised, in 1417, to supply so that his feoffees of Lancaster lands should be assured of his last wishes. The fact that it was written 'in haste' on the very eve of his departure, and was 'interlined and blotted', may mean that it must have looked very much like a rough draft, with insertions of the kind which the king himself, as well as his clerks, were wont to write into memoranda and draft letters. But it was, he asserted, to have full authority, and was not to be regarded as any less authoritative than the more formal instruments of his will.

In his last will, dated at Dover on 10 June 1421, drawn up in formal Latin, he again adopted the formulas that had been adopted in his first and second wills, stating:

We have drawn up the above [suprascriptam] in writing, and sealed [signari] it with our privy seal, and the signet of the eagle on the dorse [a tergo] and the signet of our arms . . . and have appended our great seal, and confirmed it by subscription in our own hand.[78]

---

[76] RP, iv, pp. 299–300; from C 65/87, m. 4 headed: 'Pro episcopo Dunelm de deliberatione testamenti Henrici quinti' (at the Leicester Parliament, 18 Feb. 1426): 'in quadam Cedula Papirea Manu eiusdem Regis scripto, et signeto suo de l'Egle signato, ac infra dictum Testamentum incluso', dated 9 June 1421. Only the beginning and end of the document were spelt out on the Parliament Roll.

[77] RP, iv, p. 300; Strong & Strong, 'The Last Will and Codicils of Henry V', pp. 81–2: 'I have made this will be myself, and written yt in hast with myn owen hande, thus enterlynet and blotted as it is, ye ix day of Jun'.

[78] Eton College MS 59, fo. 6r, near-contemporary copy (soon after Oct. 1423?), parchment, Latin: 'suprascriptam in scriptis redigi ac sigillo nostro privato et signeto aquile a tergo et signeto armorum nostrorum ext' . . . signari nostrique sigillo magni appensione, ac proprie manus subscriptione fecimus [robora?]ri'. The will and codicils are edited and printed in Strong & Strong, 'The Last Will and Codicils of Henry V', pp. 89–100.

With the exception of the more specific reference to the signet of the eagle *a tergo*, the wording of this authenticating clause in the 1421 will is more or less identical to that of 1415. A codicil, drawn up on his deathbed at Vincennes on 26 August 1422, simply stated that it was 'given at the castle of Bois de Vincennes' without any further indication – on the surviving copy – of seal, sign manual or signature.[79] But the recurrent emphasis in all his formal wills and testaments on their confirmation and 'strengthening' 'by subscription in our own hand' is telling. We are dealing with a process which is far more than a simple bureaucratic routine or an empty, formulaic shell. From this time onwards, the use of signs manual, and passages written in the ruler's own hand, became part of the normal currency and vocabulary, as it were, of political, social and diplomatic intercourse. That crucial development, although not initiated by him, owed much to Henry V.

I have, in the previous and present chapters, sought to describe and account for the procedures and modes of action and intervention which formed part of the everyday business of Henry V's kingship. The content and context of those actions and interventions have been set out. However impressionistic it may be, this examination of his style and manner of governance may convey some idea of the range of issues with which a fifteenth-century ruler was obliged to engage. These included: first, the redress of his subjects' grievances and complaints which, it was claimed, could not be resolved by the common law and its courts, or – where appropriate – by the laws and customs of the crown's overseas possessions; secondly, the granting of favour, dispensation, compensation and pardon; and, finally, the exercise of charity, prompted by the dictates both of the Church and of the individual's conscience. None of these categories were necessarily mutually exclusive, and there could be a considerable degree of overlap between them. But a note of scepticism about the extent to which fifteenth-century rulers were genuinely concerned for the well-being of their subjects has often

---

[79] Eton College MS 59, fos 6v–7v.

been sounded by historians. It has, however, been pointed out, in a study of the government of the Milanese state under the Visconti and Sforza, that:

> It is quite easy to find specific cases which demonstrate the hypocrisy of the concern for justice and welfare constantly expressed by the dukes of Milan. It would be no less easy to find evidence to show that their concern was perfectly genuine.[80]

Yet both approaches, it is argued, only produce 'abstract judgements', which are 'unhelpful for the understanding of either the men or the pressures on them'.[81] We might apply similar criteria in attempting to understand Henry V and the conditions of his time. Like the Italian rulers of his age, his primary concern had to be the survival of his regime in essentially unstable political conditions. To achieve that end, the well-being and interests of his subjects had constantly to be considered. The 'personalised' kingship of Henry V, with its concern for justice, and its 'most unvisionary attention to detail',[82] was in many ways a model, exemplar and yardstick for what was to follow. If nothing else, his conception and exercise of governance were regarded – even by those hard-pressed and heavily burdened lieutenants, officers and agents who survived him – as a gold standard, however unattainable, by which other, later regimes, might be judged. The reign of his son was often witness to nostalgia for the days of 'the king that dead is'.[83] Henry V may, or may not, have been 'the greatest man that ever ruled England' but he was certainly a very hard act to follow.

---

[80] Bueno de Mesquita, 'Place of Despotism', p. 317.

[81] Bueno de Mesquita, 'Place of Despotism', p. 317. For discussion of the value of such judgements in the case of Henry V, see I. Mortimer, *1415: Henry V's Year of Glory* (London, 2009; 2nd edn 2010), pp. 528–38. Much of the Conclusion (pp. 519–51) of Mortimer's book seems, however, despite some disavowals (e.g. pp. 529–31), to represent an urge to pass abstract judgement on the king's character and behaviour.

[82] McFarlane, 'Henry V: a Personal Portrait', p. 125.

[83] Morgan, 'The Household Retinue', p. 72: 'the kyng that ded ys'. The phrase is cited from the Parliament Roll for Mar. 1428: *RP*, iv, p. 326.

Chapter 3

THE KING AND THE ENGLISH LANGUAGE

The 'personalisation' of kingship under Henry V has already been discussed in the previous chapter. It was expressed, in part, through the application of the king's own hand, as well as his personal seal – the signet – to letters issued in his name.[1] But the language in which he expressed his wishes and intentions could also now be described as 'personalised', and might stem from personal choice. Later medieval society was a multilingual one, in which languages often indicated differences of status and discharged different functions.[2] There was therefore a degree of linguistic choice offered to rulers and those who served them. As a result of the Norman Conquest of 1066, the spoken and, over the subsequent three or so centuries, written language of the ruling classes in England was French. Under Henry V this was undergoing a significant change. In order to explain this change, we

---

[1] See above, chapter 2, esp. pp. 67–9.

[2] See, for a general account, D. Trotter, *Multilingualism in Later Medieval Britain* (Cambridge, 2000). Also, for a telling case study, A. Putter, 'The French of English Letters: Two Trilingual Verse Epistles in Context' in *Language and Culture in Medieval Britain: the French of England, c. 1100–1500,* ed. J. Wogan-Browne et al. (York, 2009), pp. 397–408, esp. pp. 403–4. Questions of multilingualism, from a European perspective, are treated in *Medieval Multilingualisms: the Francophone World and its Neighbours,* ed. C. Kleinherz & K. Busby (Turnhout, 2010).

need to establish how, when and why the English language first became an acceptable and viable medium of government, politics and administration. The first half of the fifteenth century has been regarded as witnessing a crucial stage in this development. And the first successful, consistent and sustained introduction of English for these purposes has been observed during the reign of Henry V. What then was the personal role – if any – of the king himself in the process? Or was the language, or languages, in which the written instruments of the king's will were drawn up, simply determined by the needs and interests of his bureaucrats and advisers?[3]

The reign of Henry V has been identified as significant and seminal in the creation – for the first time since the Anglo-Saxon era – of an English-language idiom, or medium, of government, politics and administration.[4] This was a highly significant development. The process by which this came about, and the reasons for it, certainly deserve our attention, and it has been suggested that, once this has been done, 'Henry V will be seen to have played his not inconsiderable part, not only as a user of that idiom, but also as a focus of the thoughts and feelings which the idiom came to express'.[5] So, it is claimed, a double legacy stemmed from his reign: first, the adoption of English for some forms of governmental, administrative and diplomatic activity; and, second, the commemoration, in an English language and idiom, of the king's reign and achievements, often couched in eulogistic and nostalgic terms.[6]

There was no questioning Henry's personal literacy, in both reading and writing.[7] He was not only literate (*litteratus*) in the traditional

---

[3] The latter argument is put forward in J.H. Fisher, *The Emergence of Standard English* (Lexington, Massachusetts 1996), esp. pp. 9–12: e.g. 'Chancery English was created by government officials as a language of government, business and literature in the fifteenth century' (p. 10).

[4] See, e.g. M. Richardson, 'Henry V, the English Chancery and Chancery English', *Speculum*, 55 (1980), pp. 726–50.

[5] D.A.L. Morgan, 'The Household Retinue of Henry V and the Ethos of English Public Life' in *Concepts and Patterns of Service in the Later Middle Ages*, ed. A. Curry & E. Matthew (Woodbridge, 2000)', p. 68.

[6] See above, pp. 41, 81; below, pp. 267, 278–9 for the 'after-life' of Henry V, and the literature and imagery through which it was represented.

[7] See above, chapter 2, pp. 67–75.

medieval sense of being proficient in Latin, but was also conversant with both written and spoken French, at least in its Anglo-Norman form, as well as with the Middle English that was now regarded as the 'birth tongue' of English people.[8] There is some evidence that previous kings were also literate in Latin and French – or were expected to be – perhaps to a greater extent than has sometimes been assumed. The adage that 'an unlettered king is a crowned ass' (*rex illiteratus, asinus coronatus*) had already appeared in William of Malmesbury's *Gesta regum* in the mid-twelfth century.[9] But 'whatever their pretensions to literacy, it would be absurd to imagine any of the Plantagenet kings bent for very long over their books'.[10] War and the hunting field dominated their activities. This stands in apparently stark contrast to the lives of some of their successors.

The present chapter tackles three major questions: first, what was the state, status and function of spoken and written English at the time of Henry V's birth; that is, in the mid- to late 1380s? Second, how do developments during his reign relate to more general tendencies in the development of the written language? Did his reign see the forging of a new form of the language? Finally, what was the king's own role in the process? We cannot, however, begin to describe and explain the significance of the changes which took place during the reign – and in its aftermath – without at least outlining the background and context of this aspect of the 'rise of the vernacular'.[11]

---

[8] For the general nature and extent of lay literacy during this period see M.B. Parkes, 'The Literacy of the Laity' in *Scribes, Scripts and Readers,* ed. M.B. Parkes (London, 1991), pp. 275–97.

[9] See N. Vincent, 'The Great Lost Library of England's Medieval Kings? Royal Use and Ownership of Books, 1066–1272' in *1000 Years of Royal Books and Manuscripts,* ed. K. Doyle & S. McKendrick (London, 2014), pp. 73–112, esp. pp. 82–3.

[10] Vincent, 'The Great Lost Library', p. 83.

[11] The theme continues to inform and stimulate contributions both from historians and from scholars in other disciplines. See, for recent instances, W. Cohen, 'The Rise of the Written Vernacular. Europe and Eurasia', *PMLA*, 126 (2011), pp. 719–29; M. Vale, 'Language, Politics and Society: the Uses of the Vernacular in the Later Middle Ages', *EHR*, 120 (2005), pp. 15–34; J. Saltzstein, *The Refrain and the Rise of the Vernacular in Medieval French Music*

The prelude to, and preconditions for, that sudden flowering of English vernacular literature known as the 'Age of Chaucer' (*c.*1370–1400) can be traced back to an earlier stage in the fourteenth century. Much has been made in recent writing of the emergence of a sense of English identity, which in some cases is seen to date back to the mid- and late thirteenth century.[12] Anglo-French, as well as Anglo-Scottish, Anglo-Welsh and Anglo-Irish, relations and the issues they raised have been identified as important elements in the evolution of 'national' sentiment.[13] It is claimed that the identity of a people is often shaped by awareness of the 'other', as well as by xenophobia, and that the existence of a common enemy has played its part in the construction of both national and regional identities. The war with France which began in 1337 has therefore, perhaps too simplistically, been taken by historians as a prominent milestone along the road as they chart the process of 'shaping the nation' during the following century.[14] Yet it was not only *war* with France that may have played a determining part in that process. From 1340 onwards, an arguably valid claim to the French throne was not only voiced, made fact, by Edward III of England's assumption of that title. The title was never

---

and Poetry (Woodbridge, 2013); & J.H. McCash, 'The Role of Women in the Rise of the Vernacular', *Comparative Literature*, 60 (2008), pp. 45–57.

[12] For a good example of this approach see M.N. Taylor, ' "Aultre manier de language": English Usage as a Political Act in 13th-century England' in *Medieval Multilingualism*, ed. Kleinherz & Busby, pp. 107–26, emphasising what the author sees as the choice of English as a political tool in the conflict of crown and baronage, while the significance of relations with France and the use of French is stressed in T. Turville-Petre, *England the Nation: Language, Literature and National Identity, 1290–1340* (Oxford, 1996). For a critique and further comment see my *The Ancient Enemy: England, France and Europe from the Angevins to the Tudors, 1154–1558* (London, 2007), esp. pp. 73–80. For another, even more sceptical view, which sees little evidence for a sense of national identity in medieval England, see K. Kumar, *The Making of English National Identity* (Cambridge, 2003), esp. pp. 52–58 for the later Middle Ages.

[13] From a very extensive secondary literature see esp. R.R. Davies, *The First English Empire: Power and Identity in the British Isles, 1093–1343* (Oxford, 2000) & R. Frame, *The Political Development of the British Isles, 1100–1400* (Oxford, 1990).

[14] The interrelated themes of a developing sense of national identity, of war as a 'national enterprise', and of the growth of a 'politically integrated society' underlie the recent, excellent volume on this period in the *New Oxford History of England*. See G. Harriss, *Shaping the Nation. England 1360–1461* (Oxford, 2005), esp. the Conclusion on pp. 650–3.

explicitly renounced until 1802. This meant that, for the first time, the prospect – however remote it might have seemed – of a joint, dual monarchy which united the two kingdoms, was in sight.[15] Unless a peace could be negotiated diplomatically, war with France, or rather with those within France who did not recognise the Plantagenet claim, was more or less inevitable. But all wars require longer-term objectives, post-war settlements and, if unsuccessful, exit strategies. Some kind of peace with France was thus a fundamental consideration, war or no war. The form which that peace might take was a constant underlying issue in Anglo-French relations for well beyond the century of the so-called 'Hundred Years War' (1337–1453). If a viable union of the two (very different) kingdoms was ever to take place, their relative status, nature and condition had to be taken into account, perhaps redefined and, if necessary, firmly established by law and custom. And if, as we shall see, each kingdom, as well as each people, within the union was to retain some sense of its own identity, language might become a significant factor in both creating, and expressing, that identity.[16] The English language, it could be argued, was beginning to fulfil at least some of those functions during the reign of Edward III but there were still obstacles and impediments littering the road towards what has been called the 'triumph of English'.[17]

---

[15] For the 'propaganda campaign' launched in support of the dual monarchy from 1422 onwards see J.W. McKenna, 'Henry VI of England and the Dual Monarchy: Aspects of Royal Political Propaganda, 1422–1432', *JWCI*, 28 (1965), pp. 145–62, esp. pp. 151–62.

[16] See below, pp. 124–5, 276. A recent, closely argued essay makes a plausible, if sometimes a little overstated, case for the irrelevance of the war with France to the evolution of English national – and linguistic – identity, but does not consider Henry V's possible motives for linguistic choice in any detail. See D. Hardy, 'The Hundred Years War and the "Creation" of National Identity and the Written English Vernacular: a Reassessment', *Marginalia*, 17 (2013), pp. 18–31, esp. pp. 30–1. The theme of communal and individual identity is taken up, from a literary point of view, in D. Aers, *Community, Gender and Individual Identity: English Writing, 1360–1430* (London, 1988).

[17] See, for a work which celebrates what the author saw as the 'redemption' of English from servitude to 'foreign' tongues, B. Cottle, *The Triumph of English, 1350–1400* (London, 1969), e.g. 'For anyone who speaks English, the most exciting thing about the period is . . . the redemption of our language' (p. 15).

At the time of Henry V's birth (in the late 1380s) it was, for example, abundantly clear that English was not used at all for governmental or administrative purposes. Latin and French (in its Anglo-Norman form) served as the written languages of government and of 'business'.[18] Anglo-Norman had achieved acceptable status as a medium of written correspondence and of diplomatic and social communication in the course of the thirteenth century.[19] Though never entirely displacing Latin for such purposes, it had gained considerable ground by 1300. But, with the exception of a single return in Anglo-Norman to Henry II's Inquest of Sheriffs (c.1170), for instance, the written French language was scarcely employed at all by English central or local government before the mid-thirteenth century.[20] Otherwise, 'business' Latin was still universal, found throughout England as a language of record, business transactions and communication in court rolls, estate documents, deeds, charters and writs.

What then were the functions and uses of English by the later fourteenth century? The evidence of John Trevisa's (c.1342–1402) translation of Ranulph Higden's *Polychronicon* from Latin to English (1384–7) provides a good account of the state of the question at the time of Henry V's birth.[21] Trevisa was in the service of Thomas, Lord Berkeley, as a 'priest and bedesman'. He also translated the *De proprietatibus rerum* (by Bartholomeus Anglicanus) and *De regimine principum* (by Giles of Rome) into Middle English. Under the rubric *De incolarum linguis* (Concerning

---

[18] For what has become a classic account of the evolution of languages of record in England see M.T. Clanchy, *From Memory to Written Record. England, 1066–1307* (2nd edn Oxford, 1993), esp. pp. 197–223.

[19] See H. Suggett, 'The Use of French in England in the Later Middle Ages', *TRHS*, 4th ser., 28 (1946), pp. 60–83 and, more recently, *Language and Culture in Medieval Britain: the French of England, c.1100–1500*, ed. J. Wogan-Browne et al. (York, 2009).

[20] See H. Suggett, 'An Anglo-Norman Return to the Inquest of Sheriffs', *BJRL*, 27 (1942–3), pp. 179–81, citing TNA, C 146/10018: a return to the inquest for Manasser de Dammartin, for lands held in Suffolk; also H. Richardson (*née* Suggett), 'A Twelfth-century Anglo-Norman Charter', *BJRL*, 24 (1942), pp. 168–72.

[21] See *Polychronicon Ranulphi Higden, monachi Cestrensis, together with the English translations of John Trevisa*, ed. C. Babington & J.A. Lumby (London, RS, 1869), ii, pp. 159–63.

the languages of the inhabitants), in his translation of the *Polychronicon*, Trevisa claimed that, as a result of mixing with Danes and Normans, the 'birth tongue' of the English was impaired (appayred) and that

> this impairing of the birth tongue is because of two things: one is that children in school, unlike the custom and manner of all other nations, were compelled to put aside their own language, and to construe their lessons and their subjects in French, as they have been since the Normans first came to England. Also, gentlemen's children were taught to speak French from the time that they were rocked in the cradle, and could speak, and play with a child's toy; but countrymen ['oplondysch men'] also wished to be like gentlemen, and were greatly concerned to speak French, in order to be held in respect.[22]

Trevisa continued by noting changes which had taken place since the first onset of the great plague (1348–9), claiming that this form of instruction in French was 'much used before the first plagues, but since then is some-what changed'. He attributed the change to two main causes. The first was educational and pedagogic: he claimed that one John Cornwall, 'a master of grammar, changed the practice in grammar schools, from the construing of Latin in French to its [acquisition and] construing in English; and Richard Pencriche learned how to teach this from him, and taught other men to do so'. This meant that 'now' (that is, in 1385, the ninth year of Richard II's reign), 'in all the grammar schools of England, children put aside French, and construe and learn Latin in English, thereby gaining advantage in one respect but disadvantage in another'. The role of both Cornwall and Pencriche may have been exaggerated by Trevisa, who was himself Cornish, and other grammar masters, such as John Leland (*fl.* 1401–28) may have played as influential a part through their short,

---

[22] *Polychronicon*, ii, p. 159. The Modern English versions are mine.

popular treatises and manuals of grammar.[23] But, as Trevisa pointed out, there were both advantages and disadvantages accompanying this development. An advantage lay in the fact that 'they [English children] learn their grammar in less time than children were wont to do', but there was a disadvantage in that 'now children in grammar school know no more French than their left heel, and that is harmful to them, if they pass over the sea and work in foreign lands, and in many other places'.[24] For those who were to ply their trade as merchants abroad, or serve in the overseas dominions of the English crown, or simply travel for purposes of pilgrimage, diplomacy or even warfare, there were evident losses.[25]

A second reason which Trevisa adduced for the decline of French language learning was perhaps more a result of changes in English society. He asserted that 'also, gentlemen are much less concerned to have their children taught French'.[26] As an English translator and author, it was obviously to Trevisa's advantage that his best audience and clientele should have their children schooled in English grammar and vocabulary rather than French. But if it was true that members of the upper classes – nobility and

---

[23] See, for qualification of Trevisa's observations and a general survey of grammar teaching in England, N. Orme, *Medieval Schools: from Roman Britain to Renaissance England* (London/ New Haven, 2006), esp. pp. 87–8, 105–6, & (for Leland) pp. 106–8.

[24] *Polychronicon*, ii, pp. 159, 161. Master John Cornwall taught Latin grammar at Oxford, was recorded there between 1341 and 1349, and is found at Merton College in 1347, as is Pencriche some years later. See 'The Grammar Schools of the Medieval University', in *VCH, County of Oxfordshire, iii, University of Oxford*, ed. H.E. Salter & M.D. Lobel (London, 1954), pp. 40–3. The teaching of French was subsequently enforced by university statute. For the work of Thomas Sampson, who taught the *ars dictaminis* in French at Oxford in the mid-fourteenth century, influencing the form and style of letters and petitions, see Dodd, 'Kingship, Parliament and the Court', pp. 527–8. See also A.C. Baugh & T. Cable, *A History of the English Language* (Englewood Cliffs, 1993), p. 147; and J. Beal, 'Mapping Identity in Trevisa's *Polychronicon*' in *Fourteenth century England III*, ed. W.M. Ormrod (Woodbridge, 2004), pp. 67–82, esp. pp. 73–4.

[25] A similar set of reasons for the study of French was adduced in his *Donait françois*, a French grammar book for English-speakers, by John Barton (1409): see D.A. Kibbee, 'Institutions and Multilingualism in the Middle Ages' in *Medieval Multilingualisms*, ed. Kleinherz & Busby, pp. 76–7.

[26] *Polychronicon*, ii, p. 161: 'Also gentil men habbeth now moche y-left for to teche here children Frensch'.

gentry – had begun to withdraw from having their children taught French, this may also betoken the beginnings of a more general acceptance of the English language among them. A rise in its status was clearly taking place from the mid-fourteenth century or so onwards. Some distinctions may have to be drawn, however, between the uses of the spoken and the written language at this time. There was no doubt of the continued primacy of French as a medium of written communication in England.[27] But, if the value of English as a practical instrument for transactions, as a written language capable of embracing theological and philosophical concepts, and – ultimately – as an idiom of government, politics and administration, was now recognised, then a knowledge of French was evidently less vital. It would also mean that there was now an audience and readership for the written word in Middle English among those 'schooled' in the language.

In order to become a language of government, Middle English had to overcome a degree of bias and prejudice which associated it, among the governing, educated and upper ranks of English society, with 'low' or 'lewd' persons from the lower orders. Dante, in his *De vulgari eloquentia*, revealed similar prejudices against some vernaculars in Italy, while arguing for what he described as a higher-status 'illustrious', 'cardinal', 'aulic' and 'curial' vernacular.[28] An analogous, and related, hostile attitude characterised a growing body of (largely clerical) opposition, in part a response to the threat posed by the Wycliffite heresy,[29] to vernacular theology and to the translation of anything more than a small number of selected religious texts into Middle English. This attitude arguably became more prevalent after Archbishop

---

[27] See, for its continued use, and for the development of a more elevated French style in letters and petitions, G. Dodd, 'Kingship, Parliament and the Court', the Emergence of a "High Style" in Petitions to the English Crown, *c.* 1350–1405', *EHR*, 129 (2014), pp. 515–16, 527–31. It was not, however, without its critics: see pp. 540–2. See also J. Taylor, 'Letters and Letter Collections in England, 1300–1420', *Nottingham Medieval Studies*, 24 (1980), pp. 57–70.

[28] See Dante Alighieri, *De vulgari eloquentia*, I. xi, xiv, for the 'vile jargon' of the Roman vernacular and the deficiencies of those of the March of Ancona, Spoleto, Treviso and elsewhere. I owe this suggestion to Dr Hannah Skoda.

[29] For the measures taken to counter the Wycliffite, or Lollard, threat see below, chapter 5, pp. 186–9.

Thomas Arundel's *Constitutions* of 1409, which sought to limit religious discussion and curb vernacular religious writing. Pearls of clerical learning were not to be cast before lay swine. It has, moreover, been argued that the need to keep Scripture and other religious texts, and their interpretation, from the 'vulgar populace' (*populus vulgus*) cut short the great flowering of vernacular devotional literature of the previous half-century or so. In these clerical denunciations,

> [e]rror is seen as the inevitable result of translation into a barbarous tongue like English, with its small vocabulary, lexigraphical oddities, tendency towards monosyllable, and lack of inflection, which make it grammatically and rhetorically inadequate as a vehicle for truth.[30]

A similar degree of apprehension informed views about the suitability of Middle English as a language of government, administration and, indeed, more general culture. As in some other European aristocracies, the language of culture, of 'polite' society and of communication between themselves, was – traditionally – French.[31] Now the status and functions of Anglo-Norman French since the Norman Conquest, as a spoken as well as written language, and as a lingua franca for the English themselves, had been commented upon – and sometimes lamented – at an earlier date. Similar sentiments to those expressed by Trevisa are found almost a century earlier (*c*.1294–1300), in the vernacular metrical chronicle of Robert, a monk at St Peter's, Gloucester. In his Middle English rhyming couplets, he asserted, as Trevisa was to do later:

[30] N. Watson, 'Censorship and Cultural Change in Late-medieval England: Vernacular Theology, the Oxford Translation Debate, and Arundel's Constitutions of 1409', *Speculum*, 70 (1995), p. 842.

[31] For the francophone culture of European courts see M. Vale, *The Princely Court. Medieval Courts and Culture in North-West Europe, 1270–1380* (Oxford, 2001; 2nd edn 2003), pp. 282–94.

The Normans spoke nought but their own speech,

And spoke French . . . and did their children teach;

So that high men of this land, that of their blood came,

All speak this tongue, that they took from the same,

For unless he speaks French, a man's worth is less,

As low men holden to English, and their own speech confess.[32]

A further stumbling block placed inconveniently in the way of rendering Middle English into a written, as well as spoken, language was the prevalence of its many variants and dialects, some of which were akin to languages in their own right. Trevisa joined a growing body of lament when he remarked:

It seems a great wonder how English, that is the birth tongue of Englishmen, and their own language and tongue, is so varied in sound in this island, while the language of Normandy derives from another land, but has only one kind of sound among all who speak it correctly in England.[33]

Incomprehension, across the country, of the varied forms of spoken English other than an individual's own particular dialect, as well as the absence – given the prevailing dominance of Latin and Anglo-Norman – of a universally understood or 'standard' written English language, clearly retarded the emergence of the 'birth tongue' as an instrument of government and administration.

Thus Trevisa says that the 'Mercii', that is, the men of 'myddel Engelond' ('middle England') understand both northern and southern English

[32] *The Metrical Chronicle of Robert of Gloucester*, ed. W.A. Wright, 2 vols (London, RS, 1887), ii, ll. 7537–43.

[33] *Polychronicon*, ii, p. 161. For the significance of Anglo-Norman as a lingua franca see M.D. Legge, *Anglo-Norman Literature and its Background* (Oxford, 1963), pp. 3–6, 162–75, 278–310.

dialects better than northerners and southerners understand each other; men of the 'middle' also understand those of the west and the east better, as their dialects are more in accord than those of north and south.[34] Also, he claimed, northerners' dialects were less well understood in the south, as the kings of England were largely based and rooted in southern England, because 'there may be more fertile land there, more people, more noble cities, and more profitable ports' ['hit may be better corne londe, more peple, more noble citees, and more profitable havens'] in the south.[35] There may here be some implication on Trevisa's part that the location and activities of the monarchy had some influence, however intangible, upon the evolution, status and functions of language. If English was to become an acceptable medium of exchange and communication among the upper classes, then the role of the monarchy, he seems to be suggesting, could be significant. It might therefore be a southern or midland English form of the language that established itself as that acceptable medium.[36] In effect, this is more or less what happened between *c*.1370 and 1420.

In terms of the acceptance of the written, as well as the spoken, language, Geoffrey Chaucer's role and influence were here, it is argued by various scholars, decisive. It was acknowledged by contemporaries that he 'began first to magnify our tongue, and adorn it with his eloquence' by means of his poetry.[37] What has been called the 'new literary language and its

---

[34] *Polychronicon*, ii, p. 163.

[35] *Polychronicon*, ii, p. 163.

[36] For recent summaries of the linguistic developments of the period see T.W. Machan, *English in the Middle Ages* (Oxford, 2003); L. Mugglestone (ed.), *The Oxford History of English* (Oxford, 2006); J. Wogan-Browne et al. (eds), *Language and Culture in Medieval Britain: the French of England, c. 1100–1500* (York, 2009). Also A. Butterfield, *The Familiar Enemy: Chaucer, Language and Nation in the Hundred Years War* (Oxford, 2010), pp. 328–35.

[37] John Lydgate, *Troy Book*, ed. H. Bergen, 3 vols (*EETS Extra Series*, London, 1906–35), iii, ll. 4238–43. For the problems which beset attempts to create a 'courtly', literary style in the English vernacular see Watson, 'Censorship and Cultural Change', p. 839; L. Benson, 'Chaucer and Courtly Speech' in *Genres, Themes and Images in English Literature from the 14th to the 15th Century*, ed. P. Boitani, A. Torti & L.D. Benson (Tübingen, 1988), pp. 11–30. Also Dodd, 'Kingship, Parliament and the Court', pp. 520, 536 where Chaucer's difficulties are thought to be rather less problematic.

Westminster derivative'[38] absorbed Latin and French words, expressions and terms with relative ease and established itself with perhaps surprising rapidity. Exponents of vernacular theology, similarly, pointed to the extent to which the relatively limited vocabulary of Middle English could be substantially expanded through borrowing.[39] A new generation of writers – apart from Chaucer – in verse, and now prose, adopted an English vernacular which could be both supple and subtle. They included Langland, Gower, Thomas Usk, Sir John Clanvowe, Wycliffe, the poet of *Sir Gawain*, Trevisa, Walter Hilton and Dame Julian of Norwich. All were writing between *c.*1370 and 1400. All were meeting a demand from an increasingly literate laity for books, treatises and tracts in Middle English. And the extent to which that demand was stimulated and fuelled by movements within the Church, especially in the realms of pastoral theology and ministry, should never be underestimated. Before the onset of an apparently more repressive regime after *c.*1410, works of English vernacular theology, pastoral care, and translations of continental European texts, proliferated. Preaching to the laity (and, indeed, the clergy) in the vernacular, and the dissemination of sermons, homilies and other written devotional texts in Middle English, had both created and sustained a lay audience and readership for such works.[40]

---

[38] J. Catto, 'Written English: the Making of the Language, 1370–1400', *P & P*, 179 (2003), p. 38.

[39] A defence (dateable to 1401) of the translation of biblical, theological and devotional texts into English, as set out by the Oxford theologian Richard Ullerston, made this point. See Watson, 'Censorship and Cultural Change', pp. 844–6; A. Hudson, 'The Debate on Bible Translation, Oxford 1401', *EHR*, 90 (1975), pp. 1–18, esp. pp. 9–11, 14, 15. Some of his arguments and examples were appropriated by Lollard apologists for translation: see R. Copeland, *Pedagogy, Intellectuals and Dissent in the Later Middle Ages. Lollardy and Ideas of Learning* (Cambridge, 2004), pp. 115–17 & K. Ghosh, *The Wycliffite Heresy: Authority and the Interpretation of Texts* (Cambridge, 2004), pp. 86–92. For Ullerston's connection with Henry V, see below, chapter 4, pp. 126–7.

[40] See, among a copious secondary literature, much of it transatlantic, A.J. Fletcher, *Preaching, Politics and Poetry in Late Medieval England* (Portland, Oregon, 1998); H.L. Spencer, *English Preaching in the Late Middle Ages* (Oxford, 1994); V. Gillespie, 'Vernacular Books of Religion' in *Book Production and Publishing in Britain, 1375–1475*, ed. J. Griffiths and D. Pearsall (Cambridge, 1989), pp. 317–44; & *The Idea of the Vernacular. An Anthology of Middle English Literary Theory, 1250–1520*, ed. J. Wogan-Browne et al. (Exeter, 1999), pp. 4–6, 335–7. The allegedly less liberal climate after *c.*1410 is analysed in Watson, 'Censorship and Cultural Change', esp. pp. 840–57.

It has furthermore been argued that, by the later thirteenth century, a form of non-Latin prose specifically designed for governmental, legal and diplomatic purposes had emerged, not in Middle English, but in Anglo-Norman French. This was what has been called a 'curial style' or 'curial prose'. It was not, it is asserted, a 'literary' style but rather 'a set of formal features used in legal and diplomatic documents with the functional purposes of precision in reference and ceremony of tone'.[41] Some features of this idiom then formed part of what has been termed a 'high style' of written French which became increasingly current, from the mid-fourteenth century onwards, in England.[42] It was deemed to be a worthy substitute for, and alternative to, Latin. As a model for a future written Middle English style, Anglo-Norman – as well as Latin – thus provided a useful and fruitful source. This, it is argued, made the transition from one language (Anglo-Norman French) to the other (Middle English) more easily bridgeable and negotiable.[43] The evidence of petitions also suggests that Anglo-Norman models and formulas lay behind the earliest surviving examples drawn up in English.[44] But the result was not achieved without some difficulties which, if a viable English idiom was to be created, had to be overcome. The language that first emerged, especially when used in an epistolary form, for both private and 'business' letters, has been characterised as possessing an 'intractability ... as a medium for accurate statement'.[45] In March 1420, Thomas Chaucer, the poet's son, had told Henry V that Bishop Henry Beaufort had sent the king a 'bill the wyche

[41] See J.W.D. Burnley, 'Curial Prose in English', *Speculum*, 61 (1986), pp. 593–614, esp. p. 595.
[42] For a recent survey of its nature, status and development see Dodd, 'Kingship, Parliament and the Court, pp. 515–48.
[43] Burnley, 'Curial Prose', p. 594. For linguistic questions see W. Rothwell, 'The Missing Link in English Etymology: Anglo-French', *Medium Aevum*, 60 (1991), pp. 173–96.
[44] Dodd, 'The Rise of English, the Decline of French', pp. 126–7.
[45] McFarlane, 'Henry V, Bishop Beaufort and the Red Hat, 1417–1421' in *England in the Fifteenth Century Collected Essays,* ed. G.L. Harriss (London, 1981)', p. 96. The idea has not, however, commanded universal assent, e.g. see Burnley, 'Curial Prose', pp. 596, 604.

ye may well knowe who yt ys by hys voyde langage' (a bill whose author you may well recognise by his vacuous language). [46] Beaufort's 'insufferable wordiness' might be well represented by the 'void' or 'empty' language in which he wrote. To render this somewhat intractable tongue into an acceptable and effective medium of public discourse and communication was a task to be undertaken in Henry V's reign, in part at the king's own behest and following his own example. [47] That task had, however, to a very limited extent, begun a little earlier.

Between 1388 and 1399, only four documents in the English language appeared on the Rolls of Parliament. The documenting and enrolment of Parliamentary business, by Lords and Commons, was conducted, and continued to be conducted, almost entirely in Anglo-Norman French, with a few Latin entries interspersed among the overwhelmingly French records. The four English entries were: a petition from the Mercers' Company of London, complaining about the behaviour of Nicholas Brembre, mayor of the city, in February 1388, and three other entries, all of them containing reports, judgments and confessions relating to treason accusations. [48] The use of English for these purposes may reflect the accurate recording of the spoken or dictated word or – as, for example, in the confession of Thomas of Woodstock, duke of Gloucester – the words 'by his own hand fully and plainly written', as reported by William Rickhill, the king's justice, in the Parliament of September 1397. [49] In similar vein, the words spoken by another justice, William Thirning, informing Richard II of his deposition, are recorded on the Parliament Roll of

[46] TNA, SC 1/60/9; printed by McFarlane, 'Henry V, Bishop Beaufort and the Red Hat', p. 95.
[47] See below, pp. 109–10, 114–15, 121–25, 125. A somewhat similar problem was faced by the translators of the Wycliffite English Bible, where the need to achieve and establish a 'stable theological language', employing universally recognised terms to express concepts accurately, was imperative; see Catto, 'Written English', p. 52.
[48] RP, iii, pp. 225–6 for the Mercers' petition. This was originally, apparently, drawn up in Nov. 1387 and presented to the Lords Appellant. The Cordwainers' Company also submitted a petition, as did other guilds, but in French: RP, iii, pp. 226–7.
[49] RP, iii, p. 379.

October 1399, as well as Thirning's judgment on the cases of Aumale, Surrey, Exeter, Dorset and Gloucester in the same year.[50] The practice of recording confessions, and petitions for the king's mercy, in English, continued into Henry V's reign. In August 1415, the supplication and confession of Richard, earl of Cambridge, were recorded in this way. Cambridge confessed to conspiracy, and to causing a proclamation to be made that Edmund Mortimer, earl of March, was 'heir to the crown of England, against you, my liege lord [Henry V], called, by an untrue name, Harry of Lancaster, usurper of England'.[51] He petitioned (unsuccessfully) his 'most dreadful and sovereyne liege lord', the king, for 'your merciful and piteous grace'.[52] The adoption of the vernacular 'birth' or 'mother' tongue in this context may have given added authenticity, sincerity, and perhaps validity, to statements of considerable personal and public import – some of them clearly relating to matters of life or death. A contrast, moreover, between French artifice and English plain speaking had already begun to be made in the later fourteenth century.[53] The qualities of Middle English as a language of personal commitment and of concise, direct informality were already being praised to the detriment of French.

A similar tendency manifested itself in the taking and swearing of oaths. In the early fifteenth-century treatise known as the *Form of Coronation of the Kings and Queens of England*, one version of the oath of homage, sworn at the coronation ceremony, is recorded – as it was presumably spoken – in English.[54] It ran:

[50] *RP*, iii, pp. 424, 451–2.

[51] 'Heyre to the coroune of Yngland, ageyns yoow, my lege lord, calde, by a untrue name, Harry of Lancastre, usurpur of Yngland': *Foedera*, ix, p. 300–1 [Aug. 1415]. Original in BL, Cotton MS Vesp. C XIV, fo. 39r.

[52] The petition was addressed to his 'most dredfulle and sovereyne lege lord' for 'youre mercyfull and pyteouse grace': *Foedera*, ix, p.301. The original petition is in BL, Cotton MS Vesp. F III, fo. 7r.

[53] See Dodd, 'Kingship. Parliament and the Court', pp. 541–2.

[54] Printed in L.G. Wickham Legg, *English Coronation Records* (Westminster, 1901), pp. 172–90; for the oaths see p. 179. See also below, chapter 4, pp. 175–6.

I become your liege man of life and limb and truth. And I shall bear earthly honour to you against all men living and dead. So help me God and all saints.[55]

This was in effect a direct translation of the Anglo-Norman oath which follows in the text.[56] The personal commitment of the individual was here represented by a vernacular oath, in the 'birth tongue', which may have been thought more personally binding than one taken in another language. Consideration of matters of life and death also played its part in the making of wills. It is perhaps not coincidental that the first wills drawn up by testators in Middle English, rather than in Latin or French, date from exactly the same period. Wills and testaments could express the last personal wishes of their makers, and it may well have been as a mark of their authenticity that the 'birth tongue' was chosen. In August 1387, Robert Corn, citizen of London, drew up the first surviving will known to us in English since the Anglo-Saxon era. He was followed, in September 1392, by John Pyncheon, again a citizen (and jeweller), of London, whose will combined French and English passages.[57] The progress of English as a testamentary language appears to have accelerated after 1413 (coincidentally, the date of Henry V's accession): eight English wills had been proved in the London court of probate during the twenty-six years between 1387 and 1413; fourteen were proved in the nine years between 1413 and 1422.[58] The social status of the earliest testators was that of burgess and citizen. The first knight to make a will in English, as recorded in the

[55] Legg, *English Coronation Records*, p. 179; also Bod. MS 596, fo. 50v: 'I bycome your man liege of lyfe and lymme and trouthe, and erthelich honour to yow schal bere ayens alle men that mow lyfe and dye, so helpe me godde and holydome'.

[56] MS Bod. 596, fo. 51r: 'Serem[ent] en Frau[nceys]. Jeo devien vostre home liege de vie et de membre et de fealte. Et terrene honour a vous portera encontre toutz manere de gentz que pount vivre et morir. Si dieu me eide et toutz seyntes'.

[57] See *The Fifty Earliest English Wills In the Court of Probate, London, A.D. 1387–1439*, ed. F.J. Furnivall, *EETS*, lxxviii, (1892) pp. 1–2: Robert Corn, 8 Aug. 1387, prob. 14 Mar. 1389; & p. 3: John Pyncheon, 20 Sept. 1392, prob. 9 Oct. 1392.

[58] See *The Fifty Earliest English Wills*, ed. Furnivall, pp. 1–21.

London probate court, did so in August 1411, when Sir William Langeford, of Bradfield and Compton Beauchamp (Berks) drew up his part-Latin, part-English testament. In October 1420, the London probate court recorded the earliest will of a knight, Sir Roger Salvayn, of York, composed entirely in English.[59]

Women of aristocratic rank had preceded their male contemporaries in the making of English wills. As early as July 1395, Lady Alice West, of Hinton Marcel (Hants) had made a long and very interesting will, entirely in English. This included the bequest to her daughter Joanne of 'alle the bokes that I have of latyn, englisch and frensch', perhaps indicating a trilingual level of literacy.[60] A final sign of approbation of the use of English in a testamentary context was provided by the will of Henry IV, made at his manor of Greenwich, on 21 January 1409. This was entirely in a Middle English which was now expressive of current devotional and theological concepts, with its dedication to the Father, Son and Holy Ghost ('three persons and one God') and its description of the king himself as a 'sinful wretch', bequeathing his 'sinful soul' to God.[61]

A further coincidental event, again in the 1380s, was the appearance in the civic records of the city of London of the first entries in English. Previously those records had been kept entirely in Latin and Anglo-Norman French. An important means of communication between governors and governed within a city or town was the practice of proclamation. The criers of proclamations, by sound of trumpet or bell, preceded by the call 'Oyez! Oyez! Oyez!' (Hear ye!), had necessarily to employ the vernacular. But the texts of those proclamations, and the resolutions

---

[59] See *The Fifty Earliest English Wills*, ed. Furnivall, pp. 18–21: Langeford, 4 Aug. 1411, prob. 1 Oct. 1411; pp. 52–4: Salvayn, 26 Oct. 1420, prob. 7 Mar. 1422.

[60] See *The Fifty Earliest English Wills*, ed. Furnivall, pp. 4–10: West, 15 July 1395, prob. 1 Sept. 1395. She also prescribed the saying and singing of no fewer than 4,400 masses for the souls of herself, her husband and 'alle cristene soules' in the fortnight after her death. There is an Abstract of her will in N.H. Nicolas, *Testamenta Vetusta* (London, 1826), i, p. 137.

[61] Nichols, *A Collection of all the Wills*, pp. 203–5.

whereby civic authorities issued them, were recorded in Anglo-Norman. The proclamation was a vital medium, because it 'represented the official regulation of everyday affairs', announcing both royal and civic ordinances and decrees, prohibitions, and all kinds of measures whereby urban life was governed.[62] Given London's active role in the rising of 1381, the maintenance of order in the city demanded the regular issue of proclamations concerning the keeping of the peace and the punishment of offenders. The Letter Books of the city record, for the first time, proclamations made in English in 1383 and 1387, against 'congregations, covens and conspiracies', and against defamatory speech about the king, the queen, the lords with the king and 'those around him'.[63] From 1411 onwards, and especially after 1416, the great majority of proclamations, and the decisions to issue them, were recorded in English.[64] But the written records themselves now reproduced the precise words of the proclamations in Middle English. These were often, in effect, close translations of the Anglo-Norman French in which they had previously been recorded.[65] City ordinances, meanwhile, remained in their Anglo-Norman form. Entries concerning proclamations now began with the formula: 'Be ther proclamacioun made, that alle manere of men . . .', and the first words of the proclamation itself were 'For as much as . . .' These were recurrent formulas which were also to be found in Henry V's first signet letters in English.[66] It is here that the links

---

[62] See F. Rexroth, *Deviance and Power in Late Medieval London* (Cambridge, 2007), pp. 74–5, 122–5, quoting p. 125.

[63] See *Memorials of London and London Life in the xiiith, xivth and xvth centuries*, ed. H.T. Riley (London, 1868), pp. 480–2 (1383); p. 500 (1387).

[64] *Memorials*, ed. Riley, p. 580 (24 Aug. 1411): Latin preamble and English text: 'That no manere man ne child, of what estate or condicioun that he be, be so hardy to wrestell, or make any wrestlyng, within the Seintuary ne the boundes of Poules [St Paul's] . . .' For proclamations in English from 1416 onwards see *Memorials*, pp. 628, 629 (1416), 645 (1417), 664, 665, 668, 669 (1418), 670–2 (1419).

[65] Some cases of misdemeanour were also recorded in the Letter Books, which contain the letters, ordinances and other documents issued by the city of London, in an English that was heavily based upon Anglo-Norman, e.g. the case of the fraudulent coal merchant, John Umbergh of Shenfield, Essex, in Apr. 1419: *Memorials*, ed. Riley, p. 669, from *Letter Book I*, fo. 226.

[66] See above, pp. 79–81; below, pp. 108, 113–14, 277.

between the king's use of the language and its employment by his subjects can begin to be suggested.

We possess no specific order or command from the king himself that the English vernacular be used for certain types of document and record. But we may have some clues, however indirect, to the king's intentions and mode of thought on the subject. A letter under his signet, dated at Troyes, on 22 May 1420, enrolled on the Close Rolls, sets out his regal titles in three languages, so that the royal style is consistent throughout that documentation. The treaty of Troyes, confirming Henry's regency of France, had necessitated changes in the king's style of entitlement, as he (in English) told Gloucester and the council in England:

> And furthermore, because we must, by virtue of the said accord [the treaty of Troyes], use a new style during the lifetime of our said father [Charles VI of France], we send you in a schedule enclosed within these letters our style which we will hereafter use, both in Latin, in English, and in French, charging you that in everything that is issued during the aforesaid time under our great seal, and all our other seals, wherever it be, and in proclamations, you command that our style be used according to the content of the said schedule, and that the inscriptions on all our seals be amended thereafter in all haste . . .[67]

The English style was to run: 'Henry, by ye grace of God, kyng of England, heire and Regent of ye Rewme of France, and lorde of Irlande'.[68] It was clear from the context that the English style was most likely to be employed

---

[67] 'And furthermore, for as muche as we must by virtue of ye saide accorde, use a newe stile during ye lyf of oure saide fader, we sende youw in a cedule withyn these oure stille that we wol use herafter, bothe in Latine, in Englyssh, and in Frenssh, chargeyng yow that in al thing' that passeth during the tyme aforesaide, as wel under oure grete seel as al oure other seeles, wherever hit bee, and in proclamacions ye ordeyne that oure stille be used after ye contenue of ye saide cedule, and that ye scripture of all' oure seeles be amended therafter yn al haste': C 54/270, m. 17v; *CCR, 1419–1422*, p. 108.

[68] C 54/270, m. 17v.

when proclamations were issued,[69] but could if necessary be used in formal written documents. This was a very important step indeed on the ladder towards the acceptance of written, as well as spoken, English as a formal language of record and command.

We do not have, from Henry V's reign, any manual of guidelines or compendia of formulas for English-language documents to be used by the signet office. An alleged 'exemplar', or in effect template, for a signet letter, with notes to the recipients of the styles of address which were to be used, is in fact a draft of a privy seal writ in English, apparently dating from the reign of Henry VI.[70] Yet its instructions on appropriate forms of address may well reflect usages which had begun under Henry V. The undated draft is a letter of credence for its bearers – the king's commissioners, probably to raise loans – addressed to 'Trusty and well beloved'. Its general form and terminology would, however, not be completely out of place in a signet letter of Henry V. The notes on forms of address to be used by the clerks prescribed:

This style of 'trusty and well beloved' may be directed to one person, or to as many together as the said commissioners shall like. And it may serve for all manner of men, if need be, except bishops.

Item. The said style of 'trusty and well beloved' may serve for cities, townships and communities [*cominaltees*] after this tenor, in the tail of

---

[69] A further letter, dated 14 June 1420, to the sheriffs in England, set out the text of an English-language proclamation announcing the terms of the treaty of Troyes, using the new English style: C 54/270, mm. 12v, 11v.

[70] C 81/1326, no. 36: headed 'By the kyng', the letter begins (as do the earlier Henry V signet letters) 'Trusty and welbeloved. For asmuche as in certain matiers . . .' It is endorsed 'Ham[m] ond', probably by John Hammond, clerk in the privy seal office, active *c*.1446–55. It is misfiled with a collection of letters of protection under the privy seal dating from 1482–3. See *Anthology of Chancery English*, ed. Fisher, Richardson & Fisher text no. 1, where it is misdated and misidentified; and M. Benskin, 'Chancery Standard' in *New Perspectives in English Historical Linguistics II. Lexis and Transmission*, ed. C. Kay, S. Horobin & J. Smith (Amsterdam, 2004), pp. 14–18 for discussion of the document, and for a trenchant and uncompromising dismissal of what is in other respects a useful collection of material.

the letter, to 'our trusty and well beloved, the thrifty men, notable persons, and community of our city of A. or of the town of B. and to every one of them'.

'To the right dear in God' and 'Dear in God': each of these styles may serve for abbots, priors, deans, archdeacons . . .[71]

Although there might have been no expectation among the clerks who wrote Henry V's English missives that a standard, consistent form and usage would now prevail in the foreseeable future, precedents had evidently been established.

Outside the central writing offices and administrative departments which began to produce English-language documents at this time, there is incontrovertible evidence that the king's example in this respect was soon followed by at least some of his subjects. In July 1422, the Brewers' Company of London resolved (in Latin) that English should be adopted in its Minute Books because

[o]ur mother tongue, that is to say the English tongue, has in recent times begun to be honourably enlarged and adorned, in that our most excellent lord King Henry V has, in his letters missive and divers affairs touching his own person, more willingly chosen to declare the secrets of his will and, for the better understanding of his people, hath with diligent mind procured the common idiom (setting aside others) to be commended by the exercise of writing . . .[72]

[71] C 81/1326, no. 36. Modern English version mine.

[72] 'William Porland's Minute Book (1418–1440)', printed in *A Book of London English, 1384–1425*, ed. R.W. Chambers & M. Daunt (Oxford, 1931), p. 139, from Guildhall Library archives, MS 5440, fo. 69v: 'Cum nostra lingua materna, viz. lingua Anglicana, modernis diebus cepit in honoris incrementum ampliari et decorari, eo quod excellentissimus dominus noster Rex Henricus quintus, in lit[t]eris suis missivis, et diversis negociis personam suam propriam tangentibus, secreta sue voluntatis libencius voluit declarare, et ob meliorem plebis sue intelligentiam co[mmun]em, aliis ydiomatibus pretermissis, animo diligenti scripturarum exercicio com[m]endari procuravit'. The book is composed of paper folios, consistent with the dates to which the entries relate, and the passage quoted above is in Porland's hand. Translation mine.

It is striking that William Porland, clerk to the Brewers' Company, spoke in this way, in their Minute Book, of the 'enlargement' and 'adornment' of the English language in similar terms (to 'magnify' and 'adorn') to those chosen by Lydgate in his praise of Chaucer's contribution to the development of the literary vernacular.[73] The use of English, Porland seemed to imply, had been a deliberate and conscious choice by the king, intended, in part, to promote better comprehension of his wishes by his subjects. Those subjects had, as a result of changes introduced in the latter part of the fourteenth century, become more accustomed, especially when addressed as groups or communities, to receiving communications in English.[74] Even among the Latinate clergy, it was now expected that at least some kinds of business should be conducted in English. Hence, in February 1415, the prior of the alien priory of Deerhurst (Glos.), Hugues de Mangazon, a Frenchman, who was also a monk at the Parisian abbey of Saint-Denis, was discharged from duties which he had been given by the bishop of Worcester in the archdeaconry of Gloucester. These were to act as collector of ecclesiastical taxation – the clerical tenths – for the crown. He had petitioned Henry V for discharge 'because he had not learnt the English language, and for other reasonable causes'.[75] The fact that war with France was imminent might not have been irrelevant in this case. The king granted his request, and the (English-speaking) abbot of Oseney had been appointed in his stead.

Among other groups of his subjects, an apparent decline in multi- or bilingualism also appeared to have set in. These included the brewers of London, who could, it was claimed, both read and write English but now

---

[73] See above, p. 99.

[74] See above, pp. 93–6, for some of the educational and institutional changes that took place.

[75] TNA, E 28/30, nos 71 & 72 (14 & 26 Feb. 1415): 'a cause qil ne fust pas appris en langage de Engleys et autres causes reisonables'. Mangazon had been admitted as prior of Deerhurst in Sept. 1411. Lands held by an existing monastery there had been given by Edward the Confessor in c.1059 to the Benedictine abbey of Saint-Denis and the house remained an alien priory until its (late) denization in 1443. See 'Alien Houses: the Priory of Deerhurst' in *VCH, County of Gloucester*, ed. W. Page (London, 1907), ii, pp. 103–5.

(1422) possessed little knowledge of either French or Latin.[76] Henry's decision had also raised the status of the 'common idiom', Middle English, as a written language. Porland went on to observe that as the 'greater part' of the lords and commons had begun to record their affairs in the 'mother-tongue', the brewers should follow suit and keep their records in English. The resolution was acted upon. It is followed in the Minute Book by an exemplification, which fixed its date and served to set a precedent for subsequent entries in the record. Porland reported:

> The Thursday, that is to wete the xxxe day of the monthe of Juyll' [July], the yere of Kyng Henry the vte the xe, yn the tyme of Robert Chichele, mair of London', atte a suggestion made be [by] Richard Whityngton upon the Breweres of London', wherefore the saide mair dede sende for [the] . . . maistres of the said crafte of Breweres atte that tyme ['be (by) a sergeant' – interlined] and commanded hem to bringe with hem xj of the worthiest of the same crafte to aperen before the mair atte Gyldhall' the day and the tyme abovesaid . . .[77]

The record went on to report, in English, the death of Henry V and its aftermath, in which the Brewers' Company played its part in the funeral ceremonies and interment of the king.[78] Some other London guilds, such as

---

[76] *A Book of London English,* ed. Chambers & Daunt p. 139 & Guildhall Library, MS 5440, fo. 69v: 'Et quam plures sunt nostre Arte Braciatorum qui in dicto ydiomate anglicano habent scienciam, illud idem scribendi atque legendi, in aliis ydiomatibus, viz. Latin[o] et Franc[o], ante hec tempora usitatis, minime senciunt et intelligunt. Quibus de causis, cum pluribus aliis consideratis, in presenti quemadmodum maior pars dominorum et communium fidedignorum facere ceperunt in nostra materna lingua suas materias annotare, sic et nos, in arte nostra predicta, eorum vestigia quodamodo sequentes que nos tangent necessaria, decrevimus memorie in futurum commendare, ut patet in sequentibus'.

[77] Guildhall Library, MS 5440, fos 69v–70r: 30 July 1422.

[78] Guildhall Library, MS 5440, fo. 70v (in the same hand as above): 'In this yere, yn ye tyme of ye said Robert Chichele, mair, oure worshipfull kyng Henri ye vte passed out of this world, in ye parties of Fraunce, ye last day of August upon a Sunday, yn ye even of Seint Gyle, in ye xe yer of his regne, whos soule god assoille . . .' The detailed description of the funeral ceremonies, cortège and burial, which follows, forms an extended piece of English narrative prose worthy of a chronicler. See below, chapter 8, pp. 245–7.

the Goldsmiths, and those of other English towns, such as York (1416) and Bristol (1419), had also begun to keep their records in English at this time.[79]

Although an audience and readership for a Middle English 'common idiom' already existed, the English 'curial style' was slower to develop. It only began to gain significant ground on Anglo-Norman in the early part of the fifteenth century, and especially, under Henry V, in the early 1420s.[80] Clarity, cohesion and 'ceremoniousness' have been identified by some scholars as characteristics of this contrived style.[81] The evidence appears to indicate that the emergence of this Middle English administrative language followed and post-dated, rather than preceded, the appearance of the literary language. The Westminster world of clerks, scribes and government officers was not, however, entirely remote from that of the 'new' literary language: Chaucer and Thomas Hoccleve, the poet and privy seal clerk who attempted to imitate him, were both employed in the administration.[82]

It has recently (2003) been argued that the emergence of 'Chaucerian English' between c.1370 and 1400, as a vehicle of literary expression, 'far from being a natural development from early Middle English, . . . was effectively the artificial construct of a single generation of writers'.[83] Can a similar process be discerned in the ostensibly sudden emergence of an administrative, governmental, political and so-called 'Chancery' English under Henry V?[84] The formulas and constructs of this language clearly

---

[79] G. Dodd, 'The Rise of English, the Decline of French: Supplications to the English Crown, c. 1420–1450', *Speculum*, 86 (2011), p. 136.

[80] See above, pp. 101–2 & Burnley, 'Curial Prose', pp. 598, 611. See also M. Richardson, 'The Earliest Business Letters in England: an Overview', *Journal of Business Communication* (1980), pp. 19–31.

[81] Burnley, 'Curial Prose', pp. 596, 599, 604.

[82] For Hoccleve see above, chapter 1, pp. 22–3.

[83] Catto, 'Written English', pp. 25, 46.

[84] For a critical summary of the linguistic characteristics and development of 'Chancery' English, see Benskin, 'Chancery Standard', pp. 1–40. The term is in fact a misnomer, as so-called 'Chancery' English derived from the signet office, not from the Chancery itself, which normally employed Latin. As Benskin points out (p. 21), there was no 'Chancery' standard, except Latin.

owed much to the transfusion and influx of terms of Latin and French (especially Anglo-Norman) origin, in some cases as direct translations into Middle English.[85] A definite case can be made for an Anglo-Norman model for the first letters in English under his personal seal or signet, sent by Henry V from his recently captured castle of Touques (dép. Calvados) on 9 and 12 August 1417.[86] These were addressed, respectively, to the mayor, aldermen and 'good people' of the city of London, and to Thomas Langley, the Chancellor. In both cases the text of the letter is in Middle English. The formula of address, however, on the reverse side, is in French. This remains the case until May 1418, when we find the first signet letter in which both text and form of address are in English.[87]

In the letter of 12 August 1417, the direct Anglo-Norman derivation of some terms is abundantly clear. The clerk writing this early letter, habitually used to composing in Anglo-Norman, simply (and perhaps absent-mindedly) employs the French phrase 'en due forme' ('our lettres patentes severales *en due forme*') when the English should be '*in* due forme' or '*in* due *fourme*', as it appears in subsequent examples.[88] Further evidence of the direct borrowing of terms from Anglo-Norman occurs throughout these early signet letters. The recurrent formulas are in effect the same: 'De par le Roy' and 'Donne soubz nostre signet' become 'By

[85] See Rothwell, 'The Missing Link in English Etymology', pp. 173–6, 184–7, 194–6.

[86] See *Memorials*, p. 654, from *Letter Book I*, fo. 199; & C 81/1364, no. 34. For the use of the signet, see above, chapter 1, pp. 34–5, 44–52.

[87] C 81/1364, no. 54: at the castle of Caen, 19 May 1418. The address on the dorse is 'To ye worshipful fader in God our[e] ryhttrusty and wellbeloved ye bysshop of Duresme, our[e] Chanceller'. The French form, found on previous such letters was 'Au reverend pere en dieu, levesque de Duresme, nostre chanceller Dengleterre' (C 81/1364, no. 34). Apart from a small minority of surviving letters in French after 19 May 1418, the form of address is in English from 9 Aug. 1418 onwards, and apparently remains so until the end of the reign. See C 81/1364, nos 56, 57, 62, 65 (French), & cf. nos 66–74 (English). The series of signet letters in C 81, all of them in English, ends in Apr. 1422 (C 81/1366, no. 37).

[88] C 81/1364, no. 34 & cf. no. 13: a letter in French under the signet at Blyth, dated 5 July 1414, with the formula 'en due forme'. Even closer in date to the letter of 12 Aug. 1417 is a signet letter in French, dated 12 July 1417, which refers to 'noz lettres de commission severales en due fourme': C 81/1366, no. 17. Also C 81/1364, no. 38 for a letter in English, rendering it 'in due forme' & C 81/1365, nos 16 & 28 (both 'in due fourme').

ye kyng' and 'Yeven under oure signet'.[89] 'Volons et vous mandons' becomes 'we wol and charge yow'.[90] A consistent, stable vocabulary of address, attribution, origination and command had thus been established in Middle English, made all the easier by the immediate accessibility of such terminology in 'curial' Anglo-Norman. The extreme rapidity with which the process of transition was accomplished is thus more readily explicable. The so-called 'curial style', now expressed in Middle English rather than French, had not only been born, but had already come of age under Henry V.

Was this an 'entirely new world',[91] similar to the 'divide' between pre-1370 written English and the 'age of Chaucer' (c.1380–1400)? What role, if any, can be accorded to Henry V himself in the promotion and subsequent adoption of Middle English as a medium of communication and as a means of transmitting authority? It is known that, for whatever reasons, whether mere flattery or not, he was applauded by some contemporaries for his patronage of literary works in English. Lydgate, always ready with an obsequious phrase, explained Henry's request for an English version of the legend of Troy:

Because he wished that to high [people] and low

The noble story were openly known

In our tongue, current in every age

And written as well in our language

As it is in Latin and French.[92]

---

[89] For one example among many see C 81/1366, no. 2: 17 Mar. 1416 (French) & cf. C 81/1366, no. 1: 10 Feb. 1419 (English).

[90] Again, among many examples, see C 81/1364, no. 13: 5 July 1414 (French) & cf. C 81/1364, no. 34 (English).

[91] Catto, 'Written English', p. 36.

[92] Lydgate, *Troy Book*, Prologue, ll. 111–15: 'By-cause he wolde that to hy[gh]e and lowe/ The noble story openly wer knowe,/ In our tongue, aboute in every age,/ And y-writen as wel in oure langage/ As in latyn and frensche it is'.

The king also commissioned an English *Life of our Ladye* from Lydgate, by specific request, and owned a copy of Chaucer's *Troilus and Criseyde*, of which the manuscript dates from his time as Prince of Wales, between 1403 and 1413.[93]

A case can be made for the king playing a similarly influential and formative role in the establishment of a so-called 'Chancery' English or, more correctly, a language of government, administration and political affairs emanating, above all, from his signet office and its clerks.[94] But this has recently been challenged, and it has been argued that there is no evidence for the king's active participation in the promotion of the English language. In view of the fact that three languages – Latin, French and, as a newcomer, English – were now employed by English administrative departments, it has been claimed that 'the king in fact had little interest in the language his bureaucrats used'.[95] Although the notion of a 'language policy' under Henry V (and Henry VI) seems hard to sustain, there is certainly evidence for the king's conscious choice of English for certain instruments and memoranda – which may not amount to a 'policy', but may nonetheless be a product of deliberate action on his part.[96]

That Henry V *did* concern himself with the language, or languages, in which business was conducted in his name appears from a remarkable sequence of diplomatic exchanges which took place in December 1418.[97] These may not refer directly to the use of English, but they illustrate – beyond reasonable doubt – that the king took a keen interest in language, its

---

[93] Now New York, Pierpont Morgan MS 817.

[94] For the signet office, the king's secretary, and its clerks see above, chapter 1, pp. 27–8, 34–5.

[95] G. Dodd, 'Trilingualism in the Medieval English Bureaucracy: the Use – and Disuse – of Languages in the Fifteenth-century Privy Seal Office', *Journal of British Studies*, 51 (2012), pp. 253–83, quoting p. 255. For Henry's trilingual royal style, after May 1420, see C 54/270, m. 17v & above, pp. 107–8.

[96] For the claim that a 'language policy' can be found under the Lancastrian kings see Fisher, *The Emergence of Standard English*, pp. 16–21, 34–5. Under Henry VI, but beginning under Henry V, Fisher sees 'a plan to cultivate English as the official and prestige language of the realm' (p. 35).

[97] *Foedera*, ix, pp. 655–9. The documents are in BL, Cotton MS Tiberius B.VI, fos 31 & 32.

functions and appropriate uses. In this context, it could be very much to his advantage to do so. While conducting the siege of Rouen, in November–December 1418, Henry was also negotiating with the dauphinist side.[98] His envoys were at Pont-de-l'Arche, dealing not only with the dauphin's representatives, but with the pope's cardinal-legate, Giordano Orsini, cardinal-bishop of Albano, who was attempting to mediate between them.[99] Part of the discussion was taken up with the issue of the language, or languages, in which proceedings should be both conducted and recorded. An impasse in negotiations over that very issue had been reached. Henry and his representatives claimed that his enemy's representatives wished to negotiate in French, rather than in the Latin which was customary in such cases. Latin was, the king told Orsini, an impartial and neutral tongue ('indifferens omni nationi').[100] Diplomatic proceedings were also normally recorded, by mutual consent, in that language. Henry then made the striking claim that his envoys did not fully understand French, nor could they speak it accurately ('gallicum non intelligent, sed nec penitus loqui suavit').[101] In a subsequent letter, he told Orsini that he had only to use his eyes (and, presumably, his ears) to confirm that. The identity of Henry's envoys, however, certainly suggests that there could have been no doubting their ability to understand at least one form of French – namely the Anglo-Norman in which so many of their communications took place. Archbishop Chichele, Warwick, Salisbury, Grey, Fitzhugh, Hungerford, Master Philip Morgan, Thomas Chaucer and others habitually used Anglo-Norman, as well as Latin and English.[102]

A knowledge of French was, moreover, current among those of Henry's nobles, knights and esquires who served him in France. It seems that they

---

[98] See below, pp. 119–21. For the siege of Rouen, see Allmand, *Henry V*, pp. 122–8, & pp. 261–2 for papal attempts at mediation at this time.

[99] *Foedera*, ix, pp. 655–7.

[100] *Foedera*, ix, p. 655.

[101] *Foedera*, ix, pp. 655–6.

[102] *Foedera*, ix, p. 628 for their appointment and commission. Their instructions were given in English (pp. 628–9).

encountered few, if any, problems with the spoken language. The evidence for the taking and interrogation of French prisoners at the siege of Harfleur (August–September 1415), for example, is revealing in this respect. When he was captured by some English common soldiery outside Harfleur, Raoul le Gay, a Norman priest, said that he could not understand anything they said to him, or they anything which he said to them.[103] He was taken by them into the English camp, where a certain 'young Englishman' interrogated him in Latin, and then spoke to his captors in English, but

> he did not know what he said to them, except that he understood that he was talking about *drinch*, which is to be interpreted as *bibere* [*boire* = to drink] . . . and straightaway the English who captured him made him get up to go elsewhere, and said to him: *comine, comine* [come in], which is to say *venez, venez* [come, come].[104]

As he was being escorted through a 'great enclosure', bordering a garden, one of the 'great English lords' (who, it later transpired, was Henry V himself) there spoke to him, in French, asking him 'where are your masters, who captured you?' He then ordered his men to 'take him to the earl of Dorset'. When he reached Dorset's tent,

> [t]he man who escorted him said to him that it was their king who had spoken to him, and when they came into the presence of the said earl,

---

[103] A group of seven English soldiers took him 'lesquielz, ne aucuns deulx, il nentendoit point, pour ce que point ne parloyent francoys' ('none of whom he understood, because they did not speak French'). See L. Mirot, 'Le Procès de Maître Jean Fusoris. Episode des négociations anglo-françaises durant la Guerre de Cent Ans', *Mémoires de la Société de l'Histoire de Paris et de l'Île de France*, 27 (1900), pp. 206 (14 Dec. 1415), 256 (1 Apr. 1416). For the siege see Allmand, *Henry V*, pp. 79–82.

[104] 'Nescit tamen quid dicebat eis, excepto quod intellexit quod ipse loquebatur de *drinch*, quod interpretatur bibere . . . et statim Anglici qui ducebant eum fecerunt ipsum surgere pro eundo alibi, et dixerunt ei: *comine, comine*, quod est dicere *venez, venez* . . .': Mirot, 'Le Procès de Maître Jean Fusoris', p. 257 (1 Apr. 1416).

the man who was conducting him said to the earl: 'Here is a priest whom the king sends to you.'[105]

Le Gay, yet again under interrogation, this time by the French, after his capture with apparently compromising letters from Richard Courtenay, bishop of Norwich, in his possession, told them:

As he was passing through the [English] army, the king of England spoke to him, and asked him where he was from, and the said prisoner replied that he was from the parish of Trois-Pierres, four leagues from Harfleur; and then the king asked him if he was the prisoner of those who escorted him, and if he had been armed when he was taken . . . and he replied that he was their prisoner, but had not been taken otherwise than he was [that is, unarmed] . . .[106]

Not only did the king converse with him in French, but it was evident to Le Gay that all the 'knights, prelates, and others' in positions of authority in the English army spoke good French. Thomas Beaufort, earl of Dorset, personally interrogated him, apparently at some length, in French. Similarly, Master Jean Fusoris, canon of Notre-Dame and astrologer, when he presented an astrolabe and a 'book of practice' to the king at Winchester in July 1415, was thanked by the king in both Latin and French. Henry, he claimed, spoke to him in Latin, saying 'Magister Johannes, grates vobis'

---

[105] 'Ille qui ducebat eum dixit ei qui loquitur, quod ille erat rex eorum qui cum eo fuerat locutus, et dum venerunt ad presentiam dicti comitis, ille que ducebat eum dixit ipsi comiti: "Ecce unum presbiterum quem rex mittit vobis" ': Mirot, 'Le Procès de Maître Jean Fusoris', pp. 257–8.

[106] 'Et depuis lui alant par lost, le Roy Dangleterre parla a lui et lui demanda dont il estoit, et ledit prisonnier lui respondi que il estoit de la paroisse de Troys Pierres a quatre lieues de Harfleur; adonc le Roy li demanda sil estoit prisonnier a ceulx qui le menoyent et si il avoit este prins arme . . . et il repondit que il estoit leur prisonnier, mays navoit este prins autrement que il estoit . . .': Mirot, 'Le Procès de Maître Jean Fusoris', pp. 212–13. He said, in a later interrogation (1 Apr. 1416), that he had only 'a little knife for cutting bread', but no other weapon, when he was captured. His captors took this from him (p. 256).

('Master Jean, thanks to you') and then, in French, 'Grans mercis' ('Many thanks').[107]

Henry's point, made to Cardinal Orsini in 1418, may well have been merely a self-interested diplomatic ploy, given the evidence for a good, working knowledge of French among the English nobility and higher clergy at this time. But the king may not have been wholly disingenuous in his claim. That the form of French spoken and written in England could differ in some respects from its continental equivalent, or equivalents, had been recognised from the later thirteenth century onwards.[108] And it is quite possible that the French used in diplomatic negotiations by the dauphin's envoys was sufficiently prone to misinterpretation (or at least was perceived to be so) for a diplomatic lingua franca such as Latin to have been preferred.

These exchanges are especially interesting for what they also tell us – indirectly – about the status and functions of English at this time. Henry claimed that his envoys knew Latin and English well enough to conduct complex and often tortuous diplomatic negotiations in those languages. He was, he told the cardinal, content that the French should speak Latin or French, while his men should speak 'the idioms that they understand, that is to say, English or Latin'.[109] When written articles and points for discussion, or records of the proceedings, were to be drawn up, he was content that the French could write in French, while his envoys were to write in English or Latin. All this suggests that the king now regarded

---

[107] Mirot, 'Le Procès de Maître Jean Fusoris', p. 244. Fusoris replied to the king: 'At your pleasure, most serene prince' ('ad beneplacitum vestrum, serenissime princeps').

[108] See D.A. Kibbee, 'Institutions and Multilingualism in the Middle Ages' in *Medieval Multilingualism*, ed. Kleinherz & Busby, pp. 73–4, 76–7, where it is claimed that 'the dialect of French suitable for vertical communication [i.e. between king and subjects, or between upper and lower orders of society] in England, and the dialect of French suitable for horizontal communication across the Channel, became distinct' (p. 78) & his *For to Speke Frenche Trewely. The French Language in England, 1000–1600. Its Status, Description and Instruction* (Amsterdam, 1991), pp. 74–85, 92–3; also Clanchy, *From Memory to Written Record*, p. 200.

[109] *Foedera*, ix, p. 656.

English as an acceptable and viable medium of diplomatic negotiation and record, on a par with the Latin and French of the past. His accredited envoys could also now employ English in their letters and reports to the king. In April 1422, for instance, Henry's emissary to the Emperor Sigismund, the bilingual German knight Sir Hartung von Klux, KG, wrote to the king from the castle of Swiny (Ger.: Schweinhaus) in Lower Silesia. His letter was in English, addressed to his 'most worshipful and revered lord' and contained apparent 'Germanisms' as well as phonetic renderings of English words.[110] Such usages also suggest that Henry was a ruler who, far from being indifferent to the language, or languages, in which he conducted business (and in which business was conducted in his name), was deeply concerned by the issue. In the event, during the negotiations of 1418, a compromise, proposed by Cardinal Orsini, was agreed.[111] The protracted deadlock was broken by the adoption of a 'middle way': all written material produced by the discussions was to be in two languages – Latin and French. But if any controversy were to arise over the meaning and import of any French words, recourse was to be had to the Latin record for its resolution. The cardinal told the dauphinist envoys that Henry and his 'council' claimed not to understand French 'perfectly', and that the king insisted that Latin be used to resolve any disputes because of the 'ambiguities of French words that have more than one significa- tion' ('aequivicationes et sinomia verborum gallicorum').[112] Henry V, however, had the last word: the compromise solution to which he had so

---

[110] E.g. 'Gedirse' for 'gathers'; 'noht' for 'not'; 'lauley' for 'loyally': *Foedera*, x, p. 208 (at 'Swynes', 28 Apr. 1422). For his career in the service of the Lancastrian monarchy see R.A. Griffiths, 'Klux, Sir Hartung von (d.1445): diplomat and soldier' in *New Oxford DNB* (Oxford, 2004; online edn 2008). He was elected to the Order of the Garter in 1421. See also Chaplais, *English Diplomatic Practice*, pp. 130–1.

[111] Orsini was apparently quite well disposed towards the English side. He had been appointed papal legate to mediate peace between France and England on 2 Apr. 1418, returning to Florence from that (unsuccessful) mission on 2 Apr. 1419. See W.A. Simpson, 'Cardinal Giordano Orsini (+1438) as a Prince of the Church and a Patron of the Arts', *JWCI*, 29 (1966), pp. 135–59.

[112] *Foedera*, ix, p. 657.

magnanimously 'condescended' was to set no precedent of any kind for the course of future negotiations.[113]

What *did* set precedents was the adoption, and stabilisation, of an English-language medium and idiom of public administration, correspondence and affairs. In this process, the king's role was fundamental. It has been rightly suggested that his 'English-language proclamations, and letters missive under the signet, announcing the progress of his enterprise in France, are among the formative exercises which over the following generation brought into being an English idiom of public life'.[114] The style and format of the king's signet letters, memoranda and diplomatic instructions in effect created a new genre of English governmental and administrative documentation.[115] Their impact spread into other areas of public life, sometimes through mutual influences, so that a common vernacular language of government and politics was shaped and stabilised. In December 1417, the mayor and aldermen of the city of London wrote to the king in terms which seemed to echo his signet letters. Phrases such as 'for-as-moche as we trust verryly' or 'forasmuch, most dred sovereign liege Lord', among others, would not have been out of place in one of Henry's own missives.[116] The following reign, of his son, may not have adhered to the exclusive use of English for certain forms of communication, such as letters under the signet, but the tide in its favour never turned back. Henry was succeeded by an infant who could not express himself in any language, and the government of the realm was in the hands of a council. The mere fact that, after reversion to Anglo-Norman French after Henry V's death in

---

[113] *Foedera,* ix, p. 659.

[114] Morgan, 'The Household Retinue', p. 67.

[115] In March 1421 Henry sent letters under the signet to the Benedictine order in England, not in the customary Latin, but in English. Replies came back in the same language, suggesting that ecclesiastical correspondents now accepted English as a normal language of such communication. See *Documents illustrating the Activities of the General and Provincial Chapters of the English Black Monks, 1215–1540,* ed. W.A. Pantin, Camden 3rd ser., 47 (London, 1933), ii, pp. 104–5, nos 161, 162, 163. See below, 132, 193–7.

[116] *Memorials,* pp. 658–60.

1422, English was resumed as the language of the king's signet letters at the end of Henry VI's minority in 1437, suggests that it was the choice and preference of the individual ruler himself which determined that change.[117] Personal kingship, and the active participation and intervention of the ruler in English government, was now expressed – and, perhaps even more significantly, was expected to be expressed – in the 'birth tongue' of the English, in the written form devised under Henry V. There may not have been any discernible 'language policy', but the usages established under Henry V were, in large part, the product of deliberate choice.

The fact that the earliest of the king's signet letters in English, from August 1417 onwards, were written from France may not have been coincidental or lacking in significance. It was imperative that the king's English subjects be convinced and reassured that his enterprise in France would not be to their detriment. To address them, and to express his wishes, in their own 'birth tongue', however artificially constructed its written form might be, might make an important point. Under the terms of the future treaty of Troyes (1420), the kingdoms of England and France were to remain separate entities.[118] Henry's regency of France, established by that treaty, would have led, had he lived, to his accession to its throne; instead his son acceded in 1422. To use the English language, consistently, for English affairs, just as his major campaigns of foreign conquest – or reconquest – began, could express and exemplify a desire to emphasise the separate identities and characters of the two kingdoms. In 1417, perhaps in anticipation of the terms of a later settlement, Henry may have chosen to use English as one indication of his ultimate intent. As Edward III had assured the English Parliament, when he assumed the claim to the French

---

[117] Dodd, 'The Rise of English, the Decline of French', pp. 129–30, 141, 143.
[118] This was to be the case from the making of the treaty of Troyes (May 1420) onwards, and an awareness of its implications was apparent from that date, not only during the 'critical period' from *c.*1435–40 onwards: cf. Dodd, 'The Rise of English, the Decline of French', pp. 144–5.

crown between 1337 and 1340, each kingdom was to be governed by its own laws, usages and customs, and its systems of taxation, justice and administration were to remain in place, untouched and inviolable. In the Parliament of December 1420, the Commons petitioned that Edward III's statute of March 1340 be confirmed, stating that neither 'the kingdom of England, nor the people of the same . . . shall at any time in the future be placed in subjection or obedience to him [Henry V], his heirs and successors, as heir, regent and king of France . . .'[119] Their request was granted. Henry V had thus acted in a very similar fashion to his illustrious predecessor when he drew up the treaty of Troyes, anticipating and providing for a dual monarchy.[120] In the English-language version of the treaty's terms it was stated that it had been agreed 'to keep the laws, customs, usages and rights' of the English kingdom. But, despite the fact that both crowns should 'perpetually be together, and be in one and the same person', in all other respects neither kingdom was to lose its

> rights, liberties nor customs, usages and laws, not making one of the same kingdoms subject in any way to the other, nor putting under or subjecting the rights, laws, customs and usages of one of the said kingdoms to [those] . . . of the other.[121]

That this could now be expressed in the English language, and formally entered as a record on the English Chancery Rolls, must have given added

---

[119] *RP*, iv, p. 127.

[120] Henry's concern that his English subjects should be made aware of the terms of the treaty is reflected in his order that it be proclaimed, in English, so 'that al oure pueple may have verray knowledge therof for thare consolacion, as wel as kep hit aftir as longeth unto thayme' and that this be done 'to perpetuelle mynde to all' kristen' people and to all tho that ben' under oure obeissaunce': C 54/270, mm. 17v, 12v (22 May & 14 June 1420).

[121] 'Kepyng netheles in all' maner other thynges to ayther of ye same Roialmes here ryghtes, libertees nor custumes, usages and laws, not making subget in any manere of wise oon of the same roialmes to the thoder, nor puttyng under or submittyng ye ryghtes, laws, custumes or usages of that oon 'of the sayd roialmes to ye ryghtes, laws, custumes or usages of that other of ye same': C 54/270, m. 11v.

force and weight to the sentiments embodied in the treaty establishing a dual monarchy.

The adoption of written English for governmental purposes was a product of very many factors, none of which should be omitted from an analysis of its motivation and causation. The overseas ambitions of the English crown, and their effects, can never be left entirely out of that analysis. It is one of the paradoxes of history that the pursuit, and partial realisation, of the English crown's claim to the throne of France may have led to a heightening, among its English subjects, of a sense of their own identity. In his 'Personal Portrait' of the king, K.B. McFarlane was, it seems, puzzled by Henry's apparent promotion of the English language, writing that it was

> all the more remarkable when his conquest of France and his assump-
> tion of the succession to the French crown involved his captains in the
> use of a different language across the Channel. If it was Henry's aim to
> unite in his person the kingdoms of England and France, one would
> have thought that such a union would have been eased and enforced by
> encouraging the use of French (still the traditional language of polite
> society in England) in the government of both countries.[122]

Perhaps it was precisely because the conquest and succession involved the 'use of a different language across the Channel' that Henry furthered the adoption of English, both within England, and for communicating with its government when he was in France. The retention of a strict separation and distinction between the two kingdoms within the union formed a binding statutory obligation and, whatever might have been the case in France, the king was not above the law in England. In fact, the Anglo-French union may well have been strengthened by this emphasis upon the

---

[122] McFarlane, 'Henry V: a Personal Portrait', p. 119.

differences between the kingdoms, including their separate linguistic identities. The argument should not be overstated. But, unlike some later regimes, Henry V's proposed dual monarchy of England and France respected the fundamental characteristics of the two kingdoms. The issues it faced, however, were not entirely unlike those confronting more recent unions. It has been said that a major question for the states within the European Union of the twenty-first century is 'how to balance national sovereignty against the desire to centralise, and how to retain a cultural identity'.[123] But, under Henry V, apart from the person of the ruler, there was in effect no power centre, or centralised institution of government, that could impose any of the laws, customs and administrative practices of one kingdom on the other. Nor was there any attempt to introduce linguistic uniformity into their governance. Relations between them might well be conducted in a lingua franca (Latin or French) but Henry V, by adopting the English language to express his will and intentions when dealing with English matters, ensured that his French, as well as English, subjects retained their separate identities.[124] French – never English – was to be used for matters relating to the government of France. The paradox was complete: in the attempt to join the kingdoms of England and France in a dynastic union, the discrete sense of identity of their respective peoples was sharpened and enhanced. The final emergence of the English language, despite many setbacks and vicissitudes, as a medium of government, politics and culture, may thus have owed something to the continental ambitions of England's rulers. And in the process, Henry V's contribution was by no means negligible.

---

[123] *The Observer*, 18 May 2014, p. 36.
[124] For the subsequent efforts, largely initiated by John, duke of Bedford, to persuade both English and French subjects of the dual monarchy of its legitimacy and justification, including Laurence Calot's genealogical French poem (1423), followed by Lydgate's English version (1426) see J.W. McKenna, 'Henry VI of England and the Dual Monarchy: Aspects of Royal Political Propaganda, 1422–1432', JWCI, 28 (1965), pp. 151–3.

Chapter 4

THE KING AND THE CHURCH I
PUBLIC PIETY AND PRIVATE DEVOTION

Cant. The King is full of grace and fair regard,

Ely. And a true lover of the holy Church . . .

Cant. Hear him but reason in divinity,

And, all-admiring, with an inward wish

You would desire the King were made a prelate . . .

(*Henry V*, Act I, scene i)

The words which Shakespeare puts into the mouths of the archbishop of Canterbury and the bishop of Ely in the opening scene of *Henry V* form part of a more general, sustained eulogy of the king's qualities. Much of the Shakespearean vision and portrayal of Henry V is pure fiction – but in this particular case his characterisation may carry more than a grain of historical truth. Contemporary witnesses tend often to support this view, best represented by the clerical author of the *Gesta Henrici Quinti* (1416–17), and by the short treatise *De officio militari* (Concerning the Office of Knighthood), composed and presented to Henry, as prince of Wales, in *c.*1408 by Dr Richard Ullerston, Fellow of the Queen's College, Oxford, conciliar theorist, advocate of the vernacular translation of religious texts, and a distinguished theologian.[1] The future king's interest in and concern for the study of 'divinity' were praised. Ullerston commended Henry for applying his mind to the study of Scripture, so that 'however much you may lack in philosophical knowledge, that will be remedied, with God's help, by your concern for learned (*sapientalis*) study'.[2] The author of the *Gesta* tells us that, from the outset of his reign, he 'applied his mind with all devotion to encompass what could promote the honour of God' and 'the extension of the Church'.[3] Another contemporary observer referred to what he saw as the king's priest-like appearance and manner. At Winchester, in July 1415, the French astrologer Master Jean Fusoris, expert on the astrolabe, and canon of Notre-Dame in Paris, was introduced to Henry V by the king's confidant Richard Courtenay, bishop of Norwich. In a subsequent interrogation during his trial by the French for *lèse-majesté*, and for consorting with the enemy, Fusoris was reported to have said that

he [Fusoris] being in the said land of England, the aforesaid bishop [Courtenay] asked him what he thought of the king of England, and he replied that it seemed to him that he [Henry V] had a very princely demeanour, but it also seemed to him that he was better suited to be a man of the Church than a soldier, and that his eldest brother [Thomas, duke of Clarence] seemed to him to be more suited to being a soldier than the said king . . .[4]

---

[1] For Ullerston's career see *A Biographical Register of the University of Oxford*, ed. A.B. Emden (Oxford, 1959), iii, pp. 1928–9; and M. Harvey, 'Ullerston, Richard (d.1423)' in *New Oxford DNB* (Oxford, 2004; online edn 2008). Also above, pp. 100, 126.

[2] Corpus Christi College, Cambridge, MS 177, fo. 179v. For discussion of this work see E.F. Jacob, *Henry V and the Invasion of France* (London, 1947), pp. 37–8. Jacob speculates that Henry's choice of confessors – the Carmelite friars Stephen Patrington and Thomas Netter, both distinguished theologians – may have been prompted by his studious tendencies. For Ullerston also see above, p. 100.

[3] *Gesta Henrici Quinti. The Deeds of Henry the Fifth*, ed. F. Taylor & J.S. Roskell (Oxford, 1975), p. 3.

[4] 'Item, dit que lui, estant oudit pays Dangleterre, levesque dessus nomme lui demanda qui lui sembloit du Roy Dangleterre, et il lui respondi que il lui sembloit que il menoit bien estat de prince, et toutesvoyes il lui sembloit que il estoit mieulx dispose a estre homme deglise que

Looks could of course be deceptive, and the clerical image might mislead – the priest-like king was very soon to become the victor in a great and decisive battle at Agincourt. But Fusoris's testimony should not be dismissed out of hand.[5]

We know, for example, that Henry was, as Ullerston noted, a seeker after knowledge and learning. He was in possession not only of secular books but of a substantial collection of works of theology, both speculative and pastoral, liturgy, logic, rhetoric, canon and civil law. In May 1422 his capture of the 'market of Meaux' yielded 110 such books, possibly deriving from one or more of the convents in the town.[6] Had he lived, he might have intended to give them to one of his own religious foundations, probably to the Charterhouse at Sheen. But he was also in the habit of borrowing books for his own use. After his death, some of these had not been returned to their owners. In February 1424, John, prior of Christ Church cathedral priory, Canterbury, petitioned Humphrey of Gloucester and the minority council of Henry VI for the return to that house of a large volume, containing all the 'books composed by St Gregory the pope'.[7] This had originally been given to Christ Church by Thomas Arundel, archbishop of Canterbury (d.1414), under the terms of his will. But it had

---

homme darmes, et que laisne frère dudit Roy lui sembloit mielx estre dispose a estre homme darmes que ledit Roy': see L. Mirot, 'Le Procès de Maître Jean Fusoris, chanoine de Notre-Dame de Paris (1415–1416). Episode de négociations franco-anglaises durant la guerre de Cent Ans', *Mémoires de la Société de l'Histoire de Paris et de l'Île de France*, 27 (1900), p. 175. The record of the interrogation, at the Petit Châtelet of Paris, is in Paris, Archives Nationales, LL. 85.

[5] In the Latin version of his later interrogation (28 Mar. 1416), before ecclesiastical assessors, he said that he had not told Courtenay that he thought the king 'better suited to the Church than to war', preferring to keep that thought to himself: 'intra se cogitabat quod ipse rex melius erat dispositus ad ecclesiam quam ad guerram; sed ipse noluit hoc episcopo dicere . . .': Mirot, 'Le Procès de Maître Jean Fusoris', p. 244.

[6] See K.B. McFarlane, *Lancastrian Kings and Lollard Knights* (Oxford, 1972), Appendix C: 'Henry V's Books', pp. 233–8. The town fell into two parts, divided by the Seine – the town itself and the 'Marché' ('Market'). The religious houses at Meaux were Sainte-Celine, Saint-Faron [Pharon], Notre Dame, St Rigomer & St Saintin. The largest and wealthiest of them was the Benedictine abbey of Saint-Faron. But see below, pp. 147–8.

[7] *Foedera*, x, p. 317 (1, 6 and 12 Feb. 1424).

been delivered after Arundel's death to Henry V, so that he could 'inspect' it, by Gilbert Umfraville, knight, one of Arundel's executors. The book had remained in the king's keeping during his lifetime and was currently in the custody of his favoured house at Sheen. But the king had, in his last will, or so the petitioner claimed, bequeathed the book to Christ Church, Canterbury, 'as the property of that church'.[8] The prior of Sheen was thus ordered to surrender the book to the almoner of Christ Church, according to the terms of Arundel's will, or appear before the council to explain why this had not been done. Henry's own will was very specific on the subject of his books, especially those relating to 'divinity' and pastoral care.[9] Gregory the Great's works formed one part of a collection which would not have been out of place in a monastic or university library – and some of it certainly passed into the hands of such institutions, at Sheen, Syon and (under Henry's son) King's Hall (later College), Cambridge.[10]

Yet Henry's concern did not end with the 'inspection' of religious books and the contemplative life of study. It has been said that his personal involvement in the religious life meant that he was 'the first king since Henry III [1216–72] to have shown more than conventional piety'.[11] Be that as it may, there can be no doubt of Henry's devotion to the cause of 'true religion', as is borne out by his practice of both private and public prayer, his vigorous patronage of the more austere monastic orders, and by his essentially pragmatic approach to the reform of the Church.[12] Over a

---

[8] 'Come propre bien de mesme lesglise'. The terms of the will stated simply that 'we bequeath to the church of Christ at Canterbury a certain volume containing all the books of the blessed Gregory' ('legamus ecclesie Christi Cantuar' quoddam volumen continens omnes libros beati Gregorii'). See Eton College MS 59, fo. 3v, & P. Strong & F. Strong, 'The Last Will and Codicils of Henry V', *EHR*, 96 (1981), p. 93.

[9] See below, chapter 7, pp. 253–4.

[10] See McFarlane, *Lancastrian Kings and Lollard Knights*, pp. 233–4.

[11] J. Catto, 'Religious Change under Henry V' in *Henry V: the Practice of Kingship*, ed. G.L. Harriss (Oxford, 1985; 2nd edn Stroud, 1993), p. 106.

[12] For a recent survey of Henry's chapel and its personnel who 'ministered to the king's spiritual needs' see A.L. McHardy, 'Religion, Court Culture and Propaganda: the Chapel Royal in the Reign of Henry V' in *Henry V: New Interpretations*, ed. G. Dodd (Woodbridge, 2013), pp. 131–56.

century before Henry VIII was to assume that title, Henry V, it can be argued, was already beginning to cast himself in the role of 'Supreme Head and Governor' of the Church in England. Here was a man with a mission; one which lay far beyond mere military conquest and worldly success. Some of his aims, assumptions and ambitions may perhaps have made this warrior-king a warrior in spiritual, as well as temporal, matters. In the process, the surviving evidence of the king's direct, personal involvement and intervention in these issues will have to be closely considered.

Henry V's reign witnessed the latter phases of a great crisis in the Western Church. Previous struggles and conflicts had pitted the Church – in particular, the papacy – against secular rulers, whether they were German emperors such as Henry IV (1050–1106) or Frederick II (1194–1250), or French kings, such as Philip the Fair (1285–1314). But the Church's later medieval crisis was essentially an internal one. Although secular powers did, inevitably, become involved, and were forced to take sides when schism broke out within the Church in 1378, the solution was thought to lie with the clergy themselves. Until, that is, all hope of peace and union under one pontiff seemed to have reached an impasse. That impasse still prevailed when Henry V succeeded his father in March 1413. Two rival popes, one at Rome and the other at Avignon, refused to countenance resignation or what was described as 'cession'. An attempt to resolve the situation, through the convening of an ostensibly representative church council at Pisa in 1409, only made matters worse. Three popes were now vying with each other for the allegiance and obedience of Christian Europe, as the Council of Pisa had only succeeded in electing a third pontiff while the other two still adamantly declined to resign. Whatever the relative merits of the candidates, one salient fact had emerged: there was an immense crisis of authority – on every issue – in the Church. Who held power? Which of the contenders, if any, was to be recognised by all parties in a dispute that called for papal arbitration or mediation? Who had authority to pronounce on matters of doctrine? As secular powers aligned themselves, their allies and their policies behind rival popes, with their attendant entourages of scheming and plotting cardinals, it was imperative that some semblance of authority and order be restored to the Church. The respect of the laity for Holy Mother Church was imperilled. The Schismatic 'conciliar period' (1378–1417), as it is known, produced a spate of writings, both theoretical and practical, devoted to discussion of how to end the Schism. Many of these were of great intellectual interest and moral force, but they did not solve the problem. Breaking the impasse could be done only by the intervention of secular authority supported by a sufficient body of opinion within the clergy.

A further council was convened in November 1414, to assemble at Constance, and first met in plenary sessions in February 1415.[13] But, unlike previous efforts, it was in effect under the oversight and chairmanship of secular power. It also – at the behest of lay as well as clerical parties – had an agenda for reform of the Church, and the suppression of heresy, as well as for the ending of the Schism. The need for action, in particular, to remedy perceived deficiencies and abuses in the monastic and mendicant orders had become pressing. Criticism of them could lead to anti-clericalism which, in turn, could lead to heterodox and heretical beliefs. Jan Hus's movement in Bohemia, although in part inspired by Wycliffite doctrines, had its origin in anti-clericalism. Whether the deficiencies were the fault of the clergy themselves, or whether they were at the mercy of forces over which they had little or no control, will remain a debating point among historians until the end of time. The quality of the clergy (outside the monasteries), especially in its middle and upper reaches, was probably higher than at earlier periods: they were 'more literate, more

---

[13] For the proceedings at the council, and English arguments put forward there on Henry V's behalf, see C.M.D. Crowder, *Unity, Heresy and Reform, 1378–1460. The Conciliar Response to the Great Schism* (London, 1977) esp. pp. 108–9, 115–16, 121. For a more recent survey of the activities at Constance see P.H. Stump, *The Reforms of the Council of Constance, 1414–1418* (Leiden, 1994).

conscious of old abuses, and more moved by religious zeal (even if it was misdirected) than ever before'.[14] Whatever the case, criticism of the regulars (the monastic orders) and the mendicants (the friars) was not the sole preserve of the laity. It has been said that, in the case of the long-established, black-garbed and wealthy Benedictines, by about 1420 'criticism of the black monks was once more becoming a living force . . . chiefly in ecclesiastical circles'.[15] Self-criticism and self-laceration certainly characterised some of the exponents of reform within the Church itself. But it was, in part, at the instigation of lay powers that the lachrymose hand-wringing of some clerical apologists and critics gave way to constructive and practical efforts to find a way out of the Schism, and to reform the Church in the process.[16]

It was at this juncture that the emperor Sigismund made his entry on to the conciliar stage. He was, it has been said, 'anxious to reinforce his uncertain position as king of the Romans' (the prelude to election as Holy Roman Emperor) 'by taking the lead in restoring an effective and undisputed papacy'. But, together with clear self-interest, he also had 'a genuine vision of the emperor's role and . . . his collateral responsibility for the welfare of Christendom alongside the pope'.[17] In that respect, he was not unlike Henry V – who, also besides self-interest, had a genuine vision of his role both as a leading European ruler and as the sovereign of an island kingdom. Before 1414, the general councils of the Church had consisted of representatives drawn from four 'nations' – the French, German, Spanish and Italian, into which the various European kingdoms, principalities and

---

[14] K.B. McFarlane, *Letters to Friends, 1940–1966*, ed. G.L. Harriss (Oxford, 1997), p. 40.

[15] M.D. [Dom David] Knowles, *The Religious Orders in England* (Cambridge, 1955) ii, p. 182. See also below, pp. 193–5.

[16] For a recent, wide-ranging attempt to assess the interplay of clerical and secular responses to the crisis of the Schism, and to the reform of secular government as well as of the Church, see J. Catto, 'The Burden and Conscience of Government in the Fifteenth Century', *TRHS*, 17 (2007), pp. 83–99, especially pp. 90–4 for contrasting reactions to the crisis among clerical intellectuals and the advent of a 'new mood' after *c.*1408–9.

[17] Crowder, *Unity, Heresy and Reform*, p. 7.

city-states were divided. This changed dramatically under Henry V. His advocate, proctor and ambassador at Constance, Thomas Polton, dean of York, later bishop of Hereford, then of Chichester, argued the case – at great length, but successfully – for a separate English nation. The English had previously formed part of the German nation. In March 1417, Polton attempted to rebut French claims that the English did not constitute a conciliar nation by arguing, among other assertions, that within the wider possessions of the crown of England, five languages were spoken. There should be, he claimed 'representation of as many nations as there are distinct languages' and the English, 'as a principal nation [should] . . . represent a fourth or fifth part of the papal obedience in a general council or elsewhere'.[18] The recent crushing victory over the French at Agincourt (1415) and the beginnings of Henry's rapid expansion into Normandy and northern France put England into a much stronger position among European powers than had been the case for decades. Henry V was determined to exploit this superiority in the cause of unity within the Church and its reform.

Henry had a high personal regard for Sigismund (b.1368), king of Hungary, son of the Holy Roman Emperor, Charles IV of Luxembourg. In 1416, the *Gesta* could describe them as 'like blood-brothers' (*fratres uterini*) so desirous were they of each other's wellbeing and success.[19] Sigismund had been acknowledged by the imperial electors, both spiritual and temporal, as emperor-elect in 1411. His alliance with Henry began with negotiations in July 1414, leading to an Anglo-imperial pact, formalised by the treaty of Canterbury in August 1416, which helped to bring the Schism in the

---

[18] Crowder, *Unity, Heresy and Reform*, p. 121. See also, for Polton's role, J-P. Genet, 'English Nationalism: Thomas Polton at the Council of Constance', *Nottingham Medieval Studies*, 28 (1984), pp. 60–78; and, for Polton's career, M. Harvey, 'Polton, Thomas (d.1433)' in *Oxford DNB*. For Henry V's views on the use of English as a national language see above, chapter 3. Polton received regular payments as Henry's proctor at the curia, e.g. E 403/636, m. 6r & E 403/636, m. 3r.

[19] *Gesta*, p. 151.

Western Church to an end.[20] The scandal of a deeply divided Christendom in which, after 1409, there were three popes, profoundly influenced the decision of secular European powers to, once again, attempt to set the Church's house in order. It was largely as a result of Sigismund's diplomatic activity that the general council of the Church was convened to meet at Constance. The primary objective of the council was to end the Schism, but reform of the Church was also on its agenda. Sigismund assumed the role of sponsor or patron of the assembly, and Henry supported him, both rulers taking a position that was often contrary to the views and interests of the French. This was a significant reversal of a diplomatic status quo which had largely prevailed since the reign of Sigismund's father, Charles IV, when a Franco-imperial, rather than an Anglo-imperial, alliance, had been the norm. The *Gesta* spoke of 'Sigismund . . . than whom no man (so far as one can read) has ever laboured more zealously for the reformation of the Church, and her release from the gloomy prisons in which, long out of reach of the many sighs of Christian men, a dreadful schism has held her captive under its cruel tyranny'.[21] Accordingly, in August 1416, the archbishop of Canterbury instructed the bishop of London to 'move and induce' all the king's subjects, clerical and lay, within his diocese to perform special processions, prayers, litanies and masses, and to contribute sums of money for the peace of the Church, for the king's person, and for the 'serenity of this world'. They were especially to pray for Sigismund's efforts to achieve the peace and union of Christendom.[22]

English attendance at the councils was not, however, without its hazards, as members of the English clergy did not always speak with one mind, and could in effect become loose cannons, expressing views and

---

[20] For the treaty see TNA, E 30/391: 15 Aug. & 19 Oct. 1416. For the diplomatic context of the treaty, and Henry's dealings with Sigismund and the German princes, see above, pp. 76–7, 120, 132–3; below, pp. 188–9, 268–70, 273–4.
[21] *Gesta*, p. 13.
[22] *Foedera*, ix, p. 371: 2 Aug. 1416.

opinions contrary to the wishes of the king and the English delegation there. So William Boteler, a Franciscan friar, was peremptorily recalled by Henry from Constance, after a warning that he should 'attempt nothing prejudicial to us, our crown, nor the laws and statutes of our kingdom', nor should he 'unjustly vex any of the brothers of his order'.[23] In July 1417, the king was moved to forbid all his subjects currently at Constance to act without first taking the advice of his formal representatives there – the bishops of London, Bath and Wells, Salisbury, Coventry and Lichfield, and Norwich. Some, he claimed, wished to proceed in defiance of his instructions, given expressly to his accredited envoys.[24] The shadow of the statutes of Provisors and Praemunire may be in evidence here as – in the king's eyes – any attempt by any member of the English clergy to incline towards their repeal or abolition was to be firmly resisted. The statutes (in their latest form, of 1390 and 1393) placed substantial restraints and restrictions upon papal rights of ecclesiastical patronage and jurisdiction in England. First enacted in 1351 and 1353, they were a reaction to long-term, as well as more immediate, issues.[25] The papacy had claimed the right temporarily to suspend presentation to benefices in England and then to place the pope's nominee in the vacancy. This meant that the rights of a lay patron – often the crown, or a magnate or knight – were also suspended. The appointee was thus known as a papal 'provisor'. The thirteenth century had witnessed a series of appointments of Italians to English benefices, and the fourteenth century saw a similar pattern, during the residence of the papacy at Avignon (1309–78), in favour of French candidates.

---

[23] C 81/664, no. 665: 9 June 1416.

[24] *Foedera*, ix, p. 466. See also C 49/48/15 for a draft of Henry's instructions to the bishops (styled his 'ambassadors') at Constance which included the injunction that anyone who disobeyed them, and the king's instructions which they carried, was to return home immediately to England from the 'curia or council'. Any disagreement among the ambassadors over the interpretation of the king's wishes was, for the time being, to be resolved by majority vote (18 July 1417).

[25] See C. Davies, 'The Statute of Provisors of 1351', *History*, 38 (1953), pp. 116–33.

To some degree, the legislation of the 1350s was anti-alien in nature, as it ruled that such appointees were bound to be non-resident, and that the income and revenues they gained from their benefices would inevitably be taken out of England. Apart from the material disadvantages that might accrue, the tender consciences of some churchmen – and laypeople – were troubled by considerations of a spiritual and pastoral nature:[26] the cure of souls would not be satisfactorily undertaken by foreign, absentee incumbents; and the intentions of the original founders and benefactors of churches and religious houses would not be properly fulfilled. These were often laymen, acting as patrons, protectors and 'advocates' of the churches within their domains, with the crown as chief among them. The performance of good works, the exercise of charity, and (above all, perhaps) provision for the health and destiny of their souls would not be accomplished in, and through, the establishments under their patronage if papal intervention of this kind was accepted. Furthermore, as the right of advowson (that is, the presentation of an incumbent to a living in the Church) was, in English law, a property right, its removal from the laity was in fact a breach of the common law. As we shall see, this was to be especially the case when the temporalities, or rights to the possession of land, movable goods and rights of lordship by the Church were concerned.

The legislation of the 1350s was, to some extent, moderated by what was in effect a concordat, reached with the papacy in 1377.[27] The disposition of benefices within the English Church was to be regulated by agreement between pope and king. But the statutes remained in force, and were reissued, in new forms, in 1390 and 1393. The 1390 Statute of Provisors[28] stipulated that any benefice accepted in contravention of the 1351 statute

[26] For the apparently disturbed state of some clerical consciences about the *regime beneficial* see Catto, 'Burden and Conscience of Government', pp. 88–91.
[27] Davies, 'The Statute of Provisors', p. 132.
[28] For the text of the 1390 statute see *English Historical Documents*, ed. A.R. Myers (2nd edn London, 1995) iv, no. 382, pp. 659–62.

was immediately to be forfeited. The fundamental principles of the rulings remained intact: all elections to bishoprics were to be free; all patrons holding advowsons and rights of presentation to benefices were to have freedom of provision; and any attempt at provision by the 'court of Rome' (the papal curia) would cause the right of presentation to revert to the king. The principles of the 1390 statute were endorsed and confirmed under Henry V by the Leicester Parliament of 1414.

Appointments to bishoprics, abbacies and other positions could thus be the subject of negotiation and compromise between crown and papal curia, and were 'at the heart of dealings between England and the papacy'.[29] In the event, the balance always tilted firmly in favour of the king when an appointment proved difficult or contested. Martin V was therefore forced to conclude that 'it is not the pope, but the king of England, who governs the Church in his dominions'.[30] A quid pro quo for the repeal of the statutes, which the papacy might offer, was papal acknowledgement of the legality of the treaty of Troyes, but neither side, pope nor king, came to an agreement on the issue during (or indeed after) Henry's lifetime. Henry may at times have seemed prepared to use the abrogation of the statutes as a lever whereby recognition of the treaty might be secured. But there was, in the event, to be absolutely no departure under him from the terms of the legislation, despite papal attempts by Martin V to seek its modification, repeal or abolition.[31] Yet there was always the risk that individuals

[29] R.G. Davies, 'Martin V and the English Episcopate', *EHR*, 92 (1977), pp. 309–10.

[30] Davies, 'The Statute of Provisors', p. 133. Relations between Martin V and Henry are examined in M. Harvey, 'Martin V and Henry V', *Archivum Historiae Pontificiae*, 24 (1986), pp. 49–70; & his *England, Rome and the Papacy, 1417–1464: the Study of a Relationship* (Manchester, 1993), pp. 130–8.

[31] See K.B. McFarlane, 'Henry V, Bishop Beaufort and the Red Hat, 1417–1421', in *England in the Fifteenth Century: Collected Essays*, ed. G.L. Harriss (London, 1981), pp. 81–2 for Martin's 'obtuseness' over English prejudice and Henry V's character. For a less severe view of Martin V as a diplomat and politician see Davies, 'Martin V and the English Episcopate', pp. 313–15. The pope recommenced his campaign against the statutes in 1423, after Henry's death. See also M. Harvey, 'Martin V and the English, 1422–1431' in *Religious Belief and Ecclesiastical Careers in Late Medieval England*, ed. C. Harper-Bill (Woodbridge, 1991), pp. 59–86, esp. pp. 59–60.

among the English clergy, seeking preferment in the Church by currying favour with the pope and cardinals, might pledge, or merely hint at, their support for a repeal of the statutes. If discovered, they could receive very short shrift from the king.

Of Henry's personal piety, and his concern for the welfare of the Church, there can be little doubt. He was also stirred, it seems, by the dictates of conscience. From the beginning of his reign, wrote the author of the *Gesta*, 'so fervently had he been devoted to the hearing of divine praises and to his own private prayers' (*divinis laudibus audiendis et secretis oraculis*) 'that, once he had begun them, there was not anyone, even from amongst his nobles and magnates, who was able, by conversation however brief, at any time to interrupt them'.[32] This was clearly an exceptional case among contemporary rulers. As we shall see, there may be some argument for seeing Henry V, in at least some respects, as an English Louis IX – the intensity of their personal devotion, their fervent promotion and lavish endowment of the more ascetic religious orders, and their espousal of a higher cause than conflict between Christians suggest certain affinities between the two men.[33] Yet St Louis's sainthood stood alone. There was to be no later medieval English (or indeed French) king-saint to stand beside him, or beside the Anglo-Saxon St Edward the Confessor or St Edmund the Martyr.

It was incumbent upon all medieval rulers to give alms to the Church throughout the liturgical year. Henry V was no exception to this rule. But

---

[32] *Gesta*, p. 155 & cf. p. 34, n. 3. Also Catto, 'Burden and Conscience of Government', pp. 97–9 for Henry's concern for the application of a 'disciplined conscience', as an outward expression of inward spirituality, to affairs of state. See also above, chapter 1, pp. 17, 55, 59, 60–1. The theme of conscience had appeared in English vernacular religious literature at an earlier date (*c*.1350–80), e.g. in the treatise entitled *The Pricke of Conscience*, attributed to Richard Rolle of Hampole but now considered the work of another, anonymous author. See *The Pricke of Conscience (Stimulus Conscientiae): a Northumbrian Poem*, ed. R. Morris (Berlin, 1863); and W. Riehle, 'The Authorship of the *Prick of Conscience* reconsidered', *Anglia*, 11 (1993), pp. 1–18. The author of the work hoped that 'if a man it red and understand wele/ And ye materes thar-in hert wil take/ It may his conscience tendre make . . .' (ll. 9552–4).

[33] For Louis IX's devotions see J. Le Goff, *Saint Louis* (Paris, 1996), pp. 744–80.

the very scale of his generosity certainly put him into the first rank of
donors and benefactors to the clergy. The friars did well. As in the reign of
St Louis, there would be some grounds for claiming (as did some contemporaries) that this was a 'friars' king', or a 'priests' king'.[34] Regular gifts,
well above the normal level of expenditure on alms given at masses celebrated before the ruler, were made to Franciscans, Dominicans, Austin
friars and Carmelites who preached before the king at the major liturgical
feasts (Good Friday, Easter Day, Pentecost, Ascension Day, the Assumption
of the Virgin, and so on). The normal sum offered to them was 40s. each.[35]
Daily alms averaged 7d.[36] Henry's gifts at Passiontide to paupers were also
ostentatiously lavish. On Good Friday 1413, for instance, at Kings Langley,
in the friary church, his almoner distributed 50 l. (4d each) to 3,000
paupers.[37] The figure rose to no less than 12,000 paupers in the following
year, when the king distributed alms totalling 400 l. to them at Tewkesbury.[38]
His long residences in Normandy and France made no difference to his
habitual generosity to the poor, and in March 1419 cash was received at
Rouen for distribution of alms to paupers on Good Friday.[39] One unusual
act of piety by the king was the redistribution of 1,320 gallons of ale,
originally intended for the royal household when it was at Canterbury in
1413, which was then conveyed to Leeds Castle (Kent), and thence back
to Canterbury, where it was offered as alms to the Franciscan convent.[40]

---

[34] See Le Goff, *Saint Louis*, pp. 331–3, 823–5: 'Tu n'es que le roi des Freres' (p. 823).

[35] It is notable that these sums, over and above the daily totals for alms-giving, were spent on
preaching by the friars, rather than – as with previous rulers – on the celebration of masses.
See, for examples, M. Vale, *The Princely Court. Medieval Courts and Culture in North-West
Europe, 1270–1380* (Oxford, 2001), pp. 236–7 & Fig. 1, & Tables 6, 7, 14.

[36] This was the sum allowed to the king's chaplain for daily alms under Edward II (E 101/376/7,
fo. 5r: 8 July 1315–31 Jan. 1316).

[37] E 101/406/21, fos 19r–v.

[38] *Foedera*, ix, p. 188: 7 Dec. 1414. Figures of this magnitude were greatly in excess of distribu-
tions by previous kings. In 1315–16, for example, the total year's expenditure on alms and
oblations was 194 l. 11s. 11d (E 101/376/7). In 1304–5 it was even lower, standing at 34 l.
(E 101/367/15).

[39] E 403/638, m. 18r.

[40] E 101/406/21, fo. 19v: 29 Oct. 1413.

Such libations, offered in another beverage, could also ensure the proper celebration of divine service by their recipients. During the last year of his reign (1421–2) the king disbursed, as 'special alms', the sum of 74 l. 10s. 1½d to 'the diverse abbots, priors and brethren of various religious houses' so as to provide 21 tuns of Gascon wine for the celebration of masses in their churches. The quality of the communion wine provided by the king's chief butler Thomas Chaucer, son of the poet, is not recorded. Consumed only by the clergy, there was clearly little or no difference between liturgical wine and that enjoyed for other, more secular, purposes.[41]

Apart from the day-in, day-out offering of oblations to the Church, and more occasional gifts made on major feast days, the foundation and endowment of larger-scale religious projects was also imperative. The formal recognition by the Church of the doctrine of purgatory – a staging post between earth and heaven, or hell, in which the soul was subject to fire yet not consumed by it – was a product largely of the thirteenth century. By the latter part of that century, it has been said:

> Purgatory was now a posthumous ordeal to which [the believer's] soul would be subject, but one that (as the Church assured its members) could be mitigated by the routine of prayer offered by others on his behalf, and by the vicarious practice of good works set in motion by his will.[42]

The passage of the soul out of purgatory was eased and assisted by the saying and singing of masses for that soul, for certain other identified souls, and for all those of the faithful who had departed from this world. The chantry, serviced by priests specifically and exclusively charged with mass-saying, chanting and singing, sometimes formed into colleges of

[41] E 101/407/77, m. 3r: account for the period 1 Oct. 1421–31 Aug. 1422. For a similar grant, to the London Carthusians, see E 101/406/21, fo. 19v: 18 Aug. 1413.
[42] H.M. Colvin, *Architecture and the After-Life* (New Haven/London, 1992), p. 153.

canons, had already appeared in England in the course of the thirteenth century.[43] But it was the fifteenth century which was to see its great culmination, if not apotheosis. The Beauchamp chapel at Warwick,[44] Henry VII's chapel at Westminster[45] or, on a smaller scale, the exquisite chapel of Henry V's retainers, the Wilcotes, at North Leigh (Oxon),[46] represented the flowering of the thousands of lavishly endowed and elaborate foundations characteristic of the age. Henry V's provisions for his soul will be examined in a later chapter.[47]

Although the movement to found new monasteries had slackened its pace among lay patrons and donors by the mid-fourteenth century, a small number of new foundations was subsequently created. They tended to lie outside the older-established orders of regulars (Benedictines, Cistercians, Premonstratensians, Augustinians) and sought to sustain the more hermetic and reclusive communities of monks; above all, the Carthusians.[48] Of those who led the apostolic life outside the cloister but in the world, though ostensibly not of it, the friars (Dominicans, Franciscans, Carmelites) still attracted benefactions. But a growing lay interest in hospitals, almshouses, colleges and schools, where the good works of charity might be more visibly and effectively exercised, tended to

[43] For a succinct account of the origins and evolution of chantry chapels see Colvin, *Architecture and the After-Life*, pp. 152–89.

[44] See L. Monckton, 'Fit for a King? The Architecture of the Beauchamp Chapel', *Architectural History*, 47 (2004), pp. 25–52; & R. Marks, 'Entumbid Right Princely: the Beauchamp Chapel at Warwick and the Politics of Interment', in *Memory and Commemoration in Medieval England*, ed. C.M. Barron & C. Burgess (Donington, 2010), pp. 163–84.

[45] See *Westminster Abbey: the Lady Chapel of Henry VII*, ed. T. Tatton-Brown & R. Mortimer (Woodbridge, 2003).

[46] See K. Heard, 'Death and Representation in the Fifteenth Century: the Wilcote Chantry Chapel at North Leigh, Oxfordshire', *Journal of the British Archaeological Association*, 154 (2001), pp. 134–49.

[47] See below, chapter 7, pp. 242–6.

[48] For recent work on the contribution of the Carthusian order to lay, as well as clerical, spirituality during this period see the references in Catto, 'Burden and Conscience of Government', pp. 84–5, 96–7. See also E.M. Thompson, *The Carthusian Order in England* (London, 1928) and for the popularity of the Carthusians among lay princes and nobles, the contributions in *Princeps i reis: promotors de l'Orde Cartoixa*, ed. C. Banca de Mirabo Gralla (Palma de Mallorca, 2003).

divert funds from the mendicant orders. To found an entire monastery – not at all uncommon in the twelfth and earlier thirteenth centuries – became a much rarer phenomenon by the fifteenth century. Henry V moved decisively against that trend by seeking to endow not one, but three religious houses of his own foundation.

It has been said that Henry's intentions in founding and endowing his own houses of devotion and prayer were the result of very deliberate choice and conscious planning. Three houses of monks and nuns were proposed: one Carthusian, one Brigittine, and one Celestine. The Celestine proposal was soon abandoned, but the others came to fruition. A kind of English Escorial – the later great palace-monastery of Habsburg Spain – may have been in Henry's mind. Whatever the case, the new foundations formed, it has been claimed, a 'gigantic power-house of prayer' for the Lancastrian dynasty, creating a sort of 'spiritual (royal) household'.[49] Be that as it may, there can be no doubt of Henry's personal devotion to his new houses and the austere lifestyles they were obliged to assume. As in other areas of later medieval lay piety and spirituality, the choice of lay patrons was moving firmly in the direction of asceticism and austerity. But this was in many ways simply another form of vicarious worship, and the sponsorship of a quasi-apostolic, if not hermetic, living of the Christian life by holy men and women which had characterised the religious observances of the laity from a much earlier date. The (initially) rigorously austere Cistercians of the twelfth century had, for example, ceded much ground in the minds and actions of the laity to the Carthusians by the fourteenth and fifteenth centuries. The monks of the Charterhouses – unlike their contemporary Benedictine and Cistercian brothers – were not perceived by the laity to be

---

[49] Catto, 'Religious Change', pp. 110–11. For the foundation and early history of both Sheen and, in particular, Syon see M. Tait, 'The Brigittine Monastery of Syon (Middlesex) with special reference to its Monastic Usages' (University of Oxford D.Phil. thesis, 1975). It is to be hoped that this will soon be published, in a revised edition. I am most grateful to Dr Tait for allowing me to see the latest version of his work.

prone to corruption and non-observance of their rule.[50] As we shall see, Henry's efforts towards Benedictine reform were not to be crowned with glittering success. But the Carthusians, and their female counterparts the Brigittines, in a sense performed the laity's worship and prayer by proxy, specialists in the living of a monastic life perhaps better suited to the expectations and demands of a more literate and informed laity than their earlier medieval predecessors.

Where the later fourteenth- and early fifteenth-century laity may have differed from their ancestors lay in the extent to which a more specifically lay spirituality, grounded in inward reflection and contemplation, had been offered to them by their confessors, and by the Carthusian and other writers of devotional literature.[51] What has been called the 'complementarity of material and spiritual power', expressed in works such as Walter Hilton's (d.1396) *The Mixed Life*, enabled laypeople to live a semblance of the contemplative life while fully engaged in the active life of the secular world.[52] It was assumed that these works would be read, generally in their vernacular language, by them. It was a tendency shared with the Netherlandish *devotio moderna* ('new' or 'modern devotion'), in which a form of lay *imitatio Christi* (Imitation of Christ) was expounded. Henry V was clearly influenced by such tendencies, imbued as they were with the notion that the worldly powerful bore heavy responsibilities in their discharge of public office and duty.[53] In many cases, such considerations led to the patronage of carefully selected religious orders, and the

---

[50] For studies of the nature and popularity of Carthusian spirituality at this time see the essays collected in *Studies in Carthusian Monasticism in the Late Middle Ages*, ed. J.M. Luxford (Turnhout, 2008).

[51] See J. Brantley, *Reading in the Wilderness: Private Devotion and Public Performance in Late Medieval England* (Chicago, 2008), esp. pp. 42–5.

[52] Among what has become a very extensive scholarly literature see N.R. Rice, 'Walter Hilton's Mixed Life and the Transformation of Clerical Discipline', *Leeds Studies in English*, n.s., 38 (2007), pp. 143–69, esp. pp. 148–50. Hilton's text is published in *Walter Hilton's 'Mixed Life'. Edited from Lambeth Palace, MS 472*, ed. S.J. Ogilvie-Thomson (Salzburg, 1986).

[53] Catto, 'Burden and Conscience of Government', pp. 85, 97–9.

foundation or endowment of their houses. It was therefore not entirely surprising that what has been called 'by far the most ambitious monastic foundation attempted by an English king, designed to place the monarchy at the spiritual centre of English life' should take these forms.[54] Not since the virtual re-foundation of the Benedictine palace-monastery at Westminster by Henry III in the mid-thirteenth century had anything quite on this scale been attempted.

The royal residence at the manor of Sheen, near Richmond, had been razed to the ground by Richard II after the death of his queen, Anne of Bohemia. Henry resolved to rebuild it and to found one of his two new religious houses – the Carthusian convent of Bethlehem – there. Building work on both the residence and the monastery proceeded apace. In 1417, William Algood, the king's mason, was ordered to 'supply and acquire building stone, chalk, timber, plasterers, roofers and also carriage . . . both by land and water' and all other necessities for the construction of the manor at Sheen. These resources, both human and material, were to be purchased 'at reasonable expense' for a year from various places throughout the kingdom, the possessions of the Church being excepted.[55] The house at Sheen was consistently accorded especial favour by the king: in May 1418, Henry was petitioned by the prior and convent of 'oure house of Jhesu of Bethleem at Shene, of thordre of Chartuse',[56] for exemption from a recently granted clerical tax, which had been refused them at the Exchequer. The king ordered the Chancellor Thomas Langley, bishop of Durham, to see that they were discharged from this payment 'yn ye best wyse that ye can'. He was also to speak to Henry Chichele, archbishop of Canterbury, so that Henry's letters granting privileges to them could be

---

[54] Catto, 'Religious Change', p. 110.
[55] C 81/1542, no. 7.
[56] For an account of the motives and influences behind its foundation see N. Beckett, 'Henry V and Sheen Charterhouse: the Expansion of Royal and Carthusian Ideals', *Analecta cartusiana*, 63 (1990), pp. 49–71.

1. Profile portrait of Henry V. Sixteenth-century copy of an earlier original, dated (by dendro-chronological analysis) to c.1518–23.

2. Presentation to Henry V of a manuscript, c.1421–22, of the Latin *Meditations on the Life of Christ* by the pseudo-Bonaventure, in a French translation by Jean de Galopes. Galopes was one of Henry's French chaplains in Normandy.

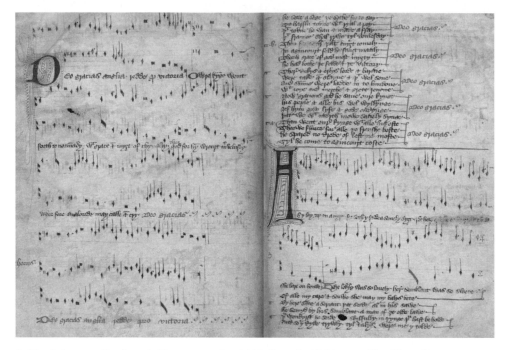

3. The Agincourt Carol, probably composed in 1415, from the 'Selden carol book', *c*.1425–50.

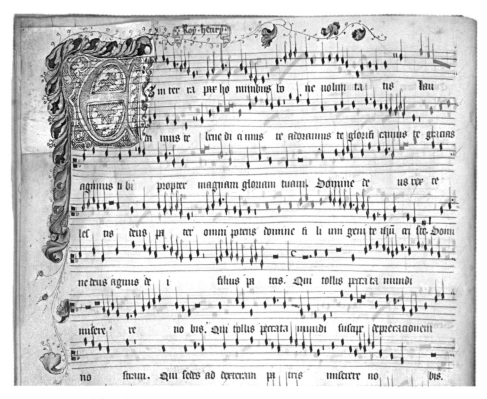

4. Mass setting of the *Gloria* by Henry V in the Old Hall MS, *c*.1415–21.

5. Part of an autograph letter attributed to Henry V, probably addressed to Thomas Beaufort, duke of Exeter. It is undated, but *c.* February–March 1418.

6. Petition by Hugh Waterton to Henry IV for the grant of some Dorset lordships and manors formerly held by the earl of March, with an endorsement, in French, in the king's own hand, 'H.R. avons grante' (*Henricus Rex* we have granted it), 20 October 1403.

7. Note in Henry V's own hand, in English, relating to the drawing-up of indentures for military service on the Agincourt campaign, April–May 1415, with the endorsement 'RH' (*Rex Henricus* or *Roy Henry*).

8. Warrant by Henry V under the signet, in English, on the payment of annuities to the masters of his ships, 12 August 1417. This is one of the very earliest examples of the use of English in documents of this kind.

9. Note (detail) on a draft memorandum concerning Henry V's negotiations with John the Fearless, duke of Burgundy, in October 1416, that the proposals were in the king's own hand: 'Choses escrites de la main du Roy touchant le duc de Burgoigne'. The document was originally sealed with the signet, of which it still bears traces.

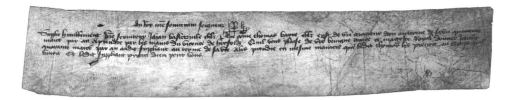

10. Petition by John Baskerville, knight, to Henry V, in French, for the grant of an annuity from Herefordshire revenues, with an endorsement 'RH' by the king, 28 February 1421.

11. Petition by John Hoggekyns, master carpenter of the king's ships, to Henry V, in French, for the grant of a life pension on account of the enfeeblement to which his service had reduced him, with 'RH' endorsement, 1 June 1421.

12. Petition by Elizabeth, wife of William Ryman, to Henry V, in French, for the grant of a Sussex manor. Endorsed, 'RH. yelding iiijd by yeere' (yielding 4d. to the Exchequer, at certain terms of the year) in the king's own hand, 6 June 1421.

13. Petition by John Kyngesley, esquire, to Henry V, in French, for the confirmation of a grant of Cheshire revenues to him by the king's late brother Thomas, duke of Clarence, killed at the battle of Bauge (22 March 1421). Endorsed, in the king's own hand, 'RH. In the forme and manere that oure brethers lettres p[ur]poten whil us lust', 9 June 1421.

14. Instructions given by Henry V, in Latin, to his ambassadors sent to negotiate with the duke of Burgundy, sealed with the king's 'secret' seal, or signet of arms, at Pontefract, 25 June 1414. The seal, in red wax, is inset and reinforced with a circular band of plaited rush.

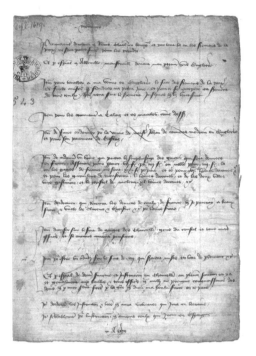
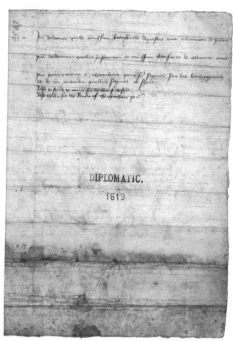

15. Memorandum and aide-mémoire by Henry V on the fulfilment of the terms of the treaty of Troyes, in French and English, with the last two lines (right) in the king's own hand, late 1420, reading, 'Also to sende to court for thabbot of Westm[inster]. Also thider for the Rendu of the chaterhous etc.'

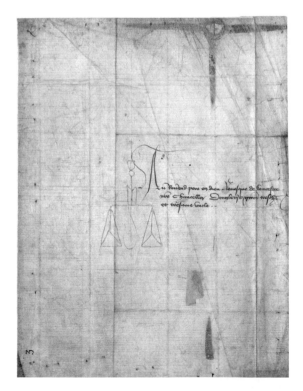

16. Warrant by Henry V to Henry Beaufort, Chancellor, in French, with traces of sealing by the signet in red wax, Mortlake, 20 March 1416. The document, on paper, carries a watermark of a balance with two triangular pans, common to the English and Burgundian secretariats at this time.

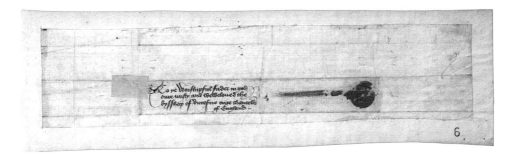

17. Warrant by Henry V to Thomas Langley, Chancellor, in English, showing the dorse of the paper document, with traces of the signet applied to its face in red wax, Rouen, 28 February 1419. It is addressed to 'ye worshipful fader in God oure trusty and welbeloved the bysshop of Duresme [Durham] oure chanceller of England'.

18. Kenilworth castle. The main complex of buildings, viewed from the west, once the site of the Great Mere, or lake. The castle was one of Henry V's most favoured residences.

19. Kenilworth castle. The site of Henry V's 'Pleasance', or pleasure pavilion, constructed between 1414 and 1417, of which only the formerly moated earthworks remain.

20. Kenilworth castle. The site of the harbour or dock for Henry V's 'Pleasance' which had to be reached by boat from the main site of the castle.

entered into his episcopal register 'if ye thinke hit goodly to be doon'.[57] In matters as mundane as the provision of household utensils to the convent at Sheen, Henry's 'special order' was implemented through payment to a London 'founder' in December 1418.[58] The house at Sheen had also been protected by Henry in March 1416, when he ordered that no one should be housed by, or take any livery from, the priory of Hayling, or on the Isle of Hayling, or from the priory of Carisbrooke, on the Isle of Wight, all of which were part of Henry's endowment of his favoured Carthusian house. Only with the prior's assent were such practices to be permitted.[59] This was followed up with a licence to the convent at Sheen for masons and labourers, with a boat, presumably to carry raw materials, to 'attend to, and remain there, employed on their works'.[60]

His particular concern for his own religious foundations was also exemplified by the care which he took to ensure that every grant made to them was drawn up in the proper documentary form. As we shall see elsewhere, this concern for due process and correct format betokened more than the usual interest in the written document and its language on the part of a ruler. Thus, in a letter under the signet, dated at Rouen on 2 March 1419, the king referred to a 'letter patent closed under our signet and sealed with our great seal' in favour of the monastic 'profession' of the new Brigittine community at Syon.[61] This document was not enrolled at its place of issue in France 'through haste', but had been enrolled in England, notwithstanding the erasure of two names. These were those of the earls of Arundel and Warwick which, Henry told the Chancellor, 'were erased because they were wrongly written, and as our said patent relates to something perpetual,

---

[57] C 81/1364, no. 55: under the signet, at Caen, 20 May 1418.

[58] E 403/638, m. 9r: payment for making 'vasis' and other utensils for the new house, 'by the special order of the king' (7 Dec. 1418).

[59] C 81/1365, no. 2: [?] 17 Mar. 1416.

[60] C 81/1366, no. 3: 20 Mar. [?] 1416.

[61] For possible influences behind the foundation of Syon, seen from the perspective of gender history, see N. Warren, 'Kings, Saints and Nuns: Gender, Religion and Authority in the Reign of Henry V', *Viator*, 30 (1999), pp. 307–22.

we wish that you write it again in a more substantial hand, and seal it under our seal, being in your keeping'.[62] Henry was determined that the 'profession' of the Syon community should be advanced and the Chancellor was urged to 'steer' and assist the process with all the powers at his command. Nothing was to stand in the way of the king's special foundations.

No detail was too small for the king's personal attention when his power-houses of prayer were concerned. The abbess and convent of Syon received many expressions of his close personal concern for their affairs. The foundation was a double convent for men and women, following the Augustinian rule, of the Brigittine order. This was a relatively recent newcomer to the ranks of the regular orders, deriving from the life and work of St Bridget (Birgitta) of Sweden (1303–73).[63] Henry V's chamberlain, Sir Henry Fitzhugh, a Yorkshire knight with close links to the exceptionally pious Scrope family, had visited the order's mother house at Vadstena in Sweden, and brought back detailed information about its organisation and practices.[64] The petitions of the abbess and convent of Syon for grants of land and property, however small or apparently insignificant, from which to sustain both divine service and themselves, were regularly granted by Henry. In July 1422, six weeks or so before his death, the king acceded to their request for a perpetual grant of a small parcel of land at the Thameside 'Eyston Wharff' (Heston Wharf?) with an adjacent pond (*stagnum*) at Isleworth.[65] Unlike some other royal and princely patrons of the religious

---

[62] C 81/1366, no. 15: 2 Mar. [?] 1419: the words were to be 'rased because they wer myssette, and for asmuche as oure saide patent is of a thing perpetual, we wol that ye do write hit agein of a more substantial hande, and seel hit under oure seel, being yn youre warde'.

[63] See, for a recent general account, C. Sahlin, *Birgitta of Sweden and the Voice of Prophecy* (Woodbridge, 2001); and also N. Beckett, 'St Bridget, Henry V and Syon Abbey', *Analecta cartusiana*, 35 (1993), pp. 125–50.

[64] Catto, 'Religious Change', p. 110; and, for Fitzhugh, pp. 85–7. The contacts had begun under Henry IV in 1406, when Fitzhugh made his visit. See Tait, *Brigittine Monastery*, pp. 3–10 & E. Andersson, 'Brigittines in Contact: Early Correspondence between England and Vadstena', *Eranos*, 102 (2004), pp. 1–29, which prints previously unpublished material. These contacts with Sweden led, among other acts, to the granting of letters of denization by Henry V to a Swedish chaplain, Magnus Hemming, a messenger from Vadstena, in 1414 (C 81/659, no. 185: 10 Feb. 1414; *CPR, 1413–1416*, p. 159).

[65] E 28/37, no. 13: endorsed: 'Le Roy lad graunte', 11 July 1422.

life, there was nothing of the misty-eyed visionary, intent only on the loftiest of other-worldly thoughts, about Henry V. Rather like some of the great abbots and priors of religious houses, keeping their grip on the endowments and assets of their communities with assiduous attention to detail, the king kept a sharp eye upon what may seem the minutest of matters. Comparisons with the administrative and managerial talents of Abbot Samson of Bury St Edmunds (1182–1211), in the twelfth century, or Prior Henry Eastry (1285–1331) of Christ Church cathedral priory, Canterbury, in the fourteenth, might not be amiss.[66] Throughout his 'policy' towards the Church and the life of the soul, a striking and consistent pragmatism and practicality reigned. Henry VII, the 'miser king' of legend, was by no means the first English sovereign to check his accounts and concern himself with the everyday business of personal rule.[67]

The king's concern for the quality of the spiritual and intellectual life in his new foundations was well expressed by his gifts of books to them. The terms of his various wills in this respect command our interest.[68] As we have seen, when the town and market of Meaux surrendered on 10 May 1422, a collection of books came into Henry's hands. The assumption that they came from one or more of the religious houses in the town could be questioned as, according to the terms of the surrender, all 'relics, jewels, books, ornaments and other movable goods being in the said market, belonging to churches, abbeys, minsters, priories or hospitals' were to be restored to the 'churches of the said market'.[69] It is not known whether these terms were fully carried out,

---

[66] For short accounts of these figures see M.D. Knowles, *Saints and Scholars. Twenty-five Medieval Portraits* (Cambridge, 1962), pp. 63–9 (Samson), 114–22 (Henry of Eastry).

[67] See above, chapter 1 for a discussion of Henry's style of government.

[68] See below, chapter 7 for Henry's testamentary dispositions.

[69] *Foedera*, x, pp. 212–14: all such items were to be gathered together and 'all the reliques, jewells, bookes, ornaments, and other goods mebles beyng in the said market, longyng to churches, abbeys, ministers, priores, or hospitals, what so they bene, in levynge hem to bene restitute in ther places of the churches of the said market, and that without fraude'. Items, including books, 'that longed to other thane to the said churches . . .' were to be separately gathered 'and that without fraude or mal engyn' (2 May 1422). The market finally surrendered, as set out in the treaty, on 10 May.

but it is at least possible that the books and other items in the collection derived from sources other than the religious houses of Meaux. Whatever the case, to the books were added some sets of liturgical vestments (a gilded and bejewelled mitre, chalices, albs, amices, stoles and maniples) as well as items of church plate. The theological, legal and devotional volumes thus entered into the king's personal possession and, together with the liturgical items, seem to have been kept in the custody of his almoner, John Snell.[70] They included a psalter (*psalterium glossatum*) which may have been the volume listed among nine other books and seven chapel service books, for which the king met the expenses of binding, 'in silk covers and with bosses' in the great wardrobe account for 1422.[71] Henry's intentions for the books must remain the subject of speculation. They were acquired only four months before his death. He may have planned to give them to one or both of his foundations at Sheen and Syon; or they may represent the book collection he pledged to the University of Oxford, but which was never received, under the terms of his last will.

Apart from his large-scale foundations, Henry established some much smaller bodies, pledged to celebrate masses for the souls of himself and others. Such were two chantries which, five months after his accession in 1413, he created at Chichester Cathedral. The Lady Chapel there housed the body of Nicholas Mortimer, 'lately our servant and *familier*' (household member). Henry established two chantries in the chapel, with chaplains to pray for the souls of himself, his father, mother and all other progenitors, 'as well as the said Nicholas', by indenture with the dean and chapter.[72] In July, the dean and chapter had already petitioned Henry for

---

[70] E 101/335/17: indenture dated 6 Oct. 1427. The list of books, but not the liturgical items, is printed in Appendix C to his *Lancastrian Kings and Lollard Knights*, pp. 233–8. See above, pp. 128, 147.

[71] E 101/407/5, m. 4r.

[72] C 81/658, no. 81: under the signet, at Henley, 11 Aug. 1413. The chaplains were to be known as 'king's chaplains' and had special privileges. See 'Chichester Cathedral: the Lady Chapel', *VCH, County of Sussex*, ed. L.F. Salzman (London, 1935), iii, pp. 113–16. The chantries were re-endowed in 1461 by Edward IV, to pray for the souls of, among others, Henry V and Nicholas Mortimer (*CCR, 1413–1419*, pp. 89, 90; *CPR, 1461–1467*, p. 110; *CPR, 1413–1416*, pp. 76–7).

the grant of an alien priory at Wilmington (East Sussex). This had lately been a cell of the Benedictine abbey of Notre-Dame de Grestain (Normandy), and was valued at 240 l. The dean and chapter requested the grant for the duration of the French war, in order to maintain the chantries.[73] Henry's dissolution of the alien priories – that is, of those religious houses whose mother house was in lands of French allegiance during the Hundred Years War – was a significant source of ecclesiastical patronage and income to the crown. As a result of the Act concerning these houses, passed in the Parliament of 1414, alien priories and their possessions were taken into royal hands. A reservoir of revenue therefore became available – in some ways a smaller-scale prefiguration of Henry VIII's later complete supression of the monasteries. The income could pass into both secular and clerical hands, while the house itself might be reassigned to the English superiors or principals of the orders to which they belonged.

Thus the Carthusian priory of Hinckley (Leics.), held by the Norman charterhouse of Notre-Dame de Lyre, was granted by Henry, on the request of his uncle Thomas, earl of Dorset, to the Carthusian priory of Mount Grace (Yorks.), founded by Dorset's family in 1398.[74] This would be sufficient to endow and sustain five monks of the order 'to perform divine services and to pray for our [spiritual] welfare and that of the said earl'.[75] Henry's closest clerical advisers and councillors also played their part in enlisting the king's support and patronage for works of piety which they initiated. Thus Archbishop Henry Chichele, who had been born at Higham Ferrers (Northants), founded and endowed a collegiate church there for eight secular canons or chaplains, eight clerks and six choristers in 1422.[76]

[73] SC 8/187, no. 9344: petition dated 21 July 1413.
[74] See 'Houses of Carthusian Monks: the Priory of Mount Grace', in *VCH, County of York*, ed. W. Page (London, 1974), iii, pp. 192–3.
[75] C 81/662, no. 478: 21 June 1415.
[76] See *VCH, County of Northampton*, ed. R.M. Serjeantson & W.R.D. Atkins (London, 1906), ii, pp. 177–9: 'Colleges: Higham Ferrers'.

The king granted to the foundation revenues from land at Higham Ferrers, and also the income from a suppressed alien priory at West Mersea (Essex), formerly a cell of the abbey of Saint-Ouen at Rouen. Chichele's foundation was dedicated to the Blessed Virgin Mary and to two English saints – St Thomas (Becket) of Canterbury and St Edward the Confessor. In August 1425, Chichele assembled all those with an interest in the new foundation, including the local parishioners, whose consent or dissent was requested.[77] No one dissented, and the new college went ahead. The spiritual function of its members was to celebrate divine service daily for the 'good estate' of Henry V, Queen Catherine and Chichele himself during their lifetimes, and for their souls after death. In July 1427, further grants were made to the college in Henry VI's name, including permission to acquire lands and rents in mortmain, as well as a stipulation that Henry V should be especially remembered in its prayers.[78] A house for 'poor men' accompanied the collegiate foundation, in which the twelve inmates, apparently chosen from the relatively well-to-do who had fallen upon hard times, were also to pray for the souls of their named benefactors.[79]

In some instances, the revenues of an alien priory could be similarly redistributed, after supplication to the king, by laypeople, as well as clergy, for devotional purposes. So, in May 1415, Isabelle de Lingen (d.1446), the formidable widow of Fulk Pembridge, knight (d.1409), told the king that she, together with two clerks, had recently (1410) founded a college of secular canons, with a chantry dedicated to St Bartholomew the Apostle, at Tong (Shrops.). The college was to consist of a warden, four chaplains, two clerks, and thirteen almspeople. One of the chaplains or clerks was to teach the others, as well as giving lessons to poor children from the surrounding area. The chaplains were, as was becoming increasingly common in lay

---

[77] The foundation ceremony is noted in E.F. Jacob, 'Founders and Foundations in the Later Middle Ages' in his *Essays in Later Medieval History* (Manchester, 1968), p. 162; also see *CPR, 1422–1429*, pp. 472–4.

[78] *CPR, 1422–1429*, p. 353 (26 July 1427).

[79] *VCH, Northants*, ii, p. 178.

benefactions of this kind, to be neither hunters nor hawkers, nor were they to keep dogs within the college precincts.[80] In her petition, Isabelle stated that her foundation was 'to sing divine service for your [Henry V's] good [spiritual] state during your lifetime, and for your soul after your death, and the soul of your . . . father, and the souls of certain others' (in fact, of her three deceased husbands), 'and of all Christians'. She asked that the revenues of the alien priory of Lapley (Staffs.), previously assigned to other beneficiaries, be granted to the warden and chaplains of her chantry, in perpetual alms. The king granted the petition in its entirety.[81] To a layperson, such a use of revenues from a dissolved alien priory might seem entirely fitting. It met a need to provide for their soul, and for those of 'all Christians' in a potentially productive manner. The good works required of the laity for the health of their souls were surely better served by such benefactions than by the retention of income by alien priories, some of dubious reputation and poor administration. Lapley provided over one-half of annual income for the college of St Bartholomew at Tong.[82] For its lay founder, that was money appropriately gathered, and it would be well spent.

Other acts of piety and charity befitting a Christian ruler abound in the recorded grants which Henry made. Apart from his exercise of rights to nominate candidates for positions in his gift in the Church, more sponta-neous acts of assistance are found. To those wishing to enter religion, or to pursue the spiritual life, he was generous. Unfree, servile tenants on royal demesne manors could be given a helping hand. Thus Thomas Colbron, son of John Colbron, 'serf [neif] belonging to our manor of Clymeslond'

---

[80] For a detailed account of the foundation and a summary of its statutes of 1410 see 'Colleges of Secular Canons: Tong, St Bartholomew' in *VCH, County of Shropshire*, ed. A.T. Gaydon & R.B. Pugh (London, 1973), ii, pp. 131–3. Also Sir William Dugdale, *Monasticon Anglicanum* (London, 1830), vi, pp. 1404–11. The alabaster tomb, with two recumbent effigies, of Isabelle and Fulk, survives in the largely rebuilt (1410–30) church at Tong.

[81] E 28/31, no. 7: endorsed 'Le Roy a grante toute la bille', 30 May 1415.

[82] *VCH, Shrops.,* ii, p. 132.

(Stoke Climsland), in the duchy of Cornwall, was permitted to enter 'the order of St Benedict, and successively the other orders up to priesthood, and then the order of priest' despite his previous villein status. Colbron was of 'firm purpose' to embrace the religious life and was to pray for the king and his kin during life, and for the king's soul after his death. Prayer service was thus a condition of the grant.[83] Grants were also made to others wishing to enter monastic orders: thus Guillaume Michel, born in Jersey, had been a secular priest until, two years earlier (in 1412?), he had entered the order of St Benedict at the abbey of Mont Saint-Michel. The island fortress-monastery was then in enemy hands, during time of war, and he had acted without seeking the licence or permission of Henry's father, or of any of his subjects. Since Henry was assured that Guillaume had done so 'because of his devotion, and also because he had heard of the great renown of the good conversation and religious life of the monks' of the abbey, Guillaume was pardoned and permitted to 'live among our enemies'.[84] Beside such support for individuals, grants were made to religious orders whose convents, for example, lay in university towns: among them, the Dominicans at the University of Cambridge. In the first year of his reign Henry confirmed the privileges of the friars at both Oxford and Cambridge, stressing direct continuity with his predecessors. Henry III's grant to the Cambridge Dominicans of 25 marks per year at the Exchequer was thus confirmed 'in honour of God, . . . for the increase of the catholic faith' and so that they could 'sustain the doctrines of the faith'.[85]

It was also within the king's rightful powers to sanction and approve matters of Church governance which some might consider to be more properly the remit of bishops and abbots. In June 1418, the prior and convent of the monastery of St Oswald's at Gloucester requested that the king grant them the right to appropriate into their patronage the church

---

[83] C 81/659, no. 124: 7 Nov. 1413.
[84] C 81/660, no. 280: 23 July 1414.
[85] C 81/659, nos 119, 142: 6 & 18 Nov. 1413.

of 'Mynstreworth' (Minsterworth, Gloucs.). This was granted, but on condition that the appropriation took place within one year.[86] No doubt this was meant to ensure that other parties would not intervene if the transaction was not concluded within the time limit normally set, for example, for suspension of presentation to a living. As we shall see, the extensive powers accorded by the rights and obligations of patronage to laymen, with the crown at their head, could – potentially – put the Church back into a position not dissimilar to that prevailing before the Gregorian reforms of the late eleventh and early twelfth centuries. There was now no question of the exclusion of lay patronage from the English Church – not only were the 'literate laity . . . taking the clergy's words out of their mouths',[87] but they were acting in ways which their earlier medieval predecessors, as 'advocates' of churches within their lands, would have recognised.

One of the justifications for the exercise of lay patronage and protection in the earlier medieval Church was the danger to which churches and religious houses might be exposed through lawlessness, disorder, the ravages of pagan Scandinavians, Magyars or Mongols, and the depredations of warfare. The Church was not able to defend itself, or so ran the argument. That function was to be assumed by the powerful laity – by kings, princes and nobles. Hence warfare, both civil and external, put the Church in peril not only of the loss of material possessions, but also of a decline, or even complete cessation, of its spiritual functions and observances. In fifteenth-century England, marcher warfare was a constant threat to the Church: in the frontier zones of the kingdom bordering Wales and Scotland the king's peace was less well kept, and the Church could suffer as a result. As we shall see, the situation was even more acute in Henry's Norman and French possessions and conquests. The king thus granted aid to religious houses damaged by war, by usurpation of their rights and

---

[86] C 81/1364, no. 62: under the signet, at the siege of Louviers, 22 June 1418.
[87] McFarlane, *Lancastrian Kings and Lollard Knights*, p. 204.

possessions, and by other misfortunes. In Wales itself, the effects of the recent rising led by Glyn Dwr were still being felt. A Franciscan house, founded in 1237, at Llanmaysi (Llanmaes; now Llanfaes)[88] on the isle of Anglesey had been 'completely desolated' (*tout desolle*) by the Welsh rebellion and wars, so that 'divine service has there been diminished and withdrawn'. In 1401 it was said to be deserted. Like many others, the house had connections with both English and other royalty, and with Welsh princes. A daughter of King John was buried there. This was Joan (d.1237), wife of Prince Llywelyn ap Iorweth and, beside her, a son of the king of Denmark; Lord Clifford and other nobles, knights and esquires 'who were killed in the Welsh wars and during the time of our predecessors' also had their tombs there. Henry V's often-stated wish to ensure the continuance of divine service everywhere he went led to the re-establishment, at his behest, of a community of eight friars in the deserted house to celebrate and to pray for the king, his brothers and others of his kin, as well as 'all Christians'. Of the eight friars, two were specified to be 'of the Welsh nation', and therefore Welsh-speaking. Harry of Monmouth was perhaps here remembering his own origins and his early career.[89]

The disturbances in Wales, as in other theatres of war and rebellion, had produced cases of theft and pillage from churches. In 1417 Henry ordered an inquiry, after petition, into the alleged theft by 'certain people' of 'an image of Our Lady, adorned with fine and rich apparel' from the chapel of 'Pylale' (Pilale, Radnorshire, in the diocese of St David's) during the Welsh rebellion. This appears to have been committed by Englishmen from the Welsh marches. They had taken the image to the Carmelite convent at Ludlow, from which, the king ordered, it should be taken and restored to the chapel, after due inquiry, and the taking of evidence on oath from the

[88] See A.D. Carr, *Medieval Anglesey* (Anglesey Antiquarian Soc., 1982, 2nd edn 2011), pp. 291–4; *RCAHMW* (1937), pp. 66–7.
[89] C 81/660, no. 265: 3 July 1414.

'worthy men' of the area, by the sheriff of Shropshire.[90] Not only were religious houses damaged by warfare or rebellion aided by the king, but also those who had fallen on hard times, who were the victims of lay assaults on their privileges, lands and goods, or whose buildings had fallen into a state of disrepair. Such was the case at the Augustinian house at Tickhill (South Yorks.),[91] founded c.1270, where the prior and convent requested aid from Henry in January 1415. Their 'poor church and other houses' were in a ruinous state, 'on the point of falling down [de tresboucher]' unless timber could be found to repair them. They accordingly asked the king – as they were his tenants, in the duchy of Lancaster – for timber from his forests, either from the royal manor of Lyndhurst (in the New Forest, Hants), or from 'Bylhare' in Sherwood Forest. The king ordered that they be given four oaks from the forest at Lyndhurst so that divine service might be maintained and increased – a very common theme in his grants of this kind.[92]

The protection of the Church and its legitimate rights sometimes demanded direct royal intervention. Some religious houses received special favour, given their foundation by the king himself or his ancestors. The convent of Our Lady (St Mary Graces) 'next to the Tower of London' was one such establishment, founded on a plot of land adjacent to the Tower by Edward III in 1350.[93] In October 1417, the abbot and convent requested Henry to act in their favour. The earl of Huntingdon, who was about to receive his inherited lands on the death of his father, intended, they claimed, to 'disturb and upset . . . [their] rightful possession . . . of certain of their manors in . . . Somerset and Devon', held in perpetuity since their foundation. Much play was made by them of their especial status, as 'your own true and immediate house' praying continually for the souls of the king and his ancestors, dependent only upon him for aid, and

---

[90] C 81/666, no. 834: 5 July 1417.
[91] For a brief history of the house see W. Page, 'Friaries: the Austin Friars of Tickhill' in VCH, County of York, iii, pp. 280–1.
[92] E 28/30, no. 50: 21 Jan. 1415.
[93] See The Cistercian Abbeys of Britain, ed. D. Robinson (London, 1996), p. 136.

'coming on their knees into the shade of your benign grace and protection'. The king ordered his justices and serjeants-at-law to adjudicate the case and, this being done, an order was sent out that the livery of lands to be granted to Huntingdon should specifically exclude the abbot's and convent's West Country manors.[94] A further general protection was issued to them in May 1418, after another supplication to the king.[95]

The house – the last Cistercian foundation to be made in England, and in effect a royal chapel – was also petitioning for Henry's protection later in 1418. On 4 September, it was still fearful for the security of its possessions and begged the king for further aid. Henry declared himself fully in support of the house, ordering Chancellor Langley to 'shewe al the favour and ese that may be doon, by lawe and conscience' to the abbot and monks, so that the community was not 'spoilled' of its possessions. The king left the Chancellor with a holding operation until he himself resolved the issue in person. He would, he wrote from the siege of Rouen, do so 'on our coming home, with God's grace, to put it in rest and quiet, as it is of our foundation, for which reason we hold it in much greater affection, according to reason'.[96] Prayer service for the royal house and its predecessors was not to be disturbed by the actions of others, clerical or lay, however exalted, high-born or powerful they were.

Other houses, although not directly founded or patronised by the crown, also sought – and gained – Henry's aid. In March 1420, the Cistercian abbot and convent of Combermere (Ches.) told the king that they were subject to the depredations of Piers Mainwaring, esquire. The Cistercian house at Combermere, originally a Savignac convent founded

[94] C 81/666, nos 864, 865: 29 Oct. 1417.
[95] C 81/666, nos 880, 881.
[96] C 81/1364, no. 68: 'yn oure hoost afore Roan' [Rouen], 21 Sept. 1418 & no. 69 for the petition. The king would act 'at oure coming hoom, with goddes grace, to put hit in rest and quiete, yn as moche as hit is of oure fundacion, for which cause we have hit moche ye more yn chierte as reson is'. The petition is printed in *An Anthology of Chancery English*, ed. J. H. Fisher, M. Richardson & L. Fisher (Knoxville, Tennessee, 1984), text no. 39. But see above, chapter 3, pp. 89, 108, 112, 115 for the problems posed by this publication.

in 1133, had not had the happiest of histories in the later Middle Ages. Plagued by problems of both internal discipline and external, local disorder, it had declined to a community of nine monks and an abbot by the late fourteenth century, and underwent successive financial crises.[97] In 1417 it was taken into royal custody, but was wracked by internal feuds, experiencing the theft by two monks, who defied all authority, of books worth 100 l. from its library, as well as the abbey's seal, which they proceeded to misuse to issue documents in their own favour in that year. Mainwaring was a member, it seems, of the prominent, if turbulent, gentry family of Mainwaring of Over Peover (Ches.).[98] This lawless scion of the gentry was allegedly using a gang of outlaws to terrorise the monks and their servants, 'menacing . . . them with decapitation, or dismemberment' (*decollier ou de trenchier en peces*), unless he was granted an annual pension for life, and a lump sum cash payment. He was already, they claimed, holding some of the abbey's lands unjustly, and this latest demand for money was yet another form of extortion which demanded redress. The king took action – Mainwaring was to be arrested and brought before him and his council at Westminster by 3 May 1420.[99] We do not know the upshot. But Combermere continued to cause problems, and the internal condition of the already much-reduced and depleted house did not improve markedly before the sixteenth-century Dissolution.

Clerical rights and privileges, as well as property, could also be the subject of lay attack or interference, and of subsequent royal intervention. In September 1417, Henry was at 'our town of Caen' (Normandy), but

---

[97] For what follows see 'Houses of Cistercian Monks: the Abbey of Combermere', *VCH, County of Chester*, ed. C.R. Elvington & B.E. Harris (London, 1980), iii, pp. 150–6.

[98] For their behaviour, and for the Cheshire gentry generally at this time, see P. Morgan, *War and Society in Medieval Cheshire, 1277–1403* (Manchester, 1987), pp. 21, 62–96 & his 'Gentry Households in Fifteenth-century Cheshire', *BJRL*, 79 (1997), pp. 21–6; also J.T. Driver, 'The Mainwarings of Over Peover: a Cheshire Family in the Fifteenth and Sixteenth Centuries', *Journal of the Chester Archaeological Society*, 57 (1970–1), pp. 27–40.

[99] E 28/33, no. 35: endorsed 'Le roy a grante la lettre que le dit Meynwaryng soit devers lui et son conseil', 26 Mar. & 3 May 1420.

received, and replied to, a 'supplication of grievous complaint' from the prior and convent of Bath abbey against the activities of the townsmen there. The king had been informed that, in time past, the usage and custom in the town had been that the priory bells were always rung before those of the town. But the townsmen had recently begun to ignore this, and blatantly rang their bells 'to the great disadvantage and prejudice of the aforesaid prior and convent'. The king's response was characteristically judicious and even-handed. If it was the case that the townsmen had so acted, they were to cease from their 'willful' behaviour and observe the ancient custom until the king returned 'into our realm of England, so that we may have full knowledge of the matter, and ordain such remedy for it as we shall then be advised by way of truth and of right'.[100] The promotion of the 'way of truth and right' and that of 'law, conscience and reason',[101] meted out to cleric and layman alike, was one of the means whereby Henry gained his impressive reputation among contemporaries for fairness and justice.

The assiduous attention paid by the king to the petitions he received from the clergy (and the laity) was, however, sometimes accompanied by a note of impatience and even irritation with his officers 'on the ground'. In July 1419, writing from Mantes, he told Chancellor Langley, bishop of Durham, in no uncertain terms, that the prior of 'our house of St Bartholomew [the Great] in West Smithfield, London', adjoining St Bartholomew's hospital, had been seeking 'on this side of the sea' (that is, in France), confirmation of all the 'gifts, grants, privileges, franchises and liberties granted . . . by our progenitors and predecessors' to that house. But Langley had not, 'by virtue of your office', taken the initiative and issued the necessary letters. The king thus demanded to know why he had been 'pursued' in this way and supposed that 'there is some reasonable cause why you have

---

[100] SC 1/43, no. 157: at Caen, 24 Sept. 1417: 'ynto oure realme of Englond, that we may have ful knowloche of ye matere, and to ordeine such remedie theruppon as we shal be than avised by way of trouthe and of right'.

[101] See SC 1/43, no. 160. See *Anthology of Chancery English,* ed. Fisher, Richardson & Fisher, text no. 73.

not done it'. If so, he demanded to know what it was; if not, the necessary letters of confirmation were to be issued in due form.[102] When acting in his role as a royal servant, and as the head of a great department of state, the prince-bishop of Durham was held directly accountable to a demanding taskmaster. Henry's abruptness of style and manner was well represented in some of his responses to petitions, and in his instructions to those who were to implement his actions. Matters were to be settled so that he heard no more of them. His reply to a petition from his 'poor chaplain and beseecher' John Morris, vicar of Hembury (Worcs.) carried the endorsement: 'the king wishes that this be done so that there is no complaint outstanding'.[103] Similar responses are found on many of the supplications presented to him. But, irritated – even angered – or not, he discharged the duty of receiving and adjudicating such requests with conscientious assiduity. It was an essential facet of the public obligations of kingship.

The relationship between the 'public' and the 'private' spheres inhabited by later medieval rulers was not, however, always demarcated by strict boundaries. This was certainly so in the case of their interactions with the Church. Henry V's behaviour in this respect was perhaps especially distinguished by his concept of 'public' piety as expressive and reflective of inward, private spirituality. His exercise of a 'disciplined conscience' informed many of his public acts towards the Church, the clergy and those laypeople who were ill-disposed – and sometimes violent – in their attitudes and behaviour towards it. No one was to be left in any doubt as to the king's desire not only to 'encompass what could promote the honour of God . . . and the extension of the Church',[104] but to engage in its reform. His personal piety was not essentially unlike that of many contemporary laymen and laywomen in the upper ranks of society. But it evidently went beyond such conventional limits as the patronage of the more austere religious orders or the promotion

---

[102] C 81/1365, no. 10: under the signet, at Mantes, 22 July 1419.
[103] E 28/36, no. 13: 14 Dec. 1421: 'the king wol this be doo[n] so ther be no plet hangyng'.
[104] *Gesta*, p. 3.

of literate and well-educated clergy to higher positions within the English Church. At a time of schism and disorder within Western Christendom, Henry's efforts to bring about institutional reform and spiritual reawakening were persistent and untiring. The warrior-king was therefore also fighting battles of a less material and less physical kind. His conception of his role required him to 'reason in divinity'[105] as well as to wield the temporal sword against his own enemies, and against those whom he saw as enemies of the true faith. Furthermore, the expansion of his territories overseas was not only part of a purely secular process; protection and patronage of churches were part and parcel of his conception of a Lancastrian continental empire. The power relations which all of these aims and ambitions, both at home and abroad, created need now to be examined.

[105] See above, pp. 126–7, 129.

Chapter 5

THE KING AND THE CHURCH II

PREROGATIVE, POWER AND THE PAPACY

We have already seen the extent to which relations between England and the papacy under Henry V were to a considerable degree determined and shaped by the operation of legislation concerning provisions to English benefices, and the prevention of appeals to Rome.[1] It can be argued that Pope Martin V, although he may not have had a very clearly formulated programme or policy, sought every opportunity to campaign for the abolition of this legislation, by persuasion, inducement or coercion. He was wont to refer to this campaign as the defence of 'ecclesiastical liberty'.[2] But there were substantial obstacles strewn across the road. Above all, there was Henry V. To what extent, in his opposition to the pope, was Henry assuming the role of 'governor', if not 'head', of the Church in England? In Henry Chichele, archbishop of Canterbury (appointed in 1414) he had an able and effective coadjutor in Anglo-papal relations. But

---

[1] See above, pp. 135–8. Also M. Harvey, 'Martin V and Henry V', *Archivum Historiae Pontificiae*, 24 (1986), pp. 49–61, 68–70. Traffic in business of all kinds between England and the papal curia at this time is examined in E. F. Jacob, 'To and from the Court of Rome in the Early Fifteenth Century' in his *Essays in Later Medieval History* (Manchester, 1968), pp. 58–78.

[2] See M. Harvey, *England, Rome and the Papacy, 1417–1464: the Study of a Relationship* (Manchester, 1993), p. 132.

Henry was usually careful to respect the rights and privileges of the see of Canterbury and of Chichele's metropolitan status.[3] Those rights and privileges, after all, enshrined the liberties of the English Church and its freedom from unwanted external (or indeed internal) interference. So, when Martin V conferred a cardinal's hat on Henry Beaufort, bishop of Winchester, in 1417, Henry forbade Beaufort to accept it.[4] The papal bull creating him cardinal-legate was impounded by the king, Beaufort was threatened with loss of his bishopric, and he in effect went into exile from England for well over a year.[5] The king was concerned, as was Chichele, that Beaufort's legatine authority, conferred by the red hat, would reduce that of the archbishop over the English Church. It might also, by extension, threaten the authority of secular government, especially in ecclesiastical matters. As McFarlane points out, Henry V 'wanted an English envoy at the papal court, not a papal envoy at the English court'.[6] If, as was indeed the case, Beaufort persuaded the pope to allow him to retain, for life, the bishopric of Winchester (their current sees were normally resigned by cardinals on their elevation), there would certainly be a papal agent within the king's own council and Parliament. Such sentiments were well, if partisanly, expressed at a later date (1440) by Henry's brother, Humphrey of Gloucester, to Henry VI, when he told the young king that Beaufort

[t]ook upon himself the state of cardinal, which was gainsaid and denied him by the king, of most blessed memory, my lord your father [Henry V] . . . who said that he would rather renounce his crown than see him [Beaufort] wear a cardinal's hat . . . for he knew full well that

[3] See R.G. Davies, 'Martin V and the English Episcopate', *EHR*, 92 (1977), pp. 310–12, 315.
[4] The best discussion of the affair remains McFarlane, 'Henry V, Bishop Beaufort and the Red Hat' in *England in the Fifteenth Century*, pp. 85–90.
[5] A (very damaged) copy of the bull is in BL, MS Cotton Tiberius B VI, fos 61r–v (dated 18 Dec. 1417). Chichele set out his objections to Beaufort's elevation in a letter to Henry in BL, Add. MS 27,402, fos 19–20 (6 Mar. 1418).
[6] K.B. McFarlane, 'Henry V, Bishop Beaufort and the Red Hat, 1417–1421' in *England in the Fifteenth Century Collected Essays*, ed. G.L. Harriss (London, 1981), p. 86.

the pride and ambition that was in him, when he was only a bishop, would have lifted him up all the more into quite intolerable pride . . . if he was a cardinal . . .[7]

Gloucester reiterated Henry V's views on Beaufort's legatine status, observing that the king considered the cardinalate to be contrary to the 'freedom of the chief church [i.e. Canterbury] of this realm which he [Henry V] worshipped duly, as ever did prince'; he would never have agreed to 'have had certain clerks of this land cardinals, they having no bishoprics in England'; and he would never have intended to insult Chichele's authority by making '[t]hem that were his suffragans . . . sit above their ordinary [superior] and metropolitan'.[8]

The pope was thus powerless to override the king's wishes, expressed with a firmness and intransigence which said a great deal about power relations in the aftermath of the Schism. Since at least the reign of Philip the Fair of France (1285–1314) it is possible to plot the emergence of 'national' churches in Europe, whose clergy were as, if not more, bound by obedience to their king as to the pope. England was no exception. If there was, in France, already a form of 'Gallicanism' (the theory and, increasingly, the reality of a Church which claimed to conduct its own affairs, in effect under the crown's direction), then a kind of 'Anglicanism' might be detected under Henry V. The Schism had, in 1398, led to the temporary

---

[7] *L & P*, ed. Stevenson, 2.ii, p. 441 from Bod. Lib., Ashmole MS 856, fo. 392. Beaufort 'toke upon him the state of cardinal, which was nayed and denyed him by the kyng of moost blessed memory, my lord your fadre . . . saying that he had as leef sette his coroune biside hym, as to se him were a cardinals hatte . . . for he knewe ful wele the pride and ambicion that was in his personne, thane being but a bishop, shulde so gretly have extolled hym more into thintollerable pride . . . [if] he was cardinal'. The document is a polemic in Gloucester's defence.

[8] *L & P*, 2.ii., p. 441. Gloucester also stated that Henry's reasoning behind the refusal of the red hat was that 'in general counsailles and in alle maters that might concerne the wele of hym and of his royaume, he shulde have promoters of his nacione, as alle other Cristen kynges had, in the courte of Rome, and not to abide in this lande as eny part of youre counsaille, as be alle other lords spirituell and temporell at the parlements and greet counsailles, whan your liste is to calle hem' (pp. 441–2).

withdrawal of the French Church from all papal obedience. It could be argued that the Provisors and Praemunire statutes were a step in a similar direction, whereby the influence of the papacy might be very greatly reduced, if not ruled out altogether. The subsequent agreement of 1377[9] between king and pope formed the basis of what was in effect a concordat between the two powers, not entirely dissimilar to the subsequent Pragmatic Sanction of Bourges (1438) which finally formalised the legitimacy of a Gallican Church in France. It would be difficult to argue that, at least under Henry V, the English crown did not have the upper hand.

The practice of papal provision could create conflict, moreover, not only between ecclesiastical and lay powers, but among the clergy themselves. A particularly striking case broke out in 1414 within the English Cistercian order. Thus Roger Frank, claiming to be 'rightful abbot of Fountains', the Yorkshire Cistercian house (whose first abbot was elected in 1132), supplicated that although he had been elected abbot (in 1410) according to the order's statutes, and had held the abbacy for three years, he had been ousted by a papal bull in favour of, and purchased by, John Ripon.[10] In his petition, which was referred from the Parliamentary Commons to the king, Frank claimed that the papal bull was 'prejudicial to the king, his crown, and to the statutes made in this Parliament, to the destruction of free elections and the great diminution [*amentissement*]' of the suppliant, his house and order, and the kingdom.[11] His rival for the abbacy, Ripon, 'present abbot of Fountains', also petitioned for redress, and had appeared in person before the king, alleging that Frank and his supporters had attempted to usurp his position and had removed certain ornaments, and other goods and chattels, from the abbey.[12]

---

[9] See above, pp. 136–7.

[10] The case is described, in detail, as 'perhaps the most distressing and contentious of election disputes in the English houses', in E.F. Jacob, 'One of Swan's Cases: the Disputed Election at Fountains Abbey, 1410–16' in his *Essays in Later Medieval History* (Manchester, 1968), pp. 79–96 and briefly alluded to in 'Houses of Cistercian Monks: Fountains', *VCH, York*, iii, pp. 134–8.

[11] SC 8/23, no. 1124 for Frank's petition; also *RP*, iv, p. 27b.

[12] SC 8/23, no. 1125 for Ripon's petition.

Although there was a case pending at the court of King's Bench, Ripon claimed that Frank was planning to murder him, or at least intimidate him by violent means. Accordingly, he claimed, before noon on Sunday 6 May (1414), on the high road at the far end of Welbeck deer park (Notts.), Frank's brother, cousin and many others, 'armed and arrayed for war', had lain in wait to ambush and kill or maim him. They shot arrows, some of them barbed, at him and his company, wounding him in the arm, where the arrowhead had remained lodged. His servants were also wounded, variously in the arm, hand, thigh and head. Such a severe disturbance of the king's peace demanded remedy, and Ripon begged consideration of the 'horrible deed', requesting the king, in Parliament, to provide redress. The king's reply was circumspect and procedurally correct. As a case was pending before his justice, both parties were to wait until the end of the trial – in Ripon's case, the king thought that he 'had sufficient remedy through the common law'. Ripon was eventually confirmed in his benefice, but not before numerous alleged chicaneries and underhand intrigues – compounded by the crisis of authority within the Church occasioned by the Schism – had taken place.[13] Henry, given the importance of the case, had finally referred the matter to his envoys at the council of Constance.[14] There could, however, in the first instance, be no plea of benefit of clergy, whereby complete clerical exemption from lay jurisdiction could be claimed. In the event, the king had withdrawn the case from the court of King's Bench, and ultimately referred it to 'a conference of secular and ecclesiastical jurists' for resolution.[15] But

---

[13] The problems posed to English monasteries by the Schism are set out in R. Graham, 'The Great Schism and the English Monasteries of the Cistercian Order', *EHR*, 44 (1929), pp. 373–87. The dispute at Fountains had been preceded by earlier conflicts, particularly at Meaux and Beaulieu.

[14] Jacob, 'One of Swan's Cases', pp. 81–2, 84–8, 94–6 and p. 97 for Henry's letter to them. Ripon was not, apparently, deposed or replaced, as he lived on as abbot of Fountains until his death in Mar. 1434. *VCH, York*, iii, p. 136. Henry required the case to be settled for 'the greater quietude of our mind', as he had been constantly and incessantly assailed by representations from both parties: Jacob, 'One of Swan's Cases', p. 97.

[15] Jacob, 'One of Swan's Cases', pp. 87–8.

rival abbots involved in lethal feuds were, in these matters, subject to the same, secular common law as their lay contemporaries and peers. That they were clergy, of relatively high rank, made no difference. And it was abundantly clear to litigants in matters relating to benefices in the English Church that the court in which to pursue their suits was not the court of Rome but that of the King's Bench in England. The king normally had the upper hand when his jurisdiction in these matters was pitted against that of the papacy.[16] But, for the king and many of his advisers, reform – especially of the monastic orders – had in some form to come, and if the Church itself was unable to achieve it, then the secular power should step in.

Many factors influenced and determined the choice of candidates for positions within the later medieval Church. Spiritual and pastoral considerations did not necessarily constitute any part of those decisions. This was the case throughout the Middle Ages – and into later periods. Clergy were clerks, in the most literal sense, and their literate and other skills, such as diplomacy, plus their schooling in law, rhetoric, accountability and the arts of persuasion, qualified them for positions in secular government, bureaucracy and administration. The king claimed rights, including the so-called *regalia*, to nominate and present to benefices; to deliver their temporalities to bishops and other prelates; and to appoint to positions within religious houses. Many of these functions formed part of the 'routine' business of government, although the king's (and his clerical counsellors') choices could clearly be significant, both for the cure of souls and for the conduct of both ecclesiastical and secular business. The common and time-honoured practice of allocating vacant benefices in the king's gift to chaplains and clerks of the royal chapel, thereby providing them with a living – although they might reside at Westminster or Windsor – was continued by Henry V.[17] Clerks and other officials in the administration would also

---

[16] For some examples, see Jacob, 'To and from the Court of Rome', p. 69.
[17] See C 81/1364, no. 38: under the signet, at Caen, 25 Sept. 1417; no. 54: 19 May 1418.

receive benefices and prebends, sometimes in the king's gift as a result of the vacancy of a bishopric, during which the temporalities of the see fell into the king's hands.[18] Similar provision was made for clerks of the king's chapel, including the choral establishment, to be appointed to prebends in royal free chapels or 'peculiars', such as that made to Thomas Gyles 'clerc of oure chapel' to the 'free chapel of Hastynges' in July 1419.[19] The costs, including the wages bill, not only of the royal chapel, but also of the royal bureaucracy were thus, in part, being met by income from the Church.

Sometimes the king intervened personally to grant a living to a favoured member of the royal household, or a royal servant, or to one of their kinsmen. Thus, in September 1420, while besieging Melun, Henry instructed the Chancellor to ratify and confirm the award of the prebend of 'Hondesoon' in Lichfield Cathedral, by the previous bishop's vicar-general, to Robert Fitzhugh, son of Henry, Lord Fitzhugh, the king's chamberlain. As the previous bishop had died before Fitzhugh was installed in the prebend, the position fell into the king's gift as part of the temporalities of the see, and so Henry scrupulously insisted that due legal process be followed. The grant was ratified, as the king intended Fitzhugh to have it unless anything to the contrary had previously been done under the king's seal.[20] Benefices in the king's gift were plentiful enough for them to supply livings to many clerical royal servants: in October 1420, for instance, Queen Catherine's doctor ('hir phisicien'), clearly in Holy Orders, was recommended by Henry, after the queen had spoken to the Chancellor, for a benefice without cure of souls, when a suitable position became available.[21]

[18] C 81/1364, nos 39, 40: grant of a prebend at Chichester to Robert Shirington, clerk of the signet office, under the signet, at Caen, 30 Sept. & at Alençon, 2 Nov. 1417; also no. 47: grant to Nicholas Wymbish 'clerc of our petit bagge' of a Chichester prebend, for the same reason; signet, at Bayeux, 22 Mar. 1418.

[19] C 81/1365, no. 11: 25 July 1419; also no. 16 for similar grants of pensions in cathedral churches to king's clerks, 10 Apr. 1420.

[20] C 81/1365, no. 23: 30 Sept. 1420.

[21] C 81/1365, no. 25: at the siege of Meaux, 29 Oct. 1420.

John Snell, the king's almoner, also benefited from this kind of patronage when, in March 1422, he received the archdeaconry of London through the king's gift.[22] The salary bill to the Exchequer for bureaucrats, civil servants and professional men in royal service was thus considerably reduced – if they were clergy, even in minor orders; and in this, as in other respects, Church and State were symbiotic.

In the provisions which he made to benefices, masterships of colleges and hospitals, prebends and other livings in the Church, the king did not always act solely on his own initiative. Advice might be sought from senior clergy, and sometimes bishops themselves might seek his approval of clerks they wished him to favour. Hence in November 1420, Richard Fleming, bishop of Lincoln, writing from 'near Stamford', requested that the prebend of Buckingham in the cathedral church at Lincoln be granted to Master Robert Gilbert, 'your well-beloved clerk'. Fleming, though a distinguished conciliarist and theologian, described himself (somewhat obsequiously, or perhaps simply with befitting modesty) as 'your lowliest liegeman and chaplain'. In a final flourish to his petition, in English rather than ecclesiastical Latin, Fleming uttered words of prayer for the king 'to whose highness, the Sovereign Prince of all princes grant ever-desired victories . . . and all manner of prosperity for the peace and ease of us all, your liegemen and servants'.[23] The endorsement of victory had been ordered by Chichele, when 25 October was declared a day of general celebration, together with the feasts of St John of Beverley, and SS Crispin and Crispinian, for the king's success 'at the battle of Agincourt . . . [where] a gracious victory was granted to the English'.[24] Such sentiments echoed those of the *Gesta Henrici*. Church and State were here at one in the pursuit of God-given victory, as well as peace and prosperity.

---

[22] C81/1365, no. 35: at the abbey of St Faron-les-Meaux, 8 Mar. 1422. Snell is found as king's almoner in May 1421 and held the office into the reign of Henry VI.
[23] E 28/33, no. 53: 9 Nov. 1420.
[24] *Foedera*, ix, p. 420: 16 Dec. 1416.

Henry's acts of patronage of this kind were, however – unlike some of those of his predecessors – not undertaken without some degree of scrupulousness. In June 1419, for example, his conscience – or so he tells us – was much exercised over the grant of the hospital of St Anthony, a royal free chapel in the parish of St Benet Fink, in the city of London, to one of his clerical servants, William Kynwolmersh.[25] Kynwolmersh was an Exchequer clerk, who had begun his career in the lowly office of cofferer, moving upwards as under-treasurer and clerk of the Receipt in 1417.[26] The mastership, or wardenship, of the hospital was in the king's gift, but he was troubled with 'a manner of doubt' about the rightness of the grant. He wished to 'avoid the peril to [our] conscience that might result from our giving, and he [Kynwolmersh] receiving, the said hospital . . . unless the title was clear in law and conscience'. Hence Chancellor Langley was instead to issue letters patent granting Kynwolmersh the deanship of the church of St Mary le Strand, but demanding surety from him that he would resign the hospital at the king's command, should the gift be found to be invalid. The Chancellor was ordered to inform the king 'in all goodly haste' if that was the case, and Kynwolmersh would then be asked whether he wished to hold either the hospital or the deanship. He could not hold both. In the meantime, until the king's 'coming home' from France, he could nominally hold the hospital as well as the deanship, but was on no account to spend any of the hospital's revenues.[27] The degree of personal attention paid to this matter – apparently seen as one of private conscience as well as pragmatic, public patronage – seems entirely typical of the king. Personal control and concern for justice, especially when

---

[25] See 'Alien Houses: the Hospital of St Anthony', *VCH, County of London*, ed. W. Page (London, 1909), i, pp. 581–4; D.K. Maxwell, 'The Hospital of St Anthony, London', *Journal of Ecclesiastical History*, 44 (1993), pp. 119–223. The hospital had originally been founded as a cell of the brethren of St Anthony of Vienne, by 1254.

[26] J. Catto, 'The King's Servants' in *Henry V: the Practice of Kingship*, ed. G.L. Harriss (Oxford, 1985; 2nd edn Stroud, 1993), pp. 78–9.

[27] C 81/1365, no. 6: endorsed 'By ye kyng', signet, at Mantes, 20 June 1419. The king wished to 'eschewe ye peril in conscience that might be unto us by ye gevying, and to hym by ye rescevyng, of ye said hospital . . . onlasse than ye title wer clere yn lawe and conscience . . .'

dealing with those of humble or 'disadvantaged' status, along with scruple, and the lawful exercise of authority – these were among the hallmarks of the reign.[28]

The nature of 'conscience' and its exercise has recently attracted scholars in history, literature and law to the seventeenth century, which many see as the 'Age of Conscience'.[29] An impressive body of historical writing on the subject has emerged.[30] In much of it, the conflict between the 'peace of conscience' and the demands of political and religious allegiance appears to be a dominant theme. It has, for example, been argued that, in the case of Charles I, his conscience was the 'essence of his kingship'.[31] The king claimed that 'the best rule of policy . . . is to prefer the peace of conscience before the preservation of kingdoms'.[32] It is doubtful whether Henry V would have entirely shared that view. A peaceful conscience could be deemed a self-indulgent, self-centred luxury that might be incompatible with the demands and duties of kingship, or with the desirable unity of Church or State. Yet the notion was clearly often uppermost in the king's mind. Shakespeare was not mistaken when, from a different standpoint, he made play with the notion, giving Henry the words: 'May I with right and conscience make this claim?' when the issue of his title to the crown

---

[28] See J. Catto, 'The Burden and Conscience of Government in the Fifteenth Century', *TRHS*, 17 (2007), pp. 97–9 for Henry's 'disciplined conscience', of which this case may be an exemplification. Also see above, pp. 60–1, 138, 159.

[29] See Keith Thomas, 'Cases of Conscience in Seventeenth-century England' in *Public Duty and Private Conscience in Seventeeth-century England. Essays presented to G.E. Aylmer*, ed. J. Morrill, P. Slack & D. Woolf (Oxford, 1993), p. 30.

[30] See, among many examples, K. Sharpe, 'Private Conscience and Public Duty in the Writings of Charles I', *Historical Journal*, 40 (1997), pp. 643–5, and the essays by him and others in *Public Duty and Private Conscience*, ed. Morrill, Slack & Woolf; also, from a largely literary standpoint, *The Renaissance Conscience*, ed. H.E. Braun & E. Vallance (New York/Oxford, 2011); C. W. Slights, 'The Conscience of the King: Henry V and the Reformed Conscience', *Philological Quarterly*, 80 (2001), pp. 37–55; and from a legal angle, R.J. Delahunty, 'The Conscience of a King: Law, Religion and War in Shakespeare's *King Henry V*', *Journal of Catholic Legal Studies* (2014): University of St Thomas (Minnesota) Legal Studies Research paper no. 14–33.

[31] Sharpe, 'Private Conscience and Public Duty', p. 649.

[32] Sharpe, 'Private Conscience and Public Duty', p. 653.

of France was raised.[33] 'Right and conscience', 'reason and conscience' or 'law and conscience' were often coupled together in the king's utterances and his questionings – sometimes self-questionings – of many kinds of decision.

It was, moreover, in the fifteenth, rather than the seventeenth, century that such appeals to conscience began more often to appear. They also began to appear in a legal, and legalistic, context.[34] Such phrases as 'as reason and conscience demand'; 'by law and conscience'; or 'by law, conscience and reason' recur with increasing frequency in the sources. The formula 'in the forum of conscience' (*in foro consciencie*) was found, for example, in papal responses to supplications to permit the ordination of the illegitimate as priests.[35] In England, as a secular juristic principle, 'conscience' is first found (in connection with the court of Chancery) in 1391.[36] A definition is hard to find, but one legal historian considers that the term 'connoted what we now call the moral law as it applied to particular individuals for the avoidance of peril to the soul through mortal sin'.[37] This quasi-theological definition might well apply to Henry V's use of the term and his understanding of its meaning and implications. To 'eschewe ye peril in conscience' that might result from a certain action, as the king himself said,[38] appears to have something in common with the language of the confessional. It has, moreover, been claimed that the usage of conscience as a juristic principle eventually came to be incorporated into the practice of equity jurisdiction, especially by the court of Chancery. Its aim was 'to do right to God and man' and to see 'fairness, equivalency,

---

[33] *Henry V*, Act I, scene ii.

[34] For a survey of the recent legal literature on the subject see D.R. Klinck, *Conscience, Equity and the Court of Chancery in Early Modern England* (Farnham, 2010), esp. chapter 2.

[35] See Harvey, *England, Rome and the Papacy*, pp. 103–4.

[36] See J.L. Barton, 'Equity in the Medieval Common Law', in R.A. Newman (ed.), *Equity in the World's Legal Systems* (Brussels, 1973), pp. 139–55; & *RP*, iii, p. 297, nos 1 & 2.

[37] A.W.B. Simpson, *A History of the Common Law of Contract: the Rise of the Action of Assumpsit* (Oxford, 1975), p. 398.

[38] C 81/1365, no. 6 (20 June 1419).

honesty and good faith' preserved.[39] And this may not, in the case of Henry V, have been mere lip service. The cynicism of historians about the motives and objectives of the powerful has to be tempered by an admission, however grudging, that we have on occasion to take them at their word. And in Henry V's case, we have – in English – what sound very much like his actual spoken words, sometimes written out in his own hand.[40] There is a ring of authenticity and immediacy about his letters dictated under the signet that leaves little doubt of his qualities.

It was normal practice in medieval England for the ruler to grant possession of the 'temporalities' of bishoprics and abbacies to their new holders, even if their appointment had been made through papal provision. This meant that the lands and movable goods, and the secular rights and privileges of lordship – the 'temporalities' – accorded to, and exercised by, the higher clergy were to be held from the crown. When a see fell vacant, the king would appoint keepers or guardians of its temporalities until such time as a new incumbent was elected, was provided by the pope or nominated by himself. Thus, after the death of Archbishop Thomas Arundel, Henry appointed such keepers of the temporalities of the see of Canterbury in February 1414.[41] An oath of fealty to the king was required before 'livery' of the temporalities to the new appointee could take place, unless special exemption had been granted to him. One such exemption was made in January 1420, when Henry commanded the Chancellor to deliver the temporalities of the see of Carlisle to Roger Whelpdale, the bishop-elect, 'as soon as his bulls are issued, notwithstanding the fact that he has not performed homage for this to us'.[42] Another was made to William Heyworth, formerly abbot of St Albans, now bishop-elect of Coventry and

[39] T.S. Haskett, 'The Medieval English Court of Chancery', *Law and History Review*, 14 (1996), p. 311.

[40] See above, pp. 34–5, 78.

[41] *Foedera*, ix, p. 117.

[42] C 81/1365, no. 13: 21 Jan. 1420: 'as sone as his bulles bee written, not withstanding that he hath not made homage therefor to us'.

Lichfield, although he had not yet been consecrated there.[43] Thus, by normal process, in July 1420, Thomas Polton, Henry's proctor and agent at the council of Constance, was provided to the see of Hereford by the pope, Martin V. In September, Polton, described as 'our clerk' by the king, was required (as was the norm) to renounce any words in the terms of his provision to the bishopric which were 'prejudicial to our crown', and to take the fealty oath required for his temporalities.[44] But this was respited by the king until he came back to England, given the important services that he was performing for the king at the papal court.[45] Polton, although a papal providee, was not in the highest favour with the pope, and was soon (on 17 November 1421) translated to the less wealthy and prestigious see of Chichester. He had recently been created the first Chancellor of the reconquered duchy of Normandy by Henry.[46] He had been an opponent of Henry Beaufort at the papal curia, where he had made many enemies, and had in consequence incurred some degree of papal disfavour.[47]

Polton's predecessor at Hereford, Edmund Lacy, a particular favourite of Henry, had been translated by the pope to Exeter in July 1420, and underwent a similar obligation of renunciation and submission. Henry's order for the restoration of the temporalities of the see to him noted that he had 'in our presence, fully and expressly renounced all words prejudicial to us and our crown in the said [papal] bulls [of provision], and has humbly submitted to our grace'.[48] Henry normally insisted upon the performance of fealty and the required renunciations from his bishops before they could assume their

---

[43] C 81/1365, no. 18: 15 Apr. 1420.
[44] C 81/667, no. 951: 22 Sept. 1420.
[45] C 81/1365, no. 29: at Shrewsbury, 11 Mar. 1421.
[46] C 81/669, nos 1114, 1115: 21 Aug. 1421. Polton's career at the papal curia, and the somewhat chequered history of his preferments, are described in Harvey, *England, Rome and the Papacy*, esp. pp. 134–6; see also her entry 'Polton, Thomas (d.1433)' in *New Oxford DNB*. See also above, pp. 70–1, 133.
[47] See McFarlane, 'Henry V, Bishop Beaufort and the Red Hat', pp. 84–5; Davies, 'Martin V and the English Episcopate', pp. 311–12, 313. For Polton's role at Constance, see above, pp. 70–1, 133; also Harvey, *England, Rome and the Papacy*, pp. 132–8.
[48] C 81/668, no. 1039: 24 May 1421.

temporalities. Some were made to give guarantees that they would not attempt to interfere in their predecessor's affairs. Although translated from Bangor to St David's in December 1417, the new bishop – Benedict Nicholls – had still not received his temporalities in March 1418. His predecessor, Henry's confessor the Carmelite Stephen Patrington, had been translated from St David's to Chichester on 15 December 1417 but had died one week later. There was apparently scope for dispute over the receipt of revenue from the temporalities at St David's, which was taken up by Nicholls. The king was asked by his brother Bedford, as his lieutenant in England, to intervene in the dispute. He dismissed the question of any 'reparacions' that might be paid to Nicholls and told Bedford that Archbishop Chichele should 'do his duty' over the issue of reparation, as he had made no such agreement with Patrington when he (Chichele) had left St David's for the see of Canterbury in April 1414.[49] But the issue had not been completely resolved by May 1418, when the king wrote to the Chancellor that Nicholls 'has given surety in our chancery that he will never vex nor disturb the executors of the testament of his predecessor, our late confessor [Stephen Patrington]'. But, as Nicholls had not brought the relevant 'bulls of his translation' into Chancery, so that he might 'make a certain renunciation . . . in conservation of our Regalia', the restoration of temporalities had been postponed.[50]

It was thus imperative that the Statutes of Provisors and Praemunire should, as far as possible, be strictly observed in appointments to English bishoprics and abbacies. The stipulations demanding renunciation of any words or phrases susceptible of subverting or diminishing them were insisted upon – in all appointments – by Henry. He was clearly determined to be master in his own ecclesiastical as well as secular house. And

---

[49] SC 1/43, no. 158.

[50] C 81/1364, no. 53: signet, at Caen, 15 May 1418. Nicholls had 'founded seurte in oure chancellerie that he shal never vex ne inquiete thexecutours of ye testament of his last predecessor, that was our confessor . . .'

bishops could exercise little, if any, authority without possession of their temporalities.

A significant change in the position of the English crown as patron and protector of the Church took place as a result of the expansion of its overseas possessions under Henry V. From 1417 onwards, rights, duties and obligations were now exercised and discharged over the churches of Normandy and what has come to be known as Lancastrian France. The crown, by virtue of its coronation, and other, oaths, vowed to defend, protect and observe the liberties, privileges and immunities of the Church.[51] This duty could also be applied to churches within its continental European lands. With this obligation, however, came certain powers, including the possession and exercise of regalian rights over its clergy. A great cathedral or collegiate church might often be referred to as 'your church' by correspondents, supplicants and petitioners to the king. The *regalia* conferred quite extensive powers upon the sovereign. At perhaps the lowest level, the king could exercise 'by virtue of our regal prerogative, at the time of our coronation', the right to nominate candidates to places within religious houses. Thus, Henry, in May 1413, put forward his nominee as a novice nun at Shaftesbury abbey, by virtue of the rights inherited from his predecessors. He nominated Ideyne [Idonia]Wodehill, as he was informed that she has 'a firm purpose and desire to put aside the world and to serve God in the said abbey'.[52] This right was not confined to his English kingdom but was also exercised in his continental possessions, that is, in his long-held, inherited duchy of Aquitaine and in his conquered (or reconquered) duchy of Normandy. Thus, at the abbey of Sainte-Croix, Bordeaux, 'founded by our noble progenitors kings of England', the abbot and monks

---

[51] For Henry's self-presentation to his Norman subjects as their legitimate duke, restoring their liberties and immunities, see A. Curry, 'Lancastrian Normandy: the Jewel in the Crown' in *England and Normandy in the Middle Ages*, ed. D. Bates & A. Curry (London, 1994), pp. 239–52, esp. pp. 248–9.

[52] C 81/658, no. 26: 16 May 1413; *Foedera*, ix, p. 16.

were bound to provide a prebend for life to the king's nominee, who must be a man 'of good life and honest conversation'.[53] The exercise of such regalian rights was greatly extended after 1417, when Henry began the systematic conquest and reduction of the duchy of Normandy and those parts of northern and central France then in the hands of his dauphinist enemies.[54] This was to bring a large body of ecclesiastical patronage into his hands.

Henry's conquest of Normandy not only reversed the Norman conquest of England in 1066: it overturned the French conquest of Normandy from its duke, John, king of England, in 1204.[55] Henry's assumption of rights of patronage, presentation and nomination to benefices in Norman and French churches began in September 1417, as his war of conquest got under way. He also assumed duties of protection for those churches, especially in war zones and war-torn areas. The ordinances which he issued to his army, apparently at Mantes, between May and August 1419 imposed rigorous penalties, including sentence of death, on those who laid hands upon the 'sacrament of God's body' or stole the 'box or vessel' which housed the Host. Nor was any member of the army to rob or pillage the Church or, unless the churchman was armed, to kill or harm any churchman, monastic or otherwise.[56] Much of the business enrolled on the newly instituted Norman Rolls, moreover, related to ecclesiastical matters. On 4 September 1417, protections were granted to 118 members of the

---

[53] C 81/658, no. 36: 30 May 1413; also C 81/659, no. 120: 7 Nov. 1413.

[54] See C.T. Allmand, 'The Relations between the English Government, the Higher Clergy, and the Papacy in Normandy, 1417–1450' (University of Oxford D.Phil. thesis, 1963) which, regrettably, remains unpublished. For a brief summary of some of its conclusions see C.T. Allmand, *Lancastrian Normandy, 1415–1450. The History of a Medieval Occupation* (Oxford, 1983), pp. 218–23, and, more recently, Allmand, 'The English and the Church in Lancastrian Normandy' in *England and Normandy in the Middle Ages*, ed. D. Bates & A. Curry (London, 1994), pp. 288–97.

[55] The most recent general account of Henry's invasion and conquest is J. Barker, *Conquest. The English Kingdom of France* (London, 2009), chapters 1–4.

[56] See S. Bentley, *Excerpta historica* (London, 1831), p. 30: ordinances 'For Holy Churche'. See also below, pp. 266–7.

Norman parish clergy, together with members of the religious orders, including the monks of the long-established houses of Saint-Étienne, and the nuns of Holy Trinity, at Caen.[57] Further protections followed in October for Norman convents, including the Carthusians at Val-Dieu, near Feings.[58] At the end of October, the first of a long series of presentations and nominations to livings in Normandy began.[59] In November, the terms of protection to the collegiate church of Saint-Rémy, and that of Saint-Étienne at Silly-le-Guillaume (a lordship soon to be held by Sir John Fastolf – one model for Shakespeare's Falstaff) declared that they were now under Henry's allegiance, and none of their crops or possessions were to be taken 'against their wish, to our use or that of others'.[60] As Norman dioceses and religious houses submitted to Henry's allegiance, their temporalities were swiftly restored to them. The king would order the local secular officer of his administration to see that the temporalities were properly restored because he did not wish that 'divine service would be unsustainable there' as a result of the seizure of the temporal goods of the house.

Many of the Norman cathedrals and other churches, monasteries, hospitals and other religious establishments had, after all, been founded by Henry's ancestors, and he considered that he was simply restoring the status quo before the 'unjust disinheritance' of his predecessors by Philip Augustus (1180–1223) in 1204. In December 1417 and March 1418, he accordingly noted that houses such as those of Saint-Étienne or Holy Trinity at Caen 'were founded by our progenitors, former kings of England,

---

[57] *Foedera*, ix, p. 488.

[58] *Foedera*, ix, p. 501.

[59] *Foedera*, ix, p. 507; pp. 516–20 for further protections; Allmand, 'The English and the Church', pp. 291–4.

[60] *Foedera*, ix, p. 516: at Alençon castle, 23 Nov. 1417. Silly-le-Guillaume was granted by Bedford to Fastolf, with the title of 'baronis de Cyllyeguillem', in 1425, so that he could sustain his status as a knight banneret. It was reckoned to be worth 1,000 marks in time of peace. See K.B. McFarlane, 'The Investment of Sir John Fastolf's Profits of War', *TRHS*, 5th ser., 7 (1957), pp. 102, 106.

and are in our patronage'.[61] It was seen as the renewal of an older order rather than as usurpation of the regalian rights of the French crown. In January 1420, a series of confirmations by Henry of the charters and letters granting privileges, rights and immunities to Norman and French churches was begun. Many of these grants had been made by his own predecessors, as dukes of Normandy or as counts of Anjou, Maine and Touraine. On 3 January 1420, he confirmed the charters granted by the Empress Matilda, daughter of Henry I of England and Normandy (1100–35) to the Benedictine abbey of the Blessed Virgin Mary at La Noe – he confirmed in perpetuity the charters granted. A stream of ratifications followed, in which charters and letters issued by Henry I, Henry II (1154–89), Robert Curthose, duke of Normandy (1087–1106), Richard I (1189–99), and John (1199–1216), were inspected and confirmed.[62] He also confirmed charters deriving from the Capetian French monarchy – described, in some cases, as 'our progenitors' – as well as from Norman and French nobles, granting lands, revenues and privileges to the Church. The churches and religious houses of Normandy, and of those parts of northern France which fell to Henry's army, brought their most important archives, some in the form of original documents, some as copies registered in their cartularies, for personal inspection and confirmation by Henry and his agents. In March 1421, Henry issued a confirmation of grants made to the church of Laval-Guion which, as with others, he seems to have seen and inspected in person. His confirmation referred to 'a certain ancient writing . . . under the seal of Louis [IX], former king of the Franks [*Francorum regis*], our progenitor, as it appears, a transcript of which we have similarly seen in a certain old register, sealed with the seal of the *bailli* of Caen'. This confirmation, in turn, inspected a charter, in French, issued by Gui de Mauvezin,[63] dated 1269.

---

[61] *Foedera*, ix, pp. 525, 548.
[62] *Foedera*, ix, pp. 834ff.
[63] *Foedera*, x, p. 38: at Rouen castle, endorsed 'By the king', 12 Mar. 1421.

Some of these documents were not in the best of condition. A grant by Dreux, count of Amiens (*c*.980–1035), to the great Benedictine monastery at Jumièges, was found, with other charters of privileges, 'among some chirographs and ancient writings', without a seal and suffering from considerable wear and tear which rendered it, in parts, barely legible.[64] The vulnerability of the Church, especially in time of war, was graphically spelt out in some of these documents. In November 1420, Henry confirmed a charter of Philip (Augustus) of France, 'our progenitor', concerning the rights of the convent of Notre-Dame du Voeu, near Cherbourg, which included the assertion by Philip that the house's charters 'at the time of the war between us and the English, were burnt by those English, when they set fire to the same monastery'.[65] On the other side, as it were, the depredations suffered by the Church at the hands of the French were also chronicled in these documents. In August 1422, a bundle of grants to Rouen cathedral was confirmed, one of which was a letter of Richard the Lionheart, dated at Rouen, in September 1194, designed to remedy 'the losses and damages inflicted by our lord Philip, king of France, on the archbishop and church of Rouen, in time of war between us and the aforesaid king'.[66] In similar vein, in December 1420, Henry himself had noted, when confirming grants by his Angevin predecessors (Henry II, Richard I and John) to the convent of Grandmont, in the forest of Beaumont le Roger, that 'the originals, through the misfortunes of war, have perished and are lost'. But the king expressed himself satisfied that 'such charters and letters did exist from ancient time' and thus he had had them newly drawn up 'in due form and in new writing', sealed with *his* seal, so that their 'validity and memory' should never be lost. He had hence

---

[64] *Foedera*, ix, p. 872: confirmation by Henry V, at Rouen castle, 28 Mar. 1420.

[65] *Foedera*, x, p. 21. The events alluded to must date from the mid-1190s to 1204. For the Anglo-French campaigns at that time see F.M. Powicke, *The Loss of Normandy* (2nd edn Manchester, 1960), pp. 94–126, 148–64.

[66] *Foedera*, x, p. 236: 15 Aug. 1422. For the events of 1194, see Powicke, *The Loss of Normandy*, pp. 97–110.

reissued the charters under the styles and titles of his predecessors.[67] This demonstrated a quite exceptional attention to detail, and an awareness of the significance of – often ancient – grants and concessions without which the Church could not survive. It may also betoken a resolve not to allow his war, as far as he was ever able, to wreak further destruction on the recorded memory of the Church, as it was vital to its mission of prayer, praise and propitiation.

The confirmations, restitutions and protections did not, however, always come without some quid pro quo or obligation. Oaths of homage and fealty, as elsewhere, were demanded for the continued tenure by the Norman clergy of their lands and worldly possessions:[68] in April 1418, for instance, Henry Beaufort, bishop of Winchester, together with his fellow bishops of Bath and Wells, Coventry and Lichfield, and the much-favoured Thomas Polton, dean of York, were empowered by the king to receive the oath for his temporalities from Jean Langret, bishop of Bayeux.[69] Sometimes, as well as a general stipulation that divine service be properly maintained, more specific prayer service could be demanded – as in March 1418, when Henry granted revenues at Caen to sustain three chaplains celebrating daily masses in the war-damaged parish church of Saint-Étienne. As a result of Henry's 'special devotion which we . . . have for the blessed Stephen', these chantry priests were to enjoy sufficient rents and other income to sustain and increase divine service, but were also to pray for the souls of Henry, his ancestors and all the faithful departed.[70] As the conquest rapidly advanced, a plethora of churches and monasteries at Caen, Bayeux, Sées, Falaise, Saint-Lô, Lessay, St Sauveur-le-Vicomte, Avranches, Lisieux, Mortagne, Louviers, Evreux, Bec-Hellouin, Coutances, Lauley, Cerisy, Rouen and Gournay received restitutions of temporalities, protections and confirmations of

[67] *Foedera*, x, p. 22: at Paris, 6 Dec. 1420.
[68] See Allmand, *Lancastrian Normandy*, pp. 218–20.
[69] *Foedera*, ix, p. 567: at Bayeux, 1 Apr. 1418.
[70] *Foedera*, ix, p. 548: at Bayeux, 3 Mar. 1418.

privileges.[71] There was therefore little or no incentive for the Norman higher- and middle-ranking clergy to defect to Henry's enemies – the dauphinist French – and his assiduous concern for their benefices, lands and privileges paid off well, not least in 1431, when they and their learned Parisian contemporaries conducted the trial of Joan of Arc.[72] Collaborators they may have been, but they were willing collaborators. Given the authority exercised by Henry and his Lancastrian successor over the Church, they knew that they owed their benefices, their incomes, the confirmation of their privileges, and those of their churches and livings, to his actions.

Henry's exercise of patronage over Norman churches and religious houses conferred very substantial powers on him. Presentations to benefices and nominations for prebends and canonries flowed freely, suggesting a degree of control over the Church perhaps even greater than in his English kingdom. The king was apparently prepared to allow papal appointment of suitable candidates to positions in the Norman Church, but adamantly refused to countenance them if they were hostile Frenchmen.[73] Benefices were filled as they became vacant, generally with Normans, occasionally with Englishmen. Hundreds of livings in the Church were confirmed, granted, exchanged and redistributed under his aegis. Names such as Manchon, Estivet, Tiphaine, Marguerie, Roussel and Alnwick, notoriously familiar from later events such as the interrogations and trial of Joan of Arc at Rouen in 1431, appeared among the direct recipients of Henry's Norman patronage.[74] In August 1418, Henry himself received further privileges and powers, to be

---

[71] See *Foedera*, ix, pp. 548–605, 618–23, 660, 676, 682, 715, 727, 757, 792, 802, for Henry's numerous acts in their favour between 3 Mar. 1418 and 25 Dec. 1419. Also Allmand, 'The English and the Church', pp. 289–91.

[72] See below, p. 263.

[73] See Harvey, *England, Rome and the Papacy*, p. 132.

[74] *Foedera*, x, pp. 17, 25, 53, 111, 171. For their part in the interrogations and trial procedure generally see *Procès de condemnation de Jeanne d'Arc*, ed. P. Doncoeur & Y. Lanhers, 3 vols (Paris, 1960, 1970–1); *La Minute française des interrogatoires de Jean la Pucelle*, ed. Doncoeur & Lanhers (Melun, 1956); and, for an English translation of extracts from the trials of both condemnation and rehabilitation, see C. Taylor (ed.), *Joan of Arc: La Pucelle* (Manchester, 2006).

exercised during his conquest, from the pope – Martin V – no doubt in recognition of, and gratitude for, Henry's advocacy of his candidacy. It has been observed that Martin 'owed his election and subsequent freedom of action to English influence and support'.[75] Like many other secular rulers and nobles, especially those whose lives demanded active, front-line military campaigning, Henry was licensed by the pope to maintain the structures and rhythms of both personal and public spiritual life. The demands of assiduous attention, at all hours, to the exigencies of government had also to be met. He was permitted to have two or more portable altars (*altaria portatilia*), or as many as might be required for 'the multitude of the faithful, coming together at any one time'. He was also granted the right to hear mass before dawn (a necessary accompaniment to soldiering, when marches and sorties could begin before daybreak); and to have mass celebrated in places under interdict and sentence of excommunication, where the church doors were closed and the church bells were silent. As was common and formulaic in such grants, the pope stated that 'because when our lord Jesus Christ, the son of God, who is the dazzling whiteness of eternal light, is sacrificed [*immoletur*] in the rite at the altar [i.e. the mass], it is fitting that it should be done not in the darkness of night, but in the light'.[76]

The pope made two further concessions to Henry at this time: first, he could transfer relics from cathedrals and other churches in the duchy of Normandy, 'and in other French regions at present subject to you, or to become subject to you at a future date', to other churches and 'sacred places' for their better (and perhaps safer) veneration. Secondly, the dean of Henry's chapel and his deputies were licensed to hear the king's confession and those of his army, when he was, the pope decreed, with his army, in camp, or at a siege, 'during a just war or battle'.[77] Divine service was to

---

[75] See Davies, 'Martin V and the English Episcopate', p. 313.

[76] *Foedera*, ix, p. 615: 18 Aug. 1418. For earlier examples of such papal grants, or indults, and their origins see Vale, *The Princely Court*, pp. 221–2, 231–2.

[77] *Foedera*, ix, p. 616.

be maintained and celebrated constantly throughout Henry's campaigns. The Norman priest Raoul le Gay, after his capture by English soldiery at the siege of Harfleur in September 1415, praised the quality of liturgical practice in the king's entourage. He told his French interrogators (in April 1416) that he had been put into the custody of Richard Courtenay, bishop of Norwich, and had been taken from Courtenay's tent to 'the king's chapel . . . and he heard the singers of the king's chapel, who performed, or so it seemed to him, a beautiful service'.[78] The spiritual lives of the king and his men when on campaign were thus not to be neglected. The regular celebration of the Eucharist, the hearing of confession, the imposition of penance, and the granting of absolution were in no way to be impeded by the disruptive business of war.

To the roles of patron and protector of the Church in his newly acquired (or reacquired) lands in France, Henry added that of reformer and disciplinarian. In this he differed from his predecessors largely in the degree to which reform engaged his personal attention and commitment. From April 1419 onwards, simultaneously with the instigation of inquiries into abuses within the English Church,[79] the king began a series of initiatives to tackle, above all, the problem of non-residence in the Norman and French Church. He ordered the bishops of Bayeux and Avranches, the archbishop of Rouen, and the deans of Coutances, Evreux and Lisieux to compel all holders of benefices in those parts of their dioceses currently outside Henry's obedience, to reside in them. They were to proceed by law against the recalcitrant. This was a draconian measure, designed to coerce beneficed clergy in areas of dauphinist allegiance, in effect, to acknowledge Henry's authority over the dioceses in which they held their livings.[80]

---

[78] Mirot, 'Le Procès de Maître Jean Fusoris. Episode des négociations anglo-français durant la Guerre de Cent Ans', *Mémoires de la Société de L'Histoire de Paris et de L'Île de France*, 27 (1900) p. 258. For the musical quality of Henry's chapel see below, chapter 6, pp. 208–12.

[79] See above, pp. 191–2

[80] *Foedera*, ix, p. 737: at Vernon castle, 24 Apr. 1419; Allmand, 'The English and the Church', pp. 292–5.

Further orders went out in March and July 1421, to all the Norman dioceses, which were now within Henry's conquest, compelling residence 'according to the institutes of canon law'.[81] But his spider's web did not end in his French lands – it extended across Europe to the papal curia and the Church councils. In February 1420, Henry appointed his representatives at Rome to receive oaths of fealty from all Norman and French clergy 'born under our lordship and power', and all those holding benefices in those places 'even if they are Italians, residing at present at the court of Rome, and wishing to enter into our obedience'. Lists and witnessed letters detailing the oaths were to be sent, all duly attested by notaries.[82] A similar process was to be followed throughout Normandy itself when, in May 1422, Henry ordered all the Norman bishops to send lists of benefice-holders within their dioceses, and to assign them a date by which they were to swear their oaths. Some, he said, were 'vagrant and wandering' and had not taken the oath, and the bishops were to take the fruits of their benefices until they returned to them.[83] The desire for accurate records to be drawn up, by which individuals and corporate bodies could be held to account, was once again entirely typical of the king. Henry was very much exercised by questions relating to the loyalty and allegiance of the clergy. There was always a quid pro quo. Patron and protector of the Church though he was, he had no truck with ideas of benefit of clergy, if those notions were at the expense of the secular authority, and certainly none with the canon lawyers' theories of clerical exemption from taxation, especially war taxation. He would have been firmly on the side of Henry II against Thomas Becket; and on that of Philip the Fair of France against Pope Boniface VIII.

In order to perform their oaths of homage, fealty and allegiance to him – or, later, to the treaty of Troyes of May 1420 – Henry required the

---

[81] *Foedera*, x, p. 84: at Rouen castle, 16 Mar. 1421; p. 147: 28 July 1421.
[82] *Foedera*, ix, p. 864; Allmand, *Henry V* (London, 1992), pp. 191–8.
[83] *Foedera*, x, p. 209: at Rouen castle, 1 May 1422.

clergy to be resident in their benefices unless granted special exemptions by him. A series of orders went out, between April 1419 and the aftermath of the treaty of Troyes in 1420, insisting that the clergy of his newly conquered – or soon to be conquered – domains reside in their benefices 'for the increase and better performance of divine service' and so that their oaths of allegiance could be taken. In May 1419, he empowered Master Nicholas Habard to receive the fealty oaths of those clergy in the recently gained *bailliage* of Cotentin who could not 'on account of poverty and various infirmities' come to the king's presence for that purpose.[84] Exemptions were sometimes made: thus in September and October 1419, respites from residence requirements were granted to those Norman clerks who were studying at the University of Paris.[85] The predicament of Norman incumbents pursuing university courses away from their benefices, as Henry's conquest of the duchy surged on apace, was well illustrated by that of Thomas Parquelee, chaplain, bachelor in decretals (canon law), curate of the parish church of Saint-Vigor at Aunay-sur-Odon (in the diocese of Bayeux). He petitioned the king in April 1422, telling him that he had been a law student at the University of Orléans for six years and more. But, the king reported, 'when it came to his ears that he [Parquelee], with others, had been called to reside in his benefice, and to swear the oath owed to us', he left Orléans without delay 'coming towards us, and our duchy of Normandy, and to his said cure [of souls]; but, because of the dangers of the roads,[86] and other obstacles which he met with on his journey, he was unable to arrive within the time limits set'. Parquelee thus begged the king that he feared the loss of the title, possession and fruits of his benefice, and requested remedy. The king accepted his account and

---

[84] *Foedera*, ix, p. 755.

[85] *Foedera*, ix, pp. 799, 808.

[86] The dangers of the routes between England, Normandy and the papal curia, for example, could also delay and impede the conduct of diplomacy and other business, as safe conducts were not always observed. The kidnapping and ransoming of English envoys was not uncommon. See Harvey, *England, Rome and the Papacy*, pp. 84–5.

desired the bishop of Bayeux, if he found the case to be valid, to restore him to his living, with all its emoluments.[87] The war took its toll in many ways, of which the king was very conscious. Loss of clerical livelihood, if the case was genuine, tended to meet with a sympathetic response. But there were other quarters from which threats to clerical livelihood came. Disendowment of the institutional Church, and deprivation of the clergy's temporalities and incomes, was one theme (among many) in the chorus of dissenting voices that grew up in and around the so-called Wycliffite heresy of Lollardy, which now claims our attention.

It is not the aim of this chapter to rewrite the history of the English crown's reaction to the movement, or movements, for doctrinal, institutional and devotional reform known as Lollardy. That has been amply accomplished by others already. Henry V's responses, however, to the threats posed by Wycliffite beliefs form a crucial part of his more general stance towards the Church and its critics. He himself was more than aware of the deficiencies of the clergy: among them, non-residence, pluralism, non-observance of their rule by members of religious orders, and the setting of poor moral examples by priests and clerks, clearly exercised him. Yet at no time does he leave us with the suspicion that he was prepared to accept or endorse views and practices which in any way undermined the doctrines and tenets of the sacramental, hierarchical Church. On such issues as Eucharistic doctrine and practice, the fundamental and exclusive role of the priest in administering the sacraments, endowment of the Church, shrines, relics, processions, and all the elaborate apparatus of later medieval devotional religion, he remained steadfastly orthodox. But this did not make him a bigot, nor was he unprepared to attempt to convince dissenters of the error of their ways. It has recently been observed that 'only in matters of faith did he significantly outstrip his predecessors, but even this had its downside, especially for those whom he allowed to be

---

[87] *Foedera*, x, p. 202: at Rouen castle, 7 Apr. 1422.

burnt at the stake'.[88] But very few were in fact burnt at the stake during his reign. There were no mass-burnings, as there had, for example, been of southern French Cathars during the reign of the saintly Louis IX, with whom he may have shared some qualities. He was no Charles V (1516–56) or Philip II of Spain (1556–98), whose reigns were to witness a spate of heretic-burning on a virtually unprecedented scale, despite Henry's affinities with Philip as a 'most Christian and Catholic king' with ambitious, Escorial-like plans for a great palace-monastery by the Thames.

The materialisation of a threat, posed by religious dissidents, not only to the Church in England, but to the secular power, received its most public expression early in the reign. Although repressive legislation had been passed under Henry's father (including the statute *De haeretico comburendo*, On the burning of heretics) in 1401, Wycliffite beliefs and practices continued to make their presence felt in certain areas of the country, and retained some following not only among the common people, but among members of the knightly class and gentry. Sir John Oldcastle, with lands in the Welsh marches, was one such exponent of their views, and his rising in 1414 represented that merging of heresy and sedition that was to doom Lollardy to a largely covert existence, outlawed as a felony, until the Reformation. Paranoia there may have been among both the higher clergy and the secular authorities, and heresy was certainly sought and (on occasion) found after 1414. But the suppression of the Oldcastle rising under Henry V, and its aftermath, effectively eliminated Lollardy as a serious threat to both Church and State. There was to be no real English equivalent, in its upshot and effects, of the radical Hussite movement in contemporary Bohemia. The Hussite Reformation was to lead to the establishment of a Czech Church which was out of communion with Rome, and to a dissolution of the monasteries one century earlier than in the rest of Europe. In England, despite the close connections

---

[88] I. Mortimer, *1415: Henry V's Year of Glory* (London, 2010), p. 520.

between Lollardy and Hussitism, anti-clericalism and demands for reform of the Church did not result in a sustainable, and sustained, doctrinal heresy.

Henry was, therefore, well aware of the dangers posed to secular, as well as ecclesiastical power by the Lollard heresy, and of the imperative to combat it wherever it emerged.[89] In December 1421, his personal instructions, drafted by him in English, to his envoys to Sigismund and the German princes, were quite specific about the priorities they should insist on.[90] When seeking aid from Sigismund against Henry's dauphinist French enemies, they 'shall require of him that, regarding first of all the matter concerning the faith against the heretics and lollards of his realm of Bohemia, which is God's cause', the combat against that pernicious evil should be given pride of place. Sigismund, writing to Henry in July 1419, had already referred to his task of eradicating the error which had arisen in Bohemia 'commonly known there as [that] of *Wiklefisiss*' (Wycliffe).[91] As in England, 'God's cause' was the fight against 'heretics and lollards' and it is revealing that Henry bracketed the two heresies and their followers together, recognising the close similarities between them. So, he told his envoys, as long as 'no mischief' would follow as a result of Sigismund's absence from the campaign against the Hussites, he should be asked to

---

[89] For a recent, critical, account of the means whereby the 1414 rising was suppressed, in part by the denial of due legal process at common law to Lollard suspects, see M. Jurkowski, 'Henry V's Suppression of the Lollard Revolt' in *Henry V: New Interpretations*, ed. G. Dodd (Woodbridge, 2013), pp. 103–30. The treatment of suspected heretics in England was, however, a relatively novel process, and inquisitorial methods, as applied in continental Europe, did not fit easily into the procedures of the English common law. Lollardy was, in any case, equated with sedition and treason, thus permitting the secular authorities to act independently of ecclesiastical courts. They were now dealing with what was seen as a felony, but a felony which threatened the foundations of secular as well as spiritual authority. See M. Aston, 'Lollardy and Sedition, 1381–1431', *P & P* 17 (1960), pp. 1–44 (repr. in her *Lollards and Reformers. Images and Literacy in Late Medieval Religion* (London, 1984), pp. 1–47).

[90] C 47/30/9/12, fo. 1r (18 Dec. 1421). Negotiations with Sigismund had been in progress since at least July 1421, when Sir Walter Pole and Master John Stokes were sent to him to negotiate 'certain secret matters' and were paid further wages in October: E 403/651, mm. 13r, 14r; E 403/653, m. 1r; *Foedera*, x, p. 143.

[91] E 30/1065: Sigismund claimed that he was prepared to aid Henry with military support in France but had first to attend to events in Bohemia (at Hagenau, 17 July 1419).

offer support to Henry against *his* enemies.[92] To conduct an ongoing pursuit of heretics did not, again, necessarily make Henry a relentless, merciless bigot. He had tried, ultimately without success, to persuade Oldcastle, at great length, of the errors into which he had fallen. McFarlane's considered conclusion about Henry was that 'his faults arose from the excess of his qualities. That he was hard, domineering and quick to ruthless action can scarcely be denied . . . [but] his merciful treatment of the humble Lollards rebuts the charge of bigotry.'[93]

This view tends to be borne out by the surviving evidence for the king's direct, personal intervention in the pardoning of those accused of heresy. In July 1414, for example, he pardoned Thomas Mason, a mason, and John Lete, a smith, of Thurlaston (Leics.) who had been indicted 'for insurrection and making a coven [*covyne*]' of Lollards with Oldcastle. They were granted full pardon and were received into the king's peace, as they were already in the hands of the bishop's ordinaries (ecclesiastical law officers) for the 'correction' of their Lollardy.[94] Gains were also made by the crown as a result of Lollard forfeitures, increasing the scope for royal intervention in appointments to vacant benefices. In June 1417, Henry ordered Henry Beaufort, as bishop of Winchester, to provide a nominee to a vacant living at Worplesdon (Surrey) upon the resignation of the incumbent, now in the king's gift 'by reason of the forfeiture of John Oldcastle, who was lately said to be lord of Cobham'. Beaufort was to install John Russell, clerk, as rector in the benefice.[95] Confiscated Lollard goods could be used

---

[92] C 47/30/9/12, fo. 1r: 18 Dec. 1421. The envoys 'shul require him that, seen furst the mater touching the faith ayen[s]t the heretikes and lollardes of his Rewme of Boeme, the whiche is goddes cause' it should be prioritised.

[93] McFarlane, 'Henry V: a Personal Portrait', p. 131. But see, for a critique, M. Jurkowski, 'Henry V's Suppression of the Lollard Revolt' in *Henry V: New Interpretations,* ed. G. Dodd (Woodbridge, 2013), pp. 104–8, 127–30.

[94] C 81/660, nos 266, 268: 3 July 1414. After Oldcastle's final capture and execution in 1417, very few Lollards were burnt, and the great majority of suspects were absolved of their alleged crimes. This might be seen as evidence for the exercise of mercy by Henry, rather than for ruthless bigotry in the battle against Lollardy, but cf. Mortimer, *1415*, p. 547.

[95] C 81/666, no. 829: 11 June 1417.

to reward servants, as in a grant to John Barton, 'servant of our armoury', of all the goods and chattels of Thomas Drayton, parson of the church of Drayton Beauchamp (Bucks.) 'forfeited to us because the said Thomas is convicted of Lollardy' to the value of 200 marks.[96] A similar grant was made to Jordan de Worsley, king's chamber valet, of the goods of the resolutely heretical London baker Richard Gurmyn, convicted before the bishop of London, who was one of the last Lollards to be burnt at this time.[97] Oldcastle's Welsh marcher captors were very well rewarded: in May 1422, the heirs and executors of Edward, lord of Powys, were given the large sum of 1,200 marks by the king for their part in the tracking down and arrest of the renegade knight.[98] Prosecution of heresy by the crown could thus increase both its ecclesiastical patronage and its reservoir of resources to reward service, when the lands and possessions of both lay patrons and beneficed clergy were sequestrated for heresy.

There is also some evidence at this time for scenes of public disrespect for the Church's practices which, although no overtly Lollard involvement seems to have been present, nonetheless suggests a degree of alienation among the laity. In 1415 the abbot and convent at Westminster had petitioned Henry for remedy, on behalf of their 'servants and tenants' at Morden (Surrey).[99] They told the king that at Rogationtide (23–25 April) a year previously, the men and women of Morden had processed around their fields, 'as other of your lieges are accustomed to do in your kingdom at that time'. The major and minor Rogation days were set aside for solemn processions invoking God's mercy, especially by blessing of the crops and fields. They also provided an occasion for 'beating the bounds', whereby the boundaries of a parish could literally be paced out. On this occasion, however, the procession had been wrecked by the men of the neighbouring

---

[96] C 81/660, no. 293: 15 Aug. 1414.
[97] C 81/663, no. 592: 28 Jan. 1416; Mortimer, *1415*, pp. 334, 357–8, 547.
[98] E 403/655, m. 4r (20 May 1422).
[99] SC 8/188, no. 9369: undated, 1415.

village of Cheam (Surrey), who assaulted those of Morden, 'seized and took away their crosses and banners, and kept them for a year'. But the archbishop of Canterbury had recovered them, and he gave them back to the men of Morden so that they could perform the Rogationtide procession once more. Yet the ringleaders of the former assault, together with a colluding local justice of the peace, once again prevented their procession, menacing them and seizing all their animals, both on the abbot's demesne and on the common land, and driving the beasts off to Cheam. The Westminster abbot and monks thus begged the king 'for the salvation of the rights of your said church', to provide a remedy in the name of God and 'in reverence for St Edward'. There may have been no whiff of heresy in all this, and the issue may well have been one of disputed parish boundaries, but the brazen insult to the Church's liturgy and observances would no doubt have impressed the king. We have no record of his response to the petition – but it would be surprising if it was not favourable.

Disrespect for Holy Mother Church, in whatever form, could not be countenanced. But, even if scandals and abuses were no worse than in previous times, the era of the councils was one in which Church reform was very much in the air. The universal Church, wracked by schism, was deemed by prominent conciliarists, such as Jean Gerson, Nicholas de Clamanges and Pierre d'Ailly, to be more than ripe for a purging of the Augean stables.[100] The Church in England was no exception, and Henry urged his representatives at the council of Constance, and within the papal curia, to act. In April 1419, a series of *capitula* (articles of inquiry) for the reformation of abuses in the English Church was granted by Martin V.[101] At the pope's command, the articles, agreed at Constance between him and the representatives of the English nation there, were registered by the papal chancery. The English bishops were to undertake inquiries into

---

[100] For Clamanges and Gerson see Nicholas de Clamanges, *La Traité de la ruine de l'eglise*, ed. A. Coville (Paris, 1936); J.L. Connolly, *John Gerson, Reformer and Mystic* (Louvain, 1928).
[101] *Foedera*, ix, p. 730: at Florence, 17 Apr. 1419.

abuses within their respective dioceses, with powers to suspend those found wanting; stricter regulations on the appropriation of churches and their patronage were to be issued; and – perhaps most important of all – dispensations for non-residence were to be more strictly limited. Absenteeism from benefices was perhaps the most damaging of abuses, if the cure of souls was either neglected or placed, through the appointment of vicars, curates and chaplains, in unworthy, unlearned and incompetent hands. Bishops' visitations were now to include inquiries into clerical morals, a subject on which the king held strong views.[102]

He also held distinctly strict and rigorous views on the state of the regulars, that is, of the monastic clergy. As well as being a founder and protector of religious houses, Henry V was a monastic reformer. The state of some monasteries in early fifteenth-century England was clearly a subject for concern. Declining numbers of novices; an unwillingness of some lay patrons and donors to endow the older, well-established orders (Benedictines, Cistercians, Augustinians, Premonstratensians and so forth) within the Church; and a persistent questioning of the lifestyles followed in some houses all played into the hands of actual and potential reformers. The crown was particularly concerned for the health and welfare of the religious houses with which it had a close, traditional connection. In 1415, conditions at the priory of Amesbury, a dependant house of the double monastery (for both men and women) at Fontevrault in Anjou, closely linked to the Plantagenet dynasty, were giving cause for serious concern. There was a previous history, dating from 1398, of conflict and disturbance at the house.[103] The abbess of Fontevrault could not intervene effectively, owing to the Schism and the war

---

[102] See Davies, 'Martin V and the English Episcopate', pp. 313–15; Catto, 'Religious Change', pp. 103–4, 106, 110.

[103] See 'Houses of Benedictine Nuns: the Abbey, Later Priory, of Amesbury' in *VCH, County of Wiltshire*, ed. R.B. Pugh & E. Critall (London, 1956), iii, pp. 242–59 for an account of the troubled history of the convent at this time. For the state of nunneries, and their patronage by the laity, largely in the diocese of Norwich, see M. Oliva, *The Convent and the Community in Late Medieval England* (Woodbridge, 1998), pp. 76–81 and pp. 99–105 for irregularities and abuses.

with France, and the 'foreign' houses dependent upon the mother house tended to lack firm administration and discipline. Henry V had acted swiftly after his accession, ordering Henry Chichele, archbishop of Canterbury, to undertake a visitation and 'to amend the faults found there'. The prioress, the aristocratic Sybil Montagu (elected 1396; died 1420), daughter of John, Lord Montagu (d.1390), had been evicted from the house and was at war with its guardians. She was, she told Chichele, afraid to enter it.[104] Her petition led to the drafting of a memorandum, dated at Westminster on 7 February 1415, recording that the king, in the presence of Chichele, had granted her 'suitable sustenance for herself and her servants from the spiritual and temporal possessions belonging to the said priory of Amesbury' until the archbishop had performed his visitation and corrected the faults found in the house.[105] There is no evidence that these measures proved successful in reforming the house – at least, not until later in the century. But Henry had directly intervened once more, in September 1420 when, after the death of Sybil Montagu, he licensed the sub-prioress and convent at Amesbury to proceed to the election of a prioress as, by legislation, the temporalities of the house, as an alien priory, were in the king's hands in perpetuity.[106] But there is no evidence that matters had improved there to any great extent before Henry's death two years later. With problems on this scale afflicting religious houses traditionally associated with the English crown, it was perhaps hardly surprising that Henry V should choose to endow new, as yet pristine and uncorrupted, foundations. Sheen and Syon both reflected a trend, and set one.

That Henry, unlike some of his predecessors, did not endow a Benedictine monastery is significant. The order was experiencing a general decline in England, and lay patronage was falling away. In March 1421, Henry was asked to undertake a reform of the Benedictines in England. As in

[104] E 28/30, no. 102: undated, but probably late 1414 or early 1415.
[105] E 28/30, no. 103.
[106] *Foedera*, x, p. 19.

other cases within the Church, if the order itself could not (or would not) set its own house to rights, it was argued, the secular power should intervene. It is not known from whom the request came, but the chroniclers cite either 'false brethren' from within the order or Robert Layton, prior of Mount Grace, the Carthusian house in Yorkshire.[107] Layton had been a Benedictine before entering the Charterhouse, and may thus have had additional cause to act as chief accuser of the order. Whatever the case, the king acted with his customary vigour, insisting that a general chapter of the order in England be convened at Westminster on 5 or 7 May 1421. His letters, containing the summons, were not in the Latin usually employed in such missives to and from the clergy, but in English.[108] They were issued at Leicester under his signet of the eagle 'in the absence of our other [signet]', and the letter addressed to the 'presidents' of the order ran as follows:

> By the king.
>
> Trusty and well beloved in God. For certain weighty matters concerning the worship of God, as well as the good of your order, with His [God's] grace, we will and charge you directly that you all come together – not just the fathers, but also those who are clerks, and others who are notable persons, from every house of the same order – in as great a number as it is possible to assemble, in our abbey of Westminster, on the fifth day of May next coming. And see to it that none of the aforesaid [persons] be excused from the said assembly, without so reasonable and evident a cause that, by all reason, they should be exempt, and as you and they desire to avoid our indignation.[109]

---

[107] There is some doubt as to the identity of the prior of Mount Grace in 1421. Candidates are Robert Layton and Nicholas Love (Luff) (d.1424), but the latter may have left the office in 1417. See M. Sargent (ed.), *Nicholas Love. The Mirror of the Blessed Life of Jesus Christ* (Exeter, 2005), pp. 2–5.

[108] See *Documents illustrating the Activities of the General and Provincial Chapters of the English Black Monks, 1215–1540*, ed. W.A. Pantin, Camden 3rd ser., 47 (London, 1933), ii, pp. 104–5, nos 161, 163. Also above, chapter 3, pp. 93, 110, 117, 121, 168.

[109] 'Trusty and welbeloved in God. For certeyn [matiers] chargeable concernyng the worshipe of God, as wele as the goode of youre ordre, with his grace, we woll' and charge you stretly that ye

In his letter of summons to the abbot of Bury St Edmunds, also under the signet of the eagle, at Leicester, the king stressed that the proposed meeting 'shall do good and profit to all your order', demanding an urgent reply 'in all haste'.[110] Whether the king actually possessed the authority to command a religious order to convene such a gathering of its own members was more than a moot point. In his reply, the abbot of Bury respectfully told the king that the next general chapter of the order in England was not due to be held for another two years. In the meantime, he apparently referred the king to the order's 'presidents', namely the abbot of Winchcombe and the prior of Worcester, before he could agree to answer the summons.[111]

But the king's order was obeyed, providing striking testimony of the extent to which the secular power could now exercise authority over the Church within its domains.[112] The assembly gathered together sixty abbots and priors and over 300 Benedictine 'monks, doctors, and proctors' during sessions of Parliament and the clerical Convocation. The assembly took place, in fact, on 7 May. It was, apparently, addressed by the king himself

do come togydyr, not only the fathers, but also thoo that ben clerk[es], and othir that ben notables persones, in every house of the same ordre, in as grete nombre as is goodly possible to assemble, to our abbey of Westmon' the vijth day of May next commyng. And seith that no suche as is before seid be excused from the seid congregacion withouten' so reasonable and evident a cause that be all[e] reason it to be except', as ye and they desire to eschewe our indignacion. Yeven under oure signett of the egle, in absence of our other, at our towne of Leycestr', ye xxv day of Marche': TNA, E 135/1/2, fo. 1v: 25 Mar. 1421; see also, for another version, *Documents illustrating . . .*, ii, p. 105, no. 163; & BL, MS Cotton Titus C. IX, fo. 18.

[110] The abbot was warned not to delay, as 'we truste to God it shal do good and proffyt to al your [or]dre. And what yee do and wul do in this matere signifieth us in al haste . . .': *Documents illustrating . . .*, ii, p. 104, no. 161 (16 Mar. 1421); BL, Cotton MS Tiberius B. IX, fo. 195r (damaged).

[111] He asked the king to 'discharge me at this tyme', while he waited for further instructions, signing himself 'your preste [priest] and oratour ye abbote of Bury': *Documents illustrating . . .*, ii, pp. 104–5, no. 162 (at Bury, 20 Mar. 1421) & MS Cotton Tiberius B. IX, fo. 195v (damaged).

[112] On 1 Apr. 1421, the 'presidents' of the order, at Worcester, issued summonses, such as that to the prior of Durham cathedral priory, to attend the assembly, according to the 'royal mandate' directed to them: *Documents illustrating . . .*, ii, p. 106, no. 164 (1 Apr. 1421). Also TNA, E 135/1/2, fo. 2r for the presidents' letter to their 'special nuncio', William Nottingham, instructing him to send letters of summons to all those included on an enclosed list (1 Apr. 1421).

who, quite exceptionally for an English ruler, admonished the assembled religious. Having, according to the chronicler Walsingham, entered the chapter house 'sufficiently humbly', he sat down to hear a suitable oration by Edmund Lacy, bishop of Exeter, his representative. Lacy, speaking in Latin, set out 'many defects . . . and abuses within the said order, as he asserted, arising at that time, which gravely distressed the king's mind'.[113] When Lacy had finished, Henry himself addressed the gathered Benedictines. He spoke 'concerning the original observance of the monks . . . and concerning the negligence and lack of devotion of the "moderns" '.[114] He noted that his ancestors had valued the prayers of ascetic monks who lived a regular life, and had made their foundations and benefactions on that assumption and to that end. He was clearly aware of the quid pro quo implicit in such endowments and gifts, and of the expectation of gaining spiritual value from the investment of material capital. This was a theme which had been found in tracts and treatises, such as *Antequam essent clerici* (Before there were clergy), since the later thirteenth and early fourteenth centuries.[115]

A small reforming committee was established, which was to confer with the Benedictines on a list of thirteen articles, proposing reform but containing a series of relatively mild requirements.[116] These related to the residence of abbots, priors and monks; the stricter observance of the order's rules about meal-taking, and the prescribed single meal per day in winter;

---

[113] *Documents illustrating . . .*, ii, p. 107, no. 165 & TNA, E 135/1/2, fo. 1r.

[114] T. Walsingham (the St Alban's chronicler), *Historia anglicana*, ed. H.T. Riley (RS, London, 1864), ii, pp. 337–8, quoted in Knowles, *Religious Orders*, ii, p. 184.

[115] For the text of this anti-clerical (and anti-papal) tract, dating from 1296, see P. Dupuy, *Histoire du differend d'entre le pape Bonface VIII et Philippe le Bel* (Paris, 1655), 3e partie, pp. 21–3 &, for an English translation, R.W. Dyson (ed.), *Three Royalist Tracts* (Bristol, 1999), pp. 4–6. The tract is discussed, with other related literature of the same period, in J. Canning, *Ideas of Power in the Late Middle Ages, 1296–1417* (Cambridge, 2011), pp. 19–20.

[116] The committee comprised Edmund Lacy, bishop of Exeter; the prior of Mount Grace, presumably Robert Layton; and the keeper of the privy seal, John Stafford, dean of St Martin's-le-Grand: *Documents illustrating . . .*, ii, pp. 107–8, and for the 13 articles, pp. 109–15; also TNA, E 135/1/2, fos 2r–6v.

the prohibition of private apartments for distinguished monks, university doctors and scholars, and of separate houses and domestic establishments for abbots; the ending of money payments instead of liveries in clothing and other necessities; and the restriction of social visits.[117] But even these less than drastic recommendations met with objections from the monks on every count: what Knowles called 'a carefully devised and practical attack on recognized abuses'[118] was in effect rejected. The chronicler of Croyland Abbey, in his account of the Westminster chapter, simply reported, blandly, that the king was 'extremely gratified at having in his kingdom so great a multitude of educated men and graduates of the said order'.[119] Benedictine self-congratulation, rather than awareness of an urgent need for reform, was in evidence here. The proposals were thus greatly watered down. An anodyne document, drawn up largely by Abbot Whethamstede of St Albans,[120] was accepted at the subsequent Benedictine chapter, after Henry's death, in 1423. What might have happened had Henry V lived longer?

The significance of Henry V's reign in the history of the Church, and of religious observance, in England deserves to be emphasised. This has been recognised, on the whole, by historians. But it was also important for the Church in France, especially in Normandy, and – more generally – for the Church in Western Europe, at a time of great crisis and potential change. In English terms, the reign has been seen as a turning point when, from 1414 to the late eighteenth century, 'religion was established and enforced by public (i.e. secular) authority, and dissentient voices were subjected to the rigours of statutory felony'.[121] Reform of public worship,

---

[117] Knowles, *Religious Orders*, pp. 184–5; *Documents illustrating . . .*, ii, pp. 110–15.

[118] Knowles, *Religious Orders*, p. 184. For the Benedictines' criticisms of the king's articles see *Documents illustrating . . .*, ii, pp. 116–21, 121–5, nos 168, 169.

[119] *Ingulph's Chronicle of the Abbey of Croyland*, ed. H.T. Riley (London, 1904), pp. 389–90.

[120] *Documents illustrating . . .*, ii, pp. 125–34, no. 170 for the 'Final articles', agreed by the order.

[121] Catto, 'Religious Change', p. 97.

organised according to a common usage (the Use of Sarum), made for greater uniformity of devotional habit and liturgical practice. This may have presaged and prefigured the growth of the notion of a common national Prayer Book, a book of common, public prayer – in Latin in the fifteenth century; in English only in the sixteenth. Or would Henry's interest in the promotion of the English language have extended, had he lived longer, into the realm of public worship? Both clerical and lay spirituality were furthered by royal example, on the whole supported by compliant, co-operative and reforming bishops. As a source of authority, the king, it has been claimed, had in effect become 'supreme governor of the Church of England'.[122] On the international stage, the 'expanding Lancastrian empire',[123] as well as the important role played by the English 'nation' and Henry's representatives at the council of Constance, made him – and his kingdom – a force to be reckoned with in European ecclesiastical, as well as secular, politics. The ending of the Great Schism was not uninfluenced by the part played by the English and their ruler. And McFarlane, in his brilliant discussion of the denial by Henry V of a cardinal's hat to Henry Beaufort, came to the conclusion that 'in the fifteenth, as in the sixteenth century, the popular ruler of a nation state was more than a match for all the forces at the disposal of the universal church'.[124]

It was a further stage in a process which had begun in the late thirteenth and early fourteenth centuries. From that time onwards, the secular power began to exert a degree of control over the Church – including the papacy – that in some measure would redress and recover what had been lost in the preceding two centuries. There could never be another Gregory VII

---

[122] Catto, 'Religious Change', p. 115.

[123] McFarlane, 'Henry V, Bishop Beaufort and the Red Hat', p. 80: 'Martin was not the man to overlook the significance of the expanding Lancastrian empire'. Beaufort's commission as legate *a latere* in England also applied to the overseas possessions of the English crown.

[124] McFarlane, 'Henry V, Bishop Beaufort and the Red Hat', p. 112.

(1073–85) or Innocent III (1198–1216), the two great reforming, author-itarian popes of the Middle Ages. Henry V takes his place beside Philip the Fair of France as a secular ruler who, perhaps for higher-minded motives than Philip's, was determined that the Church's house should be set in order. But in his personal spiritual life and its outward expression, he may have had more in common with Philip's ancestor, Louis IX. And, like Louis, he was concerned for reform of the Church and for a reformation in its moral condition. As in so many aspects of later medieval religious thought and practice, if the clergy could not do the job themselves, the lay power would do it for them.

Where historians have been less confident, and less unanimous in their verdicts, lies in the extent to which they have seen Henry's direct, personal involvement in the affairs of the Church as critical. The scepticism with which Henry's level of personal involvement and initiative in the promo-tion of English has sometimes been greeted[125] is paralleled by doubts as to his part in influencing the condition, and life, of the Church. A tendency to play down or diminish the role of the individual is evident here. This chapter has, on the contrary, attempted to suggest that Henry's part was indeed both prominent and crucial. With varying degrees of success, in virtually every area of the Church's activity – from benefice-brokering to monastic reform, and from the repression of dissent to the cultivation of inward spirituality – he was not slow to intervene. He gave the Church the backing of secular power when and where it was needed – but on his terms, and in the expectation of a return. The freedom of action of popes and bishops was to some extent curtailed by him; in other respects he and they were as one in their aims and objectives. His episcopal nominations and recommendations were sound, and his appointees, in their different capacities, served their purpose well. Under Henry V there were few, if any, rotten eggs in the English episcopal basket. In his close attention to the

---

[125] See above, pp. 114–15.

affairs of the Church, right up until the days just before his death, the warrior-king demonstrated that its concerns were very much *his* concerns. They claimed a high place on his scale of priorities.

If Henry, while advocating peace and harmony within Christendom, saw war as a necessity, it was because he was conscious that his war with France was merely part of a much loftier purpose. Failing all other means, it had to be fought. It was the sole recourse of a Christian prince when diplomacy, mediation and compromise failed. And it was, perhaps, an object of regret to him that his ends could not, or so it seemed, be attained without the 'effusion of Christian blood'. In 1435, the admittedly self-serving and partisan exponents of a Franco-Burgundian reconciliation claimed to remember that, in his last year or so, Henry, through the mediation of the duke of Savoy, had sincerely wished for peace discussions with the dauphinists, believing (or so it was alleged) that the war was consuming too many lives and too much money.[126] Anglo-Franco-Burgundian peace negotiations, mediated by Cardinal Niccolò Albergati and Amadeus of Savoy, were certainly in progress at that time. Martin V was optimistic about an agreement, citing the 'weariness' of both princes and peoples with the war.[127] But whether or not Henry V himself sought papal arbitration via Savoy is less clear. Amadeus, at a later date, complained that Henry's demands and terms had been excessive.[128] He then, after Henry's death, turned his attention to attempting to bring about a Franco-Burgundian reconciliation – but the creation of an alliance between Bedford and Philip the Good of Burgundy was soon to put an end to that. Whatever the facts

---

[126] See Harvey, *England, Rome and the Papacy*, p. 136; & J.G. Dickinson, *The Congress of Arras, 1435: a Study in Medieval Diplomacy* (Oxford, 1955), pp. 21, 209–10.

[127] See Harvey, 'Martin V and the English, 1422–1431', p. 60: Martin wrote, in high hopes, to Albergati, that both inclination and fatigue predisposed both rulers and their subjects towards peace.

[128] See Harvey, 'Martin V and the English, 1422–1431', pp. 60–1. Martin's letters are found in K.A. Fink, 'Die politische Korrespondenz Martins V nach den Brevenregistern', *Quellen und Forschungen aus italienischen Archiven und Bibliotheken*, xxvi (1935–6), nos 259, 260.

in the late summer of 1422 really were, in the instructions given to the Burgundian embassy sent to Henry VI and his council in May 1435, inviting them to send an embassy to the forthcoming Arras peace conference, it was claimed that

> to . . . arrive at the said pacification [between England, Burgundy and France] the said late king Henry – considering that the way of war is long, dangerous, perilous and very difficult, especially against such great and powerful parties, and that it was not likely that an end could be so soon put to it, without great loss and death of nobles and other people on each side, destruction of the common people and incalculable expense – divulged and declared secretly to my said lord of Burgundy [Philip the Good] and to a certain small number of his council, of whom some are still living, that he dearly wished to find a suitable way and manner of treating with the enemy side, so that the said war should completely cease . . .[129]

It was also pointed out that papal efforts (as in 1435) to achieve a lasting peace were already under way just before Henry's death in 1422. But, soon after,

> he [Henry] departed this life. And it is likely that if he had lived longer, given how well-disposed he was towards the said peace, that this kingdom [France] would soon be completely pacified, and the accursed

---

[129] Instructions (from BN, MS Bourgogne 99, pp. 422–8) printed in Dickinson, *The Congress of Arras, 1435*, pp. 209–10: 'pour . . . parvenir a la ditte pacification ledit feu roy Henry, considerant que la voye de guerre est longue, dangereuse, perilleuse et tres difficile, en especial contre si grandes et puissans parties, et nestoit pas vraysemblable que fin y peust estre sitost mise, sans tres grande perte et occision de nobles et dautres gens dun coustee et dautre, destruction de people et despense inestimable de finances, se ouvry et declara secretement a mondit seigneur de Bourgogne et a aucuns de son conseil en petit nombre, dont aucuns vivent a present, quil desiroit bien trouver voye et maniere convenable de traittier avecques la partie adverse, tellement que la dite guerre cessast du tout . . .'

impediments which had prevailed there for so long, and still prevail, would cease . . .[130]

The terms on which Henry might have agreed to such optimistic negotiations, which were perhaps born of hopeful Burgundian wish-fulfilment and self-justification at a later date, were never set out. But very similar sentiments were echoed in the justificatory statement subsequently made by Henry VI's council in 1440 when challenged by Humphrey of Gloucester over the release from captivity of Charles of Orléans, Henry's most prized prisoner. In their reply to Gloucester's accusations of their betrayal of Henry's wishes, they attributed war-weariness, and a desire to negotiate for peace with the dauphin and his party, to Henry V shortly before his death.[131] Yet, in the event, civil war in France could not, he probably believed – and certainly discovered – be brought to an end by any other means than the active prosecution of warfare. Orléans, Henry declared (or so Gloucester maintained), was not to be released until the conquest of France from the dauphinists was complete.[132] And his war had to be fought in order to bring about that peace and union, not only between but within the two kingdoms, which was a constant refrain of both his own diplomatic and other documents, and the eulogies of his

[130] Dickinson, *The Congress of Arras, 1435*, p. 210: '. . .[il] assez tost apres ala de vie a trespas. Et est vraysemblable sil eust plus longuement vesqui, veue la tres bonne disposition ou il estoit au regard de laditte paix, que pieca ce royaume fust du tout appaisie et cessassent ledit maldis inconveniens qui y ont si longuement regner et regnent encores.'

[131] See *L & P*, ed. Stevenson, ii, p. 455: 'yeet not longe tyme tofore his deth . . . he [Henry V] was so sadded of the werre and disposed in alle wises, to have entended to a paix to have be treated and made with hym that calleth hymn nowe kyng of Fraunce [Charles VII], thanne called the Dauphin, and thoo that helde his partie, as it ne is not unknowen to many that yeet lyven and were aboute hym, to whiche it liked him to open his entent in the saide mater . . .'

[132] See *L & P*, ed. Stevenson, ii, p. 447: 'my lord of blessed memorie, youre fader, (whom God assoyle!), peysing gretly so many inconveniencies and harmes that might falle oonly by his [Orléans'] deliverance, concluded and ordeyned in his last wille and utterly delivered, that unto tyme that he had accomplished fully his conquest in his royaume of France . . .' See also below (Conclusion), pp. 273–4.

biographers. If England itself was not to go the way of France, and descend into civil strife during his reign, it might have been politic to take that English propensity for warfare – and its participants – overseas. And above all else, one prerequisite for the achievement of Henry's higher purpose was an Anglo-French union, whereby the combined forces of the two kingdoms might join together to combat the enemy without. The internal citadel of orthodoxy was under threat from the forces of heresy. The external citadel of Christendom had two enemies – the enemy within, in the shape of the Bohemian Hussites; and the enemy at its gates – the Ottoman Turks, and the Muslim Mamluks of Egypt, who were in possession of the Holy Land and the places where Christ had walked the earth. Henry had, by and large, dealt successfully with his own, domestic equivalent of the Hussites – the Lollards. Again, had he lived longer, his attention might well have turned towards the enemy without. For a Christian ruler, that was indeed the highest purpose of all.

The search for peace in Europe and throughout Christendom was, as we know, not crowned with success in the fifteenth century. The Schism in the Western Church had been brought to an end, but that was all. Yet even in times of constant, if not endemic, warfare, the promotion and cultivation of the peaceful arts did not cease. It is to those arts that we now turn.

Chapter 6

THE KING AND THE PEACEFUL ARTS

Music, its patronage and practice

It seems that the virtues and accomplishments of Henry V, which have recently been drawn into the brightly colored limelight of the cinema, can be added to by a new and real one – that of a composer.[1]

The distinguished musicologist Manfred Bukofzer, quoted above, was referring to the recent appearance of the film version of Shakespeare's *Henry V* (1944), which had brought that drama, in vibrant Technicolor, to a wide, popular audience. Henry's 'virtues and accomplishments', as set out by Shakespeare, were manifold, but were not thought to include musical composition. Although well known to musicologists and historians of music, the source of evidence for this alleged accomplishment had received very little attention or notice from historians, and was completely unknown to a more general public. An attribution, which was nevertheless disputed, of two pieces of music to the hand of the 'real', not the fictitious,

---

[1] M. Bukofzer, 'The Music of the Old Hall Manuscript, Part 2', *Musical Quarterly,* 35 (1949), p. 59.

king as portrayed by Shakespeare had been made. This attribution was not without foundation, as the evidence for Henry V's musicality is quite persuasive and compelling.[2] The two pieces are to be found in a fifteenth-century collection of compositions of church music by English composers, known as the Old Hall manuscript (BL, Add. MS 57590).[3] With these two exceptions, no surviving evidence of musical composition by English kings can be found before the reign of Henry VIII (1509–47).[4] In the Old Hall collection, settings of the *Gloria* and the *Sanctus* from the Ordinary of the mass are headed with a label carrying the words 'Roy Henry' ('King Henry'). Other mass settings and related works are, unusually, similarly accompanied in the manuscript by the names of their composers.[5] It is rare to find such a substantial volume, containing so many settings by various composers, surviving both the dissolution of the monasteries and chantries, as well as subsequent Puritan and other campaigns of destruction of liturgical books. But the book's provenance, mode of compilation and manner of use have all been the subject of intense and ongoing musicological debate.

The Ordinary of the mass was (and is) that part of the Eucharist (or, in non-Roman Catholic terminology, Holy Communion, the Lord's Table or the Lord's Supper) of which the Latin texts do not vary according to the date upon which the mass is celebrated. The invariable texts are formed by the *Kyrie* ('Lord, have mercy; Christ, have mercy'); *Gloria* ('Glory be to

---

[2] See below pp. 218–19.

[3] The two pieces are in BL, Add. MS 57590, fos 12v–13r & 80v respectively.

[4] Music attributed to Henry VIII is found in BL, Add. MS 31922 (*c.*1510–20) where the song 'Pastime with good companye' is headed 'The Kynge h. viii'.

[5] A recording of the *Gloria* setting by 'Roy Henry' is included on a CD entitled *Music for Henry V and the House of Lancaster* by the Binchois Consort (Hyperion CD B00570JXCO). A reviewer in the *Gramophone* expressed the hope that the recording 'will give a more rounded picture of the victor of Agincourt as a musical patron of exquisite taste' (www.gramophone.co.uk/review/music-for-henry-v). The recording also includes pieces by other composers from the Old Hall manuscript, such as Leonel Power and Thomas Damett. A recording of a further selection of pieces from the Old Hall manuscript, by the Hilliard Ensemble, is on EMI Reflexe CD 54111 & Virgin Edition CD 61393.

God'); *Credo* ('I believe'); *Sanctus* ('Holy, Holy, Holy, Lord God of hosts'); *Benedictus* ('Blessed is He'); and *Agnus Dei* ('Lamb of God'). These unvarying words have been set to music by composers down the centuries. In the fifteenth century, the centrality of the mass in the liturgy of an essentially sacramental Church, in which the clergy's prime responsibility was the administration of the sacraments, meant that setting the 'Ordinary' offered composers of church music their main source of both inspiration and employment. Henry V, though fully conscious of the place and value of preaching – through the vernacular sermon and homily – in the Church's mission, clearly conceived of that mission in essentially sacramental terms. The continual, uninterrupted performance of divine service lay at its heart, and the anti-sacramental notions of Lollards, Hussites and other heretics were to be combated by all means in the Church's – and the secular state's – power. Without the daily celebration of the Eucharist, the work of a 'Godly preaching ministry' (as advocated by the heretics) could never fully achieve the Church's redemptive mission. It is therefore unsurprising that the king's interventions in the field of church music, if they took place at all, should be centred upon the singing of the eternal and unvarying words of the Ordinary of the mass.

The king's piety has already been noted, and his concern for the proper conduct of divine service is well known.[6] But the appearance of the name 'King Henry' ('Roy Henry') apparently as a composer, in a musical manuscript, is both unprecedented and unusual. The Old Hall volume is organised in such a way that the various settings of the constituent parts of the mass (*Gloria, Sanctus, Benedictus* and so on) are grouped together, rather than set out in complete mass cycles containing all the elements of the Eucharist. Although the name 'Roy Henry' stands at the head of the first settings of the *Gloria* and *Sanctus* (perhaps as a mark of respect) in the collection, it simply takes its place on a par with those of other,

[6] See above, chapter 4, pp. 140, 146, 154–5; chapter 5, pp. 177, 180, 182–3, 185–6.

professional church musicians, the careers of some of whom can be documented. And the fact that a layman, albeit of the very highest rank, was here performing a task normally monopolised by men of clerical status, is surely significant. The acquaintance with contemporary liturgical practice which the composer demonstrates, as well as his knowledge of sophisticated musical forms and styles, is out of the ordinary. The two compositions reveal an ability effectively to employ the techniques of choral polyphony. These were a relatively recent later medieval development and, according to scholars of music, our 'Roy Henry' displays a fluency in their use which is more than merely competent. We might perhaps expect a musically literate secular ruler to try his hand at simple Gregorian chant or plainsong (or a secular lyric), sung by a solo voice, or body of unison voices, in a single vocal line. But to find works attributed to a lay ruler in a collection 'containing, as it does, some of the most difficult and sophisticated polyphony being written anywhere at this time' is both remarkable and exceptional.[7]

The rise of polyphony, known to contemporaries as the *ars nova* ('new' or 'novel art'), in a liturgical context appears to be largely a product of the second half of the fourteenth century. It was productive of the creation of great choral foundations, including those of Oxford and Cambridge colleges. A notable representative was the poet and composer Guillaume de Machaut (*c.*1300–77), whose unique *Messe de Nostre Dame* paved the way for many subsequent polyphonic mass settings.[8] His influence, as we shall see, was still keenly felt in England during the first decades of the fifteenth century. Polyphony created a musical texture in which a number of melodic lines were simultaneously interwoven, giving rise to effects that

[7] M. Bent, 'The Old Hall Manuscript', *Early Music*, 2 (1974), p. 12.

[8] See E.E. Leach, *Guillaume de Machaut, Secretary, Poet, Musician* (Ithaca, NY/London, 2011), pp. 274, 276–9 for a discussion of the origins and purpose of this unique setting of the mass among Machaut's extant works. Formerly dated to 1364, for the coronation of Charles V, its date has been revised by more recent scholarship to the late 1350s or to some time during the 1360s.

could be almost mesmerisingly harmonious but also offered scope for dissonance and expressiveness, especially of a plaintive kind. Polyphonic works contained two, three or four vocal parts or lines. Although it never entirely replaced plainsong, or Gregorian chant, sung as a one-line melody, in the Church's liturgy, polyphonic music exploited the skills of the choral establishments of the rich and powerful as never before. And although initially grounded in plainsong, the polyphonic mass setting 'eventually attained complete musical self-sufficiency'.[9] As an *a cappella* form, that is, a purely choral medium intended for greater churches and private chapels, it called for highly trained and skilled singers, although vocal lines could on occasion be doubled by instruments. It was also more expensive to fund than chant.[10] By the time of Henry V's accession, no Chapel Royal or other princely establishment was considered properly resourced without a body of chorister clerks and boy singers competent to sing unaccompanied – or sometimes accompanied – polyphonic music. The English Chapel Royal was no exception.[11]

The view of earlier scholars, that the Old Hall manuscript was produced by and for the musicians of the Chapel Royal under Henry VI (1422–61), has been completely discarded.[12] It is now suggested that the book was largely compiled, under Henry V, between *c.*1415 and 1421, with some later additions. It is now also suggested that the greater part of the volume's contents may initially have been compiled and copied for the household

[9] See J. Caldwell, 'Plainsong and Polyphony, 1250–1550' in *Plainsong in the Age of Polyphony*, ed. T.F. Kelly (Cambridge, 1992), pp. 15–17.

[10] See Leach, *Guillaume de Machaut*, pp. 277–8 for the endowment of a Lady Mass for Machaut and his brother Jean – possibly Machaut's own *Messe de Nostre Dame* – in Rheims cathedral, funded by a 'large amount of money . . . which would have been too much for chant alone'. Also R. Bowers, 'Guillaume de Machaut and his Canonry of Reims, 1338–1377', *Early Music History*, 23 (2004), p. 43.

[11] For a recent summary of the role of music in Henry's Chapel Royal, see A.K. McHardy, 'Religion, Court Culture and Propaganda: the Chapel Royal in the Reign of Henry V' in *Henry V: New Interpretations*, ed. G. Dodd,(Woodbridge, 2013), pp. 138–42.

[12] See N. Wilkins, *Music in the Age of Chaucer* (Woodbridge, 1979: 2nd edn 1995), pp. 82–4.

chapel of Thomas, duke of Clarence, Henry V's brother, before his death in battle at Baugé in March 1421. One reason for linking the Old Hall manuscript with Clarence lies in the fact that the largest collection in the book of pieces by any one composer is made up of those attributed to Lionel Power (? *c.*1380–1445). Power was a prominent member of, and master of, the boy choristers in Clarence's chapel.[13] The quality of music attributed to him has been favourably compared to that of his more influential near-contemporary John Dunstaple (*c.*1390–1453). There are no fewer than 23 items by him in the book's first 'layer' (that is, works constituting the original corpus of the manuscript) and Clarence's chapel was evidently the establishment for which most of Power's earlier music was composed.[14] Although there is no definite proof of this, the volume could well, in the first instance, have been compiled for its use. The importance of household chapels, with their musical establishments, has been emphasised because 'the principal, if not only, identifiable users of books of liturgical polyphony were the groups of singers working in the greater churches and household chapels of the king and higher nobility'.[15] The writing down of polyphonic music was thus very closely associated with particular bodies of performers, working within specific establishments. In the case of the Old Hall manuscript, the connection with Clarence's household chapel appears to be very plausible.

In the chapels – which could be as much musical as liturgical establishments – the principal musical event was the daily High Mass, celebrated wherever the household might be at a given time. This led to the relatively large number of surviving polyphonic settings of the Ordinary of the mass, perhaps designed to impress 'diplomatic guests' with an 'edifying

---

[13] See the household accounts for Clarence in Westminster Abbey Muniments, MS 12163, fo. 14r: 'Et in denariis solutis Lionell' Power, magistro dictorum puerorum . . .' (Nov. 1418–Nov. 1419).

[14] See R. Bowers, 'Some Observations on the Life and Career of Lionel Power', *PRMA*, 102 (1975–6), pp. 109–10.

[15] A. Wathey, 'The Production of Books of Liturgical Polyphony' in *Book Production and Publishing in Britain, 1375–1475*, ed. J. Griffiths & D.A. Pearsall (Cambridge, 1989), p. 145.

manifestation of their host's piety – and wealth and power'.[16] The Old Hall manuscript is lavishly illuminated and gilded, with historiated (decorated) initials at the beginning of its main sections and 'elaborate penwork forms in the subsidiary portions'.[17] With its twenty or so members (sixteen singing clerks and four boy choristers), Clarence's musical establishment compared favourably with the Chapel Royal, which had thirty members (fourteen clerks and sixteen choristers) in 1422.[18] Clarence's household accounts for 1418–21 tell us that the provision of music played a major part in his chapel's expenditure.[19] They include payments for the 'notyng and limmnyng' ('notating and illuminating') of a 'great antiphoner' and for making good certain 'deficiencies', especially in the psalms and calendar pages of the manuscript.[20] Active searches were conducted for singers, who were then sent to join the duke and his chapel in Normandy and France during his lieutenancy there for Henry V. In 1420–1, servants and messengers were sent to the cathedrals and collegiate churches at Wells, Exeter, Crediton, Lincoln and York 'to seek clerks for the chapel'.[21] This musical establishment was 'highly competent', 'as much musical as sacerdotal',[22] with more singing clerks than chaplains, and thus well equipped

[16] Bowers, 'Some Observations', p. 126.
[17] Wathey, 'The Production of Books of Liturgical Polyphony', p. 154; also A. Hughes & M. Bent, 'The Old Hall Manuscript: a Reappraisal and Inventory', *Musica Disciplina*, 21 (1967), pp. 97–147.
[18] For payment to its members see TNA, E 101/407/4, fo. 36r; E 101/406/21, fo. 27r; E 101/45/5, m. 1; E 404/31/444; E 403/643, mm. 2–3 & E 404/35/247. Liveries of cloth were given to the members of Clarence's chapel in 1420–1:WAM 12163, fo. 17r where red cloth was bought for 24 chaplains and clerks and four boys. In 1419–20, green cloth was provided for 21 chaplains and clerks (fo. 14r).
[19] WAM, MS 12163, fos 14r–v, 16r, also transcribed in C.M. Woolgar, *Household Accounts from Medieval England, Part 2* (Oxford, 1993), pp. 604–90.
[20] WAM, MS 12163, fo. 14r: 'Et in denariis solutis pro notyng et limmyng unius antiphonarii magni . . . 100s'; 'Et in denariis solutis pro diversis salmis, kalendar' et aliis deficient' in eodem libro etc – 5s. 8d.'
[21] WAM, MS 12163, fo. 14v. One of those sent on these quests was Thomas Power, presumably a relative of Lionel Power: 'Et in denariis solutis Thomas Power, equitant' de London' usque Lincoln et Ebor' pro consimili negoc' eodem tempore etc' – 26s. 8d.' A Richard Power was also retained in Clarence's service (fo. 14v).
[22] Bowers, 'Some Observations', p. 107.

to perform the difficult polyphonic compositions which the Old Hall and other books contained. One testimony to this competence can be seen in the loan by John, duke of Berry, of one of the surviving, posthumously assembled, manuscripts of Machaut's music and poetry to Clarence on 22 December 1412, during his expedition to aid the Armagnac faction against the Burgundians.[23] It had been compiled *c*.1390, and included, among a collection of largely secular items, a copy of the *Messe de Nostre Dame*, by means of which Lionel Power 'could have become acquainted with Machaut's Mass setting'.[24]

Although the Old Hall manuscript is not specifically documented and identifiable among Clarence's chapel goods, its association with the works of Power, and contemporary composers connected with him, makes it plausible that it may have originally been compiled, during Henry V's reign, for the duke's singers. It has been suggested that the manuscript passed into the hands of members of the Chapel Royal following Clarence's death in 1421.[25] This is consistent with there being a first 'layer' of compositions in the collection, all written and copied before 1421. Identifiable members of Henry V's Chapel Royal, such as John

[23] The manuscript is now BNF, MS fr. 9221 known as MS 'E' in the Machaut corpus. See L. Earp, *Guillaume de Machaut: a Guide to Research* (London, 1996; 2nd edn 2013), pp. 92–4. For the 1412 expedition see E. McLeod, *Charles of Orleans. Prince and Poet* (London, 1969), pp. 7–87; also J.L. Bolton, 'How Sir Thomas Rempston Paid his Ransom: or the Mistakes of an Italian Bank' in *Conflicts, Consequences and the Crown in the Late Middle Ages*, ed. L. Clark (Woodbridge, 2007), pp. 103–5.

[24] Earp, *Guillaume de Machaut*, p. 92; Bowers 'Some Observations', p. 108. The mass is set out on fos 164v–170r of MS fr. 9221. For its presentation to Clarence see *Inventaires de Jean, duc de Berry (1401–1416)*, ed. J. Guiffrey (Paris, 1894), i, pp. 226–7, no. 860: 'Item, le livre de Machaut, garni de deux fermouers dargent dorez, et deux tixuz de soye vermeille, couvert de cuir vermeil empraint. Datus fuit duci Clarencie per mandatum super prima parte LXIX folii huius compoti traditum; virtute cuius dictus Robinetus acquittatur hic de eodem' ['It was given to the duke of Clarence by order recorded in the first part of the 69th folio of this account; by virtue of which the said Robinet is here quit of the same'].

[25] See Bent, 'The Old Hall Manuscript', p. 6. The unfinished and incomplete state of the 'first' layer might suggest that although it may have been intended for use by Clarence's singers, this did not happen, and Bent's earlier observation that 'there can be little doubt that the members of Henry V's household chapel were the first users of the book' may carry some conviction (M. Bent, 'Sources of the Old Hall Music', *PRMA*, 94 (1967–8), p. 26).

Cooke (*c*.1385–1442), Thomas Damett (? *c*.1390–1436/7) and Nicholas Sturgeon (*c*.1380–1454) contributed items to the collection, they and others adding their own further compositions after the volume may have passed into the king's hands following Clarence's sudden death and the dissolution of his chapel.[26] It has been suggested that a more securely date-able piece in the first 'layer' is a motet (*En Katherinae solemnia*) by Thomas (?) Byttering possibly intended for the marriage ceremony of Henry V and Catherine (2 June 1420),[27] and the Old Hall manuscript also contains motets closely associated with some of the titles of the music performed at the celebrations of the Agincourt victory in 1415.[28] Recent musicological opinion has ruled out any candidate other than Henry V for the 'Roy Henry' title: Henry IV (1399–1413) has been suggested, but 'can now be ruled out in favour of Henry V . . . who was the king at the time of writing' (of the manuscript).[29] The notion that the luxury of musical composition could not have been accommodated within the intensely active life of a warrior-king is not supported by our knowledge of the range of activities which that life encompassed. To see, as some have done, the Old Hall 'Roy Henry' pieces as products of the later years of an ailing and increasingly infirm Henry IV may also raise more problems than it solves. Unless the attribution is simply honorific, as a mark of respect for the sovereign, arguments made by Bukofzer in 1948–9 and Bent in 1974 appear to be confirmed: the identity of the monarch at the time when the bulk of the Old Hall manuscript's collection was *compiled*, rather than the date of composition of the various items within it (some dating from

---

[26] See Bukofzer, 'The Music of the Old Hall Manuscript, Part 2', p. 55. Both Damett and Sturgeon became canons of Windsor under Henry VI.

[27] The motet is set out on fos 110v–111r of Add. MS 57590 and labelled 'Bitteryng'. The connection with the marriage ceremony was, however, dismissed by Bent, 'Sources of the Old Hall Music', *PRMA*, 94 (1967–8), p. 20.

[28] See Bent, 'Sources of the Old Hall Music', pp. 22–5.

[29] M. Bent, 'The Old Hall Manuscript' in *New Grove Dictionary of Music*, www.oxfordmusiconline.com. For an earlier discussion, yet still concluding in favour of Henry V, see Bent, 'Sources of the Old Hall Music', pp. 33–5.

the reigns of both Henry IV and Henry VI), links the greater part of the collection with Henry V.[30] It was this that prompted the scribe, or rather scribes, who wrote the manuscript to use the name 'Roy Henry', that of the reigning sovereign, to identify the composer of two of the settings of the *Gloria* and *Sanctus*.

Some musicologists have detected such significant differences in style between the two settings that the notion of two separate composers has been mooted. The 'melodious and graceful' *Sanctus*[31] is thought to be less 'original', rather older in style and notation, while the *Gloria* has been described as being in an 'advanced *ars nova* cantilena style . . . smoothly and skilfully written'.[32] The notion that composers, even of mass settings, might develop as they grew older and become more attuned to contemporary musical trends may give the lie to the argument for two separate individuals at work here. The existence at this period, as at others, of 'distinct genera-tions of composing fashions' would also support that notion.[33] Whatever the case, the fact remains that these two pieces are attributed to a 'Roy Henry', undifferentiated by numbering or any other distinguishing mark. And the case for Henry V appears to be the more convincing and least subject to inconsistencies. The evidence of the *Gloria* setting supports the view that this was the work of a composer of some distinction, representing, as it does, an 'Indian summer of the *ars nova*', before both English and Burgundian musicians turned to different expressive forms.[34]

---

[30] See Bukofzer, 'The Music of the Old Hall Manuscript, Parts 1 & 2', *Musical Quarterly*, 34 & 35 (1948–9), pp. 512–32 & 36–59; Bent, 'The Old Hall Manuscript', *Early Music*, 2 (1974), pp. 2–14, esp. pp. 13–14.

[31] Bukofzer, 'The Music of the Old Hall Manuscript, Part 1', p. 530.

[32] R. Taruskin, *Music from the Earliest Notations to the Sixteenth Century* (Oxford, 2005), p. 47.

[33] Bent, 'Sources of the Old Hall Music', p. 32.

[34] Bukofzer, 'The Music of the Old Hall Manuscript, Part 1', p. 531. The discovery of an *Alleluia* four–part motet in the binding of a sixteenth-century court roll of Kempsey manor (Worcs RO, b. 705; 4 BA 54) has prompted speculation about its composer. But the refer-ence, on the face of the fragmentary document used in the binding, to the reign of 'henrici quinti' (3 July 1421), forms part of a dating clause and has no bearing on the identity of the motet's composer. See www.diamm.ac.uk/jsp/.

The Agincourt carol

The best known musical legacy of Henry V's reign lies in a zone somewhere between the ecclesiastical and secular worlds: the so-called 'Agincourt carol' celebrates a great military victory, but renders praise and thanks to God alone for that victory. Written down, notated, polyphonically set, and making contrasts between unison and divided voices, the carol is a hymn of praise and thanksgiving:

> *Deo gracias, Anglia, redde pro Victoria* ['To God give thanks, England, for the victory!']
>
> Our king went forth to Normandy, with grace and might of chivalry; There God for him wrought marv'lously, / Wherefore England may call and cry: / *Deo gracias, Anglia, redde pro victoria./Deo gracias, Anglia, redde pro victoria./*
>
> He set a siege, forsooth to say, / To Harflu town with royal array; / That town he won and made affray; / That France shall rue till Domesday: / *Deo gracias.*
>
> Then went him forth our king comely; / In Agincourt field he fought manly; / Through grace of God most marvellously; / He had both field and victory: / *Deo gracias.*
>
> There lords, earles and baron / Were slain and taken and that full soon, / And some were brought into London / With joy and bliss and great renown: / *Deo gracias.*
>
> Almighty God he keep our king;/ His people and all his well-willing, / And give them grace withouten ending; / Then may we call and safely sing: / *Deo gracias Anglia.*[35]

The combination of Latin refrain (or 'burden') and English text is perhaps significant. The use of English would not necessarily rule out the carol's

---

[35] See *Musica Britannica: A National Collection of Music, vol. iv, Medieval Carols*, ed. J. Stevens (London, 2001), p. 6, no. 8.

origins in a religious house, or possibly the Chapel Royal itself. This is not a 'popular' ballad, to be raucously bawled in the street, although its sentiments call for an emotional response from 'the people'.[36] The two- and three-part writing, and its polyphonic form, suggest that it was to be sung by trained singers.[37] Self-glorification was not part of Henry V's normal repertoire: a royal injunction, reported by the *Life and Deeds of Henry V*, attributed to Thomas of Elmham, prohibited any singers, harpists (*citharistas*) or others from making or performing songs about his victory, unless it was attributed solely to the might of God.[38] And this is precisely what the Agincourt carol, with its Latin refrain giving praise and thanks to God, does. It has recently been described as a 'festival song' and this has led to its association with the London celebrations of Agincourt on 23 November 1415.[39] It also bears comparison with the English narrative verses celebrating the event which appeared at the time, especially the *Battle of Agincourt* (BL, MS Harl. 565), where similar terms are employed to those of the carol. We know that Henry was greeted on his progress through London by groups of singers, at Bermondsey, Blackheath and Cheapside, singing '*Ave rex Anglorum*' ('Hail, king of the English!'), '*miles Christi*' ('knight of Christ') and '*Flos mundi*' ('Flower of the world').[40] We can, however, be certain that, despite some contrary opinions voiced by nineteenth-century writers, it was never intended to be sung by Henry's troops as they returned, victorious, from the field.

---

[36] Recordings of the 'Agincourt carol' have been made by Christopher Page and Gothic Voices on Hyperion CDA66238 & CDS44251/3; and, more recently, by David Skinner and Alamire on Obsidian CD709.

[37] For this, and what follows, see H. Deeming, 'The Sources and Origin of the "Agincourt Carol" ', *Early Music*, 35 (2007), pp. 23–38.

[38] *Thomae de Elmham Vita et gesta Henrici quinti*, ed. T. Hearne (Oxford, 1727), p. 72: 'Rex vero, mundanis pompis inaniter gloriari renuens, devote cordis humilitate omnem istam gloriam, et consimilia quaecumque, offert Deo, nec aliquantulum sibi, sed soli omnipotenti Deo se velle victoriam imputari, omnibus plane refert, in tantum, quod cantus de suo triumpho fieri, seu per citharistas, vel alios quoscumque cantari penitus prohibebat'.

[39] Taruskin, *Music from the Earliest Notations to the Sixteenth Century*, pp. 52, 54; Deeming, 'The Sources and Origin', pp. 26–8.

[40] Bent, 'Sources of the Old Hall Music', pp. 22–5; BL Harl. MS 565, fo. 112v for one account of the singing at the celebrations.

Where, then, did the Agincourt carol originate? The manuscript evidence suggests the possibility of an ecclesiastical source. The carol survives in two manuscript copies. One is found in a book of carols and liturgical settings (Bod. Lib., MS Arch. Selden B. 26), dating from *c.*1425–50.[41] The second contemporary source is a parchment roll (Cambridge, Trinity College MS O.3.58) containing the texts and notations of 13 English or macaronic (that is, in more than one language) carols, including the Agincourt piece.[42] Although many carol melodies were transmitted orally, a total of 130 polyphonic carols survives in written and notated form. These would be pieces 'sung by trained singers in ecclesiastical institutions' and bear comparison with contemporary liturgical polyphony.[43] A possible origin for the Trinity roll has been proposed: Mettingham collegiate church in north Suffolk is a candidate, as many carols in the manuscript are in an East Anglian dialect.[44] Mettingham is known to have had an important choral establishment at this time.[45] Alternatively, the roll may have been the property of an individual musician, possibly of Norfolk or Suffolk origin, although an ecclesiastical institutional source seems most likely. Musicological opinion appears to agree that, although a roll was easy to sing from, this example – because of its relatively fine workmanship – was not intended for the everyday use of

---

[41] The carols and liturgical pieces form fos 3r–33v of the book, and the 'Agincourt carol' is to be found on fos 17v-18r.

[42] For a description and analysis see Deeming, 'The Sources and Origin', pp. 31–3. For another description (by Roger Bowers) see *Cambridge Music Manuscripts, 900–1700,* ed. I. Fenlon (Cambridge, 1982), pp. 88–90.

[43] See Deeming, 'The Sources and Origin', pp. 25, 32.

[44] See 'Colleges: Mettingham', *VCH, County of Suffolk,* ed. W. Page (London, 1975), ii, pp. 144–5; A. Suckling, *The History and Antiquities of the County of Suffolk* (London, 1846–8), i, p. 177. For discussion of the case for Mettingham see Deeming, 'The Sources and Origin', pp. 31–3. Also *Cambridge Music Manuscripts, 900–1700,* ed. Fenlon, p. 115.

[45] See 'Extracts from the Ancient Accounts of Mettingham College, Suffolk', *Archaeological Journal,* 6 (1849), pp. 62–8: expenditure is recorded for 8–12 chaplains and a number of boys, and the writing and illumination of missals, graduals and antiphoners, including the gilding of lettering. Costs are also incurred for the purchase and carriage of an organ. The Egerton psalter, an East Anglian manuscript of *c.*1270–90, was in the collegiate church's possession in the late fourteenth century (BL, MS Egerton 1066).

minstrels.[46] The celebrations of the victory in November 1415 remain the most likely candidate for the carol's genesis and first performance.

Secular music

Besides the musical establishment in the Chapel Royal, Henry V also retained musicians for more secular purposes. His household retinue, like those of other magnates, included musicians serving in both peace and war. The martial ethos of the time was represented by the retaining of groups of trumpeters and players of drums ('nakers'). These musicians were an essential accompaniment to all military activity. But they also played an important part in court rituals, including summonses to meals and the provision of robust and festive music during feasts. Ensembles of as many as twelve trumpeters, together with a pair of what were in effect kettledrums, were not unknown.[47] The provision of splendid heraldic banners to hang from the king's trumpets was a normal item of expenditure, and in March 1420, for example, no fewer than twenty-five such banners 'stamped [*vapulata*] with the king's arms' were supplied.[48] The festive and celebratory qualities of music, as at the court, also found a place in other rituals and ceremonies of many kinds. Its absence could be significant. When, for instance, a new mayor for the city of London was chosen in October 1422, the mourning decreed for Henry V's death in the court and royal household was echoed in civic ceremony. The records of the Brewers' Company tell us that the newly elected mayor, William Walderne,

---

[46] See A. Taylor, 'The Myth of the Minstrel Manuscript', *Speculum*, 66 (1991), pp. 43–73, esp. p. 68.

[47] See H.G. Farmer, *Military Music* (New York, 1950), pp. 10–12. For the functions of music and musicians at courts see M. Vale, 'Ritual, Ceremony and the "Civilising Process": the Role of the Court, *c.*1270–1400' in *The Court as a Stage: England and the Low Countries in the Later Middle Ages*, ed. S. Gunn & A. Janse (Woodbridge, 2006), pp. 18–21.

[48] E 101/407/4, fo. 4v. The accounts contain numerous payments for trumpeters and their wages.

accompanied by the city aldermen, went up the river to Westminster by barge for his installation, but 'in black clothing, without any minstrel[sy] or any other solemnity'.[49] Secular music was clearly an intrinsic part of ritualised behaviour of many kinds.

Just as Clarence retained a musical chapel, which reflected and emulated the Chapel Royal, so other magnates – as did the king – also retained secular musicians. In November 1413, Henry confirmed grants made by the late Henry, Lord Beaumont, to his trumpeter, called Hugh, and to Nicholas Duke, 'mynstrall', as life retainers of Beaumont's underage son who was a ward in the king's custody.[50] The king himself was accompanied by his minstrels wherever he went, including during the course of his campaigns in France. In June 1415, for example, John Cliffe was retained for one year, with his seventeen 'minstrel companions', to serve on the king's voyage to France. Plate and jewels were pledged to them as securities for their payment.[51] The band of minstrels was expected to appear not only at the 'mummings' and play-acting interludes staged at the court, but on ceremonial occasions. In June 1416, the king's sixteen musicians received liveries of woollen gowns, dyed in one colour and lined with black cloth. They were to be suitably attired to play before the king, the Emperor Sigismund, the duke of Holland and other distinguished visitors.[52] Music was a constant accompaniment to the court's daily activities, and players of both 'loud' and 'soft' instruments were employed in the hall and chamber to provide appropriate incidental and occasional music.

Yet the king's musical interests extended beyond the more passive role of merely listening. Although he had in his service a liveried harper, William Corff, who – in 1415–16 – wore a hood and gown of green cloth,

---

[49] Guildhall Library archives, MS 5440, fo. 71r: the mayoral party were 'yn blac' clothing, with outen any mynstrall[cy] or eny other solempnite' (13 Oct. 1422).
[50] C 81/659, nos 129 & 132: 12 & 14 Nov. 1413.
[51] E 101/406/24: indenture of 21 June 1415.
[52] E 101/406/26, m. 5r. The account does not tell us with what colour the garments were dyed.

as did the choristers of the Chapel Royal, the king's interest in that instrument went much further.[53] It is known that Henry had, since a relatively early age, played the harp. In the autumn of 1395, for example, when he was eight, harp-strings, no doubt to replace broken ones, were bought for his use.[54] His appetite for practical music-making did not diminish with age or with the pressures of business. In September 1421, for instance, a new harp was purchased for him from John Bore, a London harp-maker, together with a set of twelve strings and a case for the instrument. They were dispatched to him in France.[55] Like the biblical King David, this was a king who did not consider it beneath the royal dignity to engage in the art of minstrelsy. Clearly, he played not only a stringed instrument but also some of the quieter wind instruments. Also in 1421, two large bags, made of canvas and linen cloth of Brabant, were acquired for the king's own recorders and 'pipes' (or flutes), plus one pound of cotton with which to line and 'stuff' the bags.[56] These wind instruments were to be played in the relative privacy of his chamber. There is no record of the kind of purely instrumental music favoured by Henry V, and none of it survives in written or notated form. But we can be certain that the secular pieces known from other European courts of the period, such as that of Burgundy, must have been popular in an establishment as musically well resourced as the English royal household. And it would be surprising if such rhythmically lively pieces as the 'Agincourt carol' were not performed by instruments – if only by pipe and tabor (small drum) – as well as voices. That the serious, hard-working, and often single-minded ruler was no killjoy is also evident from other sources.[57]

---

[53] E 101/406/21, m. 2r: William also received two pairs of red robes lined with Brabant linen.

[54] DL 28/1/6, fo. 39r.

[55] E 403/651, m. 17v: payment of 2 l. 13s. 4d for 1 'harp [*cithera*] bought from him (John Bore, harp-maker) on the king's order and sent to the . . . king in France . . . with a dozen strings [*cordarum*] for the same harp . . . and a case for the same': 4 Sept. 1421.

[56] E 101/407/4, fos 68r, 73r, 74v; E 101/407/5, mm. 4r, 8r.

[57] See below, pp. 221–3.

'Mummers' and 'mumming' – theatrical interludes usually performed by masked or disguised players – had been a feature of the English court for a long time, and Henry V's reign was no exception. Players were engaged to provide entertainment of all kinds. In 1413, on the feast day of St Peter ad Vincula (1 August), Richard Joskyn and his twenty-five companions (*sociis*) were given gifts by the king for playing before him in the park at Windsor.[58] Perhaps the setting for Shakespeare's *Merry Wives* is not totally unrelated to historical fact. But whether the masquerading and 'mumming' in the park bore any relation to Falstaff's discomfiture we shall never know. That the king did not preside over a joyless court is, however, evident from his permanent retaining of a fool – William – who was fitted out with regular summer and winter liveries and was provided with a servant. A gown, a tabard, hoods, stockings and robes were all supplied and the fact that some of these garments were lined with the expensive furs of ermine and miniver suggests that William enjoyed a relatively high status at court.[59] The king appears to have 'remained' (and retained) 'something of the old Prince Hal', and he kept 'far from gloomy company' in his court and household.[60] Pious he may have been, but he was in no way a pious prig. To characterise him simply as 'ambitious, tenacious, courageous, ruthless, pious, severe, and sometimes cruel' does no justice to the range of evidence for his behaviour which we possess.[61] It is perhaps revealing of his true character that what must have been one of his last acts in life was a grant, 'by word of mouth', as he lay dying at Bois-de-Vincennes, of life annuities, paid 'from his coffers, by the hands of the Treasurer of his chamber at that time', to his 11 minstrels.[62]

---

[58] E 101/406/21, fo. 24r: payment on 29 Oct. 1413.

[59] E 101/406/26, m. 3r: livery roll for 1415–16.

[60] K.B. McFarlane, 'Henry V: a Personal Portrait', in his *Lancastrian Kings and Lollard Knights* (Oxford, 1972), p. 131.

[61] See I. Mortimer, *1415: Henry V's Year of Glory*, (London, 2009; 2nd edn 2010), p. 538 where such qualities are accounted for by what appears to be a very speculative exercise in psychology.

[62] E 28/41, no. 72: the grant was 'par sa bouche', 'de ses couffres par les mains du Tresorer de sa chambre le temps esteant' (confirmation in the name of Henry VI on 14 May 1423).

Material culture, the arts and the apparatus of kingship

The material surroundings in which Henry V chose, and was expected by his subjects, to live do not immediately suggest those that we might expect from a hard-bitten, hard-headed, somewhat ascetic, allegedly puritanical soldier. They were far removed from anything remotely resembling the austerities and privations of the camp or the castle garrison. When engaged in the siege warfare that was so marked a characteristic of his conquests in France he was often lodged, not under canvas, but in the relative comfort of a nearby abbey or other religious house, such as Saint-Faron at Meaux or Bec-Hellouin in Normandy.[63] That he was no stranger to what contemporaries referred to as *esbatement*, that is, 'diversion' or 'enjoyment', is evident from the works he commissioned at his castle of Kenilworth, a favoured residence since his days as Prince of Wales. In 1403, he had recovered from the serious facial wound he sustained at the battle of Shrewsbury at Kenilworth, and it clearly retained a special place in his affections.[64] According to the chronicler John Strecche, it was there that he received the tennis balls insultingly sent to him by the French, mocking his relative youth and immaturity, early in 1415.[65] Strecche was an Augustinian canon of St Mary's priory, Kenilworth, so his testimony does command support, at least to the extent that some such tale may have been circulating at that time. Henry is known to have been at Kenilworth, apart from his visit in 1403, in the spring of 1408; intermittently between January and March 1414; and for the Christmas and Epiphany period from

---

[63] See above, pp. v, 50, 128; below, pp. 255–6.
[64] For the successful treatment and surgical procedures which he underwent there at the hands of Thomas Bradmore see J. Cummins, 'Saving Prince Hal: Maxillo-facial Surgery, 1403', *Henry North History of Dentistry Research Group Publications*, 19 (2006) [http://history-ofdentistry.co.uk/index_htm_files/2006N]; & H. Cole & T. Lang, 'The Treating of Prince Henry's Arrow Wound, 1403', *Journal of the Society of Archer Antiquaries* (2003), pp. 95–101. See above, pp. xiv–xvi.
[65] See F. Taylor, 'The Chronicle of John Strecche for the Reign of Henry V (1414–1422)', *BJRL*, 16 (1932), p. 150.

17 December 1416 to 25 January 1417.[66] It was included, as the 'delightful castle of Kenilworth' on his itinerary through the kingdom in 1421, when he revisited what was described as 'his manor of Plesantmaris there which [he] . . . had firmly built in the marsh'.[67] This was evidently a place at which to retire briefly from the cares of kingship and to celebrate the great feasts, especially in the light of the works he had undertaken there from 1414 onwards.

Henry's 'works' at Kenilworth were largely centred on the 'Pleasance' or 'Le Plesans en Marais' which he created between 1414 and 1417.[68] This was essentially a timber-framed pleasure pavilion and banqueting hall, with attached service quarters, in a drained area beyond the castle's vast defensive lake known as the Great Mere. It stood on a rectangular site, surrounded by a double moat linked by a canal to the Mere, and was furnished with its own small harbour or basin so that access to it could be gained by boat from the main castle site. The buildings were enclosed by a stone wall, on a site of four acres or so (1.2 hectares), with a formal garden, flanked at each corner by square towers.[69] Later building and repairs accounts speak of a 'tower called Plesauntmares' and of carpenters' work 'within the manor of Plesaunce on a tower called Clarence Tower'.[70] In January 1415 works were apparently well advanced, and 250 'waynscotes' (wainscoting panels) and timber for doors and windows were supplied for the king's works 'both within and beneath the castle of Kenilworth, newly constructed'.[71] This was a place of *esbatement*, close to excellent

---

[66] Taylor, 'The Chronicle of John Strecche', p. 141.

[67] Taylor, 'The Chronicle of John Strecche', p. 142: 'castellum dilectum de Kenileworth' & 'manerium suum de Plesantmaris quod ipse rex de palude solidoverat'.

[68] For a comprehensive account of the building works at Kenilworth see H.M. Colvin et al., *The King's Works* (London, 1963), ii, pp. 682–5.

[69] See J.H. Harvey, *Medieval Gardens* (London, 1980), pp. 106–7; H.M. Colvin, 'Royal Gardens in Medieval England' in *Medieval Gardens*, ed. E. B. MacDougall (Dumbarton Oaks, 1986), p. 11.

[70] J.H. Harvey, 'Side-lights on Kenilworth castle', *Archaeological Journal*, 101 (1944), pp. 102, 104 citing Duchy of Lancaster receivers' accounts for 1441–2 and 1464–5.

[71] E 403/620, m. 11r: 'infra quam subtus castrum de Kylyngworth de novo construend' (Jan. 1415).

hunting in the surrounding deer parks, and may have drawn its inspiration from existing sites such as the pleasure park, garden and pavilion in the *Marais*, or marsh, at Hesdin in Artois, created by the counts of Artois at the end of the thirteenth century.[72] Nothing except the residual traces of earthworks survives at Kenilworth today, but the outlines of Henry's substantial scheme can be traced on the ground. Had it survived, we would have had a far better appreciation of this aspect of Henry V's contribution to the peaceful arts. And the completion and survival of his major contribution to ecclesiastical building – the great palace-monasteries by the Thames at Sheen and Syon – might have given him a place perhaps comparable to that of his predecessor Henry III in the patronage of church architecture.[73]

The maintenance of royal dignity, and of a suitably fitting ambience of splendour and magnificence, was a necessity – especially for the usurping dynasty that the Lancastrians were, and it was an expensive one. But it was also necessary for a prince to cultivate the mind, as well as the external image of majesty, and this might be achieved through reading. It was a contemporary belief that the practice of reading had a large part to play in correction, reform and what has been called 'self-transformation'. Texts were to be 'studied for action'.[74] The poet Thomas Hoccleve advised the heretical Sir John Oldcastle to read books of chivalry, of the legends of Troy and Thebes and of Arthurian romance, rather than 'climbing too high' by attempting personally to interpret Holy Writ through his own reading.[75] But, under proper guidance, the cultivation of the habit of reading was to be encouraged, especially in kings and princes. Henry V's

[72] For the park at Hesdin see A. Van Buren, 'Reality and romance in the park of Hesdin' in *Medieval Gardens*, ed. MacDougall, pp. 117–34; Vale, *The Princely Court*, pp. 228–9, 279–80, 281–2.

[73] For the building works at Sheen and Syon see above, pp. 142, 144–5.

[74] See C. Nall, *Reading and War in Fifteenth-century England: from Lydgate to Malory* (Woodbridge, 2012), pp. 1–2.

[75] Hoccleve, 'Address to Sir John Oldcastle' in *Hoccleve's Works: the Minor Poems*, ed. F.J. Furnivall, *EETS, Extra Series*, lxi (London, 1892), ll. 193–200. Cited by Nall, *Reading and War*, p. 1.

possession of a substantial collection of books on theology, liturgy, patristic thought and canon law is well documented.[76] His known religious and devotional practices were to some extent fed and guided by his reading. The habit of more general reading had been instilled in him at an early age, and this extended to secular works of law, philosophy, what we would call political thought, and imaginative literature.[77] Instances of the acquisition, binding, 'covering' and transport of books in his wardrobe and household accounts are numerous, suggesting the ownership of a well-stocked travelling library. In 1415–16, for example, 'various of the king's books' were 'covered' in bags which were in turn covered with velvet cloth of gold, silk, and motley cloth, and lined with satin of various colours.[78] In 1420–1, books were carried from Windsor to Westminster, then to Winchelsea and Dover, while ten others were bound, and seven books for the king's chapel were repaired with silk covers and bosses on their bindings.[79] In 1422, a 'book of Chivalry' was copied for the king, and a 'book called *Bede on the deeds of the English*' apparently in Anglo-Norman French, was received, as well as another containing 'Sunday (Lord's day) sermons'.[80] Henry's reading was nothing if not eclectic, and this can be demonstrated by the works which he is known to have commissioned and the writers whom he patronised. In this way the peaceful arts profited.

The passive habit of reading was accompanied by active patronage of authors and the ordering of copies of existing works. Richard Ullerston

[76] See McFarlane, *Lancastrian Kings and Lollard Knights*, Appendix C, pp. 232–8 & above, pp. 128, 147–8 for the inventory of his collection of largely theological, devotional and generally didactic books taken at the siege of Meaux in May 1422.

[77] For an attempt to list all books owned, commissioned and borrowed by Henry V and his kinsmen and women see J.E. Krochalis, 'The Books and Reading of Henry V and his Circle', *Chaucer Review*, 23 (1988), pp. 50–77.

[78] E 101/406/26, m. 4r.

[79] E 101/407/5, m. 4r.

[80] E 101/407/5, mm. 4r & 5r: 'Pro scripture unius libri de Chevalri pro Rege' (m. 4r); '1 libr[um] voc[atum] Beda des gestes Angl' & '1 libr[um] voc[atum] de sermonis dominical-ibus' (m. 5r). For Middle English cycles of 'dominical sermons', in part inspired by the offensive against Lollardy, see *A Late Fifteenth-century Dominical Sermon Cycle*, ed. S. Morrison, *EETS*, orig. ser., 337 & 338 (Oxford, 2012).

wrote his *De officio militari* ('Concerning the calling of knighthood') for Henry, as prince of Wales.[81] As king, in *c.*1420, he commissioned one of his French chaplains, Jean Galopes, dean of the collegiate church of Saint-Louis de la Saussaye in Normandy, to translate the *Meditations on the Life of Christ* of the pseudo-Bonaventure into French.[82] Galopes, whose living, as he told Henry in his dedicatory preamble to the text, lay in the *comté* of Harcourt, 'belonging to . . . my lord the duke of Exeter, your fair uncle',[83] also endorsed the value of reading to a ruler. Citing the Old Testament Book of Proverbs, he advanced the view that 'the glory of kings who wish wisely to govern themselves and their subjects is to investigate and seek the meaning of the divine Word'. Honour would thus be accorded to 'intellectual' as well as 'moral' virtue and it was by means of reading that this might be achieved.[84] He reminded the king that he had translated the text from Latin into French 'at your command'.[85] Active intervention, rather than the unsolicited receipt of works dedicated to a prospective patron, was at work here.

In similar vein, John Lydgate, the Benedictine monk of Bury St Edmunds, produced his *Troy Book* (begun in 1412) in Middle English, recounting the Trojan legend, and an English *Life* of the Virgin Mary,

---

[81] There are two surviving manuscripts: Cambridge, Trinity Coll., MS B 15. 23, fos 16v–22r & Corpus Christi Coll., MS 177, art. 26, fos 179–84. See above, pp. 126–7.

[82] There are two surviving high-quality illuminated manuscripts: BL, MS Royal 20 B. IV & Cambridge, Corpus Christi Coll., MS 213: a sixteenth-century inscription in the latter manuscript (fo. 159v) claims that 'This wasse sumtyme King Henri ye fifeth his Booke'. A partially erased note on the flyleaf (fo. iv) appears also to refer to Henry's ownership. For MS Royal 20 B. IV, see *The Genius of Illumination*, ed. S. McKendrick (London, 2011), cat. no. 29.

[83] 'Appartenant a . . . monseigneur le duc Dexcetre, vostre beaux oncles . . .' (fo. 1r).

[84] 'La gloire des Roys, que sagement veulent eulx et leurs subgiez gouverner, est de encercher et querir le sens de la parole divine, le quel sceu ils sont a honourer comme il soit ainsy que honneur est deue a vertu homme tant seulement morale, mais a celle qui est intellectuale' (fo. 1v).

[85] 'Je cest livre ay translate de vostre commandement de latin en francoys soubz vostre commission au bien de tous et a le honneur de Dieu . . .' (fo. 2v). For Galopes see M. Boulton, 'Jean Galopes, traducteur des *Meditationes vitae Christi*', *Moyen français*, 51 (2002–3), pp. 91–102.

both at the king's request.[86] It has been pointed out that the terminology and vocabulary which Lydgate uses in his *Troy Book* to describe the Trojan war bear strong resemblances to the language that justified Henry's French campaigns, stressing 'peace, just cause, unity and reason, not wilfulness'.[87] Other surviving manuscripts that can be identified and which appear to have been in Henry's ownership include a copy of Chaucer's *Troilus and Criseyde*;[88] a Book of Hours;[89] a bible, dating from *c.*1300–10, which he gave to his Carthusian foundation at Sheen;[90] and a manuscript of Helinand de Froidmont's *Chronicon*, captured at Meaux.[91] Other manuscripts may in time come to light which can be attributed to Henry's patronage or ownership, but the current tally, while in no way exceptional for a fifteenth-century ruler, tends to suggest a particular interest in didactic literature, composed in Latin, French and English. From the surviving evidence (which may, of course, be partial and incomplete) the works of Italian humanists and poets are conspicuous by their absence – there is no Petrarch, no Boccaccio, no Salutati. It was Henry's younger brother Humphrey who was to take up that cause and introduce many of these authors to an English audience. But the range of literature with which the king seems to have been familiar is not unimpressive. The life of the mind was evidently being cultivated. But beside the difficult demands of a bookish, contemplative life, never easily met by secular rulers, the

---

[86] Lydgate, *Troy Book*, ed. H. Bergen, 3 vols, *EETS, Extra Series* xcvii (London, 1906), esp. Prologue, ll. 111–151 & pp. 3–4 for Henry's role in the creation of the work; for the *Life* of the Virgin see *A Critical Edition of John Lydgate's Life of Our Lady*, ed. J. A. Lauritis (Pittsburgh/Louvain, 1961).

[87] See Nall, *Reading and War*, p. 9.

[88] New York, Pierpont Morgan Library, MS 817. See *The Pierpont Morgan MS M.817: a facsimile/introduction*, ed. J. Krochalis (Norman, Oklahoma, 1986).

[89] Cambridge, Trinity Coll. MS B. 117.

[90] Paris, Bibliothèque Mazarine MS 34. See L.F. Sandler, *Gothic Manuscripts, 1285–1385. A Survey of Manuscripts illuminated in the British Isles* (London, 1986), ii, pp. 31–2, no. 25.

[91] BL, Cotton MS Claudius B. IX. It is no. 24 in the inventory of books taken at Meaux: McFarlane, *Lancastrian Kings and Lollard Knights*, p. 236. Helinand (*c.*1150–*c.*1239), a Cistercian monk, produced a world chronicle from which the more celebrated Vincent of Beauvais derived some of his material.

obligations of an active life of external display had also to be fulfilled. This required very substantial outlay.

Expenditure on plate and jewels, luxury textiles, expensive garments and lavishly appointed furnishings was prodigious. However much they might occasionally complain about its costs, the king's subjects nevertheless expected that this level of conspicuous consumption should be part and parcel of the exercise of kingship. Outlay on such items averaged around 7,500–8,000 l. per year, sometimes more, when the separate, daily costs of the household, including food, drink and pious alms and oblations, averaged about 11,000 l. per annum.[92] Constant payments to London goldsmiths for objects in precious metal, including tableware marked with the king's arms, as well as shields and escutcheons, and items such as 'a great alms dish called the *Shipp*' (presumably a *nef* or boat-shaped vessel) were plentiful.[93] Such items could also serve another purpose – as pledges and securities for loans, or for the forthcoming payment of wages and fees, a practice employed notably in the preliminaries to the Agincourt campaign.[94] Marks of ownership of these objects, engraved, embossed or enamelled, could take the form of the king's heraldic devices or badges, as well as the hereditary coat of arms of England and France.[95] One of Henry's badges was the antelope, and in May 1419, 200 gold

---

[92] See, for examples, E 101/406/21, fo. 35v; E 101/407/4, fo. 76v.

[93] E 101/406/21, fo. 21r (Mar.–Oct. 1413). In July 1416 an alms dish 'in the shape of a silver-gilt ship' was delivered to the clerk of the king's jewels and plate, probably the same item (E 101/406/15, m. 8r).

[94] E 101/406/24: items, including two silver-gilt ewers, one decorated with the arms of England, the other with stags, as well as a reliquary and a spice plate were pledged for the payment of the king's minstrels during the campaign (21 June 1415). See J. Stratford, '"Par le special commandement du roy". Jewels and plate pledged for the Agincourt expedition' in *Henry V: New Interpretations*, ed. Dodd, pp. 157–70.

[95] These are found, in very great quantities, throughout the surviving documentation. For the vast accumulation of plate and jewels in the king's possession at his death see the inventory of Aug. 1423 in C 65/85, mm. 8–22, printed in *RP*, iv, pp. 214–41 and a subsequent indenture of Apr. 1426 in E 101/408/2. These documents would repay a great deal of further study and deserve a new, fully annotated and commentated edition, equivalent to that for Richard II's inventory of 1398–9 in J. Stratford, *Richard II and the English Royal Treasure* (Woodbridge, 2012). Henry V was still in possession of some of the items of Richard's treasure at his death (pp. 121–7, 423–4).

antelopes, presumably for distribution as the constituent parts of a livery to his household, were acquired from a London goldsmith, while in July 1421 other items of solid gold, including a cup and ewer, a gold clasp garnished with a sapphire in its middle, and a *balais* (ruby) with six large pearls around its border were also bought.[96] The purchase was completed by 200 'great pearls for the king's use'. A similar level of expenditure was maintained on textiles, furs and luxury fabrics. Apart from the never-ending round of cloth and fur purchases to provide summer and winter clothing for his household and for many of the officers in his service, the king was obliged to furnish his residences with costly hangings, tapestries, bed covers, curtains, canopies and upholstered furniture, as well as ensuring a sufficiently copious provision of textile banners, standards and pennons for his armies and his ships.[97] One supplier of embroidered, painted and embossed textiles was Rose Tenterden, a female painter (*pictrix*), who produced tunics 'stamped' with the king's arms, banners, and pennons 'stamped' with ostrich feathers.[98]

The royal barges, which carried the king, his guests and members of his household on the Thames and the Seine, also required outlay on fabric. In 1416, a covering or awning of scarlet cloth was provided for one of them, embroidered with the king's arms and with those of the Emperor Sigismund, who was brought up the Thames from Westminster to Windsor in it for the Garter ceremonies.[99] In 1420, the barge received a covering of black cloth, apparently decorated with what appear to be gilded figures of armed men striking bells with hammers (*jakemas, jaquemarts* or 'Jacks of the clock'), again for the Garter festivities.[100] It was on these occasions

[96] E 403/640, m. 2r (1 May 1419); E 403/651, m. 14r (17 July 1421).

[97] See E 101/407/4, fos 2v, 3v, 51r–v for a grand total of 837 banners, standards, pennons and pennoncells supplied in 1421 by John Cavendish, the king's 'broudator'.

[98] E 101/407/4, fo. 71v.

[99] E 101/406/26, m. 4r.

[100] E 101/407/4, fo. 67v: for '1 nigr' coopert' jakemas adaur', with two cushions of 'baldaquin' and a hanging, for the feast of St George. See F. Godefroy, *Lexique de l'ancien français* (Paris, 1901), p. 292: *jaquemart*.

that some of the most visually striking effects were achieved through the costumes worn by the king and his immediate kinsmen. In 1416 he appeared with his three brothers (Clarence, Bedford and Gloucester), all wearing similar doublets of velvet cloth of gold and damask lined with 'cloth of Rheims' and 'fortified' with Flemish cloth. The St George's Day feast of that year was exceptionally lavish, and no fewer than 4,920 blue garters of silk and gold were acquired for the garments of kings of Portugal and Denmark, the dukes of Holland and Bavaria, the king and his brothers, and the other earls, barons and knights of the order.[101] For the 1420 Garter celebrations at Windsor, John Cavendish, the king's 'broudeur' (embroiderer) supplied 3,322 garters with letters of Cyprus gold spelling out the motto *Hony soit qui male y pense* to be sewn on to the robes worn by the king, the duke of Bedford, the twenty-four Garter knights, the queen and the countess of Huntingdon.[102] By 1421, the number of embroidered garters supplied to the participants reached 4,638 and, as in 1420, the king's body of nine 'henchmen' – young esquires serving him – were given gowns of scarlet and green damask adorned with motifs the meaning of which is now difficult to fathom. In 1420 they had been embroidered with 'silver cages', 'besants and carbuncles' (or bosses); in 1421 they displayed 'hop branches' (*ramis de hopes*), perhaps echoing the 'camomile branches' (*duplicibus ramis de camanyll*) with which one of the king's doublets for the occasion was adorned.[103] That the king himself took a personal interest in the quality of the materials supplied for such purposes is evident from a chance reference in the wardrobe accounts to a man with four packhorses taking velvet and furs from London to Rochester 'to show them to the king'.[104] The king's concern for detail is once again apparent.

---

[101] E 101/406/26, m. 5r.
[102] E 101/407/4, fo. 2r: the garters were of 'tartarin, bokeram et carde', and the letters of silk and gold, bearing the 'dictamine *Hony soit qui male y pense*' (20 Feb. 1420).
[103] E 101/407/5, m. 3r (1421); E 101/407/4, fo. 2v (1420).
[104] E 101/407/4, fo. 73v: 'eidem domino Rege monstrand'.

The keeping up of a suitably regal 'estate', or mode of life and deportment, necessitated investment in other kinds of textile. Among these were the hangings and tapestries which provided the ubiquitous wall furniture and source of visual imagery in all later medieval residences of the rich, powerful or simply well-to-do.[105] After Henry's death, in August 1423 a comprehensive inventory was made of all the plate, crowns, jewels and textiles, including the 'cloths of Arras and tapestries' held by the late king.[106] It ran to twenty-one parchment folios. The total valuation of the contents in this Aladdin's cave of treasure was estimated by competent experts as reaching the very large sum of 18,804 l. 4s. 10d sterling.[107] It contained seventy-five items of tapestry or other textile hangings, all with indications of their subject-matter, some of them inherited – including items that had been acquired by confiscation from treasonable magnates in previous reigns – others purchased or captured by the king during his lifetime. These included items confiscated from Thomas of Woodstock, duke of Gloucester, under Richard II; from Henry, Lord Scrope; and booty from Henry V's French war, taken from the duke of Bourbon and from the capture of Meaux in May 1422. The images in the tapestries offer us an intriguing insight into what was presented visually, on a daily basis, to a later medieval ruler, his household, his guests and to all who entered the precincts of a royal residence. Many of the subjects which the tapestries displayed cannot (as yet) be identified, but there are sufficient grounds for recognising some familiar – and less familiar – themes from both religious and secular sources. Most had inscriptions and extracts from texts woven into them, which form a primary iconographical source of great value.[108]

[105] For tapestries in England during this period see S. McKendrick, 'Tapestries from the Low Countries in England in the Fifteenth Century' in *England and the Low Countries in the Late Middle Ages*, ed. C. Barron & N. Saul (Stroud/New York, 1995), pp. 43–61.

[106] C 65/85, mm. 8–22; *RP*, iv, pp. 214–41.

[107] *RP*, iv, p. 241.

[108] For inscriptions (in French and Latin) on tapestries see T.P. Campbell, *Tapestry in the Renaissance: Art and Magnificence* (New York, 2002), pp. 1–12, 55–64.

The contemporary repertoire of epic, romance and didactic literature was well represented. A very large tapestry, described as a 'piece of arras', 22 yards (66 feet) long and 4 yards (12 feet) deep, depicted the '*duszeperes*', or twelve peers of France, the legendary paladins of Charlemagne, with a text beginning 'Dieu vous doit'.[109] Others represented stories from historical, allegorical, didactic, epic and romance literature, and included Bevis of Hampton,[110] Antenor (from the legend of Troy),[111] Sir Percival, Ptolemy, king of Egypt, the Nine Worthies, Abraham and Isaac, the 'Five Joys of Our Lady', Gingebras, 'king of spices',[112] the Seven Ages of Man, St Edward and St Oswald, the apostles, St George, the emperor Octavian, Pharamond, king of the Franks, Charlemagne, Gloriant, duke of Brunswick, and the tale of Renart the Fox.[113] The appearance of Gloriant, a figure found largely in Middle Dutch literature and drama, suggests a specifically Netherlandish origin for that piece of 'arras d'or'.[114] The spectator of this very miscellaneous collection was sometimes invited by the texts depicted on the hangings to 'See the story', 'See love remembered', '[See] so you can picture in [your] memory', 'See the tree of youth', 'See Pharamon, first king of France', 'See ladies of noble station', 'See a tournament beginning', 'See here king Charlemagne', or 'See the noble duke Gloriant'. Some of the tapestries and their texts refer to more specifically

---

[109] C 65/85, m. 15r; *RP*, iv, p. 229, no. 681. E 101/408/2 has 'douseperes'.

[110] This was one of the most popular of Middle English romances, probably composed in *c*.1324, deriving from a thirteenth-century Anglo-Norman French version of the tale. See A.C. Baugh, 'The Making of Bevis of Hampton' in *Bibliographical Studies in honor of Rudolf Hirsch*, ed. W.E. Miller & T.G. Waldman (Philadelphia, 1974), pp. 15–37.

[111] For visual representations of the Trojan theme see S. McKendrick, 'The Great History of Troy: a Reassessment of the Development of a Secular Theme in Late Medieval Art', *JWCI*, 54 (1991), pp. 43–82.

[112] 'Gingebras', originally meaning 'preserved ginger' in both Old French and Middle English, was in use for 'gingerbread' by the fifteenth century. The inventory entry (no. 761) refers to 'I autre pece darras dor qc commence en lestorie: "Chist roys Gyngebras nomme"'.

[113] *RP*, iv, nos 689, 692, 690, 754 ('Come Theolomoun'), 757 ('de ix. Puissances'), 760 ('de la v. joies de Nostre Dame'), 761–3, 764, 765 ('Le Octavian Roye de Rome'), 785 ('Vees Farman'), 842, 947.

[114] See *Het abel spel Gloriant van Bruuyswijc en de sotternie De Duskenblazer na volghende*, ed. G. Stellinga (Tjeenk Willink/Noorduijn, 1976); & L. Muir, *Love and Conflict in Medieval Drama: the Plays and their Legacy* (Cambridge, 2007), pp. 82–3.

English versions of these themes. One depicted 'Haukyn', the sinful 'active man', and his soiled coat or mantle (*Sus Haukyn mantelet*), derived from William Langland's *Piers Plowman*;[115] another alluded to 'Amans en consolacion', perhaps a reference to John Gower's *Confessio Amantis*.[116] That such objects could be sources of instruction and edification seems beyond doubt, and two didactic poems by John Lydgate describe tapestries with precisely that purpose. In his poems on the *Life of St George* and the *Fall of Princes* Lydgate quotes the opening lines of the texts found on tapestries in exactly the same manner as in the inventory.[117] 'See here' and 'Lo!' or 'Lo here!' replicate the texts, and one might wonder whether Lydgate had himself seen some of the king's tapestries, or very similar examples. None of them survives to this day, but similarities with existing examples, and with representations of their themes in manuscript illumination, can be detected.[118] Thus the injunction 'See how the sole desire' (*Vessi coment le sole desir*) on a tapestry forming part of a set which included a tournament, reminds one of the motto '*A mon seul desir*' ('My only desire' or 'only wish') on the later (*c.*1490–1505) *Dame à la licorne* (Lady with the unicorn) series, depicting the five or, according to some interpretations, six senses.[119] The two pieces of arras described as 'Of a lady who plays the harp' may simply refer to an anonymous subject, but the figure of

---

[115] *RP*, iv, no. 784. For Haukyn and his coat see Langland, *Piers Plowman: A New Annotated Edition of the C-text*, ed. D. Pearsall (Exeter, 2008), xiii, ll. 228–9.

[116] *RP*, iv, no. 841: 'Vessi amans en consolacion'. For 'Amans' and consolation see J. Gower, *Confessio Amantis*, ed. A. Russell Peck (Toronto, 1980), esp. pp. xi, xxviii & P. Nicholson, *Love and Ethics in Gower's 'Confessio Amantis'* (Michigan, 2005).

[117] See E.P. Hammond, 'Two Tapestry Poems by Lydgate', *Englische Studien*, 43 (Leipzig, 1910–11), pp. 10–26, esp. pp. 22–3.

[118] For a set of Tournai (?) tapestries (*c.*1475–95) representing scenes from the Trojan war, with French inscriptions, now in the Metropolitan Museum of Art, New York, see Campbell, *Tapestry in the Renaissance*, cat. nos 2, 3 (pp. 55–64). Also A. Cavallo, *Medieval Tapestries in the Metropolitan Museum of Art* (New York, 1993), cat. no. 13, pp. 229–49, especially pp. 236–9 for the inscriptions.

[119] *RP*, iv, no. 798: 'le fole desir', a misreading of 'sole desir'. For the *Dame à la licorne* series see J-P. Boudet, '*La Dame à la licorne* et ses sources médiévales d'inspiration', *Bulletin de la Société nationale des Antiquaires de France*, séance du 10 fev. 1999 (1999), pp. 61–78 & 'Jean Gerson et la *Dame à la licorne*' in *Religion et société urbaine au moyen âge: études offertes à Jean-Louis Biget*, ed. P. Boucheron & J. Chiffoleau (Paris, 2000), pp. 551–62.

Sempronia playing the harp found in Boccaccio's *De mulieribus Claris* ('Concerning illustrious women') might (perhaps unrecognised by the compiler of the inventory) conceivably lie behind the image.[120]

Whatever the case, the existence of Old French, Anglo-Norman and, to a lesser extent, Middle English versions of virtually all the 'stories' (*estoires*) in the tapestries suggests that the visual image and the written text here combined to produce a medium of instruction, edification and entertainment with which Henry V was very familiar. The wall hanging was not solely a functional, or even an aesthetic, object. It told a story, and could impart didactic and moralising messages. Some of the texts on both textiles and items of plate and jewellery listed in the 1423 inventory look very like mottoes, such as the phrase 'I love you faithfully' (*Je vous ayme loialment*) on a bench- or seat-cover;[121] or 'Without fail' (*Saunz departier*);[122] or 'To love and serve' (*Amer et server*).[123] The motto, or *mot*, in the fifteenth century, as at later periods, could represent a deliberate choice, a statement of intent, or a characterisation, often related to the personal and emotional life of the individual.[124] But, as with the Renaissance emblem, maxim or conceit, they could be deliberately ambiguous, susceptible to multiple interpretations.[125]

Henry had his own mottoes and visual devices, and these appeared in many — and sometimes unexpected — places. The evidence of his mottoes

---

[120] *RP*, iv, no. 693 ('1 pece darras pur le cuppebord del estorie "Dun dame qe harpe"'); no. 841 ('1 autre tapite darras saunz ore, qe istorie: "Dun dame qe harpe ung note" '). For an image of Sempronia as harpist see BNF, Ms. Fr. 599, fo. 68v.

[121] *RP*, iv, no. 700.

[122] *RP*, iv, no. 107 (1 collar of green fabric with the embroidered words 'saunz departier'). The words 'saunz departyr' are found with the sign manual of Richard II, in the king's hand, on a letter of 15 Nov. 1389, as 'Le Roy R. S. saunz departyr'. See Hardy, *Handwriting of Kings and Queens*, p. 14 & frontispiece; also N. Saul, *Richard II* (London, 1997), fig. 7 where it is described as 'a kind of motto'. Hardy, however, rendered its translation as 'without fail', with the meaning 'without failing to do so' ordering the recipient to do what he had been ordered.

[123] *RP*, iv, no. 479 (a gold chain with an enamel cross with a motto [*reso[u]n*] 'amer et server').

[124] See F. Salet, 'Emblematique et histoire de l'art', *Revue de l'Art*, 87 (1990), pp. 22–5.

[125] For a virtuoso display of erudition on this subject see E. Wind, *Pagan Mysteries in the Renaissance* (London, 1967), pp.12–16, 98–112.

and their possible meanings has given rise to at least one recent interpretation of the very nature of his personal kingship. On 20 February 1415 a payment was made to William Soper of Southampton, keeper of the king's ships, 'for the painting of the king's great ship, lately constructed at Southampton, with swans and antelopes and various other devices, and also with the king's motto: *une sanz pluis* ('one and no more') in various parts of the said ship'.[126] Five years or so later, the motto appeared again, this time embroidered on a covering of red cloth for the king's barge. On this occasion it was coupled with another motto: *humblement le requier* ('I humbly request it'). It was said that these were 'for the king and the queen'.[127] The posthumous inventory of August 1423 also referred to 'a covering for a barge, of red cloth, embroidered with the mottoes (*resuns*) of the king and the queen'.[128] In 1421, the second motto, *humblement le requier*, had also been embroidered on a tunic of blue and white satin, together with 'double branches of camomile', worked in gold thread and silk, 'for the king'.[129] The possible sources and derivations of these two expressions, and the reasons for their coupling, warrant investigation. Mottoes, personally chosen though they were, can be misleading, telling us more about conventional attitudes and their expression than about the heartfelt sentiments of an individual. But in the case of Henry V his use of a motto has given rise to what appears to be an ingenious, though

---

[126] E 403/620, m. 10r: Soper was paid 7 l. 6s. 8d 'super picture magne navis Regis apud Sutht' nuper facte, viz. cum signis et antelopes et aliis diversis armis, necnon cum verbo Regis vocat' *une sanz pluis* in diversis partibus eiusdem navis' (20 Feb. 1415). It is not clear from the entry whether the 'great ship' was the *Holy Ghost* or the *Saint Clare of Spain*, recently built at Southampton (see m. 4r).

[127] See E 101/407/5, m. 3r: payment for 'unius coopertorii fact' de panno rubeo pro Bargea Regis, superoperat' in brouder' cum istis dictaminibus: *une sanz pluis* et *humblement le requier* fact' pro Rege et Regine'. A virtually identical entry is found on m. 9r.

[128] C 65/85, m. 18r : 'Item, 1 coveryng pur ung barge, de drap rouge, enbroudes ovec les resuns du roy et de la royne, pris ensemble 6 l. 13s. 4d'; *RP*, iv, p. 234, no. 803.

[129] E 101/407/5, m. 3r: payment 'super opere et broudatura unius gitoun de satyn blodio et albo, superoperato cum duplicibus ramis de camamyll' et iste dictamine: *humblement le requier* de auro de cipr' et serico, pro eodem Rege', again repeated on m. 9r.

unconvincing, argument about the nature of his kingship which, it is claimed, demonstrates beyond all doubt 'he saw as being both divinely authorised and justified in its authoritarianism'.[130]

It has been suggested that the provenance of Henry's *une sanz pluis* (modern Fr. *une* or *un sans plus*) motto lies in the epic and heroic literature of the ancient world:

[I]t almost certainly comes from a medieval French version of Homer's *Iliad* (which Henry would have heard in French). The arrogance of the message is quite breathtaking: '*d'avoir plusieurs seigneurs aucun bien je n'y vois/ qu'un sans plus soit le maistre et qu'un seul soit le roi*' ('As for having several lords, I see no good therein/ let one and no more be the master, and that one alone be the king'). It is difficult to read this as anything other than Henry's determination to exercise complete authority – over France as well as England, and over his religious subjects as well as his secular ones.[131]

Unfortunately for this argument, there *was* no 'medieval French version of Homer's *Iliad*' and Henry could never have 'heard it in French'. The first recorded French edition and translation of Homer's epic appeared more than 120 years after Henry V's death, in 1545.[132] Even then, the passage cited is not rendered in anything like the same way until the appearance of the humanist Étienne de la Boétie's *Discours de la servitude volontaire*,

[130] Mortimer, *1415*, p. 541.
[131] Mortimer, *1415*, p. 97 and n. 72 on p. 576. My underlining. A reference to the *Iliad*, ii, ll. 204–5 is given there, but no edition is cited. The motto is used to support a more general argument about the authoritarian, if not absolute, nature of Henry's kingship, with the claim that 'there were plenty of men and women in Europe who saw him as a tyrant, and quite a few in England too' (pp. 540–1). For another interpretation of Henry's style of kingship see above, pp. 17–20.
[132] See M. Bizer, *Homer and the Politics of Authority in Renaissance France* (Oxford, 2011), p. 18.

composed probably in about 1548 but not published until 1574.[133] The extract is taken from Odysseus's speech to the Greeks restraining them from taking action individually and 'playing the king'. It has been argued that the speech 'links Homer's authority to the idea of monarchy being the best form of government' but that la Boétie was, in fact, attacking the use of Homer to support and buttress the absolute authority of kings.[134] The French, he urged, were not to be 'enslaved' by being put under Homer's spell by the apologists for absolutism. We can therefore conclude that Henry V's choice of the motto *une sans plus* had absolutely nothing to do with any concept of kingship, authoritarian or otherwise. He may well have harboured notions of arbitrary and unbridled rule, but they could not have been bolstered by a non-existent French translation of a great poem from classical antiquity. Henry was no proto-Charles I or James II, let alone a Louis XIV. The sources of his motto must be sought elsewhere.

The linking of the two mottoes *une sans plus* and *humblement le requier*, apparently after the king's marriage to Catherine of France, may provide some clue as to the context in which they could be set. It is known that a motto attributed to his brother Duke Humphrey of Gloucester was *Sans plus vous belle*, which associates its meaning with a love-dedication.[135] The motto *une sanz plus* is also found, twice, among a series of mottoes recorded as marginalia in a volume containing poems by Lydgate and Hoccleve's *Regement of Princes*, where it is rendered '*Une sanz plus, pur le Roy*' ('one and no more, for the king').[136] It is perhaps in this world, rather than in

---

[133] The translation, by Hugues Salet, rendered the text as 'Pas n'est raison que tous ayons honeurs . . . /Quand elle n'est que par ung seul guydee/Donc soit ung Roy (lequel Juppiter donne)/Tresobey, en tout ce quil ordonne': H. Salet, *Les dix premiers livres de l'Illiade d'Homere, prince des poetes* (Paris, 1545), p. lxiiii. For la Boétie's version of the passage (which is presumably that cited by Mortimer) see *Oeuvres complètes d'Estienne de la Boétie*, ed. P. Bonnefon & G. Gounuilhon (Bordeaux, 1892), p. 1; and M. Rothstein, 'Homer for the Court of François I', *Renaissance Quarterly*, 59 (2006), pp. 732–67 for the dating of la Boétie's treatise.

[134] Bizer, *Homer and the Politics of Authority*, p. 4.

[135] See H.N. MacCracken, 'Additional Light on the *Temple of Glas*', *PMLA*, 23 (1908), p. 136.

[136] MacCracken, 'Additional Light', pp. 129, 130. The other rendering of the motto is in the somewhat cryptic form '*Une sanz plus, fortune allas*'.

that of Homeric rhetoric, that we may seek explanation for the choice of such mottoes. It suggests that Henry's motto may have taken the form of a love token, or resolution, of exclusive fidelity to one above all others. Whether this represented a resolve, after his accession to the throne, to renounce the alleged disorderliness and even promiscuity of his earlier years can only be a matter for speculation. Alternatively, the motto might simply be an injunction to moderation and restraint.

Whatever the case, the context of the motto appears to lie within the field of personal relationships rather than authoritarian concepts of kingship. This might be supported by the coupling of the motto with the 'humble request' with which it was being paired by 1420. That phrase comes directly out of the vocabulary of petitioning and supplication: in 1421, a petitioner and his wife could 'humbly request pardon', and literary examples of its constant use are plentiful.[137] One of Machaut's ballades began with the lines: 'Lady, I humbly request your mercy if I have wronged you in any way'.[138] In the *Mystere du roy Ademar* by Jean du Prieur, the petition is found: 'Ha, my good friend and my brother, I humbly request and pray you . . .'[139] An almost identical phrase is used by Henry V's Agincourt prisoner, Jean, count of Angoulême, in his French verses addressed to the crucifix: 'I humbly pray and request you to protect me from harmful things'.[140] Similarly, in the Arras *Mystère de la Passion*, Christ

---

[137] See PPC, ii, p. 307: petition of Sir John Mortimer and his wife Eleanor to John, duke of Bedford, as Henry V's lieutenant in England: 'que humblement vous requier pardon de vostre desplesir' (15 Nov. 1421).

[138] See Y. Plumley, *The Art of Crafted Song: Citation and Allusion in the Age of Machaut* (Oxford, 2013), pp. 279–307. The ballade by Machaut begins: 'Dame, mercy vous requier humblement/Se j'ay vers vous nulle chose meffait' [http://jechante.exeter.ac.uk/archive/text].

[139] See Jean du Prieur, *Le Mystere du roy Ademar*, ed. A. Meiller (Geneva, 1970), p. 115, ll. 2626–7: 'Haa, mon bon amy et mon frere/Humblement te requier et prie . . .'

[140] See E. Charavay, *Jean d'Orléans, comte d'Angoulême* (Paris, 1876), p. 11, *Oratio ad Crucifixum*, ll. 7–8: 'Humblement te prie et requier/Que tu me gardes d'encombriers'. For Jean d'Angoulême's period of captivity in England see *Charles d'Orléans in England (1415–1440)*, ed. M-J. Arn (Woodbridge, 2000), pp. 27–8, 37–9, 42–3, 48–50, 50–2.

is asked to 'hear my petition, [as] I humbly request pardon' and the phrase recurs throughout the play.[141]

If the motto *humblement le requier* can be linked to Queen Catherine, as its appearance in the 1420s seems to suggest, then a context of love promises and tokens might be sustainable. If the two mottoes are seen as a statement and a response, then the king's assertion of fidelity, on the one hand, and the queen's request for it, on the other, might make sense of the puzzle. Or perhaps the exchange of sentiments was deemed to be mutual. The feminine *une sans plus* may (despite a certain inconsistency in the use of verbal male and female forms, noted by Mortimer) simply confirm that we are in the world of courtly love and amorous sentiment, however formal and conventional that might be. In 1430, the lubricious and distinctly unfaithful Philip the Good of Burgundy, credited during his lifetime with 26 recorded bastards, adopted the motto *Aultre n'aray* ('I will have none other'), although a possibly more political and diplomatic significance has been suggested for it.[142] But Henry V, as contemporaries testified, was a different kind of being. His newly found gravity, discretion and self-discipline were admired by the chroniclers and led to a belief that 'from the day of his father's death [in 1413] until his marriage . . . in June 1420, Henry is said to have kept himself entirely chaste'.[143] And, if his

[141] See *Le Mystere de la Passion*, ed. J.M. Richard (Arras, 1891), p. 194, ll. 16611–14: 'Sire, ma parole exauchiez/Et oyez ma petition,/Humblement vous requier pardon'. Similar phrases are found in ll. 16655–8, 17840, 21882 & 22172.

[142] The chronicler Georges Chastellain stated that Philip was 'durement lubrique': cited in J-C. Delclos, *Le Témoignage de Georges Chastellain. Historiographe de Philippe le Bon et de Charles le Téméraire* (Geneva, 1980), pp. 112, 142. See Salet, 'Emblematique et histoire de l'art', p. 24. Salet suggests that the motto implying exclusive intent or allegiance may not have related to Philip's marriage of 1430 but to his creation of his own Order of the Golden Fleece in that year, which enabled him to refuse election to the English Order of the Garter, or indeed any other order. But the notion that the motto was in some sense a prediction of his return from English allegiance to an exclusive devotion to the Valois French crown (as happened in 1435) may stretch credibility a little too far.

[143] McFarlane, 'Henry V: a Personal Portrait', p. 124, and see the chronicle references on pp. 123 & 124.

motto was to have any meaning at all, it could signify that he was, in this and other respects – as contemporary writers observed – 'a new man'.

For a ruler whose traditional and popular reputation rests upon his role as a 'warrior-king', Henry V's contribution to the peaceful arts was not unimpressive. Music, literature, ecclesiastical and secular architecture, and the applied arts, all benefited from his engagement, patronage and (in the case of music) practice. Some of this involvement was conventional, incumbent upon any ruler. But in some respects Henry's active engagement, as both prince and king, was broadly consistent with other aspects of his behaviour. The taking of personal initiatives, such as his requests for translations and Middle English versions of particular texts, along with his composition of musical settings of parts of the mass, correspond well with that directness and single-minded pursuit of objectives observable in so many other aspects of his life and rule.

Chapter 7

LAST WILL AND LEGACY

This book has set out to portray Henry V not only as an exponent of the active life, whether by choice or necessity, but also as an advocate of the inner life of contemplation. The contemplative, reflective streak in the character of even the most active of 'the great ones who live in the world's eye'[1] is often brought out when they contemplate their death. The making of a will can represent both their farewell to this world and a glimpse into their ultimate intentions and preoccupations. The declared wishes of a testator may reveal much about them. Especially at times in history when people rarely speak to us in their own voices, the words recorded in their wills and testaments, it has been said, 'deserve the closest scrutiny'.[2] In the later Middle Ages, disclosure of their last wishes can enable us to come closer to the true beliefs, intentions and preoccupations of individuals than

---

[1] K.B. McFarlane, 'Henry V: a Personal Portrait', in his Lancastrian Kings and Lollard Knights (Oxford, 1972), p. 132.

[2] The observation was made by McFarlane in his discussion of the will and codicils of Henry Beaufort, bishop of Winchester, in his essay 'At the Deathbed of Cardinal Beaufort', in *Studies in History presented to F.M. Powicke* (Oxford, 1948), pp. 405–28 repr. in *England in the Fifteenth Century*, ed. G.L. Harriss (London, 1981), vi, pp. 115–37, esp. p. 121.

any other source. 'Depend upon it, sir,' said Dr Samuel Johnson, 'when a
man knows he is to be hanged in a fortnight, it concentrates his mind
wonderfully.'[3] The ability of the prospect of mortality to 'concentrate the
mind wonderfully' appears to have played its part in determining the form
and content of the last wishes of rulers, as well as of their subjects. Henry V
was no exception to this rule. As the author of three wills – the second of
which is in fact simply a declaration, before departing for France in 1417,
of his wishes for the administration of his duchy of Lancaster estates and the
payment of debts – the king leaves us in little doubt of his intentions. His
first full and complete will was drawn up at Southampton, on 24 July 1415,
before his embarkation on the Agincourt campaign.[4] The second 'will',
dated 21 July 1417, was also drawn up on the eve of his departure 'to
recover by help of God, my rights there [in France] to me belonging'.[5] His
last complete will was made at Dover on 10 June 1421, when he was again
about to set sail for France. A set of codicils to the will was then appended
to it, on his deathbed, at the castle of Bois de Vincennes, on 26 August
1422.[6] He died between 2 and 3 a.m. on 31 August 1422.[7]

The wills are of particular interest not only for what they tell us about
the king's intentions for the salvation of his soul and the disposal of his

---

[3] J. Boswell, *The Life of Samuel Johnson* (New York, 1946), p. 143, letter to Boswell, 19 Sept. 1777.

[4] The original, in Latin, is lost but the will survives in a late seventeenth-century copy in Gonville & Caius Coll., Cambridge, MS 392: 'Miscellaneae Collectiones Mag. Hare', ii, pp. 1–10: 'Testamentum Henrici V'. Printed in *Foedera*, ix, pp. 289–93.

[5] E 23/2: the original, in English, with holograph endorsement by the king himself. Printed in J. Nichols, *A Collection of all the Wills . . . of the Kings and Queens of England* (London, 1780), pp. 236–43.

[6] ECR MS 59, fos 1r–7v, a near-contemporary copy, made soon after Oct. 1423, in Latin. Printed in P. Strong & F. Strong, 'The Last Will and Codicils of Henry V', *EHR*, 96 (1981), pp. 79–102. The will and codicils were rediscovered among the Eton muniments in 1978. The terms 'will and testament' are used interchangeably here to mean declarations whereby a testator names executors and provides for the distribution of real and movable property on death. 'Codicils' are used in the sense of documents that supplement, modify or partially revoke existing or earlier wills.

[7] See *Foedera*, x, p. 253.

worldly goods, but for the evidence they offer of changes in those intentions over his short lifetime. A significant difference between his first
(1415) and last (1421, 1422) wills lies in the extent to which French issues
and considerations are present in the later will. St Denis is now included
among the four named martyr-saints, and St Rémy among the three
confessor-saints, both closely associated with France and the French royal
house.[8] Obviously the French prisoners taken at Agincourt and elsewhere
could not feature in the first will, given its date. But they are dealt with, in
some detail, in the last will.[9] In the codicils to that will, drawn up as he lay
dying – but apparently still sound in mind – at Vincennes, specific bequests
were made by Henry, as 'heir and regent of the kingdom of France', to the
abbey of Saint-Denis 'near Paris', so that his memory 'be held in their
prayers and other devout works of piety'.[10] The monks received an altar
furnishing with 'images and figures of radiant suns', three copes of the
same set, or the nearest to them, and 'a great cross which was accustomed
to stand on the altar in our chapel'. The items given to Saint-Denis were
listed in a later inventory (of June 1425), where the cross was described as
being of silver gilt, with a 'great standing base'.[11] Henry's executors had
also delivered to Saint-Denis a 'high altar frontal' and a 'low altar frontal',
in red velvet, embroidered with gold leaves; an apparel decorated with
pearls and with the arms of England; the three copes mentioned above,
also of red velvet, embroidered with gold roses, lions and lily flowers; two
tunics and a chasuble of the same cloth and colour; three albs with 'parures',
stoles and 'fanones' (liturgical banners) of the same cloth and colour, and
a pair of curtains of red 'tartaryn'. Further gifts of vestments, altar furnishings and cloth of gold were given to churches at Mantes, Vernon, Rouen,

---

[8] ECR, MS 59, fo. 1r; Strong & Strong, 'The Last Will and Codicils of Henry V', p. 89.
[9] ECR, MS 59, fo. 2v; Strong & Strong, 'The Last Will and Codicils of Henry V', p. 92.
[10] ECR, MS 59, fo. 7r; Strong & Strong, 'The Last Will and Codicils of Henry V', p. 100: 'ut
nostri memoria ibidem in orationibus et aliis devotis pietatis operibus habeatur'.
[11] Nichols (ed.), *A Collection of all the Wills . . .*, pp. 415–16; *Foedera*, x, p. 346: 28 June 1425:
'cum magno pede stante'.

Arques, Eu, Hesdin and Thérouanne.[12] The role of Henry V as creator of Lancastrian France was here being emphasised.

As ruler of Lancastrian England, the king commended in his last will the 'prosperity and peace' of his successors, and of the kingdom, to God. It was his prayer and wish that God should 'protect, safeguard and defend' it not only from 'divisions and dissensions' but also 'from all kinds of heretical errors'.[13] The Lollard threat, though marginalised and much diminished by Henry's actions and those of his bishops, was still present in 1421. The king's wishes for his funeral ceremony and burial, and provisions for his personal salvation, command a considerable amount of space in both his first and last wills. In their final form, these clauses take us as close as we will ever get to Henry V's concept of the kingly office, its pious obligations, and the scale on which intercession for the soul was to be undertaken. The king prayed for redemption, and expressed the hope that he might be 'received into Abraham's bosum', to be redeemed 'not by my own merits, because I am a sinful man', but through the 'passion of our lord Jesus Christ'. An army of saints, martyrs, archangels and angels was assembled to intercede for his soul: of these, twenty-six are specifically named from the whole host (who were also to be included in their entirety) and, in suitably regal style, all the residents of 'the court of heaven' (*totius celestis curie*). Of the chosen saints, six were either English themselves or had strong English connections: George, Alban, Edward the Confessor, John of Bridlington (a particular favourite), Winifred and Etheldreda. The king's identification with his Plantagenet predecessors was made plain by his wish that his mortal body be buried at Westminster 'among the tombs of kings in the place where the relics of saints are kept'.[14] This meant the

---

[12] *Foedera*, x, p. 346: at Rouen, two pieces of red cloth, embroidered with gold falcons, no doubt part of a secular hanging, were given 'from which to make vestments' ('pro vestimentis inde faciendis').

[13] ECR, MS 59, fo. 1r; Strong & Strong, 'The Last Will and Codicils of Henry V', p. 89: 'a divisionibus, dissensionibus, et ab omni specie hereticorum fallacia protegat, visitet et defendat: amen'.

[14] ECR MS 59, fo. 1v; Strong & Strong, 'The Last Will and Codicils of Henry V', p. 90.

east end of the abbey church at Westminster, close to the high altar and the shrine of St Edward the Confessor. Unlike his father, who had been buried at Canterbury, Henry chose Westminster, having brought the body of the last Plantagenet – the deposed Richard II – to the abbey church for fitting burial. Continuity with the past, and the 'colonisation' of the abbey as *the* site of the royal mausoleum in future, was thereby ensured.

The specific instructions which he left for the site and construction of his tomb are significant. The tomb was to be an essential part of what was in effect a chantry foundation, and his last will speaks at length of an elaborate sequence of masses to be celebrated at Westminster to assist his soul's passage through purgatory and into paradise.[15] These stipulations admirably illustrate 'that preoccupation with the after-life which was so marked a feature of late medieval society'.[16] An altar dedicated to the Annunciation to the Virgin Mary, and to All Saints, was to be erected 'contiguous to our tomb' in such a way that 'the priests, celebrating there, could be seen by the people, so that their devotion in praise of God would be more fervently aroused, and He would be more often glorified through his creations'.[17] This public display of intercession for a ruler's soul was unusual, and may accord well with the view that Henry V showed a concern for the devotional lives of the laity, of which he himself was a member, as well as for the formal ministrations of the clergy. Those formal ministrations were of a highly elaborate and specific kind. The knowledge of liturgical practice revealed by his last will is nothing if not impressive. Unlike his father, who was content, in his last will, merely to found a perpetual chantry at Canterbury 'to sing and pray for my soul . . . in such a place and after such ordinance as it seemeth best to my . . . cousin of Canterbury', that is,

---

[15] For chantries and their endowment see above, pp. 148–9.
[16] H.M. Colvin, *Architecture and the After-Life* (New Haven/London, 1992), p. 189.
[17] ECR MS 59, fo. 1v; Strong & Strong, 'The Last Will and Codicils of Henry V', p. 90: 'quod sacerdotes inibi celebrantes videri a populo ut eius devotio in Dei laudem ferventius accendatur, et Deus in creaturis suis sepius glorificetur'.

Archbishop Thomas Arundel,[18] Henry V's wishes could hardly be more precise and specific. Three clearly defined masses per day were to be celebrated for him by the monks of Westminster until the end of time, each carefully stipulated to take place at a certain hour on each day.

Of the three daily masses,[19] the 'middle' one was always to be the mass of the day, whatever the occasion. Every Sunday, the first mass was to be of the Assumption of the Virgin, the last to be that of the Resurrection. A weekday cycle was set out: on Mondays, the first mass was to be of the altar's dedication, that is, of the Annunciation, the last to be of 'the Angels'. On Tuesdays, the first was to be of the Nativity of Christ, the last of the Nativity of the Virgin. On Wednesdays: the Holy Spirit and the Conception of the Virgin; on Thursdays: the body of Christ and the Purification of the Virgin; on Fridays: the Holy Cross and the Annunciation; on Saturdays: All Saints and a Requiem Mass for the king's soul and those of his parents, and of all the faithful departed. The first of the three daily masses was to be celebrated at 'about the seventh hour' when 'the monks of the said church are wont to rise'; the second at 'about the ninth hour'; and the third after the reading of the Gospel at the abbey's daily High Mass, at whatever hour of the day all were 'gathered together to hear masses and to give praise to their creator'.[20] These very exact prescriptions bear comparison with the wishes of other members of the ruling house and higher nobility – but they remain exceptionally specific. The consistent devotion to the Virgin Mary is particularly striking. Others among the king's kinsmen and companions-in-arms followed suit. In his will of 8 August 1437, Richard Beauchamp, earl of Warwick, appears to follow, if not to emulate, the terms of Henry V's wishes for the celebration of masses.[21] In his newly founded chantry chapel

---

[18] See Henry IV's will, dated at Greenwich, 21 Jan. 1409, in English, printed by Nichols (ed.), *A Collection of all the Wills*, pp. 203–5.

[19] ECR, MS 59, fos 1r–v; Strong & Strong, 'The Last Will and Codicils of Henry V', p. 90, for the stipulations that follow.

[20] ECR MS 59, fo. 1v; Strong & Strong, 'The Last Will and Codicils of Henry V', p. 90.

[21] His will is printed in *Historia vitae et regni Ricardi II*, ed. T. Hearne (Oxford, 1729), pp. 240–9, for what follows see pp. 241–2.

at St Mary's, Warwick, the earl also requested three masses per day, until the end of the world, one to be sung, the other two to be said 'without note'. On Mondays, his third mass was to be 'of the Angels' (as was the king's); on Wednesdays, Thursdays and Fridays they were (as were the king's) to be of the Holy Spirit, the Body of Christ, and the Holy Cross respectively.

Unlike his requests for the celebration of masses, Henry's instructions in his last will for the conduct of his funeral ceremonies are less precise than many of their time. They, and their cost, were to be at his executors' discretion, but were to be such as would 'maintain the honour of regal dignity' while 'avoiding superfluity'.[22] Despite this injunction – apparently urging restraint – there can be little doubt that the obsequies were unstinting in their display of the muted splendour customary at royal and noble funerals. No fewer than 222 cloths of gold were offered by members of the Lancastrian dynasty and higher nobility at the funeral and burial rites on 6 and 7 November 1422, and the abbey received 200 torches to be lit during the ceremonies.[23] The account in the minute book of the Brewers' Company reported that

at the *dirige* on the Friday and at the mass on the Saturday, there were offered 200 cloths of gold and more in Westminster church upon the corpse of the said king . . .[24]

A full chivalric and heraldic ritual was observed, closely comparable with those devised for Edward, the Black Prince, in 1376 and Louis de Mâle,

[22] ECR MS 59, fo. 2r; Strong & Strong, 'The Last Will and Codicils of Henry V', p. 91. For the funeral ceremonies see W.H. St John Hope, 'The Funeral, Monument and Chantry Chapel of King Henry the Fifth', *Archaeologia*, 65 (1913–14), pp. 129–86; also C. Allmand, *Henry V* (New Haven/London, 1992; 2nd edn. 1997) pp. 174–8. The abbey's sacrist's accounts for 1422–3 contain detailed entries of receipts and expenses for the funeral and burial, including wax for candles and torches, cloth of gold, black mourning robes, timber for barriers around the hearse, black cloth to drape over the hearse, and oblations: see WAM, MS 19663, mm. 1r–2v.

[23] WAM, MS 19663, mm. 1r–v.

[24] Guildhall Library, MS 5440, fo. 72r. The *dirige* was the service for the dead, in which the first words of the antiphon were 'Dirige dominus'.

count of Flanders, in 1384.[25] This demanded the appearance of four warhorses, bridled, saddled and harnessed, one ridden by a knight in full armour, bearing a sword, wearing a surcoat of the king's arms and with a crown on his head.[26] The four horses were covered with trappers or caparisons, one of blue velvet embroidered with gold windmills and antelopes; another of red and black velvet with white swans; a third of black velvet with white ostrich plumes (the tournament badge of the Black Prince, inherited by every subsequent prince of Wales); and a fourth of blue and red velvet with the arms of England and France.[27] In the cortège which processed through the abbey, four 'great standards' were also borne, as well as fifteen 'small standards' or banners, and thirty-nine pennoncells.[28] All this equipment, including the surcoat and sword, as was customary by this time, was handed over to the abbey, and the abbot, the sacrist and the keeper of the vestry received the various items. Some were to hang over the king's tomb – as over the Black Prince's tomb at Canterbury – for centuries to come.

Although 'superfluity' was to be avoided, the provision of 'lights' to burn both at the funeral rites and at subsequent celebrations and commemorations of the king was hardly made on a small scale. At least 400 pounds of wax were received by the abbey for the continuous burning of four great candles around his tomb for 296 days after his death.[29] On the day of his funeral, a total of fifteen large wax candles, of varying sizes, was to be placed on and around his hearse or bier.[30] But the highest level of expenditure was

---

[25] For these, and other such ceremonies since the later thirteenth century, see M. Vale, *The Princely Court. Medieval Courts and Culture in North-West Europe, 1270–1380* (Oxford, 2001: 2nd edn 2003), pp. 240–4 & M. Vale, *War and Chivalry. Warfare and Aristocratic Culture in England, France and Burgundy at the End of the Middle Ages* (London, 1981), pp. 88–94.

[26] Guildhall Library, MS 5440, fo. 72r.

[27] The helm, crest and trappers for the four warhorses and other funeral equipment are listed in the great wardrobe account in E 101/407/5, m. 8r.

[28] WAM MS 19663, mm. 2r–v. A fifth trapper, of green velvet, with antelopes on a 'floor' or 'stage' with gold branches, was given to the abbey after the ceremonies by the king's executors.

[29] WAM MS 19663, m. 1r.

[30] ECR MS 59, fo. 2r; Strong & Strong, 'The Last Will and Codicils of Henry V', p. 91.

reserved for the perpetual round of prayer service to be provided by the monks of Westminster. The major costs of the perpetual masses to be celebrated for the king's soul were to be borne by rents and other revenues from estates and appropriated churches held, or to be received if necessary, by the abbot and convent at Westminster.[31] These included the revenues from lands acquired as a result of the dissolution of alien priories. In 1445, the abbot and convent of Westminster requested that Henry VI confirm a grant to them of the manors of Offord Cluny (Hunts.) and Letcombe Regis (Berks.), formerly held by the great French abbey of Cluny, to meet these costs. They were

> to be held by them and their successors for evermore, and they are to find certain monks of their said monastery there perpetually to sing and pray for the soul of the most noble prince your honourable father king Harry the fifth, whom God redeem, and also for to hold and keep his obit [service on the anniversary of his death] with certain distributions to poor people and other divers deeds of alms and great charges there, yearly to be done perpetually . . .[32]

Under the terms of the king's last will, the abbot and convent at Westminster were also to display, daily and in perpetuity, eight burning wax candles around his tomb, at the time of the daily High Mass and at vespers, on all the five feast days of the Virgin Mary, and all day on every Good Friday.[33]

---

[31] ECR MS 59, fo. 1v; Strong & Strong, 'The Last Will and Codicils of Henry V', p. 90.

[32] WAM, MS 3798: petition, in English, to Henry VI from 'your humble, povere and continuell' oratours Edmond, abbot, and the priour and convent of the monasterie of Seint Peter of Westm', undated, but *c.* July 1445. See, for Offord Cluny, 'Parishes: Offord Cluny', *VCH, County of Huntingdon*, ed. W. Page et al. (London, 1932), ii, pp. 319–22; & *CPR, 1441–1446*, p. 30; & for Letcombe Regis 'Parishes: Letcombe Regis', *VCH, County of Berkshire*, ed. W. Page & P.H. Ditchfield (London, 1924), iv pp. 222–8 & *CPR, 1422–1429*, p. 77. For alien priories see above, pp. 148–51.

[33] For the costs of wax and candles for these purposes see the Westminster sacrist's roll for 28 Sept. 1422–29 Sept. 1423: WAM, MS 19663, m. 1r–v.

It was incumbent upon the rich and powerful to leave charitable gifts to the indigent and needy. Pious donations to the poor took two forms in Henry's last will: first, on the anniversary day of his death, every year, the office of the dead (*exequia*) was to be celebrated, with a sung Requiem Mass on the morrow, at which twenty-four poor men were to hold twenty-four torches provided by the abbot and convent. Each pauper was to receive 5d at the office of the dead (or 'year's mind') and another 5d at the Requiem. The abbot and convent were also to distribute, annually, the sum of 20 l. 'of legal English money' to the indigent poor 'for our soul, the souls of our parents, and of all the faithful departed'.[34] Secondly, for a whole year from the date of his burial, thirty 'very poor' men were to be fed and clothed. Each one was to recite 'the psalter of the Blessed Virgin' and, at the end, to add, in English, the words 'Mary, mother of God, remember your servant Henry, who places all his hope in you'.[35] This was personal piety at its most explicit, just as the king had called upon the aid of the Virgin with the words, in English, 'Lady Mary help' in his first will.[36] That will had also distributed liberal gifts, including one of 10,000 l., especially to his old and impoverished servants who, at the time they received their sums of money, were to be told: 'Our king bequeaths this to you for your good service'.[37] In his last will, the king specified that a sum of up to 10,000 l. be allowed, if funds sufficed after the completion of its terms, to be given to members of his household, namely to those 'poor esquires, valets, grooms and pages who were with us every day . . . at the time of our death'. A further sense of obligation also moved the king to ordain that

[34] ECR MS 59, fo. 1v; Strong & Strong, 'The Last Will and Codicils of Henry V', pp. 90–1.

[35] 'Et in fine subjungat, in vulgari suo, "Mater Dei Maria memento famuli tui Henrici qui totam spem suam in te posuit" ': ECR MS 59, fo. 2r; Strong & Strong, 'The Last Will and Codicils of Henry V', p. 91.

[36] See above, pp. 82–3.

[37] *Foedera*, x, p. 292: 'dicatur cuilibet ipsorum: "Ista legavit tibi dominus noster Rex pro bono servitio tuo"'.

Our old servants, who by reason of weakness and infirmity shall be absent from our obsequies, shall benefit from the said sum, according to our executors' discretion, if and in so far as during their lifetimes insufficient provision was made for their livelihood . . .[38]

There could be no doubt of the provenance of this bounty, and the soul's journey was eased by such good works, especially if, as in the king's last will, they were to be accompanied by the prayers of paupers addressed to the Virgin Mary.

A further provision for the celebration of masses reached a high point in the seven clauses of the king's last will devoted to the ministrations of the Church during the year immediately following his death.[39] A total of 20,000 masses was prescribed. While not unprecedented in later-medieval pious legacies, this was a very large number. In his will of 3 July 1338, with a codicil of 6 December 1341, Bernard d'Escoussans, lord of Langoiran in the Bordelais, had requested a total of 35,000 masses to be celebrated for his soul and those of his kin, within one year of his death.[40] His Gascon near-contemporary, Jean III de Grailly, captal de Buch, in a will of 6 March 1369, prescribed a record-breaking 50,000 over the same period, an estimated average of 137 masses per day.[41] This was at a time when the average provision for masses found in the

[38] ECR MS 59, fo. 4v; Strong & Strong, 'The Last Will and Codicils of Henry V', pp. 95–6: 'Et volumus quod antiqui servientes nostri qui propter inbecillitatem et invalitudinem de nostris obsequiis discesserunt, habeant regardum de dicta summa secundum discretionem executorum nostrorum, si et quatenus nobis viventibus eis pro eorum vita non fuit competenter provisum . . .'

[39] For what follows see ECR MS 59, fo. 2r; Strong & Strong, 'The Last Will and Codicils of Henry V', p. 91.

[40] See *Archives Historiques de la Gironde [AHG]*, xxvi (1888–9) p. 229. Of these masses, 25,000 were for his own soul and 10,000 for those of his father, mother and 'lignage'.

[41] See *AHG*, lviii (1929), pp. 1–18; also R. Boutruche, *La Crise d'une société: seigneurs et paysans du bordelais pendant la Guerre de Cent Ans* (2nd edn Paris, 1963), p. 276 & his 'Aux Origines d'une crise nobiliaire: donations pieuses et pratiques successorales en Bordelais du xiiie au xvie siècle', *Annales d'Histoire Sociale*, 1, no. 2 (1939), pp. 161–77, 257–77, esp. p. 164. The number of masses requested by Jean de Grailly is based on the sum allocated for their celebration. Boutruche stressed the burdens imposed on heirs and executors by such legacies, which contributed substantially to what he identified as a 'crisis' in noble incomes.

wills of the 'middle' Gascon nobility normally ranged from 2,000 to 5,000.[42] In England, something approaching a norm of 1,000 masses immediately after death seems common for members of the higher nobility. This number was prescribed in the wills of Eleanor de Bohun, duchess of Gloucester (1399), Edward, duke of York (1415), and Thomas Beaufort, duke of Exeter (1426).[43] A higher number of masses was, however, requested by Richard Beauchamp, earl of Warwick (1437), who instructed his executors to ensure that 5,000 masses were to be said 'in all haste, after my decease'.[44] Henry's Tudor successor, Henry VII, asked in his will for 10,000 masses immediately after his death, and endowed one of the most expensive chantry foundations of the age at Westminster.[45] Of the 20,000 masses requested by Henry V, 3,000 were to be in honour of the Holy Trinity; 5,475 in honour of the popular cult of the Five Wounds of Christ; a further 5,000 in honour of that of the Five Joys of the Virgin Mary; 900 in honour of the orders of angels; 300 in honour of the three patriarchs; 1,200 in honour of the twelve apostles; and 4,125 in honour of All Saints. This meant that an average estimated fifty-five masses per day for one year were to be celebrated for the king's soul. His executors were requested to see that these were performed 'as soon as possible', and that they should 'in a diligent state of mind' consider how 'sacred and salutary is the thought of praying for the dead'. All who esteemed him in life should never let remembrance of his soul be forgotten. The power of redemptive prayer was to be channelled through the multiple mass-saying and singing of the institutional Church. This was provision for the soul on an almost industrial scale. But each and every one, clerical and lay, was also to remember the king's soul in their own devotions, as many clearly did.

[42] Boutruche, 'Aux Origines d'une crise nobiliaire', p. 165.

[43] Nichols (ed.), *A Collection of all the Wills*, pp. 179–80, 218, 246–7, 250.

[44] *Historia vitae et regni Ricardi II*, ed. Hearne, p. 242. Also, for the effects of such legacies on the overall fortunes of the nobility see M.A. Hicks, 'The Beauchamp Trust, 1437–1481', *BIHR*, 54 (1981), pp. 139–42.

[45] See Colvin, *Architecture and the After-Life*, pp. 172–4 and the essays in *Westminster Abbey: the Lady Chapel of Henry VII*, esp. pp. 35–46, 73–80.

The obligation to undertake good works extended to the support of the Church in the most practical of ways. Westminster again took first place among the king's pious bequests, receiving a maximum of 6,000 marks (4,000 l.) for the completion of 'new work' to the fabric.[46] His chantry chapel there was to be constructed 'on high', reached by means of two stair-towers, and masses were to be celebrated at the altar of the Annunciation 'before our tomb'.[47] This very particular endowment was to receive three sets of white, red and blue vestments, together with the necessary liturgical equipment: chalice and paten, holy water pitchers, a pax and a bell of pure gold, and a pair of silver-gilt candelabra, all to be used on feast days.[48] An intrinsic element in this consecrated space in honour of the Virgin was a silver-gilt cross, to be flanked on each side of the altar of the Annunciation by images of Mary and the angel Gabriel. These were to be fixed at the front of the altar and to remain there in perpetuity. Henry's Marian devotion could not be more plainly set out and commemorated.

It was unsurprising that his new, incomplete monastic foundations of Brigittines at Syon and of Carthusians at Sheen should be well provided for in his last will.[49] The Brigittine double monastery (for women and men) 'of the Holy Saviour at Syon near Sheen', observing the Augustinian rule, was given 1,000 l. to further its construction 'of stone, or at least of the tiles called "brick" ', and his executors were to appoint a supervisor of the works

---

[46] ECR MS 59, fo. 2v; Strong & Strong, 'The Last Will and Codicils of Henry V', p. 92.

[47] For a detailed survey of the construction, architectural history and subsequent restorations of Henry's tomb and chantry chapel see A. Fehrmann, *Grab und Krone. Königsgrabmaler im mittelalterlichen England und die posthume Selbstdarstellung der Lancaster* (Munich, Berlin, 2005), esp. chapter IV: 'Das Grabmal und die Kapelle König Heinrichs V (+1421)', pp. 119 ff.

[48] The pax or *pacificale* normally took the form of a Eucharistic tablet, often in precious metal, on which the kiss of peace was given. For liturgical equipment and its functions see E.P. McLachlan, 'Liturgical Vessels and Implements' in *The Liturgy of the Medieval Church*, ed. T.J. Heffernan & E.A. Matter (Kalamazoo, 2001), pp. 369–429. Documentary evidence is usefully brought to bear in A. Mand, 'Liturgical Vessels in Medieval Livonia in the Light of Written Evidence' in *Art and the Church: Religious Art and Architecture in the Baltic Region in the 13th–18th Centuries*, ed. K. Kodres & M. Kurisoo (Tallin, 2008), pp. 82–103.

[49] For the two foundations see above, pp. 143–8.

to account to them when required.[50] The convent housed a total of eighty-five inmates, sixty of them women and twenty-five men. A near-identical provision was made for the 'house of the Carthusian order of Bethlehem near Sheen', which was to receive 1,000 marks for the construction of the monastery, to house fourty monks. The sisters at Syon were also bequeathed a bible, with glosses, in three volumes. The abbess and convent were to keep all the king's books currently in their custody, except for 'our great Bible' which had belonged to Henry IV and was to remain in the hands of the as yet unborn Henry VI.[51] After a series of bequests of books to others, all remaining volumes 'whether they concern meditations or are useful for preaching the Gospel' were to be divided between the king's two founda-tions at Syon and Sheen. But the community of Syon were alone to receive those of his books which were 'useful . . . for preaching', because the Carthusians in the Charterhouse at Sheen were prevented by their rule from doing so.[52] By August 1422, as he neared death, the king added a codicil to his last will which laid down that neither the Brigittines at Syon nor the Carthusians at Sheen should have any books of identical content; nor were any books of sermons to be given to the prior and convent at Sheen.[53] These stipulations betoken a close awareness of the difference in function between the two houses and in the nature of the monastic orders which they housed. Henry's foundations were to some degree complementary: one inclined towards evangelism, the other towards contemplation.

The king's pious bequests to religious orders and individual members of the clergy included a further gift of books, to Christ Church cathedral

---

[50] 'De lapidibus, vel saltem tegula vocat' "bryk" ': ECR MS 59, fo. 3r; Strong & Strong, 'The Last Will and Codicils of Henry V', p. 93.

[51] ECR MS 59, fo. 3v; Strong & Strong, 'The Last Will and Codicils of Henry V', p. 93. For the 'Great Bible', and a general survey of Henry's books, see *The Cambridge History of the Book in Britain*, ed. L. Hellinga et al. (Cambridge, 1999), p. 263.

[52] ECR MS 59, fo. 4r; Strong & Strong, 'The Last Will and Codicils of Henry V', p. 94. Henry's executors were to be advised in this matter by 'clerks and religious'.

[53] ECR MS 59, fo. 7v; Strong & Strong, 'The Last Will and Codicils of Henry V', p. 100.

priory, Canterbury;[54] a vestment and 'our breviary [*portiforium*]' (that is, a service book containing liturgies prescribed for the canonical hours), in two volumes, written by the scribe John Frampton, formerly owned by Henry IV, to Henry Beaufort, bishop of Winchester; a vestment to Henry Chichele, archbishop of Canterbury; a missal (mass-book) and breviary, given to the king by 'our dearest grandmother, the countess of Hereford', to Thomas Langley, bishop of Durham;[55] a distribution to four of the king's chaplains of a missal or breviary each; and 200 l. of gold to be divided equally among the clerks of the king's chapel.[56] These formal – if not more or less statutory – legacies to the higher clergy were offset by a bequest to John London (d. 1429), the long-standing 'recluse' of Westminster.[57] The Westminster recluses were anchorites, living in relative isolation from the rest of the monastic community, and their prayers were particularly valued by high-status laypeople.[58] Henry's bequest to him was to consist of all the apparatus for an altar, of blue damask cloth, which the king wished to be made for him, with a special exhortation that he pray for the king's soul.[59] Henry had consulted another Westminster recluse or anchorite at the time of his father's death, and the 'ankerhold', or anchorite's cell, in the abbey clearly had a special significance for him. John London had temporarily left his cell between

---

[54] ECR MS 59, fo. 3v; Strong & Strong, 'The Last Will and Codicils of Henry V', p. 93. For the disputed ownership and status of this volume, which contained eight books of the works of Pope Gregory the Great, see above, pp. 128–9.

[55] For the gifts to Chichele, Beaufort and Langley see ECR MS 59, fo. 4r; Strong & Strong, 'The Last Will and Codicils of Henry V', pp. 94–5.

[56] ECR MS 59, fo. 4v; Strong & Strong, 'The Last Will and Codicils of Henry V', p. 95. The four clerks were his almoner John Snell, Master Walter Trengough, Master John Holbrooke and Master Roger Gates.

[57] For him see L.H. McAvoy, *Medieval Anchoritisms: Gender, Space and the Solitary Life* (Woodbridge, 2011), pp. 137–8 & M.C. Erler, ' "A Revelation of Purgatory" (1422): Reform and the Politics of Female Visions', *Viator*, 38 (2007), p. 332. He received a legacy of 10 l. in the will of Thomas Beaufort, duke of Exeter, in 1426: Nichols (ed.), *A Collection of All the Wills*, p. 250.

[58] See 'Alien Houses: Hermits and Anchorites of London', *VCH, County of London*, ed. Page, i, pp. 585–6.

[59] ECR MS 59, fo. 3r; Strong & Strong, 'The Last Will and Codicils of Henry V', p. 93.

1415 and 1419 in order to oversee the setting up of the king's Brigittine convent of Syon.[60]

Henry's last will reflected the character and mood of his piety well. Apart from the palace-monastery at Westminster, no Benedictine house received a bequest; nor did the once-austere Cistercians. His own role as a founder of new religious houses meant that they were – of necessity – accorded a paramount place in his pious bequests. It was in Normandy and the kingdom of France that cathedral and collegiate churches received legacies from him, not in England.[61] The orders of friars – Dominicans, Franciscans, Carmelites – received nothing from his will. But they had benefited from his charitable giving during his lifetime.[62] In some ways he reflected the tendency of his time towards endowment of Carthusian and Augustinian foundations at the expense of older-established orders such as the unreformed Benedictines or Cistercians. The Carthusians, the various convents observing the Augustinian rule, and anchorites: these found especial favour in the eyes of many of the rich and powerful among the laity. The royal and princely houses of Lancaster, Burgundy and Visconti of Milan stood at the head of those high-status founders and patrons of charterhouses.[63] Austerity and a stricter observance of their rule marked the Carthusians out from some, but not all, of their co-religious among the monastic orders. Henry V's personal piety both reflected and furthered that final movement towards monastic reform which characterised the century before the Protestant Reformation.

---

[60] McAvoy, *Medieval Anchoritisms*, p. 137.

[61] See above, chapter 5, pp. 176–83 for his dealings with the Church in Normandy and Lancastrian France.

[62] See above, chapter 4, pp. 139, 152.

[63] The Charterhouses of Champmol, near Dijon, and Pavia were founded in 1383 and 1396 by Philip the Bold of Burgundy and Giangaleazzo Visconti of Milan respectively. See *Studies in Carthusian Monasticism in the Late Middle Ages*, ed. J.M. Luxford (Turnhout, 2008), esp. L.D. Gelfand, 'A Tale of Two Dukes: Philip the Bold, Giangaleazzo Visconti, and their Carthusian Foundations', pp. 201–23. Also S.C.M. Linquist, *Agency, Visuality and Society at the Chartreuse de Champmol* (London, 2008), pp. 20–7.

Besides an overriding concern for the fate of his or her soul in the next world, a later medieval testator might be moved by the dictates of conscience to make amends for any unremedied transgressions committed during his or her earthly life. Henry V was no exception. Debts of all kinds were to be fully repaid, restitution made to anyone found to have been wronged or unjustly dispossessed, and his executors' consciences were quite specifically to be 'burdened' with these duties.[64] One striking method of debt repayment was, as he requested, the deployment of any proceeds from the ransoms of his high-born French prisoners to clear those debts. There were two exceptions to this rule: Charles, duke of Orléans, and Charles of Artois, count of Eu were to remain in the keeping of his heir or successor. His executors were to have custody of all the remaining prisoners and, if ransomed, the proceeds were to go towards repaying the outstanding debt of 19,000 marks still owed by his father's executors. That paid, any residue was to be used to pay the king's household, chamber and wardrobe debts.[65] But Orléans and Eu were to be held by his heir (in the event, by the 'protector and defender of the realm of England', during the minority of Henry VI). Should it be decided to release them, both were to swear to observe the terms of the 'peace between that illustrious prince our father [in-law] Charles, by the grace of God king of France, and us' – that is, the treaty of Troyes (1420).[66] In that event, Henry's heir or successor was to have one quarter of the ransom, and his executors the rest.

Much of the remainder of the king's last will concerned the disposal of his worldly goods. His widow, Catherine of France, was to receive all the jewels, plate and vestments in his chapel, as well as the beds, furnishings and

---

[64] ECR MS 59, fo. 2v; Strong & Strong, 'The Last Will and Codicils of Henry V', pp. 91–2: 'super qua re executorum nostrorum consciencias oneramus'. For the operation of 'conscience' see above, pp. 138, 143, 169–72.

[65] ECR MS 59, fo. 3v; Strong & Strong, 'The Last Will and Codicils of Henry V', p. 92.

[66] ECR MS 59, fo. 2v; Strong & Strong, 'The Last Will and Codicils of Henry V', p. 92. Both were exceptionally long-lived, Orléans dying in 1465 and Eu in 1472. They were released in 1440 and 1438 respectively, when the terms of the treaty of Troyes were no longer sustainable.

'ornaments' in his chambers and hall. She was also to keep a gold crucifix containing a piece of the wood of the True Cross 'which we were accustomed to carry'.[67] It is not known in what form or manner this relic was worn or carried by the king. The practice was not uncommon, but to keep a fragment of the instrument of Christ's passion on one's person, on a daily basis, acted as a constant reminder of that sacrifice and its redemptive power. It carried strong crusading associations.[68] It also served as a talisman to protect against the forces of evil. A matter-of-fact quality informs much of the remainder of the last will: beds and horses are to go to his brothers and to his uncle Thomas, duke of Exeter; his ships 'for the defence of our realm' are bequeathed to the infant Henry VI, as are many items of gold and silver plate, as well as 'that beautiful jewelled reliquary which was the duke of Bourbon's'.[69] An array of gold cups, beds, furred robes, horses and sums of money is bequeathed to the members of his household, including Fitzhugh, Willoughby, Hungerford, Robessart, Beauchamp, Leventhorpe and Wilcotes, all of whom were among the king's executors.[70] He was particularly exercised by the need to pay all arrears and debts owed to his household officers and servants. Indeed, he stipulated that once all his debts – and those of his father – had been paid, a sum of at least 4,000 l. should be distributed among his household servants.[71]

It has been demonstrated just how crucial Henry V's household retinue was to his exercise of kingship, especially to the emergence of what has been called an 'ethos of English public life', which was 'at the heart of the

[67] ECR MS 59, fo. 3v; Strong & Strong, 'The Last Will and Codicils of Henry V', p. 94: 'una pecia ligni sancta crucis in custodia sua modo existen' quam portare solebamus'.
[68] See A.V. Murray, 'Mighty against the Enemies of Christ: the Relic of the True Cross in the Armies of the Kingdom of Jerusalem' in *The Crusades and their Sources: Essays presented to Bernard Hamilton*, ed. J. France & W.G. Zajac (Aldershot, 1998), pp. 217–38.
[69] ECR MS 59, fo. 6v; Strong & Strong, 'The Last Will and Codicils of Henry V', p. 99: 'illud jocale pulcrum reliquiarum quod fuit ducis Burbon'. This was bequeathed in the codicil of 26 Aug. 1422.
[70] For their service in Henry's household see D. Morgan, 'The Household Retinue', pp. 69–72. The bequests are in ECR MS 59, fo. 4v; Strong & Strong, 'The Last Will and Codicils of Henry V', pp. 95–6.
[71] ECR MS 59, fo. 5r; Strong & Strong, 'The Last Will and Codicils of Henry V', pp. 96–7.

king's enterprise', displaying a 'behavioural pattern of solidarity and cohesiveness'.[72] As guardians of his memory, his household knights, esquires, clerks and chaplains would remain unanimously loyal. They had served him with unwavering devotion and commitment during his lifetime, and in turn were duly remembered in his will. Their solicitude for the king and his welfare was illustrated by evidence such as that presented by John Merston, his household servant and *familier*, in a petition of May 1423, after the king's death.[73] Merston told Henry VI's council that Henry V had granted him, in the presence of Louis de Robessart, Lord Bourgchier, Thomas Swynford, Thomas Porter 'and many others of his chamber', an annuity of 12 l. for life. This had been done 'shortly before his illness, from which he would die'. Merston went on:

> And because of the said illness, the said suppliant, so that he should not be seen to be vexatious in the pursuit of the said grant, refrained from pursuing our late sovereign lord in order to gain mandates for [the issue of] such letters as relate to the said grant, until such time as it should please our lord to take him into his company.[74]

He requested Henry VI's council to confirm the grant – which they did. Lucid until the end, one of the king's very last acts in life was to make a grant to another household servant, Richard Whitehede, 'valet of the crown', of a daily payment of 6d for life on 26 August 1422, five days before Henry's death.[75] Henry's trust in his household staff was exemplified

---

[72] D. Morgan, 'The Household Retinue of Henry V', pp. 71, 72.

[73] Merston became keeper of the king's jewels under Henry VI, from 1427 onwards. See R.A. Griffiths, *The Reign of King Henry VI: the Exercise of Royal Authority, 1422–1461* (Berkeley/Los Angeles, 1981), p. 65, n. 32.

[74] E 28/41, no. 31: 'Et obstant ladicte maladie, le dit suppliant, affin que ne feust veu estre annoyeux en la pursuit dudit octroie, differeit a poursuir pardevers nostre feu soverain seignur pour avoir commandemens de telles lettres que appartenoient audit octroie, tant quil pleust a nostre seignur le prendre en sa compaignie' (7 May 1423).

[75] C 81/670, no. 9: at Vincennes, under the privy seal, 26 Aug. 1422. The grant was confirmed by Henry VI's council.

by his insistence in his last will that, although his brother Humphrey of Gloucester and his uncle Thomas of Exeter were to have the guardianship and tutelage of his infant heir, his two senior household officers – Fitzhugh (d.1425), as chamberlain, and Hungerford (d.1449), as steward – were to remain always in his son's household.[76] Henry's memory and his legacy were, on the face of it, in safe hands. Subsequent events were to prove otherwise, through no fault of most of his legatees. The news of his death was greeted, variously, with shock, bewilderment, dismay and disquiet not only by his subjects, friends and allies, but also by some of his enemies.[77] He left behind him much unfinished business, with which his brothers, and his infant son's minority council, had to grapple. His last will and its legacy were never completely fulfilled. Although his aims and ambitions did not die with him, the mere fact of his premature death deprived them of their greatest single driving force. And a force of that kind and character was rarely, if ever, to be seen again in the history of English rulership.

[76] ECR MS 59, fo. 7r; Strong & Strong, 'The Last Will and Codicils of Henry V', p. 100 (codicil). For Fitzhugh see *Henry V: New Interpretations*, ed. Dodd, pp. 42, 84–5; for Hungerford see Allmand, *Henry V*, pp. 352–3.

[77] See Griffiths, *The Reign of King Henry VI*, pp. 11–15 for reactions to his death and the disruption which immediately followed it.

CONCLUSION

W̶e have become accustomed to seeing Henry V as, perhaps, the
supreme English war leader of the Middle Ages, for whom war and
its waging was an unparalleled way of life. This was *the* warrior-king, it has
been claimed, a 'warlord . . . who clearly enjoyed campaigning and felt most
at ease in the company of his comrades-in-arms'.[1] This book has tried to
suggest that there were other facets to his character and personality, which to
some extent offset and modify the war-making stereotype that often emerges
from the literature. There is, for example, little in the surviving evidence
stemming directly from the king himself to suggest any great relish for an
exclusively military life. In his younger years, he was not considered a natural
military leader. For martial qualities and a lust for soldiering, his younger
brother Thomas, duke of Clarence, was a more likely candidate. He had
been preferred to Henry as a military commander by their father, charged
with leading what turned out to be a less than glorious expedition to France
in the late summer of 1412.[2] And it would be difficult to find anything in

---

[1] K. Dockray, *Warrior King. The Life of Henry V* (London, 2004; 2nd edn 2007), p. 224.
[2] See K.B. McFarlane, *Lancastrian Kings and Lollard Knights* (Oxford, 1972), pp. 110–11 for
the events of 1412 and the rift between Henry and Clarence at that time; also above, p. 211.

Henry's correspondence quite like the evident enthusiasm for warfare and its conduct expressed in the letter which Thomas Montague, earl of Salisbury, wrote to him in June 1421. Salisbury told him (in English) that his

> captains here do well their diligence as well in sure keeping of their places as in stirring and annoying of your enemies . . . I, your humble liege man, came home from a journey which I had made into Anjou and Maine [enemy territory]; where . . . I had assembled with me a great part of the captains of your land. And, blessed be God, we sped right well; for your people is greatly refreshed with this road [raid, foray]; for they say in common, they were never more in such road. And we brought home the fairest and greatest prey of beasts that as all those said that saw them, that they ever saw . . .[3]

The gathering of booty and plunder, here expressed in terms of livestock, gave material form and substance to the celebration of the merits of waging war in what was believed to be a just cause. But it was not a theme to be found in the surviving body of Henry V's own recorded utterances and observations.

Nor would the effusive glorification of the ennobling qualities of war found in literary works such as Jean V de Bueil's *Le Jouvencel* (*c.*1466) sit very easily on Henry V's lips. In this allegorical military romance, after an evening's dining with his comrades, the hero exclaims:

> What a joyous thing is war, for many fine deeds are heard and seen in its course, and many good lessons learnt from it . . . You love your comrade so much in war . . . When you see that your quarrel is just and your blood is fighting well, tears rise to your eyes. A great sweet feeling of loyalty and pity fills your heart on seeing your friend so valiantly exposing his body to execute and accomplish the command of our

---

[3] *Foedera*, x, p. 131 (21 June 1421).

Creator. And then you prepare to go and live or die with him, and for love not to abandon him. And out of that there arises such a delectation, that he who has not tasted it is not fit to say what a delight it is . . .[4]

A man of few words, mistrustful of rhetoric and hyperbole, the king's early experience of war may have made him well aware of its less glorious aspects, and every utterance we possess from him on the subject attributes his later successes very largely to God's grace and might. He might even have had some sympathy for the Duke of Wellington's famous remark, on the morrow of Waterloo, that

I hope to God, I have fought my last battle. It is a bad thing to be always fighting. While in the thick of it I am too much occupied to feel anything; but it is wretched just after. It is quite impossible to think of glory . . . and I always say, next to a battle lost, the greatest misery is a battle gained.[5]

In the event, for both men this was to be their last battle. Henry's *first* battle may have had lasting effects which went beyond those of a very severe, and no doubt very traumatic, physical injury. There may have been lasting neurological damage. His potentially fatal wounding, and near escape from death, at Shrewsbury in July 1403 may have had longer-term effects. That closeness to mortality may have made him more than normally aware, for his time, of his state of health. The high risks involved in

---

[4] Jean de Bueil, *Le Jouvencel*, ed. C. Favre & L. Lecestre, 2 vols (Paris, 1887–9), ii, pp. 20–2: 'C'est joyeuse chose que la guerre; on y oit, on y voit beaucoup de bonnes choses, et y apparent moult bien. On s'entrayme tant a la guerre . . . Quant on voit sa querelle bonne et son sang bien combatre, la larme vient a l'ueil. Il vient une doulceur au cueur de loyaulte et de pitie de veoir son amy, qui si vaillament expose son corps pour faire et accomplir le commandement de nostre Creteur. Et puis, on se dispose d'aller mourir ou vivre avec luy, et pour amour ne l'abandonner point. En cela vient une delectacion telle que, qui ne l'a essaiee, il n'est homme qui sceust dire quell bien c'est . . .'.
[5] Wellington to Lady Frances Shelley, 19 June 1815 cited in *A Dictionary of Military and Naval Quotations*, ed. R.D. Heidl (Annapolis, 1966; 2nd edn 2013), p. 26.

campaigning, not only of death in battle, may have led him to make three wills, each on the eve of his departure to France. It was, after all, of illness on campaign, not from 'active service', that he was to die.

That his health may not have been as robust as has been assumed might be inferred from the substantial and recurrent entries for purchase of medicaments in his household accounts as prince.[6] As king, he often appears to have consulted university-trained physicians, and the names of Masters Peter de Altobasse, John of Coventry, Jean Tiphaine, Gilbert Kymer and Jacopo of Milan recur through the household accounts.[7] During his last illness, his need for skilled medical attention was indicated by the summons, on the king's express order, of Master John Swanwych, MA, Bachelor in Physic, from England to France, to 'do him service'. Henry's physicians, given the fever from which he was suffering, had apparently been afraid to give him medicines to be taken internally, and he seems to have taken action on his own initiative. Swanwych was, on 14 July 1422, paid 100s. 'which the . . . king, with the assent of his council, ordered to be paid to the same master, to have as his gift for his expenses in coming [to him] for the aforesaid reason'.[8] The regular provision at this time of portable urinals, housed within the king's 'privy seat' (*privata cathedra*), transported in leather cases, might suggest a response to urgent medical needs.[9] And the 'chronic intestinal condition' from which he was to die had certainly manifested its

---

[6] See TNA, E 101/ 404/23, fos 4v, 5r.; also A. Curry, 'Henry V's Misspent Youth', *BBC History Magazine*, 14 (Mar. 2013), pp. 18–23.

[7] For some instances see E 403/636, m. 7r (1418); E 101/407/4, fo. 40v (1421); E 28/35, no. 35 (1421). Kymer became dean of Salisbury and served as Humphrey of Gloucester's physician, while Tiphaine became Anne of Burgundy, duchess of Bedford's, doctor and attended the trial of Joan of Arc. See F. Getz, 'Kymer, Gilbert (d.1463)', *Oxford DNB* (Oxford 2004; online edn 2008).

[8] E 403/655, m. 11r (14 July 1422). He entered the service of Humphrey of Gloucester, and was presented to the benefice of Bradfield (Berks.) in Jan. 1423. See *Foedera*, x, p. 264 (21 Jan. 1423).

[9] See E 101/407/4, fo. 68r : provision of an 'urinal' coton' apert', et cas[ula] de correo bullito pro dicte urinale imponend', pro private cathedre Regis'; fos 73v–74r: another case for the king's urinal and purchase of two further urinals; E 101/470/5, m. 7r: provision of '1 privata cathedra plicabil' de maeremio fact', et lin' cum panno nigro long' pro Rege ordinat' infra cameram suam'.

severe symptoms by mid-June 1422, when he became too ill to ride.[10] An earlier testimony of Richard Courtenay, bishop of Norwich, a close intimate of the king, to the astrologer Jean Fusoris, in 1415, is noteworthy in this respect.[11] Courtenay was apparently concerned for Henry's state of health and requested Fusoris to draw up the king's horoscope, or birth chart, thereby offering some prognosis.

His experience of battle at Shrewsbury might also have made Henry especially conscious of the plight of those who suffered in war. In November 1413, for example, he granted Thomas Huntley and his wife Agnes a pension of 8d per day for the term of their lives, drawn on revenues in Essex and Hertfordshire. Thomas had, like the king himself, been wounded at Shrewsbury and 'could not earn his living, nor did he have anything on which to live, as it is said'.[12] Later in the reign, the king had made provision for those left wounded and deprived of sufficient means by their service in his French war. Shortly after his death, it was recorded that he had given sums of money 'at various times' to 'certain soldiers, wounded [*mutulatis*] in the king's service, and reduced to poverty through the weakness of their bodies'.[13] His executors discharged their duties and cleared the debts thus incurred. Les Invalides (founded in 1670) and Chelsea Hospital (founded in 1682) clearly had precedents, if less institutionalised ones.

For a 'warrior-king', the fact that he took part in only two pitched battles – Shrewsbury and Agincourt – in his military career is cause for reflection.[14] His personal courage, exemplified on both occasions, is not in

---

[10] See C. Allmand, *Henry V* (New Haven/London, 1992; 2nd edn 1997), pp. 169–73 for an account of Henry's final illness and its course.

[11] See above, chapter 3, pp. 127–8. Mortimer dismisses Courtenay's evidence as 'disinformation' intended to mislead the French court, to which Fusoris was assumed to report back: I. Mortimer, *1415: Henry V's Year of Glory* (London, 2009; 2nd edn 2010), p. 87.

[12] C 81/659, no. 140: 24 Nov. 1413.

[13] E 101/407/7, m. 3r (household account for 1 Oct. 1421– 8 Nov. 1422): to 'diversis soldariis mutulat[is] in servicio Regis et in paupertate per debilitatem corporum suorum detent', per diversas vices per manum ... nuper Regis de elemosina sua ... 119 l. 4s. 31/2d.' The payment was made on the orders of Thomas, duke of Exeter and other of the king's executors.

[14] For a recent discussion of this point, and of Henry's military experience in general, see S. Cooper, *Agincourt: Myth and Reality* (Barnsley, 2014), pp. 33–4.

question. But an aversion to battle in the field, and its enormous risks, was not entirely uncommon among later medieval commanders – the lessons of Courtrai (1302), Bannockburn (1314), Crécy (1346), Poitiers (1356), Najera (1367), Aljubarrota (1385), or Tannenberg/Grünwald (1410) were certainly learnt by some of them. Henry's attempts to negotiate himself and his army out of the predicament in which they found themselves on the very eve of Agincourt suggest a certain reluctance to put his quarrel to the test of God's judgment in those adverse conditions.[15] His subsequent war in France was to be one of sieges, economic warfare and attrition, not even punctuated by pitched battles. With the exception of the ill-judged fight at Baugé (1421), for which Clarence paid with his life, the conquests of 1417–22 were gained by the steady and patient reduction of fortified places, generally along the river valleys of Normandy and the Île-de-France. This form of warfare was especially well suited to the king's abilities and talents. A concern for logistics, for the effective deployment of siege artil-lery, together with close supervision of military organisation and finance,[16] and an insistence on the conduct of war by a disciplined force, backed up by an uncompromising administration of punitive, drumhead justice, all played to his skills and aptitudes. None of these measures was carried out without some concern for the non-combatant and 'civilian' population. It was imperative to gain their respect and their acquiescence, if not their loyalty, if any kind of conquest and occupation was ever to succeed.[17] It has recently been argued that 'the expulsions at Harfleur and the pillaging of Caen were . . . uncharacteristic of Henry's actions in Normandy, and his subsequent treatment of Norman towns was marked by conciliation and

---

[15] E.F. Jacob, *Henry V and the Invasion of France* (London, 1947), pp. 99–101.

[16] One of the best accounts of Henry's financing, organisation and provisioning of his armies in Normandy remains R.A. Newhall, *The English Conquest of Normandy, 1416–1424. A Study in Fifteenth-century Warfare* (New Haven/London, 1924), esp. chapters IV, V & VI.

[17] See above, chapter 5, pp. 175–86; also C. Allmand, *Lancastrian Normandy, 1415–1450. The History of a Medieval Occupation* (Oxford, 1983), pp. 14–17.

clemency'.[18] Much the same could be said of his behaviour towards other areas in his French conquest.

The king's efforts to limit the ravages and excesses of war in the country over which it was fought do not immediately suggest any resort to policies of devastation, laying waste or 'scorched earth'. The terror tactics, as they have been called, of English raiding armies in the fourteenth century were not to be repeated under his aegis. Given the very limited ability of command structures in medieval armies to contain, let alone control, the behaviour of the soldiery, Henry's ordinances of war (1419), and his attempts to prevent the worst manifestations of the violence of men-at-arms, stand out for their rigour in the imposition of exemplary punishment.[19] A recent close study of the ordinances, of which versions were probably also issued in 1415, 1417 and (perhaps) 1421, has concluded that his 'reputation for the enforcement of military discipline is well evidenced in both chronicle and administrative records'.[20] His concern for the condition of the Church in war zones has already been discussed.[21] In the application of the laws of war – many of them harsh and uncompromising – his behaviour was in no way out of line with that of his contemporaries.[22] His order to kill prisoners at Agincourt, for example, was paralleled on other occasions, particularly by João I of Portugal at

[18] N. Murphy, 'War, Government and Commerce: the Towns of Lancastrian France under Henry V's Rule, 1417–22' in *Henry V: New Interpretations*, ed. Dodd (Woodbridge, 2013), p. 251; also pp. 259–64, 272.

[19] The ordinances are traditionally thought to have been issued by Henry at Mantes, between May and August 1419. But for a recent detailed discussion of the texts and dates of the ordinances see A. Curry, 'The Military Ordinances of Henry V: Texts and Contexts' in *War, Government and Aristocracy in the British Isles, c.1150–1500*, ed. C. Given-Wilson, A. Kettle & L. Scales (Woodbridge, 2008), pp. 214–49. For the text see *The Black Book of the Admiralty*, ed. T. Twiss (London, 1871), i, pp. 459–72; BL MS Lansdowne 285, fos 141r–147r; also G. A. Lester, *Sir John Paston's 'Grete Book'* (Cambridge, 1984), pp. 36–9.

[20] Curry, 'The Military Ordinances of Henry V', p. 238.

[21] See above, chapter 5, pp. 175–82.

[22] For the laws and usages of war at this period see M.H. Keen, *The Laws of War in the Late Middle Ages* (London, 1965), & for Henry V's application of them, as well as a discussion of his ordinances of war by a modern international lawyer, see T. Meron, *Henry's Wars and Shakespeare's Laws. Perspectives on the Law of War in the Later Middle Ages* (Oxford, 1993), esp. pp. 91–4, 143–6.

Aljubarrota in August 1385.[23] To allege that Henry was in some way a 'war criminal' completely misreads and misunderstands the context in which he lived.[24] It has been rightly said that 'his conduct of war compares favourably with the political assassinations which disfigured the record of both parties [in France] to the feud of Burgundians and Armagnacs'.[25] Subsequent eulogies and 'memorialisations' of his life and achievement were no doubt exaggerated, indulging in a nostalgia which may have been to some extent misplaced. But, given the prevailing climate in which deeds of military prowess were revered and honoured, this cannot be a cause for adverse comment.[26]

Too much can be made of what are often conventional expressions, in our sources, of intentions to limit and restrain the worst effects of warfare. But it is noteworthy that Henry V could demonstrate a real concern to reduce, if not minimise, casualties, especially when non-combatants and civilians were involved. In September 1415, he told the mayor, aldermen and worthy citizens of the city of London (in French) that he was inclined to accept an offer by the inhabitants of the besieged town of Harfleur to parley 'to avoid the effusion of human blood on the one side and the other'.[27] Again, in another letter under the signet to the city, in August 1417, he told them that he had taken the castle of Touques 'without shedding of Christian blood or defence made by our enemies'.[28] A month later,

---

[23] See C. Taylor, 'Henry V, Flower of Chivalry' in *Henry V: New Interpretations*, ed. Dodd, p. 236. For an account of the battle see P.E. Russell, *The English Intervention in Spain and Portugal in the Time of Edward III and Richard II* (Oxford, 1955), pp. 357–99.

[24] Shakespeare's favourable depiction of the king has prompted reactions such as that found in *Henry V: War Criminal? And Other Shakespearean Puzzles*, ed. J. Sutherland, C. Watts & S. Orgel (London, 2000).

[25] McFarlane, 'Henry V: a Personal Portrait' in his *Lancastrian Kings and Lollard knights* (Oxford, 1972), p. 130.

[26] For a useful summary of differing views, many of them in response to Shakespeare's treatment of the ethos of the fighting man, see R.H. Wells, *Shakespeare on Masculinity* (Cambridge, 2000), esp. chapter 1: 'The Chivalric Revival: *Henry V* and *Troilus and Cressida*', pp. 31–60.

[27] *Memorials of London and London Life in the xiiith, xivth and xvth centuries*, ed. H.T. Riley (London, 1868), p. 619, citing Letter Book I, fo. 143.

[28] *Memorials of London*, p. 654, citing Letter Book I, fo. 199.

he wrote again (in English), instructing them to give thanks to God for the taking of the town of Caen, by assault, but 'with right little death of our people'.[29] By August 1419, with his conquest already well advanced, the king wrote to the city from Pontoise, thanking them for their apparently spontaneous offer of financial aid for the war effort. His signet letter told them that 'we have written to all our friends and allies throughout Christendom . . . to have aid and succour from them', so that 'we will have a good end of our said war in a short time, and . . . come home to you . . .'.[30] This concern for the establishment of a durable peace became even more marked towards what we know, but he did not, would be the last year of his reign. The treaty of Troyes (1420) had, in his eyes, paved the way towards that 'final peace' which had been the ostensible aim of all Anglo-French negotiations for a long time. But that hoped-for, impending solution to the Anglo-French conflict was, again in his eyes, prevented and thwarted by the actions of his dauphinist enemies. In December 1421, he dispatched an embassy to seek the aid of the emperor Sigismund and the German princes of the Empire for his war effort. The treaty of Canterbury (1416) had in effect recreated an Anglo-imperial alliance which had largely lapsed since Edward III's short-lived, anti-French treaty with the emperor Ludwig of Bavaria between 1338 and 1341. The highly specific instructions – undoubtedly drawn up by the king himself – which he gave, in English, to his envoys, offer some insight into what may have been his true aims, as far as we shall ever know them.

His envoys were to seek 'aid and succour of men', that is, of troops, for his war and were to tell Ludwig, duke of Bavaria, and other of the electors

---

[29] *Memorials of London*, p. 657, citing Letter Book I, fo. 200 (5 Sept. 1417). Despite his attempts to limit the casualties, Henry's assault accounted for the deaths of many of the town's inhabitants. See McFarlane, 'Henry V: a Personal Portrait', p. 130: Henry 'did his best to ensure that women and clerks were spared'. Also see Murphy, 'War, Government and Commerce', p. 251.

[30] *Memorials of London*, p. 674, citing Letter Book I, fo. 237 (17 Aug. 1419).

of the Empire that 'he is now at the [final] point and conclusion of his labours and, through God's grace and the help of his allies and friends, shall soon bring his war to an end'.[31] They were also to declare:

> After a long-continued war, over many years, between the realms of England and of France, as it pleaseth God, a peace is now established and concluded between the king and his father [in-law] of France, and the two said realms . . . to be confirmed and sworn by the Three Estates of the realm of France.

But the dauphin Charles and his adherents, he asserted, were resisting and attempting to frustrate his efforts to bring about a settlement. Further prosecution of the war was therefore unavoidable. Henry's awareness of the wider European scene, demonstrated as it had been by his role in conciliar diplomacy from Constance onwards, re-emerged at this juncture, when he told his envoys to dwell upon

> what good and profit might arise if there were peace and rest among Christian princes, for then might they together act against miscreants, for the increase and augmentation of the Christian faith, as well as for the good of the Church.

---

[31] For this and the following quotations from this source, see C 47/30/9/12, fo. 1r. I have modernised the Middle English original. The original text runs: 'considered that he is now in the point and conclusion of his labour, and thorow goddes grace, and helpe of his allies and frendes, shal soone have an ende of his werre . . . after long werre continued, many yeres, betwixt the rewmes of England and of France, as it pleseth god, ther is a pees now appointed and concluded betwixt the kyng and his fader of France, and the two saide rewmes, the whiche pees thown to be confermed and sworne by the thre estats' of the rewme of France, thit ther been certain persones that wolde lette it, as he that clepeth hym Dauphin and his adherents . . . Item, they shul declare what good and profit might ryse if there were pees and rest among' christen princes, for thanne might they togeder entende ayeins mescreants', in encrece and augmentacioun of Christien faith, as wel as to the goode of the chirche . . . Item, wherefore the kyng, considering that he is now in the point and conclusion of his labour, and thorow gooddess grace trusteth, with succurs of his allies and frendes, to have goode and hasty ende . . .'

Whether this meant the launching of a joint crusade by the powers of Western Christendom against the infidel Ottoman Turk or Mamluk, or against the 'miscreant' heretics in Bohemia – or all of them – we will never know. Nor can we measure the seriousness of his assertion, on his deathbed, that once his great work in France was at an end he would have 'built again the walls of Jerusalem'.[32] But there can be little doubt that he was actively considering the possibility of intervention, with the aid of 'allies and friends', in both eastern Europe and the Near East. In the aftermath of the treaty of Troyes, which he clearly considered to be potentially viable as a peace agreement between England and France, with vital Burgundian support, his thoughts were turning towards the frontiers of Christendom. He had already established good relations with the Christian (and, in the case of Lithuania, recently Christianised) rulers in Prussia, Poland, Lithuania and Wallachia. In April 1419, the ubiquitous Sir Hartung von Klux, and two other envoys, had been dispatched to negotiate with both Sigismund and Ladislaus Jagellio (c.1362–1434), king of Poland.[33] This may have been the source of a notarial copy of the documents recording the treaty of Torun between Poland, Lithuania and the Teutonic order, dated 12 and 14 May 1419, in the English archives.[34] One objective of subsequent English missions to eastern Europe was to inform the Christian princes of the region that an Anglo-French peace was in the process, however painful, of creation. Accordingly, on 4 May 1421, the Burgundian knight, diplomat and soldier Ghillebert de Lannoy, a 'hyper-active devotee of the chivalric ethos',[35] left Sluys in Flanders as the accredited envoy of Henry V, Charles VI of France and Philip the Good

[32] Allmand, *Henry V*, p. 174; McFarlane, 'Henry V: a Personal Portrait', p. 125.
[33] E 403/640: payment to Klux, John Walden, a Carmelite friar and Typrand Shellemer in advance of their embassy (20 Apr. 1419).
[34] E 30/1243: notarial instruments, dated 12 & 14 May 1419.
[35] D.A.L. Morgan, 'Lannoy, Ghillebert de (1386–1462)', *Oxford DNB* (Oxford, 2005; online edn 2009).

of Burgundy.[36] His mission he described as his 'embassy of the peace [on behalf] of the two above-mentioned kings' to the Christian rulers, leading on to a detailed military reconnaissance of Egypt and the Holy Land.[37] He was to give particular attention to fortified places, rivers, and to the ports which might prove valuable for crusading purposes.

Lannoy was already experienced in Anglo-French and Anglo-Burgundian negotiations. He was among the Burgundian delegation which secured Philip the Good's assent and commitment to the treaty of Troyes in 1419–20.[38] He had already made a pilgrimage to the Holy Land in 1401–3, and fought with the Teutonic order in 1413. His commission of 1421 from Henry and Charles VI took him first to Poland and Lithuania, where he presented jewels and other gifts to King Ladislaus and the Grand Duke Witold (1350–1430). Together with Henry's letters of commendation, on 24 June 1421, at 'Oziminy', between Sambor and Drohobycz, he presented Ladislaus of Poland with Henry's gifts which, according to the Polish chronicler Jan Długosz, consisted of jewels, a woven tunic of cloth of gold, a helm with a gilded crest, and two English longbows.[39] That Henry himself was no stranger to the practice of archery is evident from entries in his wardrobe accounts and, despite (or perhaps because of) his early experience of its effects, he evidently considered the weapon fit for princes.[40] A delighted Ladislaus not only gave him a safe conduct, 'of his own free will',

---

[36] For his life and travels see R. Arie, 'Un Seigneur bourguignon en terre musulmane au xve siècle', *Le Moyen Âge*, 83 (1977), pp. 283–302; A. Bertrand, 'Un Seigneur bourguignon en l'Europe de l'Est: Ghillebert de Lannoy', *Le Moyen Âge*, 196 (1989), pp. 293–309. For Burgundian crusading schemes and activities see J. Paviot, *Les Ducs de Bourgogne, la Croisade et l'Orient* (Paris, 2003).

[37] Ghillebert de Lannoy, *Oeuvres*, ed. C. Potvin (Louvain, 1878), pp. 52–5.

[38] See Morgan 'Lannoy, Ghillebert de' in *Oxford DNB*; *Oeuvres*, ed. Potvin, pp. 20–2.

[39] *Oeuvres*, ed. Potvin, pp. 53–5; J. Długosz, *Annales et Cronicae incliti regni Poloniae*, xi (Warsaw, 2000), pp. 54–6: Lannoy presented to 'Vladislai Poloniae regi, ex parte Henrici, Anglorum regis, literis commendatitiis et muneribus, viz. stamino atlantico auro in texto, galea ferrea crista aurea insigni et duobus anglicis arcubus, presentatis . . .'

[40] See E 101/407/4, fo. 23r: payments to the king's bowyer for quivers, 'bags for bows' and 'a coffer for the king's bows' (1421).

to travel through his own dominions, but also letters of commendation to assist him in travelling into the territories of the Turkish sultan. In the course of the following year, Lannoy was at Constantinople, where he presented Henry's gifts of jewels to the Byzantine emperor and his son, 'together with the letters of the peace of France and England'. He also expressed the two kings' desire 'to advance the union of the Roman and Greek churches'.[41] At Rhodes, he had to leave jewels and other gifts behind, and was unable to present Henry's gift of a gold clock to the sultan Mahmoud because the latter had recently died and his territories were said to be in a state of turmoil.[42] But he went ahead and reconnoitred Egypt and Syria, reaching Alexandria, where he began to record his observations, copies of which he prepared for Henry V and Philip the Good. The *livret*, or 'small book', which resulted was headed:

> This is the report that *messire* Ghillebert de Lannoy, knight, drew up on the visitations of many towns, ports and rivers made by him, both in Egypt and in Syria . . . at the command of the very high, very powerful, and very excellent prince king Henry of England, heir and regent of France, whom God pardon.[43]

Henry did not live to receive it, so Lannoy reported back to Henry VI's minority council at London, in 1423, when he also returned the gold clock that he had been unable to present to the sultan.[44] He confessed – to Bishop Henry Beaufort – to having been overpaid for his expenses, for which he had falsely claimed what in effect amounted to a double payment,

---

[41] *Oeuvres*, ed. Potvin, p. 65.
[42] *Oeuvres*, ed. Potvin, p. 67.
[43] *Oeuvres*, ed. Potvin, p. 100. The text is on pp. 99–162; also printed by J. Webb, 'A Survey of Egypt and Syria, undertaken in the Year 1422, by Sir Gilbert de Lannoy, Knight . . .', *Archaeologia*, 21 (1827), pp. 281–444, from Bod. Lib. MS Hatton 90.
[44] *Oeuvres*, ed. Potvin, pp. 161–2.

and this still troubled his conscience later in life.[45] But, unwittingly defrauded or not, there can be little doubt that Henry V was a prime instigator and promoter of Lannoy's mission to the East. Later medieval Western rulers have sometimes been said to have paid 'lip-service' to the crusading idea (and ideal). But, had he lived and had political circumstances permitted, Henry might have demonstrated the seriousness of his intentions.[46]

Whatever the case, an Anglo-French peace settlement was evidently seen by Henry as a prerequisite for any such venture. The war had to be brought to an end, if necessary by military means, but also by diplomacy. Again, when they met Sigismund, his envoys of December 1421 were to emphasise that the king

> is now at the [final] point and conclusion of his labour, and through
> God's grace trusteth, with the succour of his allies and friends, to bring
> a good and hasty end [to it]. . .

The 'succour' from his 'allies and friends' did not in the event materialise before his premature death, and Henry himself acknowledged that Sigismund and his imperial vassals were obliged to give absolute priority to the conflict with the 'heretics and lollards', that is, the Hussites, in Bohemia.[47] Aid from his German 'allies and friends' came, before his death, only in the shape of a consignment of saltpetre, for the making of

---

[45] The circumstances of the fraud, and Henry VI's subsequent confirmation of Lannoy's pardon, were set out in letters patent of 10 Mar. 1443. See *Foedera*, xi, p. 22: 'Concerning exoneration of conscience over the fraud and deceit committed against the king's father'. Lannoy had received a total of 400 l. rather than the 200 l. which he had been granted by Henry V.

[46] For a discussion of the issues see C. Tyerman, 'New Wine in Old Skins? Crusade Literature and Crusading in the Eastern Mediterranean in the Later Middle Ages' in *Byzantines, Latins and Turks in the Eastern Mediterranean World after 1150*, ed. J.Harris, C. Holmes & E. Russell (Oxford, 2012), pp. 265–90.

[47] C 47/30/9/12, fo. 1r. See also above, chapter 5, pp. 188–9.

gunpowder, sent by the archbishop of Cologne in July 1422.[48] Nor, of course, did the expected 'hasty end' to his French war come to pass. But that did not mean that its failure to materialise was a foregone conclusion, or an historical inevitability. His final intentions remain unclear. The promotion of peace, harmony and unity must have played a part in them. Whether he would ultimately have settled for some form of partition of the kingdom of France between the houses of Lancaster and Valois can never be known. His strictures, in his last will, on the subject of the release of his most significant French prisoners and the fulfilment of the treaty of Troyes, suggest that he would not.[49] A Lancastrian dual monarchy of England and France, in some form, might for him have represented a minimum requirement below which, in the circumstances of 1421 and 1422, he would not go. Counterfactual speculation will continue to intrigue us with its 'what might have beens'. But Henry's alleged search for peace in the last year or so of his reign bears serious further investigation.[50] The jury is still out on that issue.

That the peace of Christendom was a matter to which both the king and his eulogists often alluded is hardly cause for surprise. Henry was a child of a period of schism in the Western Church.[51] The alignments adopted by secular powers towards the rival parties within the Church often echoed their internecine conflicts. Until such time as a resolution of the Schism was achieved, the possibility of joint or concerted action against the infidel, whether by military action or diplomatic negotiation, was effectively ruled out. A papacy that could no longer effectively exercise its mediating function between warring secular powers, because there was no single source of papal authority, condemned the West to

---

[48] See E 403/655, m. 11r: payment of 266 l. 13s. 4d to Theodoric, archbishop of Cologne, for saltpetre sent from his lands for the king's war in France (15 July 1422).
[49] See above, chapter 7, pp. 242, 256.
[50] See above, chapter 5, pp. 200–3.
[51] See above, chapter 4, pp. 130–4, 160.

the expectation of a permanent state of constant warfare. The threat of further division within the Church, even after the election of a single, broadly recognised pope in 1417, was exacerbated by the growth of heretical movements. But England did not go the way of Bohemia, and, as we have seen, Henry V played a major part in ensuring that Lollardy, though in many ways akin to Czech Hussitism, did not capture the allegiance either of the clergy or of the nobility and gentry in his kingdom. His role in its repression, however, was not that of, for example, the Habsburg monarchy of the sixteenth century. There were no mass burnings or autos-da-fé in England.

The Oldcastle rising of 1414 bore no relationship in scale, or in effects, to the tidal wave of heretical belief that overcame the Bohemian kingdom. The great majority (sixty-nine people) of those rebels who were condemned were executed as traitors, not as heretics, leaving only seven convicted Lollards to die as martyrs to their religious beliefs.[52] The king's clemency and lack of vindictiveness were evidenced by his issue of pardons to individual Lollards, then groups, and finally a general pardon, between January and March 1414.[53] He had previously pleaded, at length, with Oldcastle to renounce his heresy. And his behaviour on 5 March 1410, as prince, when he witnessed the burning of the Lollard artisan John Badby, was not that of a zealot intent on the extirpation of a heresy by punitive sanctions rather than persuasion. Horrified at the sight, he stopped the execution and attempted to persuade Badby to recant, offering him a daily pension and support if he would do so.[54] It was perhaps characteristic of him that, even in these extreme circumstances, he named

[52] Allmand, *Henry V*, p. 299; J.A.F. Thomson, *The Later Lollards, 1414–1520* (Oxford, 1965), pp. 6–7.

[53] *CCR, 1413–1419*, pp. 176–7; Allmand, *Henry V*, p. 300.

[54] For the prosecution of Badby and his execution see P. McNiven, *Heresy and Politics in the Reign of Henry IV. The Burning of John Badby* (Woodbridge, 1987), esp. chapter 11; Allmand, *Henry V*, pp. 290–1; I. Mortimer, *The Fears of Henry IV. The Life of England's Self-made King* (London, 2007), pp. 331–3.

a specific sum – threepence per day – as he was to do in some of the responses annotated on petitions which he received as king.[55] But it was to no avail: Badby refused, the fire was relit, and he was subjected to what was tantamount to death by roasting in a barrel. Though rigorously orthodox, the king's engagement with religion was not that of 'a bigot of near-heroic mould whose intense religiosity equalled only his intense legalism over feudal property rights'.[56] Such judgements seem fundamentally misplaced.

Besides war and religion, another of the king's preoccupations was the use of language, or languages. It is a contention of this book that a permanent legacy of Henry V's reign was the emergence, acceptance and stabilisation of the English language as an idiom of government, politics and administration.[57] For the first time since the Anglo-Saxon era, the vernacular became, in part through the king's active promotion, a vehicle for the expression of his wishes, and an accepted and acceptable medium of communication emanating from central government. Among many causes of this development, the need to address his English subjects in their own 'birth tongue', rather than – as in the past – in Anglo-Norman French, became all the more necessary after he began his war of conquest and was instated as 'heir and regent of France' in 1420. The two realms of England and France were to be kept strictly separate under the terms of the treaty of Troyes, and their laws, customs and institutions were, despite their union in a dual monarchy, to retain their separate identities. Equally important, it seems, was the idea that the cultural identity of the kingdoms, now expressed through their languages, should also be confirmed. The acceptance of Middle English as a medium not only of literature, theology and philosophy, but also of governance and political thought had finally been established.

---

[55] See above, pp. 24–5, 79–80.
[56] J.R. Lander, *Conflict and Society in Fifteenth-century England* (London, 1969), p. 58.
[57] See above, chapter 3, pp. 114–15, 119–22, 124–5.

What Henry began was continued into much later periods of English history. Formulas of address and salutation, first found in his signet letters, such as 'Trusty and well-beloved, we greet you well', or the command 'we wol and charge you', echoed down the centuries, adopted by his Yorkist, Tudor and later successors.[58] Royal Letters of Assent to Acts of the British Parliament to this day (2016) still carry the address 'Trusty and well-beloved'.[59] Similarly, the practice of applying the ruler's own hand, or autograph, to authenticate and verify letters, usually issued under a personal seal, or signet (though not entirely unknown before Henry's reign), was greatly furthered and accelerated by him. It did not require the services of Renaissance humanists, the influence of Erasmus or the growth of Renaissance 'self-fashioning' to create a 'conceptual link between authorship and authority' demonstrating a 'monarch's engagement in the affairs of state' through the writing of holograph letters by rulers, and the application to them of their signature or sign manual.[60] 'Subscription', as Queen Elizabeth I (1558–1603) was to observe, whereby the ruler's own hand 'fortified' a letter or other missive, was not an invention of the sixteenth century.[61] Henry V had already adopted precisely this by the latter years of his reign.

This book, as indicated at the very outset, does not take the form of a conventional, narrative biography. Nor, as far as is ever possible, does it

---

[58] See J. Otway-Ruthven, *The King's Secretary and the Signet Office in the xvth century* (Cambridge, 1939; repr. 2008), pp. 26, 45–52.

[59] See F. Bennion, 'Modern Royal Assent Procedure at Westminster', *Statute Law Review*, 3 (1981), pp. 138–9.

[60] Rayne Allinson, *A Monarchy of Letters: Royal Correspondence and English Diplomacy in the Reign of Elizabeth I* (London, 2012), pp. 16–17; also her ' "These latter days of the world": the Correspondence of Elizabeth I and James VI, 1590–1603', *Early Modern Literary Studies*, 16 (2007), pp. 1–27. For Erasmus's influential views on letter-writing see *The Collected Works of Erasmus: Literary and Educational Writings 4*, ed. J.K. Sowards (Toronto, 1985), xxv, pp. 391–2.

[61] See and cf. A.R. Bertolet, 'The Tsar and the Queen: "You speak a language that I understand not" ' in *The Foreign Relations of Elizabeth I*, ed. C. Beem (London, 2011), p. 110; Allinson, *A Monarchy of Letters*, p. 35; and I. Lubimenko, 'The Correspondence of Queen Elizabeth with the Russian Czar', *American Historical Review*, 19 (1914), pp. 525–42.

seek to pass judgement on its subject. Attempts to analyse the behaviour of medieval rulers exclusively in terms of 'success' and 'failure', of sincerity and hypocrisy, or of 'good' and 'bad' kingship, though often entertaining, are not always helpful. They tend to depend upon absolute, abstract, artificial and often anachronistic criteria.[62] Prompted by scepticism about McFarlane's claims for Henry V's 'greatness', the question has recently been asked: 'was Henry the least flawed man ever to rule England?' And the reply has been: 'no, he was deeply flawed'.[63] But, despite those flaws, even the most critical of recent commentators can admit that he 'did . . . achieve something extraordinary'.[64] Whether the historian should seek to discover 'flaws' in the character, personality and behaviour of past rulers is certainly debatable. Another recent, balanced assessment sees Henry as 'brave but flawed'.[65] However hard to achieve, historical writing ought not to be a form of advocacy in which denigration and the exposure of alleged inadequacies have a primary role to play. Nor, on the other hand, should eulogy and the lavishing of praise be given their unbridled head. So much may appear obvious. But the historian, sometimes quite unwittingly, can sit in self-appointed judgement on 'the great ones that live in the world's eye'.[66]

The abstract judgements that tend to be produced in this way do not necessarily illuminate or explain the attitudes and behaviour of those who walked, and rode, the earth in the relatively remote past. Sometimes such verdicts are inevitably heavily dependent upon contemporary narrative sources, such as chronicles and memoirs, from which bias and partisanship are rarely excluded. Hence this book has sought out evidence for the direct

---

[62] See above, chapter 2, pp. 13, 14, 87.
[63] Mortimer, *1415*, p. 551. Cf McFarlane, 'Henry V: a Personal Portrait', p. 133: 'Take him all round and he was, I think, the greatest man that ever ruled England'.
[64] Mortimer, *1415*, p. 551.
[65] A. Curry, 'Henry V's Misspent Youth', *BBC History Magazine*, 14 (March 2013), p. 23.
[66] McFarlane, 'Henry V: a Personal Portrait', p. 132.

action and engagement of its human subject wherever it can be found. To seek his authentic voice, to hear the promptings of his conscience and expression of his thoughts, can only be achieved by recourse to the original archival evidence. And that evidence has largely to be drawn from the formal, and informal, documents in the records of government and administration. Much of this book has attempted to interpret these materials and, in the process, has necessarily had to explain their nature, origin, purpose and the kinds of question that we can reasonably ask of them. That they can give us only a partial and incomplete picture is inevitable. But to read what Henry V himself read, handle what he himself handled, and sometimes trace his own hand on a letter, or petition, or memorandum, with one's own, may bring us as close as we will ever get to that remarkable individual.

APPENDIX

Chapter 1

[1.] Signet warrant of Henry V to the Chancellor, Thomas Langley, bishop of Durham; 1 folio; parchment; English; 12 February [1419] (TNA, SC 1/43, no. 162)

By ye kyng

Worshipful fader in God, right trusty and welbeloved. We are enfourmed that the kyng of Castel maketh a grete armee of vessel, whiche shuld be redy in short tyme, as is sayde, for to doo harme ayenst us and oures that thay may, whiche god defende, and in especiale that thaire purpose is to doo thaire p[uissance?] for to brynne and destrue oure s[hippes?] and the navie of oure lande, and namely oure shippes at Hampton, and also thaire ordnance is to lande in oure reaume for to doo thannoye that thay may. Wherefore we wol and charge yow that by thavys of oure brother of Bedford, and of other suche as semeth to youre discreccion, ye ordenne in alle haste for the gouvernance of oure lande, and for the saufwarde of seurkepyng [security and safe-keeping] of oure saide vesselx at Hampton, and in other places where as ever thay bee, and that thay of the portes and of the see coost al about be warned hereof in alle haste, and charged to be wel awaytyng and redy at al tymes if any suche thing happen.

Yeven under oure signet in oure castel of Rouen, ye xij day of Feverer [1419].

* * *

[2.] Signet warrant of Henry V to the Chancellor, Thomas Langley, bishop of Durham; 1 folio; paper; English, with a note in French on the dorse; 22 May [1419] (TNA, SC 1/43, no. 159)

By the king

Chanceller. There is oon Thomas Walwenes wyf, which hath maad a grievous compleynt unto uss upon Sir John Skydmore, and for asmuche as we had ordained bothe parties for to bee before us or oure conseil for to [have] had knowloche of the matere that thay stande in debat fore, and for to have made an ende thereof, and hit ys soo now that we may nat g[. . .]dly an ende thereto at this tyme, as ye bo[. . .] considered oure hasty departing hens, we wol that [not]withstanding that we suppose she standeth not in the right, because s[he is?] sumwhat a descla[nder]ouse woman, and also that we kepe no more to be we[ight?]ed with hir encombrous poursuites, th[a]t ye doo send for bothe the saide parties to come before yow at suche day as yow semeth resonnable, for to here the saide matere of controversie, and make an ende therein, as we shal telle yow tomorwe more pleinely by mouthe. But alyates geven hem tomorwe here day whanne they shal be with yow.

Yeven under oure signet of the Egle, at Lambehith, this day yee xx day of May [1419].

Colyngton

Dorse: Soyt mys en la chancellerie

* * *

[3.] Petition of Robert Gunthorpe to the king, 1 folio; parchment; damaged; original in French; with endorsement and note on the issue of letters granting the supplication; 14 February (?) 1419 (TNA, E 28/32, no. 61)

To the king our sovereign lord

Your poor liegeman Robert Gunthorpe, servant and carter of a certain Robert Hawkyn of London, humbly petitions that a cart, of which your said suppliant had charge and governance, was loaded with two barrels of your ale, to be carried and brought to the Tower of London, for the expenditure of your honourable household and, just as your said suppliant was coming with the said cart, duly loaded, [towards the Tower] . . . the horses who were harnessed to the said cart bolted, because of the great fear that they had of the noise of the lions [in the Tower menagerie], and the said cart was over-turned, and the said barrels broken and all the ale wasted, so that your said poor petitioner, unless he receives your merciful grace and succour . . . will be forced to pay for the said ale . . . and, as he is only a poor labourer who has to work for his living, and has nothing with which to pay . . . for the said ale . . . [without] your abundant alms, [he requests the king] to pardon him for the default and wastage of the said two barrels of ale so lost, and to order his officers to discharge both himself and his master for it, without . . . harming . . . [his] body or goods on account of the loss of the said ale, bearing in mind that otherwise your said petitioner will for ever remain without recourse, and that this [be done] for God and as a work of charity.

Endorsed: 'The king has granted it'.

Chapter 2

Letter, attributed to the king's own hand, probably addressed to Thomas Beaufort, duke of Exeter; 1 folio, paper, incomplete, lacking beginning and conclusion; undated, but probably February–March 1418. (BL, Cotton MS Vespasian F iii, fo. 8r)

Furthremore, I wold that ye com[e]end [communicate] with my brother, with the Chanceller, with my cosin of Northumbrelond and my cosin of Westme[r]lond, and that ye set a gode ordinance for my north marches, and specialy for the duc of Orlians, and for alle the remanant of my prisoners of France; and also for the k[ing] of Scotelond, for as I am secrely enfourmed by a man of right notable estate in this lond, that there hath ben a man of the ducs of Orliance in Scotlond, and accorded with the duc of Albany, that this next somer he schal bring in the maumet of Scotlond to sturre what he may, and also that ther schold be founden weys to the having awcy specialy of the duc of Orlians, and also of therl' [the earl], as welle as of the remanant of my forsayd prysoners, that god do defende. Wherefore I wolle that the duc of Orliance be kept st[i]lle within the castil of Pontfret, withowte [go]yng to Robertis place[1] or to any other disport, for it is better he lak his disport [t]hen we were disceved[. . .] of alle the remanant, dothe as ye thenketh.

---

[1] See also, for an autograph [?] letter of Henry V, undated, to Robert Waterton, on the keeping of the duke of Orléans at Pontefract rather than 'Robert's place', at Methley Hall, *Calendar of Signet Letters . . .*, ed. Kirby, no. 881.

BIBLIOGRAPHY

Primary sources

Manuscript sources

CAMBRIDGE
   Corpus Christi College, MSS 177, 213
   Gonville and Caius College, MS 392
   Trinity College, MS B 15.23
ETON
   Eton College Records [ECR], MS 59
LONDON
   British Library [BL]
      Add. MS 57590
      Cotton MSS Caligula D. V; Claudius B. IX; Cleopatra F. III; Julius B. VI; Tiberius B. VI; Tiberius B. IX; Titus C. IX; Vespasian C. XIV; Vespasian F. III; Vespasian F. XIII
      Harleian MS 565
      Royal MS 20 B′. IV
      Sloane MS 2272
   Guildhall Library, MS 5440
   The National Archives [TNA]
      C 47/28/7; 28/10; 30/9
      C 49/30/18, 19; 48/15, 18; 53
      C 54/270
      C 61/38, 118
      C 65/85, 87
      C 76/45
      C 81/658, 659, 660, 661, 662, 663, 664, 665, 666, 667, 668, 669, 670, 1137, 1326, 1358, 1362, 1364, 1365, 1366, 1542, 1543
      DL 28/1/6
      E 23/2
      E 28/29, 30, 31, 32, 33, 34, 35, 36, 37, 41

E 30/391, 397, 398, 1065, 1067, 1068, 1071, 1243, 1273, 1345, 1351, 1414, 1531, 1609, 1619, 1746

E 101/45/5; 69/7; 321/27; 335/17; 376/7; 376/15; 404/23; 406/15; 406/21; 406/24; 406/26; 407/1; 407/3; 407/4; 407/5; 407/6; 407/7; 407/10; 408/2

E 106/12/32, 33

E 135/1/2

E 403/620, 636, 638, 640, 643, 651, 653, 655, 658

E 404/31, 35

PSO 1/4; 1/61

SC 1/43; 57; 60; 62

SC 8/23; 24; 104; 174; 187; 188; 290

Westminster Abbey Muniments [WAM]
  MS 3798
  MS 12163
  MS 19663

NEW YORK
  Pierpont Morgan Library, MS 817

OXFORD
  Bodleian Library [Bod. Lib.]
    Ashmole MS 856
    Ashmole MS 1393
    Bodleian MS 596
    Hatton MS 90

Printed sources

Anglo-Norman Letters and Petitions from All Souls MS 182, ed. M.D. Legge (Oxford, 1941).

Anthology of Chancery English, ed. J.H. Fisher, M. Richardson & J.L. Fisher (Knoxville, Tennessee, 1984).

Archives Historiques de la Gironde (1888–9), xxvi.

A Bibliographical Register of the University of Oxford, A.B. Emden (Oxford, 1959), iii.

The Black Book of the Admiralty, ed. T. Twiss (London, 1871), i.

A Book of London English, 1384–1425, ed. R.W. Chambers & M. Daunt (Oxford, 1931).

The Book of Margery Kempe, ed. B. Windeatt (Woodbridge, 2014).

Bueil, Jean de, *Le Jouvencel*, ed. C. Favre & L. Lecestre, 2 vols (Paris, 1887–9).

Calendar of Letter-Books preserved among the Archives of the Corporation of the City of London at the Guildhall, Letter-Book I, c. A.D. 1400–1422, ed. R.R. Sharpe (London, 1909).

Calendar of Signet Letters of Henry IV and Henry V, ed. J.L. Kirby (London, 1978).

Chronicle of Adam of Usk, 1377–1421, ed. C. Given-Wilson (Oxford, 1997).

Clamanges, Nicolas de, *Le Traité de la ruine de l'église*, ed. A. Coville (Paris, 1936).

Cochalis, J., *The Pierpont Morgan MS M.817: a facsimile and introduction* (Norman, Oklahoma, 1986).

A Collection of all the Wills Now Known to Be Extant of the Kings and Queens of England, ed. J. Nichols (London, 1780).

Complete Illustrated Catalogue. National Portrait Gallery, London, ed. D. Saywell & J. Simon (London, 2004).

Corpus des Sceaux français du Moyen Age 2: Les sceaux des rois et de regence (Paris, 1990).

Documents Illustrating the Activities of the General and Provincial Chapters of the English Black Monks, 1215–1540, ed. W.A. Pantin, Camden 3rd ser., 47 (London, 1933), ii.

English Coronation Records, ed. L.G. Wickham Legg (Westminster, 1901).

English Historical Documents, ed. A.R. Myers (2nd edn, London, 1995), iv.

Excerpta historica, ed. S. Bentley (London, 1831).

The Fifty Earliest English Wills in the Court of Probate, London, A.D. 1387–1439, ed. F.J. Furnivall, *EETS*, lxxviii (1892).

Fink, K.A., 'Die politische Korrespondenz Martins V nach den Brevenregistern', *Quellen und Forschungen aus italienischen Archiven und Bibiliotheken* (1935–6), xxvi, pp. 172–244.

Gesta Henrici Quinti. The Deeds of Henry the Fifth, ed. & trs. F. Taylor & J.S. Roskell (Oxford, 1975).

Gower, J. *Confessio Amantis*, ed. A. Russell Peck (Toronto, 1980).

Handbook of British Chronology, ed. F.M. Powicke, E.B. Fryde, D.E. Greenway, S. Porter & I. Roy (3rd edn London, 1986).

Walter Hilton's 'Mixed Life'. Edited from Lambeth Palace, MS 472, ed. S.J. Ogilvie-Thomson (Salzburg, 1986).

Historia vitae et regni Ricardi II, ed. T. Hearne (Oxford, 1729).

Hoccleve's Works, The Minor Poems, i, ed. F.J. Furnivall, *EETS Extra Series*, lxi (1892); ii, ed. I. Gollancz, *EETS Extra Series*, lxxiii (1925).

Hoccleve's Works, The Regemen of Princes, ed. F.J. Furnivall, *EETS Extra Series*, lxii (1897).

Household Accounts from Medieval England, part 2, ed. C.M. Woolgar (Oxford, 1993).

Ingulph's Chronicle of the Abbey of Croyland, ed. H.T. Riley (London, 1904).

Inventaires de Jean, duc de Berry (1401–1416), ed. J. Guiffrey (Paris, 1894), i.

Langland, William, *Piers Plowman: A New Annotated Edition of the C-text*, ed. D. Pearsall (Exeter, 2008).

Lannoy, Ghillebert de, *Oeuvres*, ed. C. Potvin (Louvain, 1878).

Lauritis, J.A. (ed.), *A critical edition of John Lydgate's Life of Our Lady* (Pittsburgh/Louvain, 1961).

Letters and Papers illustrative of the Wars of the English in France during the Reign of Henry the Sixth, king of England, ed. J. Stevenson, 2 vols (RS, London, 1861–4).

Lettres de rois, reines et autres personnages des cours de France et d'Angleterre, ed. J.J. Champollion-Figeac, 2 vols (Paris, 1839–47).

Lydgate, John, *Troy Book*, ed. H. Bergen, 3 vols, *EETS, Extra Series* xcvii, ciii, cvi (1906–35).

Memorials of London and London Life in the xiiith, xivth and xvth centuries, ed. H.T. Riley (London, 1868).

Morrison, S., *A Late Fifteenth-century Dominical Sermon Cycle, EETS, Original Series*, cccxxxvii, cccxxxviii (Oxford, 2012).

Musica Britannica: A National Collection of Music, vol. iv, Medieval Carols, ed. J. Stevens (London, 2001).

Original Letters Illustrative of English History, ed. H. Ellis, 1st ser., i (London, 1825); 2nd ser., i (London, 1827).

Polychronicon Ranulphi Higden, monachi Cestrensis, together with the English translations of John Trevisa, ed. C. Babington & J.A. Lumby, 2 vols (RS, London, 1869).

The Pricke of Conscience (Stimulus Conscientiae): a Northumbrian Poem, ed. R. Morris (Berlin, 1863).

Proceedings and Ordinances of the Privy Council of England, ed. N.H. Nicolas, i, ii, iii (London, 1834).

Register of Henry Chichele, Archbishop of Canterbury, 1414–1443, ed. E.F. Jacob, Canterbury & York Society, 42, 45, 46, 47 (1938–47).

Rotuli Parliamentorum, ed. J. Strachey et al., iv, v (London, 1783). [Also available online as PROME: www.sd-editions.com/PROME or www.british-history.ac.uk>Sources>Primary].

'The Ryalle Book' in *The Antiquarian Repertory*, ed. F. Grose & T. Astle (London, 1807), 4 vols pp. 296–341.

Rymer, T., *Foedera, conventiones, literae, et cujuscunque generis acta publica* (London, 1727–35).

Rymer, T. *Foedera, conventiones, literae, et cujuscunque generis acta publica*, ed. A.G. Clarke & F. Holbrooke, 4 vols (London, 1816–30).

Statutes of the Colleges of the University of Oxford, ed. E.A. Bond, 2 vols (Oxford/London, 1853).

Stowe, J., *Annales of England* (London, 1592).

Stratford, J. (ed.), *Richard II and the English Royal Treasure* (Woodbridge, 2012).

Strong, P & F. Strong (eds), 'The Last Will and Codicils of Henry V', *EHR*, 96 (1981), pp. 79–102.

Taylor, F. (ed.), 'The Chronicle of John Strecche for the Reign of Henry V (1414–1422)', *BJRL*, 16 (1932), pp. 137–87.

Thomae de Elmham, Vita et Gesta Henrici Quinti Anglorum Regis, ed. T. Hearne (Oxford, 1727).

Titi Livii Foro-Juliensis, Vita Henrici Quinti regis Anglie, ed. T. Hearne (Oxford, 1726).

Walsingham, Thomas, *Historia anglicana*, ed. H.T. Riley (RS, London, 1864), ii.

Wavrin, Jean de, *Recueil des croniques et anchiennes istories de la Grant Bretaigne*, ed. W. Hardy, 2 vols (RS, London, 1868).

Secondary works

Aers, D., *Community, Gender and Individual Identity: English Writing, 1360–1430* (London, 1988).

Allinson, R., *A Monarchy of Letters: Royal Correspondence and English Diplomacy in the Reign of Elizabeth I* (London, 2012).

Allmand, C., 'The Relations between the English Government, the Higher Clergy and the Papacy in Normandy, 1417–1450', unpublished University of Oxford D.Phil. thesis, 1963.

Allmand, C., *Lancastrian Normandy, 1417–1450. The History of a Medieval Occupation* (Oxford, 1983).

Allmand, C., 'The English and the Church in Lancastrian Normandy' in *England and Normandy in the Middle Ages,* ed. D. Bates & A. Curry (London, 1994), pp. 287–97.

Allmand, C., *Henry V* (New Haven/London, 1992; 2nd edn 1997).

Andersson, E., 'Birgittines in Contact: Early Correspondence between England and Vadstena', *Eranos,* 102 (2004), pp. 1–29.

Arn, M-J. (ed.), *Charles d'Orléans in England (1415–1440)* (Woodbridge, 2000).

Aston, M., 'Lollardy and Sedition, 1381–1431', *P & P,* 17 (1960), pp. 1–44 [repr. in *Lollards and Reformers. Images and Literacy in Late Medieval Religion* (London, 1984), pp. 1–47].

Banca de Mirabo Gralla, C. (ed.), *Princeps i reis: promotors de l'Orde Cartoixa* (Palma de Mallorca, 2003).

Barker, J., *Agincourt* (London, 2006).

Barker, J., *Conquest: the English Kingdom of France* (London, 2009).

Barton, J., 'Equity in the Medieval Common Law' in *Equity in the World's Legal Systems* (Brussels, 1973), pp. 139–55.

Bates, D. & Curry, A. (eds), *England and Normandy in the Middle Ages* (London, 1994).

Baugh, A.C. & Cable, T., *A History of the English Language* (Englewood Cliffs, 1993).

Beal, J., 'Mapping Identity in Trevisa's *Polychronicon*', in *Fourteenth-century England III,* ed. W.M. Ormrod (Woodbridge, 2004), pp. 67–82.

Beckett, N., 'Henry V and Sheen Charterhouse: the Expansion of Royal and Carthusian Ideals', *Analecta cartusiana,* 63 (1990), pp. 49–71.

Beckett, N., 'St Bridget, Henry V and Syon Abbey', *Analecta cartusiana,* 35 (1993), pp. 125–50.

Bennion, F., 'Modern Royal Assent Procedure at Westminster', *Statute Law Review,* 3 (1981), pp. 133–47.

Benskin, M., 'Chancery Standard' in *New Perspectives in English Historical Linguistics II,* ed. C. Kay, S. Horobin & J. Smith (Amsterdam, 2004), pp. 1–40.

Benson, L., 'Chaucer and Courtly Speech' in *Genres, Themes and Images in English Literature from the 14th to the 15th Century,* ed. P. Boitani, A. Torti & L.D. Benson (Tübingen, 1988), pp. 11–30.

Bent, M., 'Sources of the Old Hall Music', *PRMA,* 94 (1967–8), pp. 19–35.

Bent, M., 'The Old Hall Manuscript', *Early Music,* 2 (1974), pp. 2–14.

Bent, M., 'The Old Hall Manuscript' in *New Grove Dictionary of Music* [www.oxfordmusiconline.com].

Bertelot, A.R., 'The Tsar and the Queen: "You speak a language that I understand not" ' in *The Foreign Relations of Elizabeth I*, ed. C. Beem (London, 2011), pp. 109–12.

Bizer, M., *Homer and the Politics of Authority in Renaissance France* (Oxford, 2011).

Blair, C., *European Armour* (London, 1958).

Boudet, J-P., 'Jean Gerson et la *Dame à la licorne*' in *Religion et société urbaine au Moyen Âge: études offertes à Jean-Louis Biget,* ed. P. Boucheron & J. Chiffoleau (Paris, 2000), pp. 551–62.

Boulton, M., 'Jean Galopes, traducteur des *Meditationes vitae Christi',* *Moyen français,* 51 (2002–3), pp. 91–102.

Boutruche, R., 'Aux Origines d'une crise nobiliaire: donations pieuses et pratiques successorales en Bordelais du xiiie au xvie siècle', *Annales d'Histoire Sociale,* 1, no. 2 (1939), pp. 161–77, 257–77.

Boutruche, R., *La Crise d'une société: seigneurs et paysans du Bordelais pendant la Guerre de Cent Ans* (2nd edn Paris, 1963).

Bowers, R., 'Some Observations on the Life and Career of Lionel Power', *PRMA,* 102 (1975–6), pp. 103–27.

Bowers, R., 'Guillaume de Machaut and his Canonry of Rheims, 1338– 1377', *Early Music History,* 23 (2004), pp. 1–48.

Bradley, P.J., 'Henry V's Scottish Policy: a Study in Realpolitik' in *Documenting the Past. Essays in Medieval History presented to George Peddy Cuttino,* ed. J.S. Hamilton & P.J. Bradley (Wolfeboro/Woodbridge, 1989), pp. 177–95.

Brantley, J., *Reading in the Wilderness: Private Devotion and Public Performance in Late Medieval England* (Chicago, 2008).

Britnell, R.H. & Pollard, A.J. (eds), *The McFarlane Legacy* (Stroud, 1995).

Brown, A.L., 'Authorization of Letters under the Great Seal', *BIHR,* 37 (1964), pp. 125–56.

Brown, A.L., 'Privy Seal Clerks in the Early Fifteenth Century' in *The Study of Medieval Records: Essays presented to Kathleen Major,* ed. D. Bullough & R.L. Storey (Oxford, 1971), pp. 260–81.

Bueno de Mesquita, D.M., 'The Place of Despotism in Italian Politics' in *Europe in the Late Middle Ages,* ed. J.R. Hale, J.R.L. Highfield & B. Smalley (London, 1965), pp. 301–31.

Bueno de Mesquita, D.M., 'The Conscience of the Prince', *Proceedings of the British Academy,* 65 (1979), pp. 417–41 [repr. In *Art and Politics in Renaissance Italy*, ed. G. Holmes (Oxford, 1993), pp. 159–83].

Bukofzer, M., 'The Music of the Old Hall Manuscript, Part 1', *Musical Quarterly,* 34 (1948), pp. 512–32; 'Part 2', *Musical Quarterly,* 35 (1949), pp. 36–59.

Burnley, J.W.D., 'Curial Prose in English', *Speculum,* 61 (1986), pp. 593–614.

Butterfield, A., *The Familiar Enemy: Chaucer, Language and Nation in the Hundred Years War* (Oxford, 2010).

Caldwell, J., 'Plainsong and Polyphony, 1250–1550' in *Plainsong in the Age of Polyphony,* ed. T.F. Kelly (Cambridge, 1992), pp. 15–17.

Cambridge Music Manuscripts, 900–1700, ed. I. Fenlon (Cambridge, 1982).

Campbell, T.P., *Tapestry in the Renaissance: Art and Magnificence* (New York, 2002).

Canning, J., *Ideas of Power in the Late Middle Ages, 1296–1417* (Cambridge, 2011).

Carr, A.D., *Medieval Anglesey* (Anglesey Antiquarian Society, 1982; 2nd edn 2011).

Catto, J., 'The King's Servants' in *Henry V: the Practice of Kingship,* ed. Harriss, pp. 75–95.

Catto, J., 'Religious Change under Henry V' in *Henry V: the Practice of Kingship,* ed. Harriss, pp. 97–115.

Catto,. J., 'Written English: the Making of the Language, 1370–1400', *P & P,* 179 (2003), pp. 24–59.

Catto, J., 'The Burden and Conscience of Government in the Fifteenth Century', *TRHS,* 17 (2007), pp. 83–99.

Cavallo, A., *Medieval Tapestries in the Metropolitan Museum of Art* (New York, 1993).

Chaplais, P., *Essays in Medieval Diplomacy and Administration* (London, 1981).

Chaplais, P., *English Diplomatic Practice in the Middle Ages* (London, 2003).

Charavay, E., *Jean d'Orléans, comte d'Angoulême* (Paris, 1876).

Clanchy, M.T., *From Memory to Written Record: England, 1066–1307* (2nd edn Oxford, 1993).

Cochalis, J., 'The Books and Reading of Henry V and his Circle', *Chaucer Review*, 23 (1988), pp. 50–77.

Cohen, W., 'The Rise of the Written Vernacular. Europe and Eurasia', *PMLA*, 126 (2011), pp. 719–29.

Cole, H. & Lang, T., 'The Treating of Prince Henry's Arrow Wound, 1403', *Journal of the Society of Archer Antiquaries*, 46 (2003), pp. 95–101.

Colvin, H.M., 'Royal Gardens in Medieval England' in *Medieval Gardens*, ed. E.B. MacDougall (Dumbarton Oaks, 1986), pp. 7–22.

Colvin, H.M., *Architecture and the After-Life* (New Haven/London, 1992).

Colvin, H.M. et al. (eds), *The King's Works*, ii (London, 1963).

Connolly, J., *John Gerson. Reformer and Mystic* (Louvain, 1928).

Cooper, S., *Agincourt: Myth and Reality* (Barnsley, 2014).

Copeland, R., *Pedagogy, Intellectuals and Dissent in the Later Middle Ages. Lollardy and Ideas of Learning* (Cambridge, 2004).

Corbett-Smith, A. (Major), *The Marne – and After* (London, 1917).

Cottle, B., *The Triumph of English, 1350–1400* (London, 1969).

Crowder, C.M.D., *Unity, Heresy and Reform, 1378–1460. The Conciliar Response to the Great Schism* (London, 1977).

Cummins, J., 'Saving Prince Hal: Maxillo-facial Surgery, 1403', *Henry North History of Dentistry Research Group Publications* (2006) [http://historyofdentistry.co.uk/index_htm_files/2006/N].

Curry, A., 'Lancastrian Normandy: the Jewel in the Crown' in *England and Normandy in the Middle Ages*, ed. D. Bates & A. Curry (London, 1994), pp. 239–52.

Curry, A., *The Battle of Agincourt: Sources and Interpretations* (Woodbridge, 2000).

Curry, A., 'The Military Ordinances of Henry V: Texts and Contexts' in *War, Government and Aristocracy in the British Isles, c.1150–1500*, ed. C. Given-Wilson, A. Kettle & L. Scales (Woodbridge, 2008), pp. 214–49.

Curry, A., 'Henry V's Misspent Youth', *BBC History Magazine*, 14 (March 2013), pp. 18–23.

Curry, A. (ed.), *Agincourt 1415* (London, 2000).

Dalton, J.P., *The Archiepiscopal and Deputed Seals of York, 1114–1500* (York, 1992).

Davies, C., 'The Statute of Provisors of 1351', *History*, 38 (1953), pp. 116–33.

Davies, R.G., 'Martin V and the English Episcopate', *EHR*, 92 (1977), pp. 309–44.

Davies, R.R., *The First English Empire: Power and Identity in the British Isles, 1093–1343* (Oxford, 2000).

Deeming, H., 'The Sources and Origin of the "Agincourt Carol" ', *Early Music*, 35 (2007), pp. 23–38.

Delclos, J-C., *Le Témoignage de Georges Chastellain. Historiographe de Philippe le Bon et de Charles le Téméraire* (Geneva, 1980).

Dickinson, J.G., *The Congress of Arras, 1435: a Study in Medieval Diplomacy* (Oxford, 1955).

Diggelmann, L., 'Hewing the Ancient Elm: Anger, Arboricide and Medieval Kingship', *Journal of Medieval and Early Modern Studies*, 40:2 (2010), pp. 249–72.

Dockray, K., *Warrior King. The Life of Henry V* (London, 2004; 2nd edn 2007).

Dodd, G., *Justice and Grace: Private Petitioning and the English Parliament in the Late Middle Ages* (Oxford, 2007).

Dodd, G., 'Patronage, Petitions and Grace: the "Chamberlain's Bill" of Henry IV's Reign' in *Henry IV: Rebellion and Survival*, ed. G. Dodd & D. Biggs (Woodbridge, 2008), pp. 105–34.

Dodd, G., 'Thomas Paunfield, the Heye Court of Rightwisnesse and the Language of Petitioning in the 15th Century' in *Medieval Petitions: Grace and Grievance*, ed. W.M. Ormrod, G. Dodd & A. Musson (York, 2009), pp. 135–55.

Dodd, G., 'The Rise of English, the Decline of French: Supplications to the English Crown, *c.*1420–1450', *Speculum*, 86 (2011), pp. 117–50.

Dodd, G., 'Trilingualism in the Medieval English Bureaucracy: the Use – and Disuse – of Languages in the Fifteenth-century Privy Seal Office', *Journal of British Studies*, 51 (2012), pp. 253–83.

Dodd, G., 'Henry V's Establishment: Service, Loyalty and Reward in 1413' in *Henry V: New Interpretations*, pp. 35–76.

Dodd, G., 'Kingship, Parliament and the Court: the Emergence of a "High Style" in Petitions to the English Crown, *c.*1350–1405', *EHR*, 129 (2014), pp. 515–48.

Dodd, G. (ed.), *Henry V: New Interpretations* (Woodbridge, 2013).

Driver, J.T., 'The Mainwarings of Over Peover: a Cheshire family in the Fifteenth and Sixteenth Centuries', *Journal of the Chester Archaeological Society*, 57 (1970–1), pp. 27–40.

Earle, P., *The Life and Times of Henry V* (London, 1972).

Earp, L., *Guillaume de Machaut: a Guide to Research* (London, 1996; 2nd edn 2013).

Emden, A.B. (ed.), *A Biographical Register of the University of Oxford* (Oxford, 1959).

Farmer, H.G., *Military Music* (New York, 1950).

Fehrmann, A., *Grab und Krone. Königsgrabmäler im mittelalterlichen England und die posthume Selbstdarstellung der Lancaster* (Munich/Berlin, 2005).

Ferguson, J.T., *English Diplomacy, 1422–1461* (Oxford, 1972).

Fisher, J. H., *The Emergence of Standard English* (Lexington, Massachusetts, 1996).

Fletcher, A.J., *Preaching, Politics and Poetry in Late Medieval England* (Portland, Oregon, 1998).

Fletcher, C., Genet, J-P. & Watts, J. (eds), *Government and Political Life in England and France, c.1300–c.1500* (Cambridge, 2015).

Fletcher, J.M., 'Tree Ring Dates for some Panel Paintings in England', *Burlington Magazine*, 116 (1974), pp. 250–8.

Foronda, F., J-P. Genet & J-M. Nieto Soria (eds), *Coups d'état a la fin du Moyen Âge* (Madrid, 2005).

Fraenkel, B., *Signature: genèse d'un signe* (Paris, 1992).

Frame, R., *The Political Development of the British Isles, 1100–1400* (Oxford, 1990).

Galbraith, V.H., 'The Literacy of the Medieval English Kings', *Proceedings of the British Academy*, 21 (1935), pp. 201–38 [repr. in *Kings and Chroniclers* (London, 1982), pp. 78–105].

Gamier, F., 'Production et diffusion du papier bourguignon aux xve et xvie siècles', *Annales de Bourgogne*, 79 (2007), pp. 211–28.

Gelfand, L.D., 'A Tale of Two Dukes: Philip the Bold, Giangaleazzo Visconti, and their Carthusian Foundations' in *Studies in Carthusian Monasticism in the Late Middle Ages*, ed. Luxford, pp. 201–23.

Genet, J-P., 'English Nationalism: Thomas Polton at the Council of Constance', *Nottingham Medieval Studies*, 28 (1984), pp. 60–78.

Ghosh, K., *The Wycliffite Heresy: Authority and the Interpretation of Texts* (Cambridge, 2004).

Gillespie, V., 'Vernacular Books of Religion' in *Book Production and Publishing in Britain, 1375–1475*, ed. J. Griffiths & D. Pearsall (Cambridge, 1989), pp. 317–44.

Graham, R., 'The Great Schism and the English Monasteries of the Cistercian Order', *EHR*, 44 (1929), pp. 373–87.

Griffiths, R.A., *The Reign of King Henry VI: the Exercise of Royal Authority, 1422–1461* (Berkeley/Los Angeles, 1981).

Griffiths, R.A., 'Klux, Sir Hartung von (d. 1445)', *New Oxford DNB* (Oxford, 2004; online edn 2008).

Grummitt, D., 'Henry VII, Chamber Finance and the "New Monarchy"', *Historical Research*, 72 (1999), pp. 229–43.

Haller, J., 'England und Rom unter Martin V', *Quellen und Forschungen aus italienischen Archiven und Bibliotheken*, 8 (1905), pp. 249–304.

Hammond, E.P., 'Two Tapestry Poems by Lydgate', *Englische Studien*, 43 (Leipzig, 1910–11), pp. 10–26.

Hardy, D., 'The Hundred Years War and the "Creation" of National Identity and the Written English Vernacular: a Reassessment', *Marginalia*, 17 (2013), pp. 18–31.

Hardy, W.J., *The Handwriting of the Kings and Queens of England* (London, 1893).

Harriss, G.L., *Shaping the Nation. England, 1360–1461* (Oxford, 2005).

Harriss, G.L (ed.), *England in the Fifteenth Century* (London, 1981).

Harriss, G.L (ed.), *Henry V: the Practice of Kingship* (Oxford, 1985; 2nd edn Stroud, 1993).

Harvey, J.H., 'Side-lights on Kenilworth Castle', *Archaeological Journal*, 101 (1944), pp. 91–107.

Harvey, J.H., *Medieval Gardens* (London, 1980).

Harvey, M., 'Martin V and Henry V', *Archivum Historiae Pontificiae*, 24 (1986), pp. 49–70.

Harvey, M., 'Martin V and the English, 1422–1431' in *Religious Belief and Ecclesiastical Careers in Late Medieval England*, ed. C. Harper-Bill (Woodbridge, 1991), pp. 59–87.

Harvey, M., *England, Rome and the Papacy, 1417–1464: the Study of a Relationship* (Manchester, 1993).

Harvey, M., 'Polton, Thomas (d. 1433)' in *New Oxford DNB* (Oxford, 2004; online edn 2008).

Harvey, M., 'Ullerston, Richard (d.1423)' in *New Oxford DNB* (Oxford, 2004; online edn 2008).

Haskett, T.S., 'The Medieval English Court of Chancery', *Law and History Review*, 14 (1996), pp. 245–313.

Heard, K., 'Death and Representation in the Fifteenth Century: the Wilcote Chantry Chapel at North Leigh, Oxfordshire', *Journal of the British Archaeological Association*, 154 (2001), pp. 134–49.

Hellinga, L., et al., *The Cambridge History of the Book in Britain* (Cambridge, 1999).

Henig, M., 'The Re-use and Copying of Ancient Intaglios set in Medieval Personal Seals, mainly found in England: an Aspect of the Renaissance of the 12th Century' in *Good Impressions: Image and Authority in Medieval Seals*, ed. N. Adams, J. Cherry & S. Robinson (London, 2008), pp. 25–34.

Hicks, M.A., 'The Beauchamp Trust, 1437–1481', *BIHR*, 54 (1981), pp. 139–42.

Hudson, A., 'The Debate on Bible Translation, Oxford 1401', *EHR*, 90 (1975), pp. 1–18.

Hughes, A. & Bent, M., 'The Old Hall Manuscript: a Reappraisal and Inventory', *Musica Disciplina*, 21 (1967), pp. 97–147.

Jacob, E.F., 'The Warden's Text of the Foundation Statutes of All Souls College, Oxford', *Antiquaries Journal*, 15 (1935), pp. 420–31.

Jacob, E.F., *Henry V and the Invasion of France* (London, 1947).

Jacob, E.F., 'To and from the Court of Rome in the Early Fifteenth Century' in his *Essays in Later Medieval History* (Manchester, 1968), pp. 58–78.

Jacob, E.F., 'One of Swan's Cases: the Disputed Election at Fountains Abbey, 1410–16' in his *Essays in later Medieval History*, pp. 79–96.

Jacob, E.F., 'Founders and Foundations in the Later Middle Ages' in his *Essays in Later Medieval History*, pp. 154–74.

Jeay, C., 'Pour une Histoire de la signature: du sceau à la signature, histoire des signes de validation en France (xiiie–xve siècles)', *Labyrinthe. Actualité de la Recherche*, 7 (2000), pp. 155–6.

Jeay, C., 'La Naissance de la signature dans les cours royales et princières de la France (xiiie–xve siècles)' in *Auctor et Auctoritas. Invention et conformisme dans l'écriture médiéval*, ed. M. Zimmermann (Paris, 2001), pp. 457–75.

Jeay, C., *Des Signatures et des rois: du signe de validation à l'emblème personnel (France, xiiie–xve siècle)* (Paris, 2003).

Jeay, C., 'La Signature comme marque d'individuation. La chancellerie royale française (fin xiiie–xve siècle)' in *L'Individu au Moyen Âge. Individuation et individualisation avant la modernité*, ed. B.M. Bedos-Rezak & D. Iogna-Prat (Paris, 2005), pp. 59–78.

Jeay, C., *Signature et pouvoir au Moyen Âge* (Mémoires et documents de l'École des Chartes, 99, Paris, 2015).

Jones, P.J., 'The End of Malatesta Rule in Rimini' in *Italian Renaissance Studies*, ed. E.F. Jacob (London, 1960), pp. 217–55.

Jones, P.J., *The Malatesta of Rimini and the Papal State. A Political History* (Cambridge, 1974).

Jurkowski, M., 'Henry V's Suppression of the Lollard Revolt' in *Henry V: New Interpretations*, ed. Dodd, pp. 103–30.

Keen, M.H., *The Laws of War in the Late Middle Ages* (London, 1965).

Kibbee, D.A., *For to Speke Frenche Trewely. The French Language in England, 1000–1600. Its Status, Description and Instruction* (Amsterdam, 1991).

Kibbee, D.A., 'Institutions and Multilingualism in the Middle Ages' in *Medieval Multilingualisms*, ed. Kleinherz & Busby, pp. 63–81.

Killick, H.K.S., 'Thomas Hoccleve as Poet and Clerk', unpublished University of York Ph.D. thesis, 2010.

Kleinherz, C. & Busby, K. (eds), *Medieval Multilingualisms: the Francophone World and its Neighbours* (Turnhout, 2010).

Klinck, D.R., *Conscience, Equity and the Court of Chancery in Early Modern England* (Farnham, 2010).

Knapp, E., *The Bureaucratic Muse: Thomas Hoccleve and the Literature of Late Medieval England* (Philadelphia, 2001).

Knowles, M.D., *The Religious Orders in England*, 2 vols (Cambridge, 1955).

Knowles, M.D., *Saints and Scholars. Twenty-five Medieval Portraits* (Cambridge, 1962).

Krochalis, J.E., 'The Books and Reading of Henry V and his Circle', Chaucer Review, 23 (1988), pp. 50–77.

Kumar, K., *The Making of English National Identity* (Cambridge, 2003).

Lander, J.R., *Conflict and Society in Fifteenth-century England* (London, 1969).

Lang, S.J., 'John Bradmore and his Book *Philomena*', *Social History of Medicine*, 5 (1992), pp. 121–30.

Lang, S.J., 'The Philomena of John Bradmore and its Middle English Derivative: a Perspective on Surgery in Late Medieval England', University of St Andrews unpublished Ph.D. thesis, 1998.

Lang, S.J., 'Bradmore, John (d.1412)', *New Oxford DNB* (Oxford, 2004; online edition Jan. 2008).

Leach, E.E., *Guillaume de Machaut, Secretary, Poet, Musician* (Ithaca, NY/London, 2011).

Le Goff, J., *Saint Louis* (Paris, 1996).

Lester, G.A., *Sir John Paston's 'Grete Book'* (Cambridge, 1984).

Lewis, P.S., 'France in the Fifteenth Century: Society and Sovereignty' in *Europe in the Late Middle Ages,* ed. J.R. Hale, J.R.L. Highfield & B. Smalley (London, 1965), pp. 276–300.

Lewis, P.S., *Essays in Later Medieval French History* (London, 1985).

Linquist, S.C.M., *Agency, Visuality and Society at the Chartreuse de Champmol* (London, 2008).

Luxford, J.M. (ed.), *Studies in Carthusian Monasticism in the Late Middle Ages* (Turnhout, 2008).

McAvoy, L.H., *Medieval Anchoritisms: Gender, Space and the Solitary Life* (Woodbridge, 2011).

McCash, J.H., 'The Role of Women in the Rise of the Vernacular', *Comparative Literature*, 60 (2008), pp. 45–57.

MacCracken, H.N., 'Additional Light on the *Temple of Glas*', *PMLA*, 23 (1908), pp. 128–40.

McFarlane, K.B., *Lancastrian Kings and Lollard Knights* (Oxford, 1972).

McFarlane, K.B., 'Henry V: a Personal Portrait' in his *Lancastrian Kings and Lollard Knights*, pp. 114–33.

McFarlane, K.B., *The Nobility of Later Medieval England* (Oxford, 1973).

McFarlane, K.B., 'Henry V, Bishop Beaufort and the Red Hat, 1417–1421' in *England in the Fifteenth Century. Collected Essays*, ed. G.L. Harriss (London, 1981), pp. 79–113 [orig. pub. in *EHR*, 60 (1945), pp. 316–48].

McFarlane, K.B., 'At the Deathbed of Cardinal Beaufort' in *England in the Fifteenth Century*, pp. 115–37 [orig. pub. in *Studies in History presented to F.M. Powicke* (Oxford, 1948), pp. 405–28].

McFarlane, K.B., 'The Investment of Sir John Fastolf's Profits of War' in *England in the Fifteenth Century*, pp. 175–97 [orig. pub. in *TRHS*, 5th ser., 7 (1957), pp. 91–116].

McFarlane, K.B., *Letters to Friends, 1940–1966*, ed. G.L. Harriss (Oxford, 1997).

Machan, T.W. *English in the Middle Ages* (Oxford, 2003).

McHardy, A.L., 'Religion, Court Culture and Propaganda: the Chapel Royal in the Reign of Henry V' in *Henry V: New Interpretations*, ed. Dodd.

McKendrick, S., 'The Great History of Troy: a Reassessment of the Development of a Secular Theme in Late Medieval Art', *JWCI*, 54 (1991), pp. 43–82.

McKendrick, S., 'Tapestries from the Low Countries in England in the Fifteenth Century' in *England and the Low Countries in the Late Middle Ages*, ed. C.M. Barron & N. Saul (Stroud/ New York, 1995), pp. 43–61.

McKendrick, S. (ed.), *The Genius of Illumination* (London, 2011).

McKenna, J.W., 'Henry VI of England and the Dual Monarchy: Aspects of Royal Political Propaganda, 1422–1432', *JWCI*, 28 (1965), pp. 145–62.

McLachlan, E.P. 'Liturgical Vessels and Implements' in *The Liturgy of the Medieval Church*, ed. T.J. Heffernan & E.A. Matter (Kalamazoo, 2001), pp. 369–429.

McLeod, E., *Charles of Orleans. Prince and Poet* (London, 1969).

McNiven, P., *Heresy and Politics in the Reign of Henry IV. The Burning of John Badby* (Woodbridge, 1987).

Marks, R., 'Entumbid right princely: the Beauchamp Chapel at Warwick and the Politics of Interment' in *Memory and Commemoration in Medieval England*, ed. C.M. Barron & C. Burgess (Donington, 2010), pp. 163–84.

Martindale, A., *Heroes, Ancestors, Relatives and the Birth of the Portrait* (Maarssen/The Hague, 1988).

Maxwell, D.K., 'The Hospital of St Anthony, London', *Journal of Ecclesiastical History*, 44 (1993), pp. 119–223.

Maxwell-Lyte, H.C., *Historical Notes on the Use of the Great Seal of England* (London, 1926).

Meron, T., *Henry's Wars and Shakespeare's Laws. Perspectives on the Law of War in the Later Middle Ages* (Oxford, 1993).

Mirot, L., 'Le Procès de Maître Jean Fusoris. Episode des négociations anglo-françaises durant la Guerre de Cent Ans', *Mémoires de la Société de l'Histoire de Paris et de l'Île de France*, 27 (1900), pp. 137–287.

Monckton, L., 'Fit for a King? The Architecture of the Beauchamp Chapel', *Architectural History*, 47 (2004), pp. 25–52.

Morgan, D.A.L., 'The Household Retinue of Henry V and the Ethos of English Public Life' in *Concepts and Patterns of Service in the Later Middle Ages*, ed. A. Curry & E. Matthew (Woodbridge, 2000), pp. 64–79.

Morgan, P., *War and Society in Medieval Cheshire, 1277–1403* (Manchester, 1987).

Morgan, P., 'Gentry Households in Fifteenth-century Cheshire', *BJRL*, 79 (1997), pp. 21–6.

Mortimer, I., *The Fears of Henry IV. The Life of England's Self-made King* (London, 2007).

Mortimer, I., *1415: Henry V's Year of Glory* (London, 2009; 2nd edn 2010).

Mugglestone, L. (ed.), *The Oxford History of English* (Oxford, 2006).

Muir, L., *Love and Conflict in Medieval Drama: the Plays and their Legacy* (Cambridge, 2007).

Murphy, N., 'War, Government and Commerce: the Towns of Lancastrian France under Henry V's Rule, 1417–22' in *Henry V: New Interpretations*, ed. Dodd, pp. 249–72.

Murray, A.V., 'Mighty against the enemies of Christ: the Relic of the True Cross in the Armies of the Kingdom of Jerusalem' in *The Crusades and their Sources: Essays presented to Bernard Hamilton*, ed. J. France & W.G. Zajac (Aldershot, 1998), pp. 217–38.

Myers, A.R., 'Parliamentary Petitions in the 15th Century', *EHR*, 52 (1937), pp. 385–404, 590–613.

Nall, C., *Reading and War in Fifteenth-century England: from Lydgate to Malory* (Woodbridge, 2012).

Newhall, R.A., *The English Conquest of Normandy, 1416–1424. A Study in Fifteenth-century Warfare* (New Haven, 1924).

Nicholson, P., *Love and Ethics in Gower's 'Confessio Amantis'* (Michigan, 2005)

Oliva, M., *The Convent and the Community in Late Medieval England* (Woodbridge, 1998).

Orme, N., *From Childhood to Chivalry: the Education of the English Kings and Aristocracy, 1066–1530* (London, 1984).

Orme, N., *Medieval Schools: from Roman Britain to Renaissance England* (London/New Haven, 2006).

Ormrod, W. M., 'Murmur, Clamour and Noise: Voicing Complaint and Remedy in Petitions to the English Crown, *c.*1300–1460', in *Medieval Petitions: Grace and Grievance*, ed. W.M. Ormrod, G. Dodd & A. Musson (York, 2009), pp. 135–55.

Otway-Ruthven, J., 'The King's Secretary in the Fifteenth Century', *TRHS*, 4th ser., 19 (1936), pp. 81–100.

Otway-Ruthven, J., *The King's Secretary and the Signet Office in the xvth century* (Cambridge, 1939; repr. 2008).

Parkes, M.B., 'The Literacy of the Laity' in *Scribes, Scripts and Readers*, ed. M.B. Parkes (London, 1991), pp. 275–97.

Parnell, G., *The Tower of London* (London, 1993).

Paviot, J., *Les ducs de Bourgogne, la croisade et l'Orient* (Paris, 2003).

Plumley, Y., *The Art of Crafted Song: Citation and Allusion in the Age of Machaut* (Oxford, 2013).

Powicke, F.M., *The Loss of Normandy* (2nd edn Manchester, 1960).

Pugh, T.B., 'The Southampton Plot of 1415' in *Kings and Nobles in the Later Middle Ages*, ed. R.A. Griffiths & J. Sherborne (Gloucester/New York, 1986), pp. 62–89.

Pugh, T.B., *Henry V and the Southampton Plot of 1415* (Gloucester, 1988).

Putter, A., 'The French of English Letters: Two Trilingual Verse Epistles in Context' in *Language and Culture in Medieval Britain: the French of England, c.1100–1500*, ed. J. Wogan-Browne et al. (York, 2009), pp. 397–408.

Rexroth, F., *Deviance and Power in Late Medieval London* (Cambridge, 2007).

Rice, N.R., 'Walter Hilton's Mixed Life and the Transformation of Clerical Discipline', *Leeds Studies in English*, n.s., 38 (2007), pp. 143–69.

Richardson, M., 'Henry V, the English Chancery and Chancery English', *Speculum*, 55 (1980), pp. 726–50.

Richardson, M., 'The Earliest Business Letters in England: an Overview', *Journal of Business Communication* (1980), pp. 19–31.

Riehle, W., 'The Authorship of the *Prick of Conscience* Reconsidered', *Anglia*, 11 (1993), pp. 1–18.

Robinson, D. (ed.), *The Cistercian Abbeys of Britain* (London, 1996).

Rothstein, M., 'Homer for the Court of François I', *Renaissance Quarterly*, 59 (2006), pp. 737–67.

Rothwell, W., 'The Missing Link in English Etymology: Anglo-French', *Medium Aevum*, 60 (1991), pp. 173–96.

Sahlin, C., *Birgitta of Sweden and the Voice of Prophecy* (Woodbridge, 2001).

St John Hope, W.H., 'The Funeral, Monument and Chantry Chapel of King Henry the Fifth', *Archaeologia*, 65 (1913–14), pp. 129–86.

Salet, F., 'Emblematique et histoire de l'art', *Revue de l'Art*, 87 (1990), pp. 13–28.

Saltzstein, J. *The Refrain and the Rise of the Vernacular in Medieval French Music and Poetry* (Woodbridge, 2013).

Sandler, L.F., *Gothic Manuscripts, 1285–1385. A Survey of Manuscripts illuminated in the British Isles* (London, 1986), ii.

Simpson, A.W.B., *A History of the Common Law of Contract: the Rise of the Action of Assumpsit* (Oxford, 1975).

Simpson, W.A., 'Cardinal Giordano Orsini (+1438) as a Prince of the Church and a Patron of the Arts', *JWCI*, 29 (1966), pp. 135–59.

Spencer, H.L., *English Preaching in the Late Middle Ages* (Oxford, 1994).

Starkey, D., 'Henry VI's Old Blue Gown: the English Court under the Lancastrians and Yorkists', *Court Historian*, 4 (1999), pp. 1–28.

Stratford, J., ' "Par le special commandement du roy". Jewels and Plate pledged for the Agincourt Expedition' in *Henry V: New Interpretations*, ed. Dodd, pp. 157–70.

Stubbs, William, *The Constitutional History of England in its Origin and Development*, 3 vols (5th edn Oxford, 1896).

Stump, P.H., *The Reforms of the Council of Constance, 1414–1418* (Leiden, 1994).

Suggett, H., 'An Anglo-Norman Return to the Inquest of Sheriffs', *BJRL*, 27 (1942–3), pp. 179–81.

Suggett, H., 'A Twelfth-century Anglo-Norman Charter', *BJRL*, 24 (1942), pp. 168–72.

Suggett, H., 'The Use of French in England in the Later Middle Ages', *TRHS*, 4th ser., 28 (1946), pp. 60–83.

Sutherland, J., Watts, C. & Orgel, S. (eds), *Henry V: War Criminal? And Other Shakespearean Puzzles* (London, 2000).

Tait, M., 'The Brigittine Monastery of Syon (Middlesex) with special reference to its Monastic Usages', unpublished University of Oxford D.Phil. thesis, 1975.

Taruskin, R., *Music from the Earliest Notations to the Sixteenth Century* (Oxford, 2005).

Tatton-Brown, T. & Mortimer, R. (eds), *Westminster Abbey: the Lady Chapel of Henry VII* (Woodbridge, 2003).

Taylor, A., 'The Myth of the Minstrel Manuscript', *Speculum*, 66 (1991), pp. 43–73.

Taylor, C., *Chivalry and the Ideals of Knighthood in France during the Hundred Years War* (Cambrige, 2013).

Taylor, C., 'Henry V, Flower of Chivalry' in *Henry V: New Interpretations*, ed. Dodd

Taylor, C. (ed.), *Joan of Arc: La Pucelle* (Manchester, 2006).

Taylor, J., 'Letters and Letter Collections in England, 1300–1420', *Nottingham Medieval Studies*, 24 (1980), pp. 57–70.

Taylor, M.N., ' "Aultre manier de language": English Usage as a Political Act in 13th-century England' in *Medieval Multilingualisms*, ed. Kleinherz & Busby, pp. 107–26.

Thompson, E.M., *The Carthusian Order in England* (London, 1928).

Thomson, J.A.F., *The Later Lollards, 1414–1520* (Oxford, 1965).

Thurley, S., *Whitehall Palace: an Architectural History of the Royal Apartments, 1240–1690* (London/New Haven, 1999).

Tout, T.F., *Chapters in the Administrative History of Medieval England*, 6 vols (Manchester, 1920–33).

Trotter, D., *Multilingualism in Later Medieval Britain* (Cambridge, 2000).

Turville-Petre, T., *England the Nation: Language, Literature and National Identity, 1290–1340* (Oxford, 1996).

Tyerman, C., 'New Wine in Old Skins? Crusade Literature and Crusading in the Eastern Mediterranean in the Later Middle Ages' in *Byzantines, Latins and Turks in the Eastern Mediterranean World after 1150*, ed. J. Harris, C. Holmes & E. Russell (Oxford, 2012), pp. 265–90.

Vale, M., *War and Chivalry. Warfare and Aristocratic Culture in England, France and Burgundy at the End of the Middle Ages* (London, 1981).

Vale, M., *The Origins of the Hundred Years War. The Angevin Legacy, 1250–1340* (Oxford, 1996).

Vale, M., *The Princely Court. Medieval Courts and Culture in North-West Europe, 1270–1380* (Oxford, 2001; 2nd edn 2003).

Vale, M., 'Language, Politics and Society: the Uses of the Vernacular in the Later Middle Ages', *EHR*, 120 (2005), pp. 15–34.

Vale, M., 'Ritual, Ceremony and the "Civilising Process": the Role of the Court, *c.*1270–1400' in *The Court as a Stage: England and the Low Countries in the Later Middle Ages*, ed. S. Gunn & A. Janse (Woodbridge, 2006), pp. 13–27.

Vale, M., *The Ancient Enemy: England, France and Europe from the Angevins to the Tudors, 1154–1558* (London, 2007).

Van Buren, A., 'Reality and Romance in the Parc of Hesdin' in *Medieval Gardens*, ed. E.B. MacDougall (Dumbarton Oaks, 1986), pp. 117–34.

VCH, County of Berkshire, ed. W. Page & P.H. Ditchfield (London, 1924), iv.

VCH, County of Chester, ed. C.R. Elvington & B.E. Harris (London, 1980), iii.

VCH, County of Gloucester, ed. W. Page (London, 1907), ii.

VCH, County of Hampshire, ed. H.A. Doubleday & W. Page (London, 1903), ii.

VCH, County of Huntingdon, ed. W. Page, G. Proby & S. Inskip Ladds (London, 1932), ii.

VCH, County of Leicester, ed. W.G. Hoskins & R.A. McKinley (London, 1954), ii.

VCH, County of London, ed. W. Page (London, 1909), i.

VCH, County of Northampton, ed. R.M. Serjeantson & W.R.D. Atkins (London, 1906), ii.

VCH, County of Oxfordshire, iii, University of Oxford, ed. H.E. Salter & M.D. Lobel (London, 1954).

VCH, County of Shropshire, ed. A.T. Gaydon & R.B. Pugh (London, 1973), ii.

VCH, County of Suffolk, ed. W. Page (London, 1975), ii.

VCH, County of Sussex, ed. L.F. Salzman (London, 1935), iii.

VCH, County of Wiltshire, ed. R.B. Pugh & E. Critall (London, 1956), iii.

VCH, County of York, ed. W. Page (London, 1974), iii.

Vincent, N., 'The Great Lost Library of England's Medieval Kings? Royal Use and Ownership of Books, 1066–1272' in *1000 Years of Royal Books and Manuscripts*, ed. K. Doyle & S. McKendrick (London, 2014), pp. 73–112.

Walford, W.S. & Way, A., 'Examples of Medieval Seals', *Archaeological Journal*, 18 (1861), pp. 49–55.

Warren, N., 'Kings, Saints and Nuns: Gender, Religion and Authority in the Reign of Henry V', *Viator*, 30 (1999), pp. 307–22.

Wathey, A., 'The Production of Books of Liturgical Polyphony' in *Book Production and Publishing in Britain, 1375–1475*, ed. J.G. Griffiths & D.A. Pearsall (Cambridge, 1989), pp. 143–61.

Watson, N., 'Censorship and Cultural Change in Late-medieval England: Vernacular Theology, the Oxford Translation Debate, and Arundel's Constitutions of 1409', *Speculum*, 70 (1995), pp. 822–64.

Watts, J.L., *Henry VI and the Politics of Kingship* (Cambridge, 1996).

Watts, J.L., *The Making of Polities: Europe, 1300–1500* (Cambridge, 2009).

Wells, R.H., *Shakespeare on Masculinity* (Cambridge, 2000).

Wilkins, N., *Music in the Age of Chaucer* (Woodbridge, 1979; 2nd edn 1995).

Wilson, C., 'The Tomb of Henry IV and the Holy Oil of St Thomas of Canterbury' in *Medieval Architecture and its Intellectual Context. Studies in Honour of Peter Kidson*, ed. E.C. Fernie & P. Crossley (London, 1990), pp. 181–90.

Wogan-Browne, J. et al., *The Idea of the Vernacular. An Anthology of Middle English Literary Theory, 1250–1520* (Exeter, 1999).

Wogan-Browne, J. et al., *Language and Culture in Medieval Britain: the French of England, c.1100–1500* (York, 2009).

Wylie, J.H. & Waugh, W.T., *The Reign of Henry V*, 3 vols (Cambridge, 1914–29).

ILLUSTRATION CREDITS

1. Royal Collection Trust, Windsor, RCIN 403443 © Her Majesty Queen Elizabeth II 2016. 2. Corpus Christi College, Cambridge, MS 213, fo. 1r © The Master and Fellows of Corpus Christi College, Cambridge. 3. Bodleian Library, Oxford, MS Arch. Selden B.26, fos 17v–18r © Bodleian Library, Oxford. 4. BL, Add. MS 57950, fo. 12v © British Library Board. 5. BL, MS Cotton Vesp. F.III, fo. 8r © British Library Board. 6. TNA, E 28/32, no. 20 © The National Archives. 7. TNA, E 101/69/7, no. 509 © The National Archives. 8. TNA, C 81/1364, no. 34 © The National Archives. 9. TNA, E 28/32, no. 66 © The National Archives. 10. TNA, E 28/34, no. 57 © The National Archives. 11. TNA, E 28/34, no. 72 © The National Archives. 12. TNA, E 28/34, no. 19 © The National Archives. 13. TNA, E 28/34, no. 10 © The National Archives. 14. TNA, E 30/1531 © The National Archives. 15. TNA, E 30/1619 © The National Archives. 16. TNA, C 81/1366, no. 3 © The National Archives. 17. TNA, C 81/1366, no. 9 © The National Archives. 18–20. © A.M.E. Wheeler.

INDEX